MOUNTAINTOPS
and
Mai Tais

MOUNTAINTOPS
and
Mai Tais

DOUGLAS M. JOHNSTON, JR.
SCALING THE HEIGHTS TOWARD A HIGHER CALLING

XULON PRESS

Xulon Press
2301 Lucien Way #415
Maitland, FL 32751
407.339.4217
www.xulonpress.com

© 2021 by Douglas M. Johnston, Jr.

Paperback ISBN-13: 978-1-6628-0879-1
Hard Cover ISBN-13: 978-1-6628-0880-7
Ebook ISBN-13: 978-1-6628-0881-4

In tribute to Doug Coe
whose spiritual walk inspired my own.

TABLE OF CONTENTS

PREFACE

Life is far more spiritual than most of us might imagine. When you stop to think about it, all of us are no more than spirits walking around occupying different shells. When the spirit is gone, the shell is useless. Yet, most of us spend the better part of our lives, worrying about the shell rather than feeding the spirit.

It is commonly assumed in some religious traditions that we humans are made in the image of God. If so, that likeness takes place in the spirit, because that is the realm in which God allegedly exists; and it seems highly unlikely that He runs around looking like any of us.

Said differently and more eloquently is this letter from Benjamin Franklin to his brother John's step-daughter, who was deeply shaken by her step-father's passing.

Philadelphia, February 22, 1756

Dear Child,

I condole with you, we have lost a most dear and valuable relation, but it is the will of God and Nature that these mortal bodies be laid aside, when the soul is to enter into real life; 'tis rather an embryo state, a preparation for living; a man is not completely born until he be dead: Why then should we grieve that a new child is born among the immortals? A new member added to their happy society? We are spirits.

That bodies should be lent us while they can afford us pleasure, assist us in acquiring knowledge or doing good to our fellow creatures, is a kind and benevolent act of God—when they become unfit for these purposes and afford us pain instead of pleasure— instead of an aid, become an incumbrance and answer none of the intentions for which they were given, it is equally kind and benevolent that a way is provided by which we may get rid of them. Death is that way.

We ourselves prudently choose a partial death. In some cases a mangled painful limb, which cannot be restored, we willingly cut off—He who plucks out a tooth parts with it feely since the pain goes with it, and he that quits the whole body, parts at once with all pains and possibilities of pains and diseases it was liable to. Or capable of making him suffer.

Our friend and we are invited abroad on a party of pleasure—that is to last forever—His chair was first ready and he is gone before us—we could not all conveniently start together, and why should you and I be grieved at this, since we are soon to follow, and we know where to find him. Adieu.

With warm regards,
Benjamin Franklin

Why does any of this matter? It matters because it affects the depth of one's story when one is seeking to give an account of his or her life's journey and what it has meant. My principal reason for wanting to do just that is to share with future generations of family some of the more humorous anecdotes and mountain-top "highs" that I experienced during my short time on planet Earth. To be sure, there were any number of valleys as well. Indeed, one might say I had more than my share – having been married three times before finally getting it right. But everyone has valleys, and they're not so fun to write about. So, with this caveat, please indulge this fading memory as it seeks to recapture the past.

There are four stages to life: youth,
maturity, "You're looking good,"
and, "My, doesn't he look natural?"

PART I
The Early Years

Chapter One

BEYOND THE BOX

*I shall pass through this world but once. Any good therefore that I can
do or any kindness that I can show to any human being, let me do it
now. Let me not deter nor neglect it, for I shall not pass this way again.*
Stephen Grellet (1772-1855)

There I was in the mountains of Pakistan meeting with 57 Taliban commanders, most of whom had crossed the border from Afghanistan to participate in the meeting. The alleged purpose of the gathering was for me to explain exactly what America wanted in Afghanistan. As one Taliban commander, who had already lost two sons in the fighting, expressed it two months earlier, "You come at us with guns, and we have no recourse but to respond in kind. We simply don't know what America wants." This had led to an invitation for me to address this question with their senior leadership. Hence the meeting.

I led off by saying I was there to see if we could build on commonly-shared religious values to develop a confidence-building measure that could point toward peace. However, for them to participate in such an initiative they would need to understand the Western perspective on the conflict and what America wanted.

After addressing this issue, the meeting morphed into a lengthy give-and-take discussion followed by a smaller planning session to develop the confidence-building measure. During the discussion period, though, there was a considerable venting of grievances on their part; and at one point, a very tough-looking gentleman stood up, pointed his finger at me, and said, "I can't talk to you unless you become a Muslim." I thought for a moment and replied, "I don't see a problem. 'Muslim' means submission to God. We all submit to God; therefore, we're all Muslims." Everyone laughed and we went on with the discussion.

It was some time later that I learned from two Muslim colleagues who had accompanied me, that they had grown visibly nervous when the above exchange took place. Apparently, the normal way for that particular scenario to play out is that one either converts or one dies. Not knowing any of this, I couldn't help but think to myself, "The Lord really does look out for fools and incompetents."

Because of the setting, one might characterize this as a mountaintop experience. There have been any number of other mountaintops as well, which I have made a central part of this book. Unlike my experience with the Taliban, though, most of the others have been of a more personal nature, with some of them quite humorous. As for the Mai Tais, they were often the preferred drink of choice in celebrating some of the latter.

By the same token, I have been asked by friends and colleagues alike to tell the story of the International Center for Religion & Diplomacy (ICRD), a non-profit organization that I founded on the back side of 60, which has had a noteworthy impact on the conduct of U.S. foreign policy. That is not quite so humorous, and I'm not certain that a blend of the serious with the not-so-serious can work as a new literary form designed to appeal to future generations of Johnstons as biography and to foreign policy practitioners as history. In a generic sense, though, the two intimately connect.

It was a lifetime of constant change and adapting to new challenges that enabled me to establish such a center without batting an eye over the fact that I had few, if any, apparent qualifications for doing so. In this regard at least, one could consider it a continuum from start to finish. Anyway, I have given it a shot to see if it can work.

In summary, my life might be described as a light-hearted journey that took a number of unpredictable turns before arriving at its final destination of advancing religious influence as an operational instrument of peace. And for several reasons, there is no small degree of irony in this particular outcome.

First, although I have significant credentials in the field of political science, I am totally unschooled in the field of religion. Second, to the extent U.S. policymakers have previously connected religion with conflict, it has almost always been through a negative lens in which religion was seen as a contributing factor to that conflict. Finally, despite being one of the more religious countries on the face of the planet, we have all-too-often let our separation of church and state serve as an excuse for not doing our homework to understand how religion influences the world views and political aspirations of others who don't similarly separate the two.

Contributing to this unlikely voyage of mine were a number of disparate personal factors, including: (1) a life-long commitment to public service, (2) an abiding interest in international relations, (3) a natural openness to things spiritual, (4) a desire to make a difference with my life, and (5) a disciplined perseverance stemming from my naval service that enabled me to overcome most of the obstacles I encountered.

Equally important was the support provided by others along the way. The road to any mountaintop is almost always paved with encouraging inputs from family, friends, colleagues, or employers; and mine was no exception. Some of these have been included in the addenda because of the inspiration they provided at the time. Their immodest nature only lends added credence to P. T. Barnum's adage about fooling some of the people some of the time. Cutting across all of this was a keen appreciation for humor, humility, and eventually empathy, all of which are good for the soul.

This book provides a roadmap for how all of the above came together and had its eventual impact on American diplomacy by taking the reader through five stages of my personal development:

- the early years of overcoming some rather extraordinary challenges and the insecurities that accompanied them,

- a phase of developing self-discipline and a sense of selflessness through military service,

- a period of enhancing personal versatility and vocational dexterity through a series of interesting jobs in different career fields,

- a parallel odyssey of finding spiritual meaning in it all, and

- a final phase of bringing it all together in birthing a new form of political and religious engagement designed to facilitate peace and promote greater understanding in a troubled world.

So, from playing tag with Soviet submarines off the coast of Russia to directing Harvard's first executive program for Flag-rank military officers to negotiating with Taliban commanders in the aftermath of 9-11 (and much in between), it has been an exciting ride.

I hope you enjoy this reading adventure. Worst case, it's a great cure for any sleeping disorders you might have. Alternatively, the paper on which it is printed could be used to re-line your canary cage. Best case, however, if the planets should happen to align, it might inspire you to reach beyond your comfort zone and pursue a higher purpose that can bring added meaning to your life and those of others.

5

Chapter Two

ROOTS ON THE RUN

Truth is stranger than fiction; fiction is obliged to stick to possibilities, truth isn't.

Mark Twain

My earliest memories date back to the age of four and are generally unremarkable until I was diagnosed with tuberculosis (TB) of the left ankle bone and sent to a TB sanitarium on Wallum Lake, a somewhat remote location in northern Rhode Island. At the time, Dad was in the Navy and stationed in Newport, at the opposite end of the state. The saving grace was the state's status as the smallest in the nation, which put me within geographic reach of weekend visits from my folks.

Into the Jungle

The prognosis going in was that I would never be able to walk again, which I thankfully didn't know at the time. Nevertheless, it was a rough adjustment as I was initially placed in quarantine for two weeks and remember the first few nights crying myself to sleep. For the next two years, I was tied to a bed with my left leg in a full-length cast. In this moribund state, I began earlier than most to learn some of life's more meaningful lessons, like how to survive in the medical jungle of a hospital ward. Although I was only four years old, there were other kids there as old as eleven; and whenever one received a "care package" from home, one needed to guard it diligently from the unwanted grasps of others.

And there were any number of other ways in which one learned to cope. For example, after the lights went out at night, I would often untie myself from the bed, hop over on one leg and join several other kids in playing cards by flashlight under a blanket beneath a nearby bed. Such was life in the hospital; but for the rest of my days, I have had to resist a too-natural tendency to cut corners or otherwise beat the system, whatever form that might take. Left unchecked, I would have had little problem adjusting to life as a con man.

The fondest memories I have from my hospital experience relate to the efforts of a wonderful nurse by the name of Mrs. Charette, who took a personal interest in me. She modeled my first memories of unconditional love, while caring for my emotional as well as physical well-being (often through reading me innumerable fairy tales). It struck me much later in life that because those fairy tales almost always ended with "They got married and lived happily ever after," that image may have contributed to my later, too-natural tendency to take marriage for granted, without fully understanding that it is not so much about finding the right person as it is about becoming the right person (and by never taking it for granted).

When the happy day of my departure from the sanitarium came, I was set loose on crutches and a shorter cast, which six months later morphed into a leg brace—and eventually to arch supports. Although the doctors later concluded that I didn't have TB after all, they never absolutely determined what I did have, so I have always assumed it was probably a mild case of polio, which was running rampant throughout the land at the time. But that is only a guess. The one lingering consequence of it all was that I have had weak ankles ever since (probably from being off my feet for those two years), requiring me to tape them up when playing serious football or having to go what seems like 120 miles an hour to stay up on ice skates.

As soon as I left the hospital, I began what seemed like an endless stream of trips across country in the back seat of a car heading to my Dad's next duty station. Early in the first trip after vacating the hospital, we stopped to see the sights in Washington DC. At one point, Dad drove away to park the car after leaving Mom and me off at the base of the Capitol steps. I still remember rather poignantly a kind gentleman who picked me up and carried me to the top (crutches and all). I don't know why such small gestures can have such a lasting impact; but ever since, I've had a special place in my heart for the city of Washington and its inspiring monuments.

Getting Started

I had some informal schooling in the hospital; but it was pretty hit-and-miss after that, with bits of schooling here and there as Mom and I spent time with various relatives over the next couple of years, while Dad was stationed in Hawaii (with the war in the Pacific not quite over yet). This transitory existence included brief stays in Vancouver, Longview and finally, for a longer stretch in Burton on Vashon Island (all in the state of Washington).

In Burton, we lived above a grocery store owned by Mom's sister and broth-er-in-law, while she herself worked at the store and handled its business at a nearby Indian reservation. I still vividly remember running into the street to celebrate the end of the war, with everyone in sight hugging and rejoicing with care-free abandon.

During this period of hopping around, we also spent some time at my grandparents' farms in Vancouver, Washington and Brush Prairie, Washington (about 12 miles apart). The Vancouver experience, where Dad grew up, was always fun because his mother was the living personification of unconditional love, often manifesting itself in unforgettable root beer floats for her favorite (read "only") grandson, made with homemade ice cream. His father was fun as well and a skilled woodworker, in addition to being a respectable farmer. My favorite memory of him was when he was milking the cows and would sometimes squirt the milk directly into their cat's mouth from a couple of feet away.

Life on Mom's farm was a bit more challenging. Her parents lived in a house that her father built at the age of 19 and lived in until he passed away in his 90s. The amenities were few. The outhouse was about a hundred yards from the main house, and when her Dad finally had an indoor toilet installed for her Mom (when she was in her 80s), he continued to use the outhouse for quite some time afterwards. He just didn't trust them newfangled inventions.

The only source of heat in the house was a wood-fired stove in the living room; and whenever I slept there, it was usually in the winter in an upstairs hallway with a heated iron wrapped in a blanket at the foot of the bed to pre-vent frostbite. Upon getting up in the morning, the established routine con-sisted of a quick trip outside to wash one's face in a pan of ice-cold water, followed by fifty turns on a handpump to transfer water from the well to a water tank that was capable of meeting household needs by gravity feed for much of the day. It was a stoic existence that placed a heavy premium on self-reliance.

My poignant memory on that front was catching foot-long nightcrawlers in the cow pasture (after midnight) for use as fish bait. One had to be quick about it, though. Despite their length, they disappeared back down their holes faster than lightning, if you weren't.

Finding entertainment in these rather bare bones settings required more than a little creativity, but somehow the memories are all the richer for it. This was "back in the day" when hand-cranked telephones mounted on the wall provided access to a "party line," and one had to wait until the line cleared before making a call. Even after all that, anyone else on that party line could eavesdrop on your conversation, if they felt so inclined. Somehow, though, iPhones and Androids just don't compare.

Finally, we were able to join Dad in Hawaii and that proved quite a memorable experience.

Sweet Aloha

Dad was stationed at the Naval Anti-Aircraft Training Center in Waianae, on the western side of Oahu, where Navy gunners would hone their skills on the Center's 40-millimeter gun mounts, shooting down target sleeves towed by low-flying aircraft. Dad was a Lieutenant Junior Grade (LTJG) at the time, having been promoted to the officer ranks during the war. He had enlisted in the Navy as a Seaman Apprentice during the depression, so that transition represented quite a step up for a farm boy from the state of Washington. The other officers at the Training Center were all about the same rank and a great group to be around. Their nickname for Dad was "Frosty", because his head was always in the refrigerator, looking for ice cream. I suspect it must have been a genetic flaw, in light of my own inexhaustible passion for the same stuff.

At one point, this great group of young officers gave me a dog as a birthday present. Spooky had more or less served as their mascot for quite some time; and although a mongrel, he was amazingly talented. I could throw a bare stone deep into some nearby woods on the darkest night; and he would retrieve it, without fail. I think my greatest sense of loss as a child was when Spooky was run over by a car, while we were walking to the local grocery store. We rushed him to the base, and the base doctor did everything he could to save him, but it was too late.

Because Waianae was quite distant from Honolulu and from the naval base at Ford Island, we were essentially living with the locals. Being the only Caucasian in my school, I came to appreciate the challenge of minority rights at an early age. Although I was eight at the time, I was placed in the first grade because the Hawaiian school system wouldn't give credit for the piecemeal education I had received up to that point. As it turned out, they concluded in short order that I was too big for the first grade and therefore advanced me to the second grade. Then, because it was almost the end of the school year, I was promoted to the third grade along with the other second graders, essentially catching up with where I should have been for my age.

One day after school, Mom noticed a ring mark on my neck and asked what had happened. I told her that a Japanese student who was several years older (and quite a bit bigger) than me had been beating me up after school. She called the Principal, and he whaled the tar out of my Japanese friend. The next morning, while waiting in line for hot chocolate and graham crackers (a mid-morning ritual at the school), this same student came up and told me he was really going to get me after school, whereupon I told the Principal, and he repeated his previous ritual. Apparently, that did the trick, because I had no further problems after that. I later concluded he must not have heard that the war was over. Petty incidents aside, I grew to love the Islands and have always relished the fact that I was able to live there long before it became a mecca for tourists.

We initially lived in a small plantation picker's hut for $25 a month, largely because Dad had become good friends with the German plantation owner before Mom and I arrived. I recall with warm feelings the typical weekend routine that would start with Mom and Dad playing tennis at some nearby courts, followed by a swim and diving for shells at the beach. This routine always concluded with a big Hawaiian breakfast when we returned home.

Interrupting the above routine was an unfortunate occurrence that took place one night when the house next door to us burned down. We had to quickly vacate our hut, so a fire truck could spray it down to prevent the fire from spreading. I vividly recall waking up and grabbing all my worldly possessions before fleeing the premises, which at that time consisted of an old cigar box containing a few dollars- worth of coins, a pair of roller skates, and eight pair of well-worn dungarees ("jeans" in today's parlance). That was it. Sadly, the fire, which apparently stemmed from an electrical problem, claimed the lives of eight people, including the Mayor of Honolulu's son to whom the house belonged.

After a year or so, we moved to Aiea Heights to live in a modest, but quite nice home overlooking Pearl Harbor. This time it was rent-free, as long as we kept the place looking good. Again, a result of Dad's friendship with the plantation owner and his wife who had been using it as their summer cottage.

Life as a Vagabond

"I never think of the future. It comes soon enough." – Albert Einstein

Growing up, life was a constant blur as we moved from one navy port to another, about equally split between the East and West coasts. Every year of high school, for example, was in a different corner of the country, from Oregon to California, to South Carolina, to Maryland. What one lacked in roots, one made up for in versatility. From getting elected to class office (but moving away before ever having to serve) to having to re-prove one's self on new sports teams, it was a never-ending challenge. Later in life, I used to comment half-jokingly that my only sense of roots growing up was the Naval Academy where, for the first time in my life, I actually spent four years in one place.

However, I wasn't totally adrift. Over the course of the various moves in my teenage years, I spent about seven of them in scouting, first as a Cub Scout, then a Boy Scout and finally as an Explorer. I put a great deal of time and effort into it and became an Eagle at age 13. A year later, I earned the Silver Award, Explorer Scouting's highest. Bob Lovell, my scoutmaster in Astoria, Oregon, who became a life-long friend, used to call me "showboat;" but I think what was really going on was a need to prove my own self-worth by addressing mild insecurities stemming from the hospital experience and the never-ending moves. At one point I was going for all 105 merit badges and got to 57 before I discovered girls, which effectively nipped that crusade in the bud. Scouting clearly had a formative impact on my life, but not without some humorous episodes along the way.

In no particular order, while living in Astoria in 1952, I was trying to earn enough money to attend the National Boy Scout Jamboree in Irvine, California by selling greeting cards from door to door. At one point, Dad asked how I was doing. I replied "not very well," and he asked what I said to people when they answered the door. I replied, "You wouldn't want to buy any greeting cards, would you?" Needless to say, I quickly changed my pitch to something like, "I'm selling greeting cards for the Boy Scouts to go to the National Jamboree in California. Can you help us out?" In short order, I had the several hundred dollars required to make the trip, but that natural instinct of not wanting to impose on others has been a constant challenge throughout life, particularly when it comes to fundraising. Left to my own designs, I would be a total failure at marketing anything in which I didn't fully believe.

On another occasion, Dick Hellberg, a good friend and fellow scout, and I were participating in a Camporee at the local armory in Astoria, with a sizable audience of locals observing. Our particular task on that occasion was to demonstrate how to make a fire without matches. In my case, from flint and steel; and in Dick's, from rubbing two sticks together. To enhance his probability of success, Dick had ground up some match heads and mixed them with a little gunpowder, which he then inserted into the circular recess of the board (in which he would rapidly rotate the stick until it generated sufficient heat to ignite the cedar shavings). So, every once in a while, as he was rubbing away, the audience was treated to a minor explosion and a puff of smoke. It certainly livened things up, but he never could get a fire going. Thankfully, that served as sufficient distraction for most observers not to notice that I wasn't doing any better. I never did figure out why I couldn't get it to light, because it worked every time I tried it at home. Must have been stage fright!

One final tale from scouting. I was the first scout from Astoria to be inducted into what is called the Order of the Arrow, an honorary brotherhood with memorable initiation rites: two days of hard work, building log bridges out of tree limbs and rope (and other similar undertakings, all with no tools), wearing only a loincloth and no talking allowed. A small bowl of oatmeal in the morning served as our sole sustenance for the day, and we slept overnight in the woods, absent any bedding, other than the loincloths we were wearing.

This rite of passage resulted in a later request to use my newly acquired supernatural powers to light the campfire at an outdoor Camporee, this time in the woods with about a hundred other scouts taking part (no civilian audience this time). So, there I was, standing in the dark in front of these scouts, all decked out in Indian garb (including a full headdress), painted appropriately, and praying in Delaware Indian language for the God of Fire to light the campfire that was laid before me.

Like Dick at the armory, I sought to enhance my chances of success by having a friend perched high in an adjacent tree prepared to light a kerosene-soaked rag wrapped loosely in a wire collar that would slide down an invisible-to-the-audience piano wire strung from the tree to the campfire. As my chanting reached its crescendo and it was time for the God of Fire to do his thing, one could hear a swish, swish, swish as my friend tried unsuccessfully to ignite the match with which to set the rag on fire and send it on its way.

After what seemed like an eternity, he finally got it lit; but as the ball of fire streaked toward earth from out of the heavens, the wire broke; and it landed a couple feet short of the campfire—-whereupon I went over and kicked it the rest of the way in with my moccasin. I made no excuse for the near-miss, leaving it to the Fire God to explain. Because the wire broke, no one ever really knew how the fire got there in the first place, keeping intact my growing mystical reputation.

Coming of Age

High school began in Astoria and later morphed to Long Beach Polytechnic in Long Beach, California. Numbering about 3,000 students, Poly represented yet another fresh start in a new location. Two things stood out from that experience. First, it was where I finally determined what I wanted to do when I grew up; and second, it was where I was introduced to the sport of water polo. Having learned to swim in the pounding surf of Oahu, the latter became a reasonably comfortable fit.

My favorite course at Poly was World History taught by Eleanor Weiherman, with whom I shared Christmas cards for the next fifty years. I recall her taking me aside one day and saying, "Douglas, I predict that one day you will become either a teacher, a preacher, or a politician." To varying extents, she proved right on all counts.

One day she was out sick, and the substitute teacher happened to be a retired Navy Captain who brought with him his Annapolis Year Book. Up until then, I had never even so much as heard of Annapolis or the Naval Academy, despite being a Navy Junior (the label affixed to offspring of Navy personnel, as opposed to Army or Air-Force "brats"). After class, I thumbed through his year book and concluded without question that the Academy was where I wanted to go.

Before that epiphany, I had pictured myself pursuing any number of different career options, ranging from forest ranger to electrical engineer, but never joining the Navy. No doubt because Dad told me at an early age that if I ever thought I wanted to go into the Navy, he was going to put me on the roof during the stormiest night of the year and have me march back and forth for four hours, rest for two, then repeat that same cycle all night long. Anyway, despite this inspiring encouragement, my mind was made up—I was going to become a Midshipman in the United States Navy.

The next year found me in the 11th grade at Charleston High in Charleston, South Carolina. Despite the mild culture shock, Charleston is one of the more charming cities in the South and was a great place for making friends, including my first romantic interest. In 1953, there wasn't much in the way of air-conditioning; but despite the intense heat and humidity, life was good.

One learning experience that stands out from my time at Charleston High was an episode that took place in my American History class. The course was taught by an elderly gentleman by the name of Mr. Griffin, whose teaching was not without a certain degree of bias when it came to discussing the "War of Northern Aggression." I recall the tears flowing down his cheeks as he described the "flower of the Confederacy" being severed at the stem in the Battle of Gettysburg.

One day, he told us that the United States had come close to adopting German as its official language, but narrowly missed by a single vote in the House of Representatives. Somehow, this didn't sound right, so I wrote the Pennsylvania Historical Society and asked if it was true. In due course, they responded by commenting that "Every now and then, this 'old wives' tale gets repeated". They said what actually happened was that a vote was taken to determine if U.S. laws should also be printed in German (in addition to

English) because of the sizable German population in the country at the time. Lingering hostility toward the British may have played a role as well, but that wasn't mentioned. The motion was ultimately defeated in a vote that wasn't recorded. Anyway, after reading the letter aloud in class, I was awarded a "D" on my next exam, despite having aced every question. Justice aside, I later concluded the "D" was a small price to pay for an important lesson in humility.

Charleston was also my first real introduction to the work force in several different capacities. First, as a caddy at the local golf course, where I grew interested in the game myself. This in turn, led to a rather humorous episode while out golfing with a friend. One of my shots went in the rough; and when I finally found my ball, it was lying beside a dead copperhead snake. Since the corpse looked fresh, I assumed that my errant ball had done the deed.

Anyway, there was an elderly couple playing behind us, which inspired me to pick up the snake and carry it to the next hole, where I wrapped it around the base of the flag, stuffing it into the hole until only the head was showing when you looked down. Then my friend and I hid in the bushes to observe the fireworks.

After the couple chipped onto the green, the man went to hold the flag for his wife as she putted out. As her ball approached the hole and he looked down, he let out a yell and literally threw the flag, pole and all, across the green and onto the fairway. Though we were lucky he didn't have a heart attack, we had a good laugh and finished our game with rather smug looks on our teenage faces.

When golf season was over, I next took a job as a stock boy in the local grocery store for 45 cents an hour, following which I worked in a women's shoe store in downtown Charleston, where I was paid on a commission basis. Because all of our customers were poor, the highest-priced shoes in the store were $3.98 a pair. Even at that, though, I was able to beat the store record on the Saturday before Easter by hitting the $300 mark. However, a mountaintop it was not.

Some shoes were out of style and commanded a bonus if you were able to sell them. While attempting to do just that during my record-breaking day, it became clear that the shoes I was trying to sell one customer were much too tight, whereupon I told her, "They're wearing them tight this year, Ma'am." Then I called the store manage over to confirm what I was saying, which he did (in response to the number of fingers I held up for only him to see: one meaning "tight' and two meaning "loose"). Anyway, the shoes were so tight that they literally exploded as she exited the front door of the store, falling apart before our very eyes. To ease my conscience, I gave her a better pair of the non-bonus variety, which fit much better, and decided that my one-finger, two-finger days were over.

My fellow salesmen were considerably older, and a pretty tough group to be around. When things were slow, they would often head to the back of the store and practice throwing ice picks at the silhouette of a man etched on a standing piece of plywood. Although I didn't drink at the time, a number of the upside-down shoe boxes on the racks contained fifths of whiskey. And on Saturday mornings before the store opened, we would amuse ourselves by racing one another from one end of the store to the other, while wearing high heels. Ever since, I've had difficulty understanding how women are able to balance themselves so well on such uncomfortable contraptions.

Dad's next duty station was the Naval Proving Ground at Dahlgren, Virginia, where the Navy test-fired the various categories of ammunition it used in the fleet. Because there wasn't an accredited high school in the vicinity, the folks decided to send me to a prep school that was reasonably close by in Silver Spring, MD. At that point, I only needed one additional credit to graduate, so I effectively spent my senior year at The Bullis School taking courses offered to high school graduates who were there for additional schooling (in order to enhance their chances for acceptance into some of the country's more prestigious academic institutions like the Ivy league schools, MIT, and the Service Academies). This was particularly true for most of the star athletes who had been recruited by the Naval Academy for its football and basketball teams.

The quality of education offered at Bullis was superb, and I soaked it up like a sponge. My goal throughout was to score high enough on the Naval Academy entrance exam to qualify for a Presidential Appointment. I had previously spent a day in Washington DC, knocking on the doors of various Senators and Congressmen, seeking a Congressional Appointment; but without political roots of any kind in any Member's district, those doors were effectively closed. The only remaining option was to compete for Presidential sponsorship, which was offered to the sons of military service members (no daughters in those days) who scored in the top 75 in the country on the entrance exam. Thanks in large part to Bullis, I scored well and in June of 1956, was sworn in as a Midshipman.

Despite having done well, that year's entrance exam posed a unique and interesting challenge. For a number of years, the test had included a significant section on English and American literature. In anticipation of this, I had taken courses in each at Bullis, which I thoroughly enjoyed. I was something of a romantic at heart, and the quality of the teaching was off the charts. When it came time to show one's stuff on the entrance exam, though, there was nary a question on literature to be found. Instead, the test included a totally new section on reading comprehension. I recall on more than one occasion reading the assigned paragraph and while attempting to answer the associated questions, wondering if I had read the right paragraph. It was by no means a walk in the park. The literature courses, however, proved helpful in other ways. Not only have the associated insights served me well in navigating the various twists and turns of life, but I was able to draw on them to good advantage in my coursework at the Academy.

An Anchor in Any Storm

On November 18, 2011, the Chicago Herald Tribune carried an article titled, "Remarkable Woman, Kate Johnston", with the accompanying subtitle, "Inner-city teacher helps kids unleash the star within." The piece was about my sister who was born when I was half-way through the Naval Academy, making her roughly twenty years younger than me and a real surprise to our parents.

At the time of the article, Kate was teaching music to high school students at a charter school in Chicago. The article itself was a tribute to her ability to inspire disadvantaged kids to reach for the stars through their involvement in musical performances. She had made as a condition of her employment that every student in the school would be required to take music as a core subject, rather than an optional elective. She was somehow able to persuade the school administrators that music was every bit a mind-expanding subject as any other academic discipline.

The last half of the piece segued into an interview, during which she was asked, "Who inspired you?" She responded by saying,

> *"I had two remarkable parents who taught me thousands of important life lessons by their strong examples. They were resourceful, humble, talented, and truly crafted a life for our family using their gifts and common sense. They did not attend college, but there was never a moment in our upbringing that we doubted that we would attend university. They were incredibly well-read and curious and never stopped learning themselves."*

Her encapsulation expressed well the reality of our home life. Dad was at sea much of the time when I was growing up, so I didn't know him as well as I would have liked. In fact, because he was away so much, I tended to put him on a pedestal; and he was always something of a hero to me. But for a stroke of good fortune, though, there may have been no pedestal on which to stand.

In 1943, Dad was transferred off of the *USS Buck (DD420)*, a destroyer on which he had served while escorting convoys of merchant ships across the North Atlantic during the Second World War. There the principal challenge was to counter the devastating lethality of the German Wolf Packs, groups of U-boats that would simultaneously launch their torpedoes at multiple targets and then slip away. Firing a large number of torpedoes in short intervals created mass confusion and made it next-to-impossible for the targeted ships to maneuver out of harm's way or for their escorts to launch successful counterattacks.

I recall Dad mentioning one particularly trying episode in which his destroyer and two English corvettes (smaller, lightly-armed vessels) were guarding a 52-ship convoy sailing from Argentia, Newfoundland to Murmansk, Russia when a Wolf Pack sank 19 of them in one night. The aftermath of such attacks was gruesome, especially when the torpedoes hit ammunition ships or tankers (in which case, the chances of finding survivors was close to zero).

On the ship's next voyage after Dad was transferred off, it was sunk by a German U-boat off the coast of Salerno, during the Allied invasion of Italy. That tragic episode was captured by Naval historian Samuel Eliot Morison in his *History of United States Naval Operations in World War II:*

> Destroyer *Buck*, patrolling the Gulf on the night of 8-9 October, got a surface radar contact shortly before midnight. As she was tracking the submarine, one or two torpedoes struck forward of her single stack and exploded with great violence. Lieutenant Commander "Mike" Klein, the much beloved skipper, and most of the officers were killed in the explosion, and the destroyer began to go down. The men launched all life rafts that were intact, put such wounded as they could find on board them, and abandoned ship. About four minutes after the hit, her stern stood straight up for 100 feet; she plunged down half way, shuddered, and then slid under. As there had not been time to set all depth charges on "safe" before they became inaccessible, some exploded, killing or wounding swimmers and blowing the bottoms out of all the balsa rafts. There were no other ships nearby. An Army transport plane spotted floating survivors at 1000 [10:00 am] October 9 and dropped three rubber life rafts, a godsend to swimming survivors. As no other planes or vessels appeared, they attempted to row ashore, 45-50 miles distant. Finally, at 2000 [8:00 pm], as a second

night was descending, a destroyer was sighted and her attention attracted by a Very Pistol [flare gun]. This was *USS Gleaves*. Shortly after, *Plunkett* and *H.M.S.LCT-170* arrived at the scene to help pick up the men still alive—only 94 out of a crew of 260.

Several months earlier, *Buck* had sunk an Italian submarine and was able to rescue 46 of its crew of 49. Sadly, the *Buck*'s crew didn't enjoy similar luck.

Dad went on to become an officer and eventually command a ship of his own. He was scheduled for promotion and command of a squadron of mine-sweepers out of Long Beach (land of my birth) when a heart attack forced his retirement from the Navy. He was only 42 at the time, so it was a rather abrupt adjustment. However, he lived a very active 27 additional years before succumbing to a second and final heart attack.

It would be difficult for me to imagine life without Dad. He had a great sense of humor and was just so darned fun to be around. From shooting golf to shooting pool, it was always a great game with lots of laughs. And as I would often say when he wasn't around, every girl from 4 to 104 fell in love with him. He could also do just about anything under the sun that needed doing. From crafting a beautiful tea cart in wood shop as a kid to overhauling an automobile engine, or repairing a camera, he could do it all. Typical of his humor is this excerpt from a letter he sent me in 1981:

> "There is this fellow I encounter at the lumber yard once in a while— we were on the school board together in '65—he asked about the family and after telling about you being a Captain now, he said 'how did such an unconscious [expletive] as you produce someone like that?' I told him I had hidden talents and that you weren't done yet, so show me a little more respect. So, he saluted me."

While Dad was a mix of Scottish and English, Mom was half-German and half-Swiss. Although she was not as humorous as Dad, she complimented him nicely with her strong sense of purpose and stoic self-resolve. She too could accomplish most anything she put her mind to. All of this is in amplification of Kate's more general description.

The Concrete Football

"A brother is a friend given by nature." — Jean Baptise Legouve (1729-1783)

Between Kate and me is our brother Mike, who is roughly ten years younger than me and ten older than her. With that sort of age difference, our folks effectively raised an "only child" for the better part of 40 years. Although Mike and I were together until he was ten years old, one's agenda as a teenager is so far removed from that of a much younger sibling that one is only minimally aware of the other's existence.

That changed a bit whenever I was home on leave from the Academy, as we tossed a football in the front yard; and I sought to make him a star. The ball we had was quite heavy — as Mike describes it, like "concrete". Most of this activity consisted of me throwing him passes that were difficult to catch, determined to one day see his name in lights as one of the country's great football stars. And, of course, during numerous interviews in that capacity, he would proudly say he owed it all to his bigger brother. That dream never quite materialized; and as he now recounts that experience in later life, he says, "I may have been small, but I was slow."

Another instance of brotherly give and take from that same period took place when I signed a piece of paper and asked Mike for comparison's sake to see what his signature looked like. He proceeded to show me, after which I lifted the top sheet of paper above his signature, revealing that he had just signed over to me all rights to any inheritance from the folks' estate — -all that is, except the greenhouse and the popcorn popper. The so-called "greenhouse" was an abysmal, almost embarrassing structure up the hill from our house in Southworth, Washington; and the popcorn popper, which was older than the hills, had probably long ago seen its last "pop". Years later, after the folks had graduated to their higher reward, Mike sent me the popcorn popper, COD.

Although we weren't that close growing up, he and I finally bonded one summer when he flew in from the West Coast, and we sailed for a week off the coast of Maine. It was a memorable time. Every day was an adventure as the six-horsepower outboard on the back of my 25-foot sloop broke down at the most unpredictable and inopportune times.

The first day was indicative of what was to come. It was rainy and quite foggy (as often happens in August), and after sailing for a while, we decided to put in at the nearest port. While we were heading in, Mike said he didn't think it was the port we had thought it was. At that point, we were in a following sea, with huge waves pushing us along, and the outboard wasn't working. I told him it didn't matter; we were irreversibly committed to wherever we were going. "Just don't tell anybody we're Naval Academy graduates."

As it turned out, we tied up in Newburyport, a delightful town about 40 miles north of Boston where we spent the night and stayed long enough to get the motor fixed. While there, I bought a pair of green sneakers for $5.00 to wear while giving my docksiders a chance to dry out. The sneakers were pretty awful-looking and have become an endless source of laughter for two brothers reminiscing about a memorable time together. And so it went for the next few days until we reached Jewel Island in Casco Bay, the northernmost point of our trip. Once there, we anchored out and made our way to shore for a hike around the island and a brief swim. Though uninhabited, it was clear the island had served as a Civil Air Patrol station in World War II.

Our return trip was every bit as exciting and once we finally tied up to our mooring in Salem Harbor, we drank a toast to what had clearly been a great experience. Beyond the fact that we had a lot of "sea stories" to share on the trip, since Mike too had attended the Naval Academy, served aboard nuclear submarines, and gone to work for the government after leaving the Navy, our life agendas at the ages of 30 and 40 respectively were much closer than had been the case when we were 10 and 20. Mike later commented that for him, the trip had been the closest thing to a spiritual experience he had ever encountered. I felt the same.

We have had any number of other experiences since then. One I recall with a chuckle is a conversation we had in my car on our way to a day of white-water rafting on the Upper Youghiogheny in the Maryland panhandle. I was tuning the radio and told Mike I was looking for a good country and western station because I particularly enjoyed how the lyrics in such songs often speak volumes in just a few words. He agreed and said his long-time favorite in that department begins with, "I'd rather have a bottle in front of me than a frontal lobotomy."

Despite the significant age difference between the three of us, we are all exceptionally close. That's undoubtedly due in large part to the influence of our parents; but without a shred of prejudice, I can safely say that Mike and Kate are two of the finest, most wonderful siblings a person could have. Their presence has been a constant blessing in my life.

Cousin Dale

The cousin I was closest to during my youth and ever since was Dale Haney. The closeness was neither geographic nor from spending all that much time together, especially since I was constantly moving from one coast to the other as Dad's naval orders dictated. Rather, it was a coincidence of interests. As adolescents, we were both hooked on Monopoly; and Dale was always the sneaky one, hiding a $500 bill here or a $100 bill there and then pulling them out at strategic moments later in the game.

As we grew older, it was sports and girls. Dale was two years older and a master at both pursuits, so I naturally looked up to him and tended to follow his lead. He earned 12 varsity letters at Battleground High (near Portland, Oregon) and the visor on the driver's side of his car sported a seemingly infinite number of hairpins, one for each of his current and past lady friends.

Anyway, once Dale graduated from high school, he attended Washington State College and made his way through by felling trees as a lumberjack in the summers. After college, he attended dental school but dropped out just prior to graduation, deciding at the last minute that he didn't want to spend the rest of his life with his hands in other people's mouths. And then his Monopoly instincts kicked in as he purchased a house via an FHA foreclosure and got some buddies to help him fix it up.

Fast forward ten years and Dale now owns about 200 rental units, two bars, and a motel. By this time, I was out of the Navy after a ten-year stint and working for the government, helping to administer the Price and Wage Controls Program under President Nixon. Part of the job required me to sell the program to the public through various speaking engagements around the country. One of these trips had me traveling to Portland, Oregon where I visited Dale at The Stone Balloon; one of his two bars (aptly named because it was the 1970's, when "getting stoned" had become a national pastime).

After visiting over lunch, Dale challenged me to a game of Foos Ball. Until I walked into his bar, I had never so much as seen a Foos Ball table. He, of course, was an ace; so, it was a very one-sided game. In fact, it soon got to the point where he had to stand on one leg, use one hand, and close one eye. For every ball he put in the goal, I paid him a dime. For every one of mine, he paid me a dollar—and he still won.

Fast forward another 30 years, and Dale had suffered a stroke that left him partially paralyzed on his left side. Soon after, I called him up and challenged him to a rematch, only this time he would have to stand on his left leg, use his left hand, and close his right eye. Upon hearing the conditions, Dale just laughed and said, "Hell, I could beat you from the casket." The sad part is that he probably could! Everyone should know the fun of such a cousin.

Meet Dad--not bad for a farm boy

Or the ship he commanded
(official U.S. Navy photo)

Or his farm girl bride

Or life 30 years later

"Showboat"

Sister Kate

The store in Burton, Washington
above which Mom and I were living
when the war ended.

Catching concrete

The spiritual journey begins

A brotherly plunge

Two wet amigos

The Three Musketeers

With the motor
actually running

My cousin, the land baron

PART II
Navy Days

Chapter Three

ANCHORS AWEIGH

Universities are full of knowledge; the freshmen bring a little in, the seniors take none away, and knowledge accumulates.

A. Lawrence Lowell
President, Harvard University (1909-1933)

The Class of 1960 took the Oath of Office with raised right hands in the front court of the Naval Academy. It did so with little awareness of what lay ahead. In immediate terms, it translated to very short haircuts (the term scalping comes to mind), countless hours of stenciling one's name and laundry number on the inside of newly-issued uniforms and other wearing apparel, and rigorous non-stop indoctrination in Navy tradition. The latter consisted of Academy history and the required responses to an endless stream of questions that would be posed by the upper classes when they returned from cruise at the end of the summer. On top of that was the constant drilling, marching, and learning the ins and outs of seamanship.

The intense pace coupled with exceedingly hot and humid weather (and the all-but-total absence of air-conditioning) helped get us in fighting trim for the months ahead. Indeed, I was down to 145 lbs. by the end of the summer, after having sweated more than enough to float a battleship.

Life as a Troublemaker

Once the rest of the Brigade returned from summer cruise, it didn't take long for me to get into trouble. In fact, on the first evening of their return, several upper classmen had us newcomers lined up in the hallway at attention. At one point, one of them cracked a joke, and I made the egregious mistake of chuckling in response. In penance for my severe lapse in judgement, I was made to "come around" to his room every night immediately following evening meal. In fact, I was supposed to be in his room five minutes after the

27

meal was over, dressed in 10 pairs of sweat gear (i.e. sweat shirts and pants). Because it was physically impossible to return to one's own room, change into even one pair of sweat gear, and make it to his room on time, all sorts of physical punishment awaited.

The most memorable of these exercises was the requirement to "swim to Baltimore," which consisted of climbing up and into a rectangular hole located high on the wall between the main room and the closet. The hole was large enough to fit one's body through and just thick enough (about 8") to support one's mid-section as one stretched horizontal and went through the motions of swimming. Custom had it that you reached Baltimore when the 25th drop of sweat had fallen off your nose. Then came the swim back. After several months of this, I was in pretty good shape.

Not all plebe year experiences were quite so masochistic. In fact, there were any number of humorous episodes that took place along the way. One of these happened during Plebe Summer when one of my roommates, a future track star for Navy, mentioned in passing that gas escaping from the lower regions of the human body was highly flammable. I had never heard of such a thing and accused him of being full of stuff. To prove his point, he leaned back on his bunk with his legs in the air, lit a match, and shortly turned into a human blowtorch. With scorched trousers and a broad grin, he had proven his point. However, our third roommate, a future oarsman on Navy's 1960 Olympic crew team, had a special gift in that same area. Upon assuming the fetal position, he could produce gas every 20 seconds, like clockwork. Only it didn't burn; so I suppose in the end, we were both right.

A few months later, while standing in ranks at attention and undergoing a formal inspection, the inspecting upperclassman asked me when was the last time I had shaved. I replied, "I've never shaved, sir!" In response, he said I was to come around to his room at 6:00 am every morning to shave while braced-up (standing at attention) and that I was to do so until hell froze over. About two weeks into this routine, Don Larsen pitched a no-hitter in the 1956 World Series and the sports page in the local paper read, "Well, folks, hell finally froze over today…". The next morning, I took him the article and after a good laugh, he let me off the hook.

On another occasion, I was eating lunch, braced up (i.e. sitting at attention) on the front two inches of my chair as all plebes were required to do, when an upperclassman began grilling me on the innumerable things a plebe was theoretically supposed to know at any given time—things like the countless facts about Navy tradition and the Academy as captured in *REEF POINTS*, a 300 page 3 ¼" x 5" "Annual Handbook of the Brigade of Midshipmen," [1] which every midshipman (mid) was issued upon taking the oath.

Also to be recited when called upon to do so: everything on the menu for the next four meals; the names of all movies playing in Annapolis and who was starring in them; the names of the players on the opposing football team that Navy would be playing that week (including standing on one's chair at mealtime and singing their fight song); the names and armaments of any Navy ships that might be in port, including the ships' dimensions and the names of their Captains. The list went on and on.

Anyway, the gent asking the questions was keenly motivated to do so because I had sassed him in response to something he had asked the day before—-so I had it coming. By some strange alignment of the planets on that particular occasion, I happened to know the right answers to all of the questions he threw at me. Finally, in frustration, he pulled out the stops and said, "Mr. Johnston. Do you see that bird over there?" I turned in my chair, still braced up, spotted a bird flying in the mess hall, and said, "Yes, sir!" He then told me to have that bird to him by evening meal or I would be "coming around" until graduation (his, not mine), which at that point was still several months off.

Now the mess hall in which we were served our meals, was a huge, T-shaped structure which accommodated all 3,600 mids at one time, with considerable room to spare. Anyway, when the meal was over, the upper classes were dismissed, during which time we plebes had to stand at attention behind our chairs until we heard "Fourth Class, march out." over the speaker system.

While waiting for our dismissal, I noticed out of the corner of my eye that the bird had landed on a nearby window screen. When the announcement finally came, I went over to the window, gently lowered it, reached up, and caught the bird. Two minutes later, I knocked on the upperclassman's door, entered the room and said, "Midshipman Johnston, Fourth Class, sir. Here's

---

[1] Illustrative of the innumerable canned responses Plebes were required to recite from memory was the prescribed answer to the question, "Why didn't you say, Sir?" "Sir, sir is a subservient word surviving from the surly days in old Serbia when certain serfs, too ignorant to remember their lord's names, yet too servile to blaspheme them, circumvented the situation by serogating the subservient word sir, by which I now belatedly address a certain senior cirruped, who correctly surmised I was syrupy enough to say sir after every word I said, Sir."

All this to be said in a single breath, while standing at attention. Here, some 60 years later, I find myself still able to do it. Though increasingly unlikely, I am ever-prepared for that next upperclassman who might happen along.

your bird, sir" and let it fly. That evening at dinner, he announced to the table "Don't ever tell Johnston to do something stupid, 'cause he'll do it."

One night I decided to get back at an upperclassman across the hall from where I roomed, so at about 3:00AM, I snuck into his room and dumped a wastebasket full of cold water over his head while he was asleep and raced out of there before he gained full consciousness. Unfortunately, the wastebasket dripped on the way back to my room. Did I ever pay a dear price for that one!

On yet another occasion as a plebe, my Spanish language section was marching back from class to Bancroft Hall, the world's largest dormitory (where all of us roomed). There was a lot of snow on the ground, and it started to rain quite hard—so hard that we began to break ranks and run. At that point, and unbeknownst to me, an upperclassman who was serving as Battalion Officer of the Watch, came running over to order us back into formation. I was in the rear of our section; and just as he approached the chaos, a huge snowball that I had thrown (hoping to hit one of several classmates as they were running away) struck him squarely in the chest and knocked him over.

After he picked himself up, he held the section in place in the pouring rain and asked who had thrown the snowball. Being more than a little concerned about the consequences, I didn't say a word. But when he started to take the Section Leader's name, probably to put him on report and assign him demerits, I stepped forward and 'fessed up. He ordered me to come around to his room that evening, and I did so, with no little trepidation. Happily, when I did, he said that he had done something similar himself when he was a plebe and let me off with a warning. Talk about living lucky!

Not all such episodes took place during plebe year. During my last year, for example, I awoke in the middle of the night to find Dave Bolden, one of my two roommates, standing beside my bed, shining a flashlight in my eyes. Dave had apparently gotten out of bed, which was in an adjacent room (where he and our third roommate, Paul Cooper, slept), walked over to my clothes locker in the main room (where I slept), picked up my flashlight from the back of my locker, and began shining it at me. All this, while he was sound asleep

Now, Dave was admittedly rather tightly-wound, and could instantly turn around and hit you, if you so much as touched him unexpectedly from behind. I recall one time during swimming practice, when I had to dive in and retrieve him from the bottom of the pool, because his muscles had suddenly locked up as he entered the water from a racing start. I forget the diagnosis of his condition, but it took a couple of weeks in the hospital for him to fully recover.

Anyway, after I woke Dave up and he found his way back to his own bed, Paul Cooper, our third roommate who occupied the bunk above Dave's, waited about ten minutes after we turned out the lights before he began chanting in a low voice, "Bolden, get your bayonet and stab Johnston." (We all had bayonets, which we affixed to our rifles during dress parades.) After repeating this chant for a couple of minutes, I began to hear movement in the other room, whereupon I barricaded myself in and spent a rather sleepless rest of the night.

The First Mountaintop

During my four years at Annapolis, I had two mountaintop experiences in terms of personal development, both occurring during plebe year (freshman year in civilian speak). The first of these related to a first-semester course in English Literature. During the final exam, I drew heavily on knowledge I had acquired at Bullis and scored a 3.96 out of a possible 4.0. Not only was that an unheard-of grade in "Bull" (the label commonly affixed to any subject taught by the Department of English, History and Government), but it propelled me to first in the class by quite a margin (out of 1050) in that particular subject.

Ironically, on my way to swim practice the afternoon of the test, I thought I might have failed the exam because 60% of the grade related to writing a thesis on one of eight possible topics; and although I had written a great deal, I felt in hindsight that I hadn't really answered the central question the thesis was supposed to address. It would be difficult to overstate the depth of my surprise when the grades were posted several days later! I could only laugh at how far I had misjudged the outcome.

I mention this particular episode not for purposes of self-aggrandizement (after all, I thought I had failed), but to acknowledge the enormous boost in self-confidence it provided. The grade itself didn't necessarily mean anything other than the fact that I had paid attention at Bullis, but it was a huge shot in the arm in terms of purging any lingering insecurities and causing me to think for the first time that I could conceivably compete with the best, if I put my mind to it.

Until that particular point in time, I had no aspirations of excelling at the Academy, only to graduate and pursue a naval career. However, once I sampled that rarified atmosphere, I wasn't about to give it up lightly; so from then on, I was inspired to do as well as I could. In hindsight, one might say that the "Bull" in Bullis had a major impact on my life.

The Second Peak

Of the half dozen courses, we took during Plebe Year, one of the more demanding was Physical Education in which we were graded in gymnastics, swimming, boxing, wrestling, and running the obstacle course. Throughout the year, I competed in these activities against Dave Bolden, my previously mentioned roommate, who was the fastest 50-yard freestyle swimmer Navy had ever recruited. In contrast, I was middle-of-the-pack; so, by competing with Dave, I was clearly aiming high.

We had going for us the fact that we were both engaged in what were called "dry-land exercises" for swimmers during the off-season. This was an exceedingly rigorous and demanding routine that helped build strength and stamina before actually hitting the pool several months later. In addition, I was also reaping the physical benefits of the rigorous hazing to which I was being subjected by various upperclassmen—certainly more so than Dave, who was considerably better at staying out of trouble.

Anyway, during the course of our friendly rivalry, we both maxed the swimming competition, which called for swimming a mile in a sailor suit within a given period of time. In boxing, I fought against Frank Clark, our third roommate at that time, who while he outweighed me by about 20 lbs., had comparable boxing ability and a nose that, when properly hit, bled like a "stuck pig." Our fights were therefore always quite bloody; and we received great scores. As for wrestling, I learned some great moves that served me well; but it was my least favorite area of competition, primarily because of the innumerable elbow burns incurred from rubbing against the mat.

I found gymnastics to be the greatest challenge because one had to compete in eight different categories: the high bar, the parallel bars, the uneven bars, the side horse, the rings, tumbling, the rope climb, and I forget what else. It took me all of three weeks to master one relatively easy maneuver on the high bar, and I sprained an ankle quite badly during the tumbling; but all in all, received pretty high marks.

Finally, there was the obstacle course, which consisted of a number of challenging obstacles spread out over the course of a half mile or so. To offset the fact that I was a slow runner, I studied each obstacle to figure out the fastest and most efficient way to traverse it. Surprisingly, I maxed the course; and at the end of the year, Dave stood first in our class in Physical Education; and I stood tenth. That standing in Phys Ed was a real mountaintop for me, especially after the doctor's prognosis some 14 years earlier of not being able to walk again.

Rights as Privileges

When I entered the Academy, our family was still living in Dahlgren, Virginia; but by Christmas leave several months later, they had moved to

Southworth, Washington, a roaring metropolis on the edge of Puget Sound consisting of a single small building, which served as the grocery store, post office, and gas station. A heart attack at the end of the summer had forced Dad into retirement, so the folks decided to settle down in their home state somewhere reasonably close to a Navy hospital.

One of the more perverse requirements of Plebe Year at the time was that plebes weren't allowed to date while at the Academy, so the only opportunity to address the hormonal pressures of youth was when one was away on leave. Upon arriving home on my first Christmas leave and not knowing a soul in the area, I managed to get ahold of the latest yearbook for Bremerton High School (which was about 30 miles away) and called the young lady who had been elected Homecoming Queen earlier that year. We went out the next evening and several nights later on New Year's Eve. Both were fun times; and after that, we maintained a long-distance relationship for the better part of a year before she broke it off. She did so because I was planning to become a Naval aviator; and she didn't want the constant worry that would go along with that.

Because I had undergone this same sequence about a year earlier with a young lady in Dahlgren, Virginia, including her breaking it off for the same reason, I was beginning to detect a pattern. The irony is that I never did become an aviator; but who knows, maybe the threat of doing so kept life a lot simpler.

Filling the Gap

One exception to the non-dating rule was what were called "tea fights", those occasions on which the Academy would bus in a bevy of young ladies from some nearby women's college, with whom we were to practice our dancing. Part of becoming God's gift to women was the requirement to be well-steeped in the social graces, including a degree of dexterity on the dance floor. I still have to chuckle when I recall the time one of my company mates by the name of Warren Hahn took dexterity to a whole new level by feigning an epileptic fit on the dance floor. His seizures looked incredibly real as he thrashed about on the floor, while his poor dance partner stared down with a very bewildered look on her face.

In another somewhat inspired attempt to close the gender gap, I leaned on the U.S. mail. Seeing an article titled "Queens of the Midwest" in a new issue of *Look Magazine*, I approached four other Mids to form a betting pool in which each of us would put up five dollars (a full month's pay) to see who would be the first to receive a reply from one of the "queens" in response to a letter from one of us. He who received the first reply would get half the pot, and whoever received the most promising reply would get the other half. We then drew straws, and I ended up with last pick. The one I chose looked like she would be the least likely to respond for two reasons: (1) she was the most attractive and (2) her picture showed her stepping down from a large rock, with a male hand helping her to do so. Within a short while, though, I received a perfumed response signed "love"; and although that turned out to be more than enough to win the entire pot, I never had the pleasure of meeting her. We corresponded for a bit, but she was from Lincoln, Nebraska, which was a bit of a stretch for a penniless mid (even one with overflowing pockets from winning the bet).

Re-approaching Normal

"Give me chastity and self-restraint, but do not give them to me yet."
St. Augustine (354-430 AD)

With the prohibitions of Plebe Year now behind me, I was finally able to start living the semblance of a normal life again. As the saying went at the time, "When you enter the Academy, the Navy takes away all of your God-given rights and slowly gives them back one-by-one over the years as privileges." One of those privileges was the right to date again. But that presented challenges of its own, with only nine dollars of spending money a month (the norm for a sophomore).

Because the Academy was quite an attraction for young ladies to "be asked to a hop in Annapolis," there was no dearth of dating opportunities, other than the tight budget. Typically, a girl would pay her own way to Annapolis on a Saturday and then pay $5.00 for a night's lodging at a "Drag House" in town (so named, because midshipmen's dates were known as "drags," since they were constantly being dragged around, first to an athletic event on campus Saturday afternoon, then to dinner in town Saturday evening, and finally to a formal "hop" that evening). On Sunday, midshipmen were tied up until about 1:00 pm, attending church (not optional) and eating lunch in the mess hall. After that, we were able to reconnect with our dates, usually taking them to a concert or a movie in Mahon Hall in the afternoon or just spending free time together. Following that, we said our good-byes; and then it was back to the normal grind of studying, sleeping, attending class and playing sports.

Somehow, I was able to make the finances work and dated almost every weekend. In so doing, I always used the same "Drag House" at 28 East Street in Annapolis, a private home owned by a dear lady by the name of Mom Cassavetes (the aunt of movie star and film director, John Cassavetes). She was in her mid-50's and had suffered a double blow some years earlier when her naval aviator son was killed when his jet exploded and her husband suffered a fatal heart attack upon hearing the news. So, her Mids were special, and she provided a delightful touch of home for all who entered.

The Joys of Summer

Some of the more memorable times took place during the summers, when we experienced first-hand what life was like out in the Fleet. Even Plebe Summer (the summer of our "swearing in"), which was spent at the Academy, provided valuable ship-handling experience aboard Yard Patrol Craft, which were akin to miniature destroyers. We also experienced the thrill of flying in the back seat of an open-cockpit, N3N bi-plane. Termed "yellow perils" because of their bright yellow paint jobs, these seaplanes were every bit as exciting to fly as one might imagine. The timing proved highly fortuitous as these World War I look-alikes were retired from active service the year after we graduated.

Youngster cruise took place following the completion of Plebe year and consisted of a two-month-immersion into the duties of an enlisted man. This involved doing all of the more menial tasks that a sailor would perform at sea—in my case, aboard a mighty battleship, the *USS Iowa (BB61),* as we cruised to South America. The experience was great, but the food left a lot to be desired. Indicative of this was an announcement that came over the 1MC general announcing system one evening while a number of us were back on the fantail (the rear of the ship) watching a movie, "Now hear this, now hear this: Will zee duty chicken report to zee galley to run through zee soup." Uproarious laughter followed, since the chicken soup that was often served seldom, if ever, contained anything resembling a piece of chicken.

A highlight of that trip was the initiation we received as we crossed the equator for the first time. The transition from "pollywog" to "shellback," involved all sorts of unmentionable punishments. The crescendo of this rite-of-passage was a requirement to kiss the belly of "King Neptune", who in this case was a 350 lb. African-American, who had coated his stomach with an extraordinarily foul-smelling substance. A couple of southerners in our ranks refused to kiss the king's belly and paid a heavy price for their racial misgivings. They were strapped to their backs and forced to swallow oysters to which strings had been attached, Once swallowed, the string was pulled, with predictable results.

Second Class Summer following our Youngster (sophomore) year had all of us heading to Little Creek, Virginia, to participate in a Marine Corps amphibious landing exercise. After hitting the beach in an LPV landing craft (seemingly designed to make one as sea-sick as possible), I had the unenviable and slightly bloody task of serving as a human bridge over the barbed-wire that had been strung along the beach to complicate the landing. Instead of merely running over me as they should, a number of my fellow trainees treated it like a competitive dive off the high board, requiring a lot of spring — hence the term "bloody."

Even more harrowing, was the opportunity to run the UDT (Underwater Demolition Team) obstacle course that was reasonably close by. This wasn't required; but it was something I volunteered to do because I had entered the Academy, hoping to go UDT. However, I later learned that this option wasn't available to Academy grads because the war-time mortality rate for these precursors to today's SEALS was considered too high to risk losing the sizable investment of an Academy education.[2]

Perhaps the most difficult of the obstacles was the "slide for life," which consisted of a thick nylon rope extending from the top of a thirty-foot tower to a pole at ground-level a hundred feet away on the other side of a pool of water. The challenge was to scale the tower, lay on top of the rope, and pull yourself head-first to the bottom without falling into the water. About three quarters of the way down, I lost my balance and ended up under the rope, finishing the trip like an upside-down spider. Of course, one could have made the trip all the way like a spider; but it was a much slower way to go and would have taken too long to qualify within the time allotted. Anyway, the course was exceedingly difficult; and when I finished, my clothes were in tatters, I was bleeding in several places and shaking all over. I couldn't believe I could be so beat up by a series of inanimate objects. Yet one more hard-earned lesson in humility.

The principal goal of Second Class Summer, though, was to expose all Midshipmen to the challenges of Naval Aviation. This exposure was broad and seemingly all-encompassing as we learned the basics in a T34, a single engine aircraft that all but flew itself (and in which we practiced take-offs and landings and performed a range of acrobatic maneuvers); took it up a notch in a T28, an overpowered fighter plane used as a bridge to piloting a jet; and topped off the sequence in a T33 jet trainer. We also spent time learning to fly a helicopter, and some of us had the opportunity to pilot a blimp as well.

The most challenging of the above to fly, at least to my way of thinking, was the helicopter in which all four of one's limbs are actively engaged at all

---

[2] That is no longer the case today as the SEALS currently recruit 24 midshipmen from each graduating class.

times, with seemingly minimal relationship between their respective functions. Most surprising, though, was the blimp and its glacial response to the
controls. One would be flying along; and as it started to nose over, pull back
on the stick to keep it level. After no apparent response, one would pull back
even further; again with no response. After several repetitions, the blimp
would suddenly over-respond and nose upward more than one wanted. An
auto pilot on one of these would certainly have its work cut out for it.

All in all, it was an exciting summer, and one came away with a good
understanding of the challenges that awaited if one opted for a career in Navy
Air upon graduation.

Sink or Swim

"Why they call a fellow who keeps losing all the time a good sport gets me."
Frank McKinney Hubbard (1868-1930)

A good friend of mine by the name of Jerry Montague and I were classmates at Bullis Prep prior to entering the Academy, and we both had a yen
for swimming. Bullis did not have, nor had it ever had, a swim team of any
sort, so Jerry and I formed a team and arranged a schedule for the season.
Our practice facilities consisted of a 20-yard pool at a Jewish Community
Center some ten miles away in downtown Washington D.C. (to which we
would hitch-hike three times a week). We had a tough schedule that included
a number of noteworthy opponents, like Catholic University, Mercersburg
Academy, and various others I can't recall. Although we had some individual
successes along the way, as a team we never won a meet (Addendum A). But
we did have a lot of fun and gave Bullis the kickstart it needed to wax aquatic.

In a somewhat similar vein while at the Academy, Jerry and I loved to
play water polo along with a number of other equally enthusiastic mids. Navy
had discontinued water polo as a varsity sport in 1948 when someone apparently lost an eye during a meet. At that time Harry Train (later Admiral Harry
Train) was captain of the team and his father (also a former Admiral) was
the coach. I paid a visit to the former coach, who lived in Annapolis; and,
seeking his guidance, told him we were trying to have water polo reinstated
as a varsity sport. He was quite enthusiastic about the possibility and offered
his encouragement.

To get something going, Jerry and I organized a team and challenged the
varsity teams of several other schools. On one particular Saturday, we played
back-to-back games against Villanova and the University of Pennsylvania and
beat both of them by wide margins. Later with stars in our eyes, we wrote

a letter challenging the New York Athletic Club (NYAC) to a meet. They had represented the United States in the previous Olympics, so we were aiming high, especially since we didn't really have a team in any true sense of the word.

Well, the NYAC accepted, so we formed a team from among those of us who were allowed to take a weekend (at that time only First and Second Classmen—Seniors and Juniors) and made the trek north. Although we lost, the score was closer than we had any legitimate right to expect. The game itself was very interesting because we had to play in the buff (Club rules), the other team spoke almost no English (being mostly Hungarians, Swiss, and Germans), and they played a very dirty game. I forget the exact score, but the difference was less than the margin by which they had beaten West Point, which did have a varsity team and which had won the AAU (Amateur Athletic Union) championships that same year. We all felt good about the game and retired to Mama Leone's, a relatively up-scale restaurant, to cheer our audacity and near success.

The more interesting part of the story came two weeks later when I was called into the Commandant of Midshipmen's Office.[3] He told me that a dear friend, who had planned a trip to the Academy to see her son and, while there, to visit him and his wife, didn't make the trip because her son said he would be away that weekend playing for the Navy water polo team. This understandably caused a raised eyebrow on the part of the Commandant, who knew Navy had no such thing. He then said he learned that I might know something about this.

I briefed him on what we had done and attempted to turn crisis into opportunity by regaling him with the many reasons water polo should be reinstated as a varsity sport. Not only did we have some world-class players who could do the Academy proud; but we had conducted a Brigade-wide poll on the matter, and 83% had indicated their support for reinstatement. Although the Commandant bought the idea, we ultimately lost out because the Director of Athletics strongly opposed it, apparently because it wouldn't be a money maker. Regardless, Jerry and I had yet another great time challenging our parent institution to get with it. He was a great swimmer and a wonderful friend. A few years after graduation, he died in a car crash in Belgium, and I still miss him to this day.

---

[3]   The Commandant is usually a senior Navy Captain, or Marine Colonel who runs the day-to-day operations of the Academy under the leadership of a Vice Admiral, who serves as Superintendent.

"The Wather Polo"

"Anyone can win—unless there happens to be a second entry."
–George Ade (1866-1944)

Another interesting water polo-related episode took place a few years earlier during my Youngster (sophomore) cruise to South America in 1957 on the *Iowa*. This was supposedly the ship's final cruise before its rumored conversion to ten million razor blades. Actually, the latter has yet to happen, since she was recommissioned for service in the Middle East under President Reagan and currently sits alongside a pier in Long Beach, California, as an impressive monument to the past.

As we entered port in Rio de Janeiro, all midshipmen were apprised of various events that would be taking place ashore, as we were set loose to enjoy liberty in this exciting port of call. I was particularly intrigued by a party that would be taking place at the U.S. Ambassador's residence to which upper-class mids were invited (but certainly not Youngsters, like myself). I persuaded a classmate by the name of Dave Mullen, who bunked in the rack below me on the *Iowa*, to join me in crashing the party.

As we set out to do so, it began to rain; and we soon found ourselves running through a bit of a downpour, shouting to locals along the way who were sitting outside on their balconies, *"Donde esta la casa del Embajador de los Estados Unidos?"* After reaching our destination by following a series of pointing fingers, we hid behind one of the front columns of the rather palatial residence, until the greeter went out to welcome the next car that drove up to discharge its passengers. We slipped in while he was tending to the new arrivals and used our handkerchiefs to wipe off our dripping uniforms. The party was every bit as good as hoped, and I met an attractive young lady, with whom I spent what free time I could during the remaining days in port.

Late in the week, I invited her to attend a water polo match between the Brazilian Naval Academy and a pick-up team from our ship, for which I had volunteered. The Brazilians had a superb team, in contrast to our own, which had never before played together. Needless to say, they beat us rather soundly. When the match was over, the sponsors graciously awarded both 1st and 2nd place medals. Because I was de facto captain of our team, I was first in line to receive a "second place" medal. I noticed that the presenters of said medals weren't paying a lot of attention to detail, so after receiving mine, I slipped to the end of my line to receive a second one (which I, in turn, passed to Marianne). She was duly impressed; and in a letter I received from her after returning to the States, she mentioned how much she enjoyed "the wather polo." Although I have never been back to Rio, 60-year-old memories linger of good times driving around in her Mercedes SL 500 in one of the more magnificent settings in the world. If you haven't been there yourself, its great grist for your bucket list!

More recently, in 1986, I played in an annual alumni water polo match against the Naval Academy varsity. As I watched the varsity warming up, they looked like cigarette boats plowing through the water (and like Adonis, when they exited the pool). Small wonder that almost all of them volunteer for duty as Navy SEALs upon graduation. The Alums ended up winning the meet but only because the Navy water polo coach, who was doing the refereeing, heavily tilted all judgement calls in our favor. Even so, being 18 years older than the next oldest alum, I had long forgotten how tough it is to swim with someone hanging on to you. Suffice it to say, it was a wet and sobering experience. Life was infinitely sweeter once it was over.

On the Road Again

Because I had no independent source of funding and we only received minimal stipends as midshipmen (ranging from $5/month the first year to $15/month the last year),[4] making the trek home to Southworth, Washington (and back) was always a bit of an adventure and usually consisted of flying in space-available hops on military aircraft heading in the right direction followed by more deliberate hitch-hiking along various highways on the final stretch.

Typical of said adventures was one trip where I was flying in a C-47, a World War II vintage propeller plane, when one of its two engines caught fire. I recall putting on my parachute and being ready to jump without a moment's hesitation. The fire was extinguished and we landed safely, so the jump never happened. Ever since, I have been struck by the seeming incongruity of my absolute willingness to parachute from a plane that's in trouble versus my ingrained reluctance to do so from one that isn't. It's on my bucket list, so we'll see.

On another occasion I had caught a flight to San Francisco and was hitch-hiking north to Seattle. At one point, I found myself just south of the Oregon border, and it being Christmas Eve, traffic was almost non-existent. Not even Santa was on the road! Although I was in uniform, with overcoat and gloves,

---

[4] These amounts were a midshipman's actual spending money, after all else had been deducted from his monthly salary (uniforms plus multitudinous other expenses). Over the years, the spending money for plebes has gradually increased to $100 a month.

it was very cold; and rather than freeze to death, I decided to stand in the middle of the highway and flag down the next vehicle, no matter what. That strategy worked, and I soon found myself traveling at break-neck speed in a car with a broken heater. The driver was a mean-spirited character who was pretty awful to his girlfriend, who was riding alongside him in the front seat. Feeling sorry for the girl, I gave her my gloves when they dropped me off in Portland. So, the remainder of my journey north became even colder.

Another time, while heading back to the Academy, I found myself on a plane out of McCord Air Force Base near Tacoma, Washington heading to an air base near Charleston, SC. Even though we landed late at night, the heat and the humidity were intense. An Air Force First Lieutenant, who had caught a ride on the same flight, suggested that we get a room at the BOQ (Bachelor Officer Quarters). We did, and after a cool shower, hit the sack. I awoke to find him sitting on the side of my bed with less than honorable intentions. So, I slugged him, grabbed my gear, and got out of there. It was about 4:00 AM in a strange land, and I can't recall exactly what I did to get back to the Academy on time; but whatever it was, it worked.

In telling this, I am reminded of a sign that appeared on an Air Force base as part of a major effort to reduce errors in all phases of its operations:

> *To err is human, to forgive divine – neither of which is the policy of the 8th Air Force.*

Finally, to round out my adventures as a free traveler, I was heading home on summer vacation after Second Class Summer (or Aviation Summer as it was sometimes called) and found myself stranded for about a week at a Naval Air Station outside of Dallas. I was in my khaki uniform, with only a small gym bag of personal articles along. Because it was quite hot and I had been waiting for the better part of a week for any space-available aircraft heading west, I decided to take a break and made my way to the base pool to go for a swim.

While in the pool, I noticed an attractive young lady swimming laps. So, I accidentally collided with her and in the course of apologizing, made her acquaintance. We went out that evening and later on, when I dropped her off, this dream encounter came to a screeching halt when her father walked in to find us waxing friendly on the couch, apparently beyond his comfort zone. He was the Base Operations Officer in control of incoming and outgoing aircraft, so it was no surprise when I magically found myself on a plane headed to LA early the next morning – just me alone with 38 women Marines. We engaged in idle banter for much of the trip, but they were a pretty rough bunch and clearly a huge step down from my swimming companion.

Orcas and Nephews

"Confidence is going after Moby Dick in a rowboat and taking the tartar sauce with you. Zig Ziglar (1926-2012)

Shortly after I began trekking back to Southworth, while on various vacations from the Academy and for many years afterward, I established a tradition of rowing from the shoreline near our home to Blake Island, a heavily-wooded, uninhabited island about a mile and a half off shore in Puget Sound. Most of the time it was just over and back, with a short hike on the island in between. Once Mike and I rowed all the way around the island on a pretty rough day, depositing yet one more memorable experience in the memory bank of life.

On one such trip in the late 1980's, I took Mike's son, Schuyler, with me. As we were leaving Blake and heading back to the mainland, I noticed a prominent bow wave coming toward us pushed along by some submerged creature and began rowing a little faster. As it drew closer, Schuyler and I both noticed that whatever it was that was causing the wave, was big and distinctly black and white in color. We concluded it must have been an Orca (killer whale), which are known to sometimes frequent the Sound. Several other observers in sailboats moored offshore were as transfixed by its presence as we were.

I considered throwing Schuyler overboard to distract the whale and make a quicker get-away; but he was very young, and I thought that doing so might tarnish my reputation, so I backed off. Not then nor to this day has anyone, including Schuyler's dad, ever believed our story. But ever since, Schuyler and I have enjoyed our honorary membership in the "Sacred Brotherhood of the Orca."

Incidentally, the day when I could even think of throwing Schuyler over the side has long since passed. A few years after that experience, we were together again in attempting to scale Mt. Rainer, along with his dad, Kate's husband and their oldest son Mark, and my youngest step-son, Pearson. Of the six of us, only Schuyler made it to the top. Years later he participated in no fewer than three *Iron Man* competitions, each consisting of a 2.4-mile swim, a 112-mile bike ride, and a 26.2-mile run.[5] No, the days of throwing Schuyler anywhere are long gone.

One of the key inspirations for me rowing to Blake in the first place was because it is supposedly where the legendary Chief Seattle took his bride on their honeymoon. I say legendary because he was the source of any number of profound and compelling insights, especially in relation to Mother Earth.

After leaving the Navy, Mike spent a highly successful career in government — working for the Environmental Protection Agency, serving for most of that time as Director of the Agency's Northwest Regional Laboratory, coincidentally located just a few miles via crow from Blake Island. Both he and I revere the legacy of the good Chief, especially as it relates to the environment. As he so eloquently put it many moons ago:

> *Humankind has not woven the web of life...we are but a part of it. Whatever we do to the web we do to ourselves. All things are bound together...all things connect. Whatever befalls the earth, befalls also the children of the earth.*
>
> Chief Seattle

---

[5] It apparently runs in the family, because Schuyler's delightful wife Tara has also tried her hand at a couple of *Iron Mans*. The two of them are now balancing full-time jobs with raising two highly precocious kids, a daughter named Logan, who is 6 years old, and a son two years younger named Conrad. One evening while sitting around the dining room table, Logan and Conrad were discussing how they weren't sure how they could ever believe anything their Daddy said, because he teased them so much. At one point, Conrad spoke up a bit louder and said, "For example, Daddy said that girl cows grow their vaginas on top of their backs." At this point, Schuyler and Tara were rolling with laughter and Schuyler said, "Conrad, I never said that." Whereupon his four-year-old son replied with an exasperated look on his face, "I know, Daddy. IT'S JUST AN EXAMPLE!"

"Yellow peril" over the Academy
(permission obtained from the artist,
LCOL William J. Pardee,
USAF (Ret), Class of 1951, USNA)

Plebe Cruise on the
USS IOWA (BB61)
(official U.S. Navy photo)

A proud institution

Aviation summer

Graduation picture
(official U.S. Navy photo)

Jerry scores one for "Navy."
(Naval Academy Public Relations photograph)

Graduation day

Dad and me at Mike's graduation a decade later

Blake Island

Chapter Four

TAKE HER DOWN

Be ever questioning. Ignorance is not bliss. It is oblivion. You don't go to heaven if you die dumb. Become better informed. Learn from other's mistakes. You could not live long enough to make them all yourself.

Hyman Rickover

When it came time to make our service selections toward the end of First Class year, deciding which service we wanted to go into (Navy, Army or Air Force) or in which branch of the Navy we wanted to serve: Navy line (surface ships or submarines), Navy Air or the Marine Corps, I was pretty set on becoming a jet pilot. However, about that same time, a unique opportunity arose in which the Navy, for the first time ever, was going to select 25 newly-minted graduates from the Naval Academy and 25 from other technically-proficient universities to be trained for service aboard nuclear submarines. A couple of years earlier the *USS Nautilus*, the world's first nuclear-powered submarine, had made headlines by completing the first submerged transit of the North Pole, so it appeared that nuclear submarines might become the wave of the future. Without hesitation, I volunteered for nuclear power training.

What made this opportunity so special was that up until then, it had typically taken three or more years to reach that same point, starting with at least a year aboard a surface ship to qualify as "Officer of the Deck" (OOD, the Commanding Officer's representative in charge of the safety and navigation of the ship). Then, if the Commanding Officer approved your application and the Navy selected you for submarine duty, you were assigned to six months of Submarine School in New London, Connecticut before reporting for duty aboard a diesel submarine, the specific choice of which keyed to your final Sub School class standing. It would then take another year or so to qualify in submarines and earn the right to wear "gold dolphins" above the left, breast pocket on your uniform.

At this point, you could theoretically apply for advanced nuclear power training. Selection for this training, however, required the personal approval of Admiral Hyman G. Rickover. The Admiral had pioneered the Navy's transition to nuclear power (for propelling all of its future submarines and a number of its surface ships) and enjoyed a legendary reputation as a very tough grader. Thus, the opportunity we were being given as fresh-caught graduates effectively bypassed most of that earlier process leading up to securing the Admiral's approval.

The catalyst for this new opportunity was the conclusion by the Office of Naval Intelligence that the Soviet Union was about to embark on a massive nuclear submarine building program. In 1960, there were fewer than a dozen U.S. nuclear subs patrolling the ocean's depths, all of them fast-attacks (SSNs),[6] with the exception of a single, long-range ballistic missile-launching submarine, the *USS George Washington (SSBN598)*. Feeling compelled to stay ahead of the forthcoming Soviet challenge, the U.S. Navy initiated its own formidable building program.

During the Kennedy Administration, it reached the point where one new SSBN was being launched every month, requiring both a Blue Crew and a Gold Crew to man and operate it. The strategic mission at that time required that each crew operate the ship on a three-month cycle—three months on duty (the first month repairing any problems from the other crew's latest patrol, followed by two months of patrolling one's self). On top of this, a number of new attack subs were also being constructed; and the available manpower to operate all of these new submarines was stretched to the breaking point. Hence the decision to take a chance on us kids.

An Exciting Juncture

"That must be wonderful; I don't understand it at all." –Moliere (1622-1673)

The personal interviews with Rickover became the stuff of legends, as he was famous for keeping interviewees as off-balance as possible, while subjecting them to mild and not-so-mild harassment in one form or another. Famous among his methods was that of making the candidate sit on a specific chair, the front legs of which had been purposely shortened to create a disquieting feeling of "falling off" while being interviewed and to ensure that the Admiral was speaking from a higher vantage point. In my own case, other

---

[6] SSN (Submarine Service Nuclear) is the designation for a general purpose, "fast-attack" nuclear submarine and SSBN (Submarine Service Ballistic Nuclear), for a nuclear-powered, ballistic missile-launching submarine.

than ordering me to cut back on my extracurricular activities, including dating so much; I emerged reasonably intact, largely because my class standing had been improving each year.

More typical, though, was the experience of the classmate in our group who stood the lowest among us. Rickover kept him cooling his heels outside his office for about four hours before he finally called him in. Without letting the candidate say a word, he commented on his low class standing and said, "Why, you're so G** D*** dumb, I can't hold an intelligent conversation with you. OUT!!" After spending another two hours outside his office, Rickover called him in again and, after thoroughly chastising his poor performance, accepted him into the Program. The irony is that this classmate stood 52nd out of a graduating class of 798. Because the Submarine Service was strictly voluntary at that point and rapidly acquiring an intimidating reputation, within a couple of years, the Navy was having to reach considerably lower in succeeding classes to meet its needs.

Nuclear school was tough, with one out of three not making it through. The attrition among those of us who were "direct inputs" was probably a bit lower since we were used to a rigorous study regime; but for those in our class who had come through the normal pipeline and had been away from the academic grind for as many as five years, it was tremendously stressful. In math alone (one of six courses that we took each day), we covered an entire math major's college curriculum during the six months of our training. When I graduated from Bullis, I received the school's top award for mathematics and was convinced there wasn't an algebra problem in the world that I couldn't solve; but when we hit quantum mechanics in Advanced Nuclear Power School, I was a mere child in a very strange land.

The Tobacco Fields

"He who devotes sixteen hours a day to hard study may become as wise at sixty as he thought himself at twenty." –Mary Wilson Little (1880-1952)

The next phase of the program consisted of another six months of "hands-on" training at a shore-based nuclear prototype. The prototype in my case was located in the Connecticut River Valley near Windsor Locks, Connecticut, where I soon found myself sharing a small rented house with six other aspiring "nukes". That too proved quite a grind, as 16-hour days quickly became the norm. Here, the roles reversed and those who had come to the training from the fleet now had the upper hand over us direct-inputs. To qualify as OOD on a surface ship and later on a diesel submarine, they had spent countless hours tracing their ship's propulsion, hydraulic, and electrical systems and becoming intimately familiar with their interdependency.

We were far too preoccupied to enjoy much of life, but I did manage to buy a used 1953 Plymouth, which had a bad habit of breaking down at the most inconvenient times. I recall with mild amusement the innumerable stops in the surrounding tobacco fields while commuting to and from the prototype, with me under the hood trying to figure out what was wrong with the carburetor. An unattractive brown in color, the car was generously christened "Dan, the tan sedan" by John Donlon, one of my six ranch mates – a senior submariner, with a wife and seven kids in Groton, Connecticut, (a little more than an hour's drive from where we were living).

I was dating a young lady—also from Groton, who I had met while in nuclear school, so I gave John a ride down there and back whenever we could get away on a weekend. John was not only a tremendously fun person to be around, but he was second to none in his command of submarine lore, which I soaked up like a sponge during those weekend jaunts. A few years ago, I traveled to New London for the 50th reunion of our Nuclear Power School class, and one of my greatest joys was seeing John again. Still fun and hadn't aged a day.

After the prototype, I attended Submarine School in New London and learned most of what there was to know about diesel submarines. It also proved to be a crucial fork in the road for me personally. When I graduated from Sub School, I had first pick of the available nuclear subs, and quickly narrowed the field to two: the *USS Skipjack (SSN585)*, the world's fastest, and the *USS Thresher (SSN593)*, the latest and greatest (the lead submarine in the latest class of fast-attacks). I had dismissed as possibilities the *Nautilus* and *Skate*, which were getting a bit worn at that point, and any Polaris Missile-carrying SSBN's, which were far less exciting to serve on than the attack boats. Fortunately for me, "world's fastest" sounded sexier, and I chose *Skipjack*. Sadly, however, two of my classmates elected to go with *Thresher*, which sank on April 10, 1963, while conducting a "deep dive" off of Cape Cod. It went down with the loss of all 112 crew members and 17 shipyard personnel, who were onboard at the time. It was the first of two US nuclear submarines ever to be lost at sea. The second was the *USS Scorpion (SSN589)*, sister ship[7] to *Skipjack*, which sank for unknown reasons in May of 1968, while transiting from the Azores to Norfolk, Virginia.

---

[7] The terms "ship," "boat," and "submarine" are used interchangeably in the Submarine Force.

The loss of *Thresher* was attributed to a combination of flooding in the Engine Room caused by a failed silver-brazed joint in a sea water piping system and an inadequate high-pressure air system for bringing the sub to the surface in an emergency (by blowing water out of the ship's ballast tanks). This tragedy led to the development of a first-ever system for inspecting the bonding of silver-brazed joints and to the installation of a higher-pressure emergency blow system, changes that set back the entire submarine building program by a full two years.

On a more personal level, the human losses were incalculable. Taking just my two Academy classmates, Jim Henry had graduated close to the top of our class and had all-but-single-handedly won two college bowl contests on national television (a quiz show that pitted a team of West Point Cadets against a team of Naval Academy Midshipmen, following the playing of the annual Army-Navy football games in the late 1950's). Ron Babcock, who also stood high in the class, had a wife who was six months pregnant at the time. In the wake of all this, I felt undeservedly fortunate and more than a little obliged to "give back" in whatever form that might take.

The Real Deal

I reported aboard the *Skipjack* while she was undergoing a seven-month overhaul at Portsmouth Naval Shipyard in Kittery, Maine. Because I was "George," (the most junior officer onboard— by a full 5 years, no less), I was assigned to be the ship's Gunnery Officer, First Lieutenant, and Commissary Officer. As Gunnery Officer, I was in charge of the Torpedo gang, a half-dozen hot-shot Torpedomen who, as rumor had it, were unrivaled in the time it took them to fire six torpedoes, drain the torpedo tubes, reload them, and shoot six more. They were good, and they knew it.

I did my best to earn their respect and think I did, although I wasn't totally certain after they invited me to attend a "shower" for one of the gang who had managed to get his girlfriend pregnant. So, there I was in a house that one of them rented, the only officer participating in this joyous occasion. The shower gifts were creative – a six pack of beer with baby nipples instead of bottle caps, and the like. At some point, early on, one of them slipped me a mickey (or Mickey Finn, as it is more properly called) — a drink doctored to render one unconscious. The next thing I knew, I was stretched out on the porch, covered with about a quarter inch of snow when a couple of the men carried me upstairs and poured me into the nearest bed, from which I emerged some 13 hours later. It was a less-than-sobering experience, and I don't know to this day if we celebrated the birth of a boy or a girl.

While aboard *Skipjack*, I had a number of interesting experiences. One of the more memorable took place during the Cuban Missile Crisis. We were about to deploy to the Mediterranean Sea to determine if a US Carrier Task Group could defend itself against a nuclear submarine (the very first such test). Accordingly, we were loaded out for a 60-day deployment.

The evening before our departure, I was out with my then fiancé when we heard President Kennedy's message on the car radio, calling for a US blockade of Cuba as the latest chess move designed to prevent the Soviets from deploying long-range missiles close to our shores. I immediately returned to the ship and spent all night off-loading exercise torpedoes and on-loading the real thing. We also took onboard another 30 days of provisions. These actions were predicated on the assumption that surely the world's fastest submarine would be called up to be part of the blockade. A totally wrong guess as it turned out. The next morning, we set sail for the Med, walking on top of coffee cans in the engineering spaces. A 90-day load-out on a 252 ft. long submarine is not without its consequences.

To prepare for our encounter with the carrier, we exchanged our IFF/UHF (Identification Friend or Foe/Ultra High Frequency) mast for an RDF (Radio Direction Finder) antenna prior to getting underway, so we could determine from afar where the Task Group was at any point in time. This proved very useful as we would maneuver to get in front of them, then close at flank speed. Our 30 knots[8] in one direction combined with the carrier's 30 knots in the opposite direction gave us a 60+ knot "relative range rate" (rate of closure). There were 16 destroyers protecting the carrier, but at that speed, they would only see a couple of blips on their sonar screens before we had fully penetrated the formation. After doing a U-turn under the carrier, we took close-up photographs of its screws, then shot flares onto the flight deck (which was totally unappreciated by the carrier's crew).

After proving unable to evade us after using every trick in their book (maneuvering into shallow waters and masking their screws, plus any number of other evasion techniques), the Admiral in charge of the Task Group boarded us to learn all he could about how we operated and to determine what, if anything, they could possibly do to redeem the carrier's invincible reputation. I was OOD when we were on the surface for the transfer and still recall catching this Admiral swinging in the breeze at the end of a helo line and steering him into the small opening on top of the sail that served as our "bridge." That

---

[8] *The term "knot" is short for nautical mile, which equates to 2,000 yards (slightly longer than a regular mile).

all went fine, but I never did hear what he concluded after spending a full day onboard.

A few days later as we pulled into the harbor at La Spezia, Italy (our first European port of call), an 0-ring seal ruptured on one of the hydraulic valves close to the diving stand, spouting oil all over the place. I was on watch as the Diving Officer at the time and dove into the manifold area to shut the valve that would stop the leak. As it turned out, I got the wrong valve. No damage done other than a slightly singed arm, a slightly bruised ego, and more than slight laughter from others over my misplaced heroics. Later, when I was on deck (in my capacity as First Lieutenant) to oversee the line handlers as we were preparing to tie up, I remember the excitement I felt about setting foot in Europe for the first time.

Living the Dream

"Sex appeal is fifty percent what you've got, and fifty percent what people think you've got." –Sophia Loren

Once we tied up in La Spezia, I was assigned to permanent shore patrol duty. Normally this is undesirable duty, hence its all-but-automatic assignment to the most junior officer onboard. In this particular case, it proved to be just the opposite. For the next eight days, I was in officer's quarters ashore, and my duty consisted of four hours of patrolling the city's bars at night to keep the sailors in line. Then I would have 20 hours off, during which I could do anything I wanted.

On my first day off, I took a tour bus to Florence, which was only a couple of hours away. While on the bus, I ran into several sailors from my sub who started razzing me about being slow on the draw. Two junior officers from some other ship were clearly making their moves on our lovely Florentine tour guide who spoke flawless English. With the sailors' encouragement, I made my own moves and ended up dating Laura del Mela until the ship set sail for France a week later. With most of the world's great art concentrated in Florence, it is a very romantic city; and, in one fell swoop, my life-long fantasizing about Europe had suddenly come to pass.

Meanwhile, back at the *Skipjack,* the other officers were standing port and starboard duty, alternately standing watch one day, and doing ship's work the next. In other words, very little time ashore. When they learned how well I had fared, one of our more senior officers volunteered to take shore patrol duty in our next port of call, which was Toulon, France. However, he experienced a much more demanding routine, with little time to enjoy himself and ended up quite frustrated. I, on the other hand, became a great fan of the French when I noticed that the diameter of the wine-fill connection on the French sub moored alongside was greater than that of our own connection for replenishing fuel oil. The French clearly had their priorities straight!

The Pucker Factor

Not long after our European cruise, we conducted what was called a Spec Op (short for "Special Operation"), Navy- speak at the time for conducting surveillance operations in Soviet waters. This consisted of transiting undetected across the Atlantic, traversing the GI (Greenland/Iceland) Gap, and patrolling off the coast of Northern Russia, often in close proximity to Murmansk, their chief submarine base.

At the ripe-old age of 22, while viewing Russia up close and personal for the first time (albeit through a periscope), I began to wonder what would happen if I got caught. We were close to shore and well within their territorial waters, so it wasn't an entirely frivolous concern. Anyway, I thought that if they pulled out my fingernails, maybe I could hang tough—but maybe not; I don't like pain. However, all they would have to do is force-feed me broccoli; and I would tell them how to build reactor plants, nuclear submarines, or anything else they might want to know. [9]

The "pucker factor" was quite high throughout the deployment. At one point, for example, while I was again serving as OOD, we detected a Soviet submarine formation and began maneuvering our way into its center. This sounds far more heroic than it actually was because we knew the Soviets didn't have any nuclear subs of their own at that time, and we also knew our submarine could outrun their fastest anti-submarine torpedo (at least in a straight-away). Even more to the point, the Soviet submarines in question were actively recharging their batteries, which meant that they were operating close to the surface, drawing in fresh air from the outside through their snorkel masts in order to run the diesel engines with which they charged the batteries. This process was inherently noisy, which made it highly unlikely they would ever be able to hear our presence in the midst of theirs.

The goal in penetrating their formation was to determine the sound signatures (noise characteristics) of the individual subs by which we would be

---

[9] In March of 1990, when President H.W. Bush was quoted as disliking broccoli, I wrote him a letter to fortify his resolve by telling him the above story. I also mentioned that I felt the same way about cauliflower, and brussels sprouts ("that vegetable in which all that is foul in a cabbage has been condensed to a single bite"). Sensing a kindred spirit, he sent back a lighthearted reply (Addendum B).

able to identify them whenever we crossed paths in the future. To the trained ear, sonar signatures can provide a great deal of information about another submarine or ship, like the kind of propulsion plant being used, the number of blades on their propeller(s), and any number of other characteristics unique to a particular ship or submarine.

Our Commanding Officer ultimately decided to back away from penetrating the formation because of an unexplained noise that suddenly began emanating from our own submarine, which he feared the Soviets might detect. The noise was later determined to have been caused by a fan in the crew's berthing compartment, which had short-circuited. By then, however, we had long-since withdrawn from the formation, and it had moved on. Despite our withdrawal, the sound information we were able to secure from outside the formation was more than adequate to have justified the total effort. Throughout this and various other encounters, there was always a degree of risk involved, made all the greater by the Soviet Navy's penchant for holding "depth charge practice" with live charges whenever they thought a U.S. submarine might be in the vicinity. No explosions ever came close, but we did occasionally hear them in the distance.

Another interesting development that took place while I was serving as OOD involved our transit into the White Sea, an inland sea in the north of Russia. At one point, I heard what sounded like a cracking sound over the underwater hydrophone and noticed a trace on the scope unlike any I had ever seen. I called the Captain to the Control Room, and he immediately identified it as ice. He had been Navigator on the *Nautilus* when she made her first transit under the North Pole, so was quite familiar with the sound. We were all surprised, though, because according to our best intelligence, there wasn't supposed to be any ice in the White Sea in August. Because *Skipjack* wasn't rigged for under-ice operations*[10], we made a U-turn and retraced our steps to open waters.

Sobering Realities

Skipjack was equipped with the first S5W pressurized-water reactor core; and because the calculations used to estimate core life for any nuclear reactor are inherently inaccurate, we had *carte blanche* to travel at flank speed (the fastest rate of speed possible) everywhere we went in order to exhaust the core as soon as possible. This would enable the Navy to determine with

---

[10] *To operate safely under ice, the top of the sail and the leading edges of the sail-planes need to be reinforced so they are strong enough to break through the ice when surfacing the submarine, should that become necessary.

greater precision how long the core would last before other similarly equipped submarines would need to be refueled with a new one. It was a particularly important calculation; because as it turned out, no fewer than 98 of these S5W reactor cores were eventually built to propel eight different classes of submarine.

The price the Navy paid for determining this more accurate picture was twofold. First, traveling at flank speed placed a heavier-than-normal burden on the engineering support systems, such as the sea water pumps used to cool the steam generators and the like. Over time, these systems on the *Skipjack* broke down faster than they would have otherwise.

The second price was the need to operate at deeper depths than normal in order to minimize one's noise signature (by reducing the noise produced by the popping of small air bubbles that form on the blades of a fast-moving propeller as it slices through the water). This phenomenon is referred to as cavitation, and the way to minimize it is by operating at deeper depths where the increased sea pressure makes it more difficult for such bubbles to form. The bottom line was that we traveled fast and deep wherever we went. That is, until the loss of the *Thresher*.

A sidebar of that particular tragedy was the fact that *Skipjack* was also operating in the same general vicinity at the time; and because the news initially broke without naming the submarine in question, there was a brief period of time in which a number of *Skipjack* families feared the worst. Following the sinking of the *Thresher*, we began transiting at shallower depths. It was thought that the suspected source of the problem that had sunk the *Thresher* (sea water leakage at a deep depth caused by failure of a silver-brazed joint) could just as easily cause other submarines to meet a similar fate.

One day, I came to fully appreciate the magnitude of this problem when I leaned against a vent on a sea water pump in the Engine Room, and it came off in my hand. It was a silver-brazed joint. Fortunately, the ship was on the surface at the time, so there were no dire consequences. However, had it happened when we were submerged during normal operations, full-pressure sea water would have shot out of that vent and probably caused a total loss of power as it shorted out the electrical systems (similar to what is thought to have happened on *Thresher*). That particular vent was pointed directly at the Maneuvering Room, from which the major engineering functions are controlled (electrical as well as mechanical). Sea pressure increases by 44 pounds per square inch with every hundred feet in depth, so it doesn't take much of a hole to have a major impact.

In addition to standing watches and performing my Division Officer duties, the first ten months of my year aboard *Skipjack* were consumed with qualifying in submarines. This was normally a year-long process, but I was anxious to become a full-fledged submariner as soon as possible. When that magic day finally arrived, Shepherd Jenks, the Commanding Officer, provided a special touch for the occasion. When he pinned on my "dolphins," he used those which he had worn when navigating *Nautilus* under the Pole in 1958.

To further celebrate the fact that I was the first officer to ever qualify in submarines aboard *Skipjack* (all of the other officers, who were considerably senior to me, had qualified elsewhere before reporting aboard), the crew added a touch of its own. I was made to wear a large 20 lb. plaque of cast-iron dolphins around my neck for 24 hours, which they had specifically designed for the occasion.

During that year and with a lot of help from the superb enlisted personnel who worked for me, we won the "E" in Gunnery (annual award for Excellence) and the Ney Award for the most outstanding mess (food service) in the Fleet. I must confess to a slight sleight of hand on the latter. When the Ney inspection team arrived, it was presented with menus that had been artificially enhanced for the occasion with a copious use of adjectives wherein "potatoes" became "oven-roasted potatoes", "peas" became "fresh, garden peas", and so on. Here, it should also be noted that submarines receive an additional food allowance for their crews in order to compensate for the fact that they typically run out of fresh provisions after the first two weeks of a patrol, at which point one finds steak and lobster creeping onto the menu.

As for the food service aspect of the inspection, for the first time ever, the crew ate off of checkered table cloths, with lit candles providing an irresistible ambiance. Transparent to be sure, but nevertheless effective. Looking back on my experience aboard *Skipjack*, it was an exciting and memorable time aboard one of the finest submarines that ever sailed.

Moments to Remember

While *Skipjack* was the world's fastest underwater, she was pretty fast on the surface as well. One small trick that boosted her on-surface performance was what we called putting her "on the step." This consisted of proceeding ahead at 19 knots and placing the stern planes on an angle of 5 degrees "rise." This particular configuration then resulted in a certain planing effect, which added an additional knot and a half of speed.

I will never forget the exhilaration I felt when standing alone on the bridge at night as OOD, gliding along on the step under a starlit sky, with the phosphorescent glow of the seawater streaming across the bow. It was me alone with the universe, fully immersed in all its majestic glory. At times dolphins would join in the fun, jumping alongside the vessel as we cut through the water. It was more than special. Even at sea level, it was mountaintop.

Time for Fun

"The Anglo-Saxon conscience does not prevent sinning; it only prevents enjoying one's sins." –Salvador de Madariaga (1886-1978)

With *Skipjack,* home-ported in New London, Connecticut; I lived in a snake ranch on the water in Groton Long Point, a semi-resort area about a half hour's drive from the ship. "Snake ranch" is a descriptive term for a group of bachelors living together, who are free to "snake" (move in on) any other ranch-mate's lady friend unless she and the ranch-mate are engaged to be married. In my case, there were seven of us living together, all junior officers serving aboard different submarines. The fact that we all qualified in submarines at about the same time was more coincidence than anything else, but it provided a wonderful excuse to hold a party to end all parties. It lasted three days and included a live rock band in addition to multitudinous other activities ranging from water skiing to flights in a small seaplane and lots in between. As would be expected, more than a little alcohol was consumed, with Fish House Punch constituting the basic staple.

At that time, there was a long-standing tradition in the Submarine Force that before you could pin on your dolphins (above the left breast pocket of your uniform) denoting your status as a full-fledged submariner, you must first put them in the bottom of a tall glass filled with various hard liquors and catch them in your teeth as you chugged the contents of the glass. Being mindful of the ritual, I snuck into the kitchen for a quick glass of milk to coat my stomach just prior to the moment of truth. As I downed the liquor and caught the dolphins, tears involuntarily flowed down both cheeks; and I formally joined the club. I heard sometime later that another submariner undergoing this same ritual actually died from the experience, the shock apparently being too much for his system; at which point the tradition switched to beer.

A Time of Transition

"The man who lives by himself and for himself is apt to be corrupted by the company he keeps." –Charles H. Parkhurst (1842-1933)

Little did I dream that my time at the ranch would have such a lasting impact on the rest of my life. At one point along the way, I complimented one of my ranch-mates on the attractive lady he was dating (and later married). He thanked me and said, "If you think she's something, you should see her sister." He then showed me the sister's picture, which was nothing short of stunning, but added, "She absolutely refuses to go out with any naval officer." Two months later we were married.

During those two months, I was transferred from the *Skipjack* to the Blue Crew[11] of the *USS Ulysses S. Grant (SSBN 631),* being built at the Electric Boat Company, across the *Thames River* from where *Skipjack* was moored. The next year proved to be a highly challenging time, working 16-18 hours days in rotating shift work, meaning that one's work hours changed every three days (thereby making it impossible to establish any sort of daily rhythm). Most of this time was spent inside the hull of the submarine, overseeing the building and testing of the ship's reactor plant systems, often in the cold, with little or no heat to speak of.

Adding to the challenge, was the fact that shortly after our marriage, Nina began suffering mightily from morning sickness. Although she and I had decided to wait a couple of years before having children, nine months and two days into our marriage, Lance Kallen Johnston was born. Strategic planning is one thing; execution quite another.

Building and commissioning a new submarine involves innumerable challenges that defy description in a single volume. Suffice it to say, the *Grant* was no exception. Adding significantly to those challenges, though, was the tyrannical nature of our commanding officer, Captain Larry From. He made life incredibly difficult for his officers to the point where the Navigator refused to eat in the Ward Room (with the other officers) in order to escape the Captain's constant criticisms. After a couple years of this, it reached the point where even I, as dedicated as I was, began to contemplate leaving the Navy. Then, from out of the blue, I received orders to report to Harvard University at a later date to pursue a Master's Degree in International Relations. It was a dream

---

[11] Under the Cold War concept of Mutual Assured Destruction (MAD), it was necessary to deter the possibility of a Soviet missile attack against the U.S. homeland by maximizing our own threat to their homeland. A highly effective way of doing that involved keeping our ballistic missile submarines at sea as much as possible, ready to launch their strategic missiles on a moment's notice, should that ever be required. As implied earlier, the best way to achieve this was to operate each of these submarines with two crews (a Blue Crew and a Gold Crew) that would alternate in taking it to sea. Both crews were equally capable of performing this function.

assignment; and although I would owe the Navy another two years of service upon completion of my studies, I decided to stay in and give it another shot.

As is true in much of life, there is often a degree of Russian Roulette involved in who you might be working for at any given point in time. This is particularly the case when it comes to military assignments. Although life on the *Grant* was often unpleasant for the reason cited, that was not the case aboard the USS *Casimir Pulaski (SSBN633)*, sister ship to the *Grant* (and also under construction at Electric Boat), which was commanded by Captain Robert Long. Because of Long's superb professional and leadership skills, he went on to become a 4-star Admiral in charge of all naval forces in the Pacific.

The opposite proved true with From, who, upon returning to port from our first patrol, refused to stay on for a second when asked to do so by higher authority. Having previously served as Commanding Officer of the Gold Crew on the USS *George Washington, (SSBN598)*, he apparently felt that yet another patrol would not be career-enhancing and opted instead for a different assignment. Ironically, his refusal probably cost him any chance he might have had for future promotion to Admiral.

To fill the leadership gap on the *Grant,* Commander Bob Dickieson, Prospective Commanding Officer of the Gold Crew of the USS *Kamehameha (SSBN642)*, then building in Mare Island, California, was temporarily assigned to take us on our next patrol. His arrival was like the Second Coming of Jesus – morale skyrocketed, and we had a great patrol.

Before setting out on that next patrol, though, Captain Dickieson asked me to see if I could get him on a space-available military flight to Saipan. I never asked him why, but gave it my best effort. Although I wasn't able to get him to Saipan, I did manage to get him on a flight to Yap, and that turned out to be a home run. The beaches on Yap were topless; and the Captain returned feeling like he had died and gone to heaven. I suspect that little excursion may have also contributed to the subsequent upsurge in crew morale.

When not at sea on the *Grant*, most of our time was spent in Hawaii where we were assigned when in an "off-crew status" (while the Gold Crew had the ship). In anticipation of these times of reuniting with our loved ones, most of us experienced a phenomenon called "channel fever", usually during the last day or two of patrol on our way back into port. It bore this label because it involved running a slight fever. The term "hot and bothered" comes to mind.

There were other adjustments associated with returning to port as well. One's first exposure to sunlight after being submerged for more than two months, was always a blinding experience. Moreover, because of the purity of the atmosphere in which we lived while on patrol (thanks to our oxygen generators, carbon dioxide scrubbers, and carbon monoxide burners), the initial smell of the salt-sea air once the outside hatch was opened was absolutely foul (air, which under any other conditions, smelled absolutely wonderful). Finally, because the concentration of carbon dioxide in the normal atmosphere is about .02% and the lowest we could get it down to with the scrubbers was 0.8%, it always took a few weeks for our body's metabolism to return to normal. Until it did, we were more susceptible than usual to coming down with colds, hay fever, and other mild ailments.

Upon returning from patrol, Nina, Lance and I would typically spend a delightful week on the beach at Bellows Air Force Base, on the windward side of the island where one could rent a cottage for $5 a day. One of our constant challenges while there was to keep Lance from running head-first into the pounding surf. Though he was only two at the time, that same fearless streak stayed with him into adulthood, including a stint in the Army as a Green Beret between high school and college.

At one point, he was an avid kickboxer, a skydiver, and a Jump Master with his Special Forces unit. It was in his sky-diving capacity that I bought him a reserve parachute one Christmas on the condition that if he ever had to use it, he would owe me dinner at a restaurant of my choice. Many paratroopers go a full career without ever deploying their emergency chute, so it seemed like a safe bet for Lance. As luck would have it, though, he had to deploy it twice during the next year, once at Fort Devens (outside of Boston) where his unit was headquartered, and a second time in Nigeria, while training Nigerians in special operations. We dined at the Bay Tower Room overlooking Boston Harbor; and when he all-but-choked on the size of the tab, I asked him what it would have said about how much I valued his life if we had eaten at McDonald's.

After Lance completed his four years in the Army, he enrolled at a community college in Bradenton, Florida, attended that for two years, and then transferred over to the University of South Florida in Tampa. He studied hard throughout; and just as he was completing his final year, he broke up with his girlfriend, which knocked him for quite a loop. His grades had been superb, and he was within sight of graduating at the top of his class (*summa cum laude*); but the break-up was clearly taking a toll on his ability to concentrate. While on an airplane together traveling to I forget where, I told him he should persevere in his studies and that the *summa* title was something that would stick with him for the rest of his life. To make sure I had his attention, I offered him a thousand dollars if he pulled it off. Happily, I am now a thousand dollars poorer.

Lance wasn't the only bright light in the Johnston harbor. One summer while vacationing at a lake in Maine, his younger brother taught me to play chess. Although Keith was only five years old at the time, I have always felt that even then, he held back in teaching me all he knew. We didn't play often, but the only time I recall beating him was several years later when it was late at night and he fell asleep on the couch, waiting for my next move. When I finally woke him up to continue the game, I finished him off. Later while playing on a plane coming back from Disney World, I thought I had him nailed for a second time until late in the game, he took my Queen with his pawn—and that was that. If you know anything about chess, a move like that is almost unheard of, unless the owner of said Queen is inept in the extreme. On that inglorious note, I retired from the game of chess.

Coincidentally, (or maybe not), Keith, also joined the Army, but did so after college. At one point, I had made a strategic blunder by taking both sons deep-sea fishing on a very rough day. And, that was all she wrote for the Navy. In Keith's case, he joined to take a year of language training in Egyptian Arabic at the Defense Language Institute in Monterey, California, which many consider to be one of the best language schools in the world. Thinking he wanted to one day become an archeologist, it made a lot of sense.

At last count, Keith has mastered a total of eight languages and at one point was teaching German to Spanish students in Barcelona. If that has anything to do with heredity, it must come from his mother because I barely do English. He has now turned into a bit of a renaissance man, teaching French and German to high school students, while training for a triathlon, competing as an American Ninja Warrior, and trying his hand at the violin. One busy fellow!

Chinese Hospitality

Back to Hawaii, both Nina and I thoroughly enjoyed our time on Oahu, which included occasional treks to town to take in the Don Ho show at Duke Kahanamoku's. Although the island had become heavily commercialized since I first lived there as a kid, the laid-back, hospitable nature of the culture remained intact. No one batted an eye if you walked through downtown Waikiki in a swimsuit, with your surfboard under your arm.

During this time, we rented a home in Makiki, a Chinese neighborhood in Honolulu. Soon after we moved there, we heard loud clicking noises and the sounds of people's voices in a wooded area behind the house. Nina baked a cake, and we followed the noise until we came across a group of Chinese neighbors engrossed in a game of mahjong. We introduced ourselves and gave them the cake. Some weeks later, just prior to departing on my first patrol, Wellington Wong, who lived next door, dropped by and gave us a sketch of the neighborhood, indicating exactly who lived where and who Nina should contact to address any kind of problem she might have while I was away (electrical, plumbing, etc.). No small part of why I have always loved the Islands.

An Unusual Challenge

Of the many challenges I faced during my time on the *Grant,* one of the more interesting occurred while serving as the ship's Diving Officer. We were heading to sea to conduct the first test-firing of the new A3 Polaris missile, which meant that five missiles would be selected at random from our 16-missile complement to shoot at a distant target. Not knowing in advance, which five would be selected created a bit of a problem. The automatic compensation systems for six of the 16 missile tubes were not functioning at the time. The purpose of these systems was to flood the right amount of sea water into the missile tube as the missile was fired in order to offset the loss of the missile's weight as it exited the tube. This was the only way the sub could maintain the neutral buoyancy required for additional shots. So, there I was the night before the test, with a college physics textbook trying to figure out how much water I would need to flood into any of the missile tubes for which the compensation system wasn't working. In other words, how much water would I need to flood into the tube through a given size hole that would equal the weight of the missile as it ignited and left the ship.

As luck would have it, when the time came to conduct the shoot, the tubes for three of the five missiles selected required manual compensation. This kept me incredibly busy throughout the test; and by the time the fifth missile had exited the tube, the ship was at its outer limits both on angle and depth for continuing to shoot. Even though we passed that test (barely); I was astounded at the final result. Three of the missiles traveled 2,000 miles to target, while one went to its maximum range of 2,500 miles, and the fifth just spun cartwheels in the sky shortly after take-off. All told, 60% accuracy for something I had expected to be much closer to 100%. Whatever the reliability, it's a miracle that neither side ever found a compelling reason to launch a missile with a real warhead. One can only pray that future generations never have to face that moment of truth.

Another Milestone

One of my final endeavors aboard the *Grant* before leaving for Harvard was to qualify for command of a nuclear submarine. This consisted of a two-stage process: first, writing a thesis that advanced the thinking on some aspect of submarine warfare; and second, actually performing the duties of a commanding officer while underway on a submarine different than one's own (and ideally one involved in challenging operations).

My thesis advocated the consolidation of several torpedo attack-related functions (at that time handled by different officers) under the auspices of a single individual and made what I thought was a compelling case for why this would be more effective than the existing arrangement. Once the thesis was accepted, I performed my underway examination aboard the *USS Carbonero (SS 337)*.

Adding to the challenge of this particular phase was the fact that *Carbonero* was a diesel-powered submarine (rather than nuclear) and I was required to perform the functions of the ship's Operations Officer and its Communications Officer (in addition to Commanding Officer) because I had never before served in either capacity. Finally, the frosting on the cake was the challenge of serving as Tactical Commander of a day-long exercise, involving our submarine, a surface ship, and two aircraft. To this day, I'm not sure how I managed to pull it off; but somehow, I did. Pretty heady stuff for a 27-year-old.

Matriculation at Harvard

"Too often we enjoy the comfort of opinion without the discomfort of thought."
–John F. Kennedy

In the summer of 1966, I emerged from the subway at Harvard Square to see a line of seven Hari Krishna disciples, hopping down the sidewalk in their long white robes, each with his hands on the hips of the one ahead, pony tails bouncing in the breeze and chanting as they went. I thought I had landed on Mars.

Born into a Navy family, educated at the Academy, and submerged in a submarine for the better part of the next six years, when I finally surfaced in Harvard Square, my world view was probably about ten degrees at most, all to the right of Genghis Khan. After the year at Harvard, though, I felt like my universe had expanded a full 360 degrees. I walked in to the right of Genghis and out with an "A" in Socialism.

That year proved to be a wonderful experience. The faculty were giants in their respective fields, and it was not at all unusual for classes to conclude with a round of applause from the students. A far cry from the Naval Academy! But whether it was Louis Hartz on liberalism, Henry Kissinger on foreign policy, Ernest May on American history, Merle Fainsod on Soviet government, Adam Ulam on Soviet foreign policy, or John Fairbank on China, they were all superb; and I reveled in the opportunity to learn from the best.

I arrived in the summer and took two courses prior to the beginning of the normal school year, one of which was "The Conduct and Control of Foreign Policy," taught by Professor William Y. Elliot. Elliot was a well-known figure both in academia and in the government (where he had played a key role in resource mobilization during World War II). I learned later that he was also Henry Kissinger's mentor. Anyway, he required a paper on some topic relevant to national security and suggested that I tackle Ballistic Missile Defense.

At the time, considerable debate was underway in government and in academic circles about whether or not the United States should erect a shield against a possible missile attack from the Soviet Union. After looking into it, almost everything I read on the topic was opposed to the idea, so I decided to make the case for building such a system.

In addition to the welcome "A" which the paper received, Professor Elliott had written all over the title page, insisting that I have the piece published in one of the leading academic or military journals. Long story short, I condensed the more than 17,000-word essay down to somewhere around 3,000 and sent it off to the *U.S. Naval Institute Proceedings* for their consideration. A couple of months later, I received a postcard, indicating they had sent it on to DOD (Department of Defense) Security Review to ensure it didn't include any classified information. Then a number of months passed, and I had totally forgotten about it until I one day received a check in the mail for $650 and a letter indicating they intended to use it as their feature article in an upcoming issue of the magazine. Having sold my first attempt at an article, I was high as a kite; and we used the money to purchase some much-needed furniture.

When the article finally appeared in print, Senator Thomas Dodd of Connecticut, who was serving on the Senate Armed Services Committee at the time and who had happened to read it while convalescing in a hospital, had it reprinted in the *Congressional Record* for future reference during the Senate debate on ABM that took place in 1967. By then, I was back at sea and found it rather amusing when I, as a lowly Lieutenant, one day received a letter from an Admiral castigating me for not having advocated a sea-based missile defense system. I remember thinking at the time, "Sea-based? Hell, I'm lucky to have even known there was such a thing as land-based." Anyway, here I am 50 years later, still enjoying some of those same furniture items.

One of the first courses I took when the school year began was Henry Kissinger's Seminar on National Security Policy. There are two things I recall rather vividly from that class. On one occasion when Henry had been particularly profound, I turned to the person next to me and said, "When I become President, I think I'm going to want this guy as my Secretary of State." Years later when President Nixon did exactly that, I chuckled and wondered, "What took him so long?"

Kissinger would periodically invite prominent government figures to speak to our seminar on topics relevant to their duties and our studies. There were only 22 of us in the class sitting around a large, round table, so these were great opportunities for meaningful dialogue. On one occasion, Secretary of Defense Robert McNamara paid us a visit. He was visibly shaken because the limousine in which he had been riding had been significantly jostled by a crowd of students venting their feelings about the Vietnam War. During the course of his presentation, he mentioned having spent sleepless nights over the slaughter of 300,000 Communists and Communist sympathizers that had just taken place in Indonesia. Because they were Communists and it was the height of the Cold War, there was little, if anything, he could have done to change that situation; but the point is that he cared.

McNamara was President of the Ford Motor Company when President Kennedy recruited him to become Secretary of Defense in order to bring greater financial discipline to the Defense Department. McNamara did so with a vengeance by incorporating at the top of the Pentagon bureaucracy an exceedingly able team of systems analysts to determine with far greater precision exactly how much of what kinds of military hardware would be required to implement the National Defense Strategy. In many respects, he attempted to bring that same discipline to bear in executing the Vietnam War.

My impression, which mirrored that of many others, was that Secretary McNamara was akin to a walking, talking Calvinistic computer. His comments on Indonesia, however, brought me up short. Although I wasn't aware of what was going on in Indonesia at the time, I felt humbled by the fact that I probably would not have lost any sleep over that situation—simply because they were Communists. From that moment onward, I had a very different impression of Robert McNamara. Many years later when I happened to have dinner with him in the wake of his documentary on *The Fog of War*, he displayed that same kind of compassion and no little remorse for his role in the Vietnam War and the enormous human costs it had incurred.

The year at Harvard was also a year of tremendous upheaval in the country. The SDS (Students for a Democratic Society) was taking hold on campuses across the country, as this movement of the New Left engaged countless students in opposing the Vietnam War. The mood was as unforgiving as it was aggressive, with the military bearing the brunt of citizen outrage in the form of jeers and insults as they returned from the conflict. In many instances, this was after having performed honorable, if not heroic, service for their country. At Harvard, those of us who were in the military never wore our uniforms – other than to graduation ceremonies at the end.

This combustible dynamic manifested itself in any number of ways. For example, I recall an instance in Michael Walzer's class on "Problems in Political Theory," when he was expressing his left-leaning views on a range of important topics, like civil disobedience should be viewed not only as one's right, but as one's responsibility and that U.S. aviators shot down over Vietnam should be treated as war criminals rather than prisoners of war. He went on to applaud the fact that students at the University of California had just taken over the Administration Building on the Berkley campus. At that point, I raised my hand and asked why that was such a good thing. What did those students know about administration? He was a bit taken aback, and that wasn't the point, of course; but the exchange was indicative of how different the drumbeats were to which so many of us were marching at that time.

Soon after enrolling at Harvard, I learned that those Army and Air Force officers who were also enrolled were given two years by their respective services to pursue their studies – the first year to obtain their Master's Degree in Public Administration, and the second to get a leg up on a PhD – after which they would be assigned to teach at West Point or the Air Force Academy. Upon learning this, I became determined to follow suit. I thought that if I could present the Navy with an impressive report card, they might let me stay for a second year. So, at the end of the first semester, I applied for and was accepted into the PhD program in Political Science. Normally, this was done at the end of one's first year of graduate studies, but I frankly didn't give it much thought until I learned some months later that they only accepted 40 applicants out of the more than 800 who had applied. On top of that, they offered me a full-tuition Fellowship to support my studies.

I was humbled by the honor and more determined than ever to get that second year. When the time came to request the extension – even with a stellar report card and the backing of a Senator and two Admirals, the Navy didn't bat an eye. It was back to sea. So much for jousting with windmills! But second year aside, the year I did spend was pure mountaintop from start to finish.

Speaking of finish, I was sitting at graduation feeling good about all I had learned, until the Valedictorian of the Harvard Class of 1967 started giving his valedictory address. He did so in Latin, and I was totally clueless as to what he was saying. Adding insult to injury, at various points in his talk, the entire assembly would break out in laughter; and I began to wonder if I was the only one in the crowd who didn't understand Latin. It was only when I turned the program over a few minutes later that I saw the English translation on the back.

A Fork in the Road

"When you come to a fork in the road, take it." –Yogi Berra

The Harvard experience lit some fires I wasn't sure the Navy could address. I was growing weary of poking holes in the ocean on uneventful Polaris patrols. By design, SSBNs go where the action isn't in order to avoid detection, so the ship will always be in position to launch its missiles if called upon to do so. Thus, unlike fast-attack submarines, there isn't much of a pucker factor other than the ever-present challenge of keeping a highly complex weapons platform patrolling the ocean's depths for two months at a stretch, without any shore support to assist in the repair of the inevitable equipment breakdowns. This, in effect, became my task when, following graduation from Harvard, I was assigned as Engineer Officer of the Blue Crew aboard the *USS James K. Polk (SSBN 645)* operating out of Rota, Spain.

Indicative of the above-challenge were the complex capabilities required to provide a seaborne deterrent against nuclear attack by a potential aggressor. At the forward end of the sub was the torpedo room, with its highly sophisticated fire control system to support the launching of multiple nuclear-capable torpedoes. In the middle of the boat, there was the Control Room, with its satellite-supported Ship's Inertial Navigation System (SINS) that provided the submarine's exact position on the face of the planet at all times. Further aft, was the equivalent of a miniature Cape Kennedy, capable of launching 16 ballistic missiles, each equipped with multiple nuclear warheads, thus enabling one to attack a number of different targets simultaneously. Finally, in the rear of the ship, was the nuclear reactor plant that provided the ship's propulsion. At that time, the SSBN was probably the most technically sophisticated ensemble of lethal capabilities known to man. Indeed, there was more firepower on a single SSBN than that collectively expended by all sides in World War II.

With my new assignment, I faced at least another three years of poking holes, owing the Navy two years of duty for my year at Harvard plus another year for the Vietnam War. The additional year resulted from President Johnson's decision that all members of the Armed Forces would serve for an additional year beyond their normal obligation to help meet the demands of that conflict. So, early-on in my new assignment, I applied for a transfer from the submarine service to Naval Intelligence, hoping to serve as a Naval

Attaché in challenging parts of the world, like the Soviet Union. My request was understandably denied, because the Navy had already invested heavily in training me for nuclear submarine duty.

One of the more pleasant aspects of serving as Chief Engineer of the Blue Crew on the *Polk* was the pleasure of turning over control of the Engineering Department to my Gold Crew counterpart, Roger Mehle, upon the completion of each patrol. Roger, also an Academy grad, was Engineer of the Gold Crew and an exceptionally fine one at that, having been the first in his year-group to be so assigned. With each turn-over, he and I would sit down with both commanding officers to provide our collective assessment of the material condition of the ship, which included the engineering challenges the outgoing crew had encountered during its patrol and those that the oncoming crew was likely to face.

Although these were serious meetings, Roger and I would typically precede our reports with effusive praise for one another, saying something like, "Captain, before giving my report, I feel compelled to compliment Roger for his superb performance during the last patrol and to note for the record that he may be the finest Chief Engineer in the entire Submarine Force." After the first couple of times, the skippers caught on to our little game and laughingly kicked us out of their stateroom until we could come back and give them a more serious-minded report.

On one of these occasions, Roger reported at some length on a major problem the Gold Crew had encountered toward the end of their patrol in which they had experienced major salt water contamination of the ship's hydraulic oil system. By the time they returned to port, this had gradually incapacitated the ship's ability to maneuver, requiring the wholesale replacement of every control valve in the system, which affected everything from the movement of the rudder and control planes to the firing of the ballistic missiles. Replacing these large aluminum block valves not only exhausted all such valves in the Navy's supply system, but required the cannibalization of existing spares from a number of other SSBNs as well. Of course, the thankless task of replacing them all fell to the Blue crew during our 28-day upkeep period prior to taking the ship on its next patrol.

Not to be outdone, the next patrol had challenges of its own. At one point, we encountered a perfect storm of mechanical malfunctions and human error, which led to a partial loss of electrical service to the reactor plant. By the time I made my way back to the engineering spaces to take control of the situation, virtually every alarm in the Maneuvering Room (engineering control room) was going off, and we were on the brink of losing propulsion.

With the invaluable support of superbly- capable enlisted watch standers, I was able to pull the fat out of the fire and avoid everyone's worst nightmare. Nevertheless, during this incident (and because of a resulting thermal shock to the system), the reactor plant demineralizer, through which the primary coolant was filtered, leaked some of its filtration material. So, at our next change of command in Rota, I commented to Roger, "Remember when you told me you had a little saltwater in the hydraulic oil? Well, to return the favor, we have a few demineralizer resin beads in the primary coolant." The burden this placed on Roger and his department during that next upkeep was every bit as onerous as that of our hydraulic-valve replacements. Without even trying, we had more than gotten even!

Here, it is worth noting that after many millions of miles of surface and submerged operations on nuclear power,, the United States Navy has never experienced a reactor accident, primarily because Admiral Rickover was every bit as hard on industry in demanding strictest adherence to exacting engineering standards as he was on those of us who were trained to operate "his" nuclear power plants. The above situation had tested to the fullest the resiliency of the men and equipment in preserving the invincible reputation of the Navy's seaborne nuclear deterrent.

In the aftermath of that perfect storm, the Blue Crew Commanding Officer, Peter Durbin, recommended that I receive a Navy Achievement Medal for my handling of the incident. When it came through, I accepted the award on behalf of the Blue Crew engineering department; but to this day feel that Roger should have received at least comparable recognition for his handling of the sea water contamination problem and the corrective action he initiated, which enabled *Polk* to complete its patrol and return safely to port.

(Not long afterwards, Roger left the submarine service to join an investment banking firm on Wall Street, and later serve as Assistant Secretary of the Treasury for Domestic Finance in the Reagan Administration. We remain fast friends to this day.)

Upon returning from a later patrol, I had a letter waiting for me from Nina, indicating that she wanted a divorce. Knowing how difficult the periods of family separation had been on both of us—especially when something major went wrong at home, like the time Lance almost died from severe anaphylaxis caused by a bee sting on his tongue— I told her I would leave the Navy to save our marriage.

I was shocked when I received her message, but this sort of thing apparently happened more often than I would have guessed, because of a phenomenon, referred to in medical circles as the "The Polaris Syndrome." I later learned that the divorce rate in the Polaris submarine force was higher than that of any other component of the military, except for the Air Force's Strategic Air Command (SAC). Although these two components shared similar strategic missions in time of nuclear war, the psychological burden placed on the families of those who were assigned to either component was also similar, but for dramatically different reasons.

In SAC, bomber crews would be called away on instant notice without any idea of when that might happen or of how long they would be away. And when they were away, there was no ability whatsoever to communicate with their families. With Polaris, on the other hand, the submarine crews knew to the hour of the day when they would be flying off to man the submarine and take it on its next patrol. While actually on patrol, they were able to receive four "family grams" from home of 15 words each, but without any ability to reply. [12]

So, although both components were essentially out of touch insofar as communicating with their families was concerned, SAC understandably suffered from the uncertainty of not knowing when one would be called away, while Polaris suffered from the exact opposite (of knowing too much). There was apparently something psychologically debilitating about operating on a three-month cycle in which one was subconsciously counting the days until the family would be together again or, alternatively, until the next period of separation would begin. It was as though one was counting one's life away. Whatever it was, apparently the totally predictable on-again, off-again nature of the Polaris cycle took a heavier than normal toll on family life, as reflected in the higher divorce rate.

Although family separation was the precipitating factor for my decision to leave, I had other misgivings about staying in as well. In addition to being bored with the endless routine of Polaris patrols, I had developed serious reservations about my moral willingness to launch our missiles in the absence of concrete evidence that the United States itself was under nuclear attack. In harboring such reservations, the concept of deterrence begins to break down; and one is probably doing one's country a disservice by continuing to serve in such a capacity. (Ironically, about 25 years later, this same moral dilemma was portrayed rather accurately in the 1995 movie *Crimson Tide*, which takes place aboard a ballistic missile-carrying nuclear submarine).

Anyway, for the above combination of reasons, I submitted my resignation from the Navy. Peter Durbin, a Harvard graduate and a terrific skipper, did his best to talk me out of it, suggesting that if I stayed in, I could become

---

[12] That has since changed for the better.

an Admiral and a statesman. In response, I half-jokingly replied that I had finally figured out that the Chief of Naval Operations—the top military job in the Navy—works for the Secretary of the Navy and that I would rather be Secretary. Six years later, while Pete was working in the Pentagon (subsequent to his command tour) and I had recently been sworn in as Deputy Assistant Secretary of the Navy, we both had a good laugh over lunch about the vagaries of life and its unpredictable nature.

(Years later, I learned that if President George H.W. Bush had been re-elected, I was in line to become Secretary of the Navy. By that time, Pete had graduated to his higher reward; but had this actually come to pass while he was still alive, we would have enjoyed more than a casual laugh over lunch.)

During Navy maneuvers, the captain was pushing his destroyer to the limit when a sailor came to the crowded bridge with an urgent message from the admiral. Proud of his performance, the captain commanded the message be "read aloud" in front of his men. The sailor obliged. It read: "Of all the blundering idiots, you nearly rammed the flagship." The captain, undaunted, looked back out to sea and replied, "Very good sailor. Now take the message below and hove it decoded!"

World's fastest "on the step"
(official U.S. Navy photo)

Receiving a special set of dolphins

"Dive, dive"
(official U.S. Navy photo)

Nina and Lance at Bellows

Soviet sub on the surface
(unofficial U.S. Navy photo)

Surfer man

Launching of my second submarine,
the *USS Ulysses S. Grant (SSBN631)*
(General Dynamics Corporation photo,
Public Relations Department, Electric
Boat Division)

Nina and Lance join in accepting award for
the Engineering Department on the *Polk*.
(official U.S. Navy photo)

Up, up, and away
(official U.S. Navy photo)

73

PART III
Shopping Around

Chapter Five

SIPPING AT THE GOVERNMENT TROUGH

*"Don't believe the world owes you a living; the world owes you nothing—
it was here first."*

Robert Jones Burdette (1844-1914)

S hortly before my last Polaris patrol aboard the *Polk*, I received a call from Harvard, indicating they might not have the money to pay for my doctoral fellowship because of their need to establish a new Black Studies Program. This precipitated a quick search on my part for other options; especially because the economy was in bad shape at the time, and I had a wife and two sons to support. Among other initiatives, I attended a Job Fair targeted for former military officers, which, in turn, led to a visit to Westinghouse headquarters in Pittsburgh. There I was given the royal treatment, lunch at the country club and interviews with three departments within their Power Systems Division. The interviews went well and apparently generated a degree of internal competition that manifested itself in a rather handsome job offer.

On another front, I responded to a job announcement posted by the President's Office of Emergency Preparedness (OEP) in Washington, DC. I was pleasantly surprised when I arrived for an interview with Steve Loftus, the head of OEP's policy shop, and he immediately asked "Are you the Doug Johnston who wrote that article on ABM (Anti-Ballistic Missile Defense) in the *Naval Institute Proceedings* several years ago?" This was long before Google, and I was amazed that he could ask such a question. At the end of the interview, he offered me a job, not because I knew anything about driving nuclear submarines, but because he happened to like something I had written years earlier. Talk about a small world!

After all was said and done, I had four excellent choices: Harvard came through with its original offer, the Westinghouse job opportunity, and OEP.

In addition, the Navy relented at the eleventh hour and agreed that I could make the transition to Naval Intelligence. By this time, though, I had made my commitment to Nina to leave the service, and I wasn't about to reverse course.

Although I had resigned with the intent of pursuing the doctorate, I subsequently reconsidered because of the unrest that plagued college campuses at the time owing to the student backlash against Vietnam (including the burning down of ROTC buildings). I knew I would probably get caught up in opposing all that, because so much of what was taking place struck me as nonsensical, if not self-defeating. For example, the related closure of Harvard's NROTC unit effectively stemmed the annual flow of 75 liberal-minded officers into the United States Navy, who could have done far more over time to advance the kinds of progressive ideas being advanced by the protestors, than would a temporary takeover of some college campus. So, I decided to set Harvard aside for a later date. Although the Westinghouse offer was the most lucrative of the three, part of my reason for leaving the Navy was to expand my horizons beyond those associated with nuclear power. So, I turned that down as well.

In many respects, the offer from OEP came closer than any of the others to testing the courage of my convictions. The Director of OEP at that time was a statutory member of the National Security Council, and part of my task would be to help prepare him for those meetings, in addition to an array of other challenging assignments.

Thus, began a seven-year career in government service that included six different jobs in three different career fields. Anyone perusing my resumé would have undoubtedly concluded "this guy can't hold a job".

The First Sip

My work at OEP was quite interesting owing to the varied nature of the agency's mission. As a precursor twice-removed to today's Federal Emergency Management Agency (FEMA), one of its central responsibilities was to coordinate all Federal assistance in addressing natural disasters and other emergency situations. I still recall my initial shock of flying over a town in the Mississippi Delta that had literally been turned into toothpicks by a major hurricane. And then there were the very early-morning attempts to summarize the nation-wide consequences of a major rail strike for the President's morning briefings.

One of my first tasks after reporting to OEP was to coordinate an international meeting on earthquakes to be held in San Francisco. In making the advance preparations, I assigned the prospective participants to one of five working groups and drafted preliminary Working Group reports before the meetings even took place. Of course, they were later modified to reflect what actually transpired; but I was amazed at how little needed changing after the fact. Another equally challenging task was the need to craft speeches for each of the six prominent personalities who were invited to speak at the gathering. Among others, these included Dr. Charles Richter (of Richter Scale fame), U.S. Secretary of Transportation John Volpe, and former actress and Ambassador to Czechoslovakia Shirley Temple Black (for what reason I can't recall). I had to dig deep to come up with that many distinctive speeches on the subject of earthquakes, but it seemed to work.

The night before the meeting, I was faced with a decision of whether or not to show a new BBC documentary at the opening reception to be hosted by Mayor Joseph Alito the following day. The film was titled, "The City that Waits to Die" and highlighted the extent to which the city of San Francisco is built over a fault zone. At one point, it featured footage (accompanied by dramatic organ music) showing a tall skyscraper sitting directly on top of the San Andreas fault line. I decided it wouldn't be politic to show it, so took a pass.

The two highlights of the event for me were the opportunity to have a substantive lunch with Dr. Richter and later go to North Beach for a non-substantive evening with Carl Gidlund, who handled the PR functions for OEP (and who was soon to become a life-long friend). For those who don't recall, North Beach was where the whole business of topless dancing originated. I found it interesting to experience how quickly forbidden fruit loses its allure in the cold glare of a spotlight, but we had a great time.

It took me about six months to fully appreciate my good fortune in being hired at OEP. The director of the agency, was a retired Army Brigadier General by the name of George A. Lincoln (or "Abe Lincoln," as he was commonly called). Lincoln had served as General George Marshall's War Plans Officer during WWII; and when the war was over, had voluntarily reverted to the rank of Colonel to head the Social Sciences Department at West Point. During the 22 years that he served in that capacity, he hand-picked the highest-caliber officers he could find to teach in his department. With laser-like precision, he would go after the best and the brightest not only from within the Army, but in some instances, the other services as well. Collectively, those so chosen joined the ranks of what later became widely known as the "Lincoln Brigade".

In 1969, Lincoln was invited by President Nixon to become Director of OEP and a member of the National Security Council because of his stellar credentials, not only in national security more generally, but in wartime mobilization and its prospective relevance to OEP's management of the nation's strategic stockpile of critical commodities. He accepted the assignment and brought with him a number of "Lincoln Brigaders" to serve as his key staff. Without being aware of any of this, I had unknowingly joined their ranks, and it proved an inspiring experience.

I don't know if it was because of the ABM article or just chance, but in addition to my policy-related duties, I was tasked with crafting some of Lincoln's speeches. I recall one speech in particular that commanded a great deal of my time. Lincoln had been invited to speak at a CINCSTRIKE Conference (Commander-in-Chief of the Strike Command) in Puerto Rico on the topic of energy security. All of the participants at this conference were 4-star Flag officers and their civilian equivalents, so it was a serious gathering. At the conference, Lincoln laid out the nation's energy picture and prophesied the energy crisis that later came to pass.

Because of the speech, the phone began ringing off the hook once we returned to Washington. But prior to returning, I was invited to go deep-sea fishing with General Lincoln and his wife, Freddie. We spent a delightful couple of days trolling the Caribbean, but the only thing we caught was a seagull that went after the bait while we were reeling it in. Despite the absence of a trophy catch, it was a special and memorable time.

Another, albeit more esoteric, mission of the agency was to maintain continuity of government and stabilize the economy in the wake of a nuclear attack. This, in turn, required the presence of an OEP office in each of the 10 Federal regions into which the country was bureaucratically divided. It was largely because of this regional capability and the agency's economic stabilization responsibilities that OEP was given the task of overseeing a 90-day freeze on prices and wages across the country when President Nixon imposed economic controls in 1971. About a week into the freeze, Lincoln called me into his office and said, "I need you to handle the incoming correspondence relating to our new task. We already have a backlog of more than a thousand letters, and are sinking under the load." I readily accepted, without the faintest clue of what to do.

A Second Sip

"If you think you're too small to make a difference, try sleeping with a mosquito in the room." –Dalai Lama

The Winder Building in which OEP was headquartered, sits directly across the street from the Old Executive Office Building (EOB) in which the National Security Council is housed and which itself sits adjacent to the White House. Before the EOB came into existence, President Lincoln allegedly used to walk across the White House lawn to visit with Confederate prisoners housed in cells in the basement of Winder. I was given two of these cells to execute my new assignment, along with a few magnetic-selectric typewriters and, over time, the aid of a small number of lower-level staff and interns temporarily secunded from different Federal agencies around town.

Although the typewriters were a far cry from today's personal computers, they did enable one to substitute canned paragraphs tailored to the different kinds of questions being asked. Long story short, within a few weeks, we were receiving incoming mail at a rate of 800 letters a day and maintaining an average backlog of less than two and a half days. This was achieved with a well-oiled team of 10 people, including several lawyers (to handle the incoming legal briefs, many of which were quite thick).

The Controls Program was initially overseen by the President's Cabinet; and when General Lincoln flashed the correspondence numbers on the screen during their daily briefings, it was met with a mild degree of skepticism. Apparently, Cabinet members weren't used to seeing this degree of responsiveness from the government. That disbelief led to a visit to the basement of the Winder Building by Donald Rumsfeld, then Counselor to the President, to see for himself how this was being achieved.

By the end of the freeze, I had signed the Director's name on outgoing correspondence no fewer than 27,000 times (3,000 of which were to Members of Congress), without any negative repercussions. I actually reached the point where I began to feel I could sign Lincoln's name better than he could—-and in his handwriting. Almost all of this mail related to technical aspects of the freeze, but every now and then a bit of humor would creep in. For example, as carried in the September 4, 1971 edition of the Pensacola Journal in Pensacola, Florida:

Pensacola Bachelor Wants to Know: Does Price Freeze Affect Hanky-Panky?

Washington—A Pensacola, Florida man has asked President Nixon's already over-worked Office of Emergency Preparedness (OEP) to decide whether or not he can legally grant a "price increase" for "hanky-panky".

No official announcement was made by the OEP regarding the request, but it came to light Thursday when two handwritten letters found their way into this reporter's hands.

Despite the somewhat peculiar nature of the request, OEP officials are following the procedure that has become standard since the office went into operation—by mailing an immediate (if somewhat nebulous) response to the Florida man.

The letter of request (the author's name is being withheld) arrived at the OEP's Washington office early this week and was referred, as have been more than 4,000 other letters, to the correspondence section. The inquiry read:

"Dear Sir: I take pen in hand to write you this letter to show I am patriotic and want to comply with the new laws of the President. So, I will just write you this and would like...a simple answer.

"My problem is that I am a bachelor who lives down here on the Florida beach in a little house trailer. Now, I have this old girl who comes in to see me once or twice a week, and, to be quite honest, she doesn't just really come by for a visit, but she spends the night with me, and, as you would guess, a little bit of hanky-panky goes on between us.

"Now she is a good old girl, and I just feel that I owe her something. So, I take her out in my pick-up and get her a hamburger (50 cents), or a fish plate (mullet, $1.25). I thought she was satisfied with this, but last night she told me she wasn't coming back unless I bought her a steak dinner ($2.50)

"Now, just to be sure that I am not breaking the law, please tell me if you would consider this a price increase and not allowed by President Nixon. I haven't seen anything, or heard anything about the possible increase in cost of the item referred to. Thank you."

The OEP response, drafted over the signature of Douglas M. Johnston, special assistant, reads:

"First let me extend my congratulations. I am sure there are a great many men in the country who would envy you your life in Florida, on the beach with frequent companionship.

"As to your specific problem, I recommend you appeal to the 'old girl's' loyalty to her country and her sense of pride in America. The President has asked all citizens to cooperate in the wage-price freeze as their patriotic duty.

"If this fails, and she still insists on the $2.50 steak, I think you should seriously consider the effect on you of another kind of freeze.

"While I can't tell you that her increase in the asking price is allowed in the law, I do say that $2.50 seems a good price; and maybe the less said the better.

"If you do wish to file a complaint, contact the nearest Internal Revenue Service office and give them the particulars of this case."

In what may have been an afterthought, Johnston added a final line of closing:

"You might send me some particulars, too, in case I get to Florida sometime."

In today's era of political correctness, I'm not sure such a piece could be published. But either way, I didn't craft the response myself and always suspected it was authored by Ray Karam, an office-mate and highly decorated Air Force pilot imbued with a great sense of humor.

When the freeze had run its course, OEP bowed out and a new government bureaucracy was born to oversee Phase II of the controls program. About this time, I was told that C. Jackson Grayson, head of the newly-formed Price Commission, had asked to have me assigned to his Commission, but that Lincoln had cut his request off at the pass. Then Rumsfeld, who had been newly appointed to direct the entire program, came after me; and Lincoln couldn't say no (because the request came from the White House). However, when I received the call from Rumsfeld's office, I said no. They said they were interested in having me become Deputy Director for Administration of the new Cost of Living Council, and I told them I wasn't interested. They asked why, and I said administration wasn't my thing. They asked what was, and I said policy planning.

The next day I received a call to interview with a smart and highly engaging economist by the name of Marvin Kosters, Director of Planning and Analysis at the Council.

The job in question was to serve as liaison between the Council and the newly-formed Pay Board, with the interview going something like this:

Q: What kind of background do you have in labor relations?

A: None, but I get along with people.

Q: How about labor economics?

*A: I had a year of economics at the Naval Academy and stood
2nd in the class, but I have honestly forgotten most of what I
learned. However, I am Scot enough to know the difference
between profit and loss.*

And so it went, close-to-dumb answers to a series of very reasonable questions. Anyway, I left quite satisfied with my performance, because I really liked working at OEP and had no desire to move elsewhere. The next day I was amazed when I was offered the position and a promotion to go with it.

Phase II Controls

"Confidence is what you have before you understand the problem."
–Woody Allen

To implement the second phase of the controls program, the Nixon Administration developed a new structure consisting of three separate offices: The Cost of Living Council (COLC) to oversee the program, a Pay Board to oversee wage controls, and a Price Commission to do the same for prices. To go along with the wage controls, George Meany, head of the AFL/CIO, extracted from President Nixon an agreement that the Pay Board would function separately and independently of the Cost of Living Council. My job as liaison between the Council and the Pay Board was to help steer the Pay Board in whatever direction the Council wanted it to go.

The Pay Board itself consisted of 15 members: five major union leaders, five captains of industry, and five distinguished academicians. I, on the other hand, was so credential-free as to pose a threat to no one. Since I was present at the Pay Board for all of its meetings, I made it a point to develop good relationships with each of the members and most of the staff (all of whom ultimately reported to the Board Chairman, George H. Boldt, a Federal District Judge from the State of Washington).

On selected occasions when I felt it absolutely necessary, I would intervene (from the sidelines) in the Pay Board's deliberations by standing up and suggesting that if they went through with what they were contemplating, it would conflict with steps the Council was about to take in that same area. In each instance, they backed off; and a short time later I would call the Council and tell them what they had to do. Thankfully, in every instance, the Council followed through as requested.

When I wasn't at the Pay Board, I was at the Council developing wage-related policies. I shared an office with Dawson Ahalt, an exceedingly sharp government official on detail from the Department of Agriculture, who served as the Council's liaison to the Price Commission (my counterpart, so-to-speak). Because the imposition of economic controls was without precedent, at least dating back to World War II, we were effectively developing policy on the run.

On my first day of work, for example, I was given an hour and a half notice to develop a policy paper on how the wages of Federal employees should be treated under the Controls Program. I recall asking Dawson to "give me a con" (as I was developing a list of "pros" and "cons" for the paper). He asked, "What's the issue?" I said, "It doesn't matter, just give me a con." He replied, "Might undermine the credibility of the program." I said, "Great" and used it. The rest of it was mainly common sense, and two hours later, I was at the White House, presenting my paper to the Cost of Living Council. My recommendations were accepted, but the abbreviated nature of the process was indicative of the degree to which we were literally flying by the seats-of-our-pants. Ironically, when I re-read that policy paper a year later (when I actually knew what I was doing), I wouldn't have changed a word. More than a little luck in those early days!

Another eye-opener for me took place one afternoon when I received a call from a Congressman from Michigan by the name of Gerald Ford, inquiring about wage provisions for the auto industry. After hanging up, I was dumbfounded by the realization that I as a middle-level bureaucrat had more influence over what was going on than he did as an elected official.

One of the more interesting aspects of my job was that relating to the public, which manifested itself in numerous speaking engagements around the country to explain the program to public audiences and various interest groups. En route to my first speaking engagement in Phoenix, I ran into Earl Rhode in front of the New Executive Office Building (NEOB), where the Council was housed. Earl, who was the COLC Staff Director (and therefore an upper-tier boss), asked where I was heading and offered some helpful advice to this PR neophyte. He said, "Just remember when someone asks you a question, chances are you will know a lot more about the topic than anyone else in the room, since you are fully immersed in the substance, and they are not. Further, 95% of the others in the audience probably won't have any interest in that particular question. So, stay relaxed, and go with the flow." It was sound advice, which I augmented with an unembarrassed willingness to say, "I don't know" whenever appropriate, followed by a pledge to find out and get back to the questioner. Then I was very scrupulous about following through.

With one possible exception, I really enjoyed the challenge of these presentations. That exception had to do with an engagement in Everett, Washington, north of Seattle, at which a total of six people showed up, four of whom were relatives. I was told that the light turnout was a result of competing with the Olympics and the Miss America Pageant, both of which were showing on television at that same time. Thankfully, I was able to recover a glimmer of dignity when an audience of about 1600 showed up at a later presentation in Seattle.

On another PR excursion, I was scheduled to make a presentation in Eau Claire, Wisconsin, followed by my first-ever television appearance. Prior to going, Tom Donnolly who was in charge of making the speaking assignments (and another life-long friend to be), called some of his JC (Junior Chamber of Commerce) colleagues in Eau Claire and told them to show me a good time because I was a "real swinger" (whatever that meant). Well, Tom's friends and I hit every bar in town the evening after my presentation; and when I made my TV appearance the next morning, not a single cell in my body was capable of being nervous. I was Mr. Calm, Cool and Collected—-all due to the numbing effects of alcohol!

Laughing Last

"The brain is a wonderful organ; it starts working the moment you get up in the morning and does not stop until you get to the office."—Robert Frost

On a more humorous note, the following is a practical joke that took place during my first months at the Council, in which I was the intended victim but which, with some clever insider help, was turned around on the perpetrators. It all began when I dropped by the office of Myron Mintz, a new COLC acquaintance who worked in the Office of the Legal Counsel. I noticed he had an autographed picture of the President on his desk and asked what had occasioned such treatment. He said that another colleague of ours by the name of Roger Kreuzer had arranged it for him and felt sure he would be happy to do the same for me, if asked. A short while later, Myron dropped by Roger's office, told him I'd probably be by to see him and urged him to play along.

When I later visited Roger, I introduced myself and said, "I hear you're the man to see about pictures." In response, Roger put his forefinger to his lips, quietly closed the door, and said, "I don't want that to become generally known around here. You understand, don't you?" After confirming that I was a loyal Republican (which was true at the time), he said he would do what he could but that I may have to wait a while. Pointing toward the White House, he said, "They're not too happy with me over there because I've been pestering them too much lately." I said I didn't mind waiting, thanked him for his trouble, and departed.

Following this conversation, Roger convened a meeting of the co-conspirators, which besides Myron and himself had expanded to include Don Smith, who worked in Public Affairs, and my office-mate, Dawson Ahalt. Dawson's job was to act as the eyes and ears of the operation and to make certain that I heard that which I was supposed to hear. He was also to report back to the group any undesirable behavior on my part. Don was charged with the task of logistical support and Myron, in addition to being principal instigator, was to serve as a technical advisor throughout. Beyond that, all participants were to stay in close touch in the further execution of the hoax.

Little happened over the next 30 days until Don Smith, consistent with his logistical responsibilities, produced the following message on a sheet of White House notepaper:

"Dear Roger,

The President will be able to meet with you and Mr. Johnston at 12:15 pm on Friday, October 6.

Mark"

With note in hand, Roger showed it to me and said, "Doug, take a look at this." I asked what it meant. He said, "It means we're going across the street for the picture." I said, "You mean he's going to give it to me himself?" to which he replied, "Hell, no. Not a picture of himself; a picture of you with him." I told him this exceeded all expectations, and he said, "It's really nothing, Doug."

Although Roger had indicated that we might get bumped because of the President's busy campaign schedule, he began having second thoughts about the spoof itself, thinking it was all-too-cruel. On October 3rd, I asked Roger if it was still on. He said it was, but said that I needed to get a haircut and wear a nicer suit. I told him I had a nice suit but that it might not quite be what was needed. He told me to wear it the next day and he'd check it out. The next day I wore it to work; and at that point Roger's conscience kicked in. He took me aside, revealed that it was all a big hoax, but suggested that we might be able to turn it around on the others. I was only too happy to do so; and from this point on in the telling, the tables are effectively turned. I later concluded that a significant reason this entire charade played out so well from beginning to end was the fact that in an earlier life, Roger had spent two years behind the lines in East Germany as an undercover agent for the Defense Intelligence Agency. Next to that, this was pretty small potatoes.

The next morning, Roger came to my office and told me in Dawson's presence that we had been bumped, because the President wouldn't be available on the 6th after all – what with it being so close to the election and all. I said,

> *"Damn, are you kidding?"*

> *"No, I'm not; what's the matter?"*

> *"Well, I was over at the White House last week delivering some papers to Ehrlichman's office and ran into my old Harvard professor, Henry Kissinger. He and I are both members of the Saints and Sinners Club and I had run into him at one of their gatherings the previous week. Anyway, I told him about the appointment to have my picture taken with the President and invited him to join us for the picture. He agreed to do so, and now it's going to be embarrassing as hell to have to tell him the whole thing is off."*

> *"Damn it, Doug, I told you explicitly not to mention the picture session to anyone. I don't want anyone to know about my association with the President."*

> *"I know, but I thought it would be all right, since he's the President's right-hand man."*

Roger appeared quite upset, and Dawson was shifting in his chair, keeping a straight face while biting hard on his pipe stem but totally unaware that his Adams Apple was vigorously bouncing up and down. Roger pulled himself together and said,

> *"I'm sorry, Doug, but you're just going to have to call Dr. Kissinger and tell him the photo session is off for tomorrow."*

> *"Damn, this is going to be embarrassing!"*

I then picked up the phone and faked a call to Dr. Kissinger's office. About 10 minutes later, Roger received an urgent call from Counselor Mintz, asking him to meet right away. When Roger arrived, Myron was at his most serious. According to Roger, he had to suppress a smile because Myron looked like someone had gently tamped a surveyor's stake up his behind, thereby forcing a ramrod posture.

"This is bad," said Dawson, with his eyes flashing and his Adams Apple doing the mambo.

"Bad! This is dynamite," Roger roared. "My God, we've gone too far. I knew something like this would happen. We're sitting on a powder keg. "

"Well," said Myron. "I think it's time to start playing this down. Personally, I think this might be a counterattack on Johnston's part. I think he might be wise to us."

"Are you kidding?" Roger blurted. "This guy is serious. Why the hell would he be wise" He's completely taken in. And now, by virtue of his acquaintance with Kissinger, each of us including Smith is skating on very thin ice."

Later that same day, Don Smith shows up, and another meeting takes place, yielding the same collective verdict: to let it die a natural death and hope that Johnston never catches on.

The following Monday I told Roger in Dawson's presence that I had bought a new suit and that it looked like a million dollars. He tried to back off, but I again expressed confidence in his ability to make it happen. Unrelated to this scenario, I had actually purchased a new suit over the weekend and wore it the next day. All three of the other hoaxers, Myron, Don and Dawson, asked if it was a new suit; and I said yes without further comment.

The next morning, I received a call from a Mr. Brewster of the Secret Service (actually Roger), inquiring about the photo session. He said he had become aware of it quite by accident from a friend in Kissinger's office and since he's charged with protecting the President, he wanted to fully understand what was going on. Looking very depressed, I then told Dawson about it (thinking he may not have overheard enough of the phone conversation). He acts completely innocent, but soon thereafter gets together with the others and they start a long, slow panic.

That afternoon, all four pranksters enter my office and confess their misdeeds. I give them hell for doing something so stupid. They talk about losing their jobs, and I indicate it's a distinct possibility. I then turn to Dawson and ask him if that happens, how he's going to make his payments on a 38- acre farm he was buying in the Maryland countryside? He said he had kept his wife apprised of the whole thing and she was already mad at him for getting involved in the first place.

They all then volunteered to go with me to meet with Brewster, but I suggested just taking Roger. Then I insisted on going alone in a selfless attempt not to involve any of them unless absolutely forced to do so. An hour and a half later, I put on my coat and faked a visit to the White House. Upon my return, I made a detailed report to the group. Looking very sullen, I told them I had attempted to make Brewster see the humor of the situation; but he didn't smile, nor would he even shake my hand. I said I didn't tell him that I worked for Rumsfeld, only that I worked in Planning and Analysis at the Cost of Living Council. Brewster, then asked, "Doesn't Don Rumsfeld head that up?" and I said, "Yes." (I threw that in, so the trio would think Brewster might tell Rumsfeld). At this point, they are really getting panicky, especially when I tell them that Brewster will be calling them within a day or two.

The Finale

"I do not mind lying, but I hate inaccuracies." —Samuel Butler (1862-1902)

The next morning I suggested that Roger call everyone together, to ensure they were all singing from the same hymnal when they told Brewster their respective stories, since I was going to be leaving town the next day for a speaking engagement. They all gathered, and we fibbed a bit longer before coming clean with the straight story. Their reaction was one of shocked disbelief followed by exhaustive relief and raucous laughter.

Roger later shared with me that he had felt a slight twinge of guilt for leading me to believe he was close to the President—guilt that soon turned to mirthful laughter when he concluded that he probably had been very close to the President when he and his parents had visited the White House on a Gray Line Tour.

And so things continued for about a year until the Controls Program was ready to proceed to the next phase. At that point, Don Rumsfeld departed for Brussels, Belgium to become Ambassador to NATO, and I was appointed Deputy Administrator of the newly established Office of Wage Stabilization. As we were parting ways, I thanked Don for his support and the long leash he had given me. He said, "Well, I have a management theory. I find good people, give them the ball, and let them run with it. If they stumble, the leash gets very short indeed." I knew the latter to be true, because I had seen first-hand how tough he could be on folks who didn't measure up to his expectations.

By the same token, it was the combination of Don's integrity and toughness that kept the Council scandal-free throughout. It wouldn't stretch one's imagination to envision the possibility of corruption taking hold in a make-shift program that had been quickly cobbled together to control the world's largest economy. But there was absolutely none of that. I recall early in the program receiving a large package from the Barber's Union full of all sorts of desirable goodies, which I immediately sent back. Thanks in large part to Don's influence, we all took pride in being purer than Caesar's wife.

In addition to the experience of working with Don, I also had the pleasure of working with Dick Cheney, who assisted Don in running some of the Council's operations. Years later, after the controls program had faded into history, I happened to sit next to then-Congressman Cheney on a plane heading West; and we struck up a conversation about the good old days. In passing, he mentioned that President Nixon had once told Don (also while sitting together on a plane) that he would one day have his (Nixon's) job. Thus, I wasn't at all surprised by Don's later run for the Presidency—nor with Dick's even later. Although neither was successful in that particular quest, they both left their respective marks on history—Don as a Congressman, White House Chief of Staff, and twice Secretary of Defense and Dick as a Congressman, White House Chief of Staff, Secretary of Defense, and Vice President of the United States. Pretty tall cotton by any standard.

Another chance encounter that also occurred several years later took place at what was then called The Lawyer's Club in Washington D.C. There I ran into Judge Boldt having lunch with some friends. Once his chairmanship of the Pay Board was over, he had gone back to being a Federal Judge in the State of Washington. After exchanging pleasantries, I congratulated him on a tough legal decision he had recently made in preserving a treaty right of Native Americans that entitled them to half of the fish caught in the rivers and tributaries of the Northwest. It had made all the newspapers; and he had been taking a lot of heat for the decision, being hung in effigy by fishermen and various other stakeholders who didn't want to share the spoils. Anyway, Boldt looked at me and said, "Oh, I don't deserve the credit for that. It was really my grandson. When I asked him what he would do, he said, 'Grandpa, it seems to me a deal's a deal." [13]

Phase III Controls

Phase three of the controls program was largely devoted to preparing for the abolishment of controls. The overriding goal from the outset had been to work ourselves out of a job, so the free market could once again work its magic. During this phase of the Program, as Deputy Administrator of the

---

[13] His decision was later upheld by the Supreme Court in July of 1979.

new Office of Wage Stabilization, I spent most of my time in policy-related meetings, (while Millard Cass, the Administrator, devoted most of his time to administering existing policy).

One of my more memorable experiences during this period was a trip to the United Kingdom to brief the British Pay Board on the latest phase of our program. The British had established an economic controls program of their own and were effectively one phase behind us in its implementation. Making the trip all the more memorable was the fact that I was accompanied by a self-proclaimed mountain woman from Denver, Colorado, who I had met a couple of months earlier.

The attempt to save my marriage to Nina by leaving the Navy had not worked, so I was now back in circulation. I had met my new acquaintance on a ski trip to Vail, and there had been an immediate attraction. Our next encounter was when she joined me on a trip to Hollywood Beach, Florida for another of my many speaking engagements. While there, I made a serious mistake while trying to impress her with my derring-do. It was about two o'clock in the morning, and we were out for a late-night swim in a salt-water pool directly behind the hotel. This particular pool had a triple-high diving platform, and I was airborne before I realized I couldn't clearly see the water-line beneath me. Consequently, I hit at a bad angle; and my back hurt for the better part of a year. Which brings to mind several other humility-inspiring episodes that took place while she and I were dating.

At one point, we were high on a mountain at Snow Mass in Aspen, Colorado when I turned to her and said, "The Germans are coming," (implying imme-diate danger of a World War II nature). Then I assumed a tuck position and started racing down the hill to escape the virtual Germans. While doing so, I caught the tip of my ski and suffered a pretty bad fall, spraining both the knee and ankle on my left leg.

The more memorable part of that experience, though, took place the fol-lowing day. By this time, I was on crutches; and we drove to Glenwood Springs to take a dip in a damned-up sulfur spring surrounded by snow, thinking that the heat might bring a degree of comfort in my infirmed state. But it did far more than that; I walked in a cripple and came out a whole man. To this day, I marvel at that transformation. Both sprains immediately disap-peared, as did the crutches.

Yet another humbling experience took place while skiing together in the back bowls of Vail. It was my first attempt at skiing in powder, and I was fol-lowing her down a rather narrow, mogul-laden trail. Unable to see my skis beneath the powder, I was going a bit slower. She had just disappeared from sight around a tight curve, when I went off the trail and ended up literally hanging upside down from my skis in a thicket of Aspens. Eventually she showed up and helped me down.

Not Quite Mountaintop

Finally, on another excursion, we went hiking on the Mount of the Holy Cross in the Northern Sawatch Range of the Rockies near Red Cliff, Colorado. The mountain came by that name because whenever it snows, the snow accumulates in indentations on the side of the mountain which, when viewed from afar, takes the form of a giant cross. Anyway, we were making our way up a rocky interface when she said, "Watch out for the rotten rock." Unfamiliar with the term, I thought she was making casual conversation and didn't take her warning seriously— that is, not until a huge chunk of rock came off in my hand as I was in the act of climbing. Now, good climbers know you should always have at least three weight-bearing points of contact with the mountain at any given point in time. With that displaced chunk in my hand, I was effectively down to a two-point stance; and it must have taken me a full minute to work up the nerve to make a short leap to gain that third hold. Although she clearly qualified as a mountain woman, I can think of no conceivable reason I could ever claim to be a mountain man!

Off to Scotland

Anyway, back to the British Pay Board. After I briefed them on the latest phase of our economic controls program, we rented an Austin Mini in downtown London and took off on a week's excursion. En route to the Scottish Highlands, we visited the small town of South Cadbury in England, where the archeological remains of King Arthur's castle had supposedly been uncovered a few years earlier. However, the farmer to whom the land belonged and who had permitted the excavation to take place, had done so on the condition that it be restored to its original state once the dig was completed. So, although there were no physical signs of the castle itself when we toured the sight, one could feel the ghostly presence of the Knights (of the Table Round) as one took in the sweeping view of the rolling countryside.

Deeper Roots

I felt more than a little at home in Scotland, probably because of the Scottish blood coursing through my veins, most of it owing allegiance to the McLeod Clan. In tribute to this particular strain of ancestry, we visited

Dunvegan on the Isle of Skye, a castle which has served as the headquarters of the McLeods for more than a thousand years. I came away impressed that they must have been one pretty tough crew. Their dungeon, for example, was located in one of the castle's turrets and consisted of a sizable 16-foot-deep pit beneath a trap door that could only be opened from above. Unless the prisoners were of royal stock and could command a ransom (in which case they would be placed in irons above the trap door), they were unceremoniously thrown into the pit regardless of how wounded they might be and left there to starve to death. Adding insult to injury, a long, narrow slit had been cut in the rock wall surrounding the pit that led back to the kitchen, thereby enabling the prisoners to smell the cooking odors as they slowly starved. Once everyone had fully expired, a gate at the bottom of the pit would be opened to let the tide from the surrounding sea carry out their remains. Then the dungeon was ready for the next batch.

On the northern side of the island sits the remains of the McDonald's castle, which only lasted about three hundred years before the McLeods wiped them out. I suspect that in addition to all else, the Scots may have invented the concept of ethnic cleansing.

One night, because it was August and the peak of the tourist season, we were unable to find lodging anywhere. Out of desperation and quite late at night, we turned down a dirt road that seemingly led nowhere, parked the car and spent the night, occasionally sipping from a bottle of single malt to stay warm. When I awoke around 5:30am, I was startled to find us parked at the foot of a huge dam that was holding back one of the surrounding lochs. I woke my travel mate, told her where we were, and said that I had read somewhere that they opened such dams every morning at 6:00am. That was a total fabrication, but it provided a good laugh and minor relief from the pain in my back that still lingered from my majestic dive on the beach in Florida.

That trip began a three-year involvement during which we skied all but two areas in the state of Colorado, did some serious hiking along the Continental Divide, and even searched for buried stagecoach loot from the Kenosha Pass stagecoach robbery a hundred years earlier. At one point, I thought we were on the brink of finding the loot and began wondering what in the heck we would do if we actually found it. When it proved to be a false alarm, I felt immediate relief from the prospective burden of retrieving and transporting all that gold. Thus, it turned out to be a win-win, the thrill of the search without any added complications.

With the end of the Economic Controls Program in sight, I found my next job on the staff of the Special Assistant to the Secretary of Defense, working for a gentleman by the name of Robert Murray.

Into the 5-Sided Palace

Working for Bob was a real pleasure, since he was incredibly sharp and had a great sense of humor. After a year of addressing the innumerable political/military challenges that typically confront the Secretary of Defense, Bob moved up to become Deputy Assistant Secretary of Defense for Manpower and Reserve Affairs(M&RA); and I became Director of Policy Planning and Management working under him. Mine was a new position, so I had the unique and quite rare opportunity of establishing an entire office from scratch and hiring a full-time staff (of 12) to fill it. Since we had some rather major mountains to move, I went after the very best—the top "one percenters", so to speak.

With this superbly capable staff, we tackled a number of important issues. Although these were serious undertakings that commanded the best thinking we could muster, there were the occasional reminders that there was more to life than work. For example, I one day received the below correspondence seemingly through official channels and on the presumed letterhead of *Playgirl Magazine*:

Playgirl, INC.
Executive Offices, 35 East 48ᵗʰ Street, New York, New York 10036

Mr. Douglas M. Johnston, Jr.
Director, Office of Policy, Planning and Management
Room 3D949, Pentagon

Dear Mr. Johnston,

We wish to thank you for your letter and Polaroid pictures which we recently received. We regret however, that we will not be able to use you as "Playgirl's Man of the Month Centerfold."

When rated by our panel of AAW (Average American Women) on a scale from 1 to 10, your body was rated minus 2. The AAW is comprised of widowed females ages 60-75 who have not been involved with sex for five years or longer.

To further justify our rating, we submitted your photographs to another panel of women in the age bracket 25-35, but we couldn't get them to stop laughing long enough to rate you.

Please be assured that should the tastes of American Women ever change so drastically that bodies of your type are in demand for our centerfold, you will be notified. Meanwhile, don't call us, we'll call you.

Sincerely,
Amanda Blake
Playgirl Magazine

To this day, I don't know who sent it, but I can't help laughing every time I read it.

Among our more serious challenges was the need to assess the efficacy of the All-Volunteer Force (AVF), which had been established the year before to finesse some of the political challenges that accompanied the draft during the Vietnam War. To get a hands-on feel for how effective the AVF was in maintaining combat effectiveness, I conducted a number of field trips, including repeat visits to the Ninth Infantry Division, headquartered at Fort Lewis in Washington State. In response to the trip report following my second visit to the Ninth, I received the below memorandum from the Army Vice Chief of Staff:

DEPARTMENT OF THE ARMY
OFFICE OF THE CHIEF OF STAFF
WASHINGTON, D.C. 20310

10 July 1975

MEMORANDUM FOR: MR. DOUGLAS M. JOHNSTON, OFFICE OF THE ASSISTANT SECRETARY OF DEFENSE (MANPOWER AND RESERVE AFFAIRS)

SUBJECT: Visit to the 9th Infantry Division

1. The observations and recommendations contained in the memorandum of your visit to the 9th Division have been reviewed by the Army Staff. We appreciate your comments and are pleased to receive your positive assessments of the success of the volunteer concept and the improvements that you noted in the quality and esprit of soldiers in the 9th Infantry Division since your visit there last year.

2. Although there have been many improvements, we agree with you that further improvements are possible. Accordingly, we are taking a hard look at the problem areas you identified; and your recommendations will be most helpful in determining ways for their solution. Through the combined efforts of both HQ DA and the 9th Infantry Division, I

feel confident that continued progress will be made to eliminate those problems you highlighted.

3.   Again, thank you for your observations and recommendations.

WALTER T. KERWIN, JR.
General, United States Army
Vice Chief of Staff

Upon receipt of said memo, I passed it on to Bob, with a penciled note in the upper right corner:

"Bob, who says they don't listen to us? A nice gesture on Army's part." Doug

Bob sent the memo back with the following notation in the margin:

Official Translation: "Here's this Johnston, at it again. Isn't he a Naval officer? What does he know about real soldiering? He's a pain in the ass! Who keeps approving his trips to the 9th? Send him a reply signed by Kerwin. Make it sound positive, and maybe he will go away. And close the gates at the 9th."

I had to admire Bob's masterful touch in keeping things in perspective.

Yet another critical issue arose when the DoD Office of Planning, Analysis, and Evaluation (a principal legacy of Robert McNamara's tenure as Defense Secretary) came forward with a recommendation to abolish the Naval Air Reserve because of inadequate carrier deck space to keep them properly trained. I immediately voiced serious opposition, insisting that the Naval Air Reserve was a national treasure, consisting of Vietnam veterans who regularly outperformed their active-duty counterparts in the annual William Tell gunnery competition. Further, because of their experience and the fact that there were no rookies in their ranks, they were instinctively better attuned to the challenges of combat.

This impasse between our respective offices led to an official test of the Naval Air Reserve's capabilities aboard the *USS Saratoga (CV60)*, a Forrestal-class supercarrier based on the East Coast. I was present for the test; and to put my money where my mouth was, flew off the carrier in an *A-3 Skywarrior*, a strategic bomber commonly referred to as *The Whale* and the heaviest aircraft capable of taking off and landing on a carrier. The pilot was a naval air reservist (or "Weekend Warrior" as they are commonly referred to by active duty fliers), and I was sitting beside him in the co-pilot's seat.

The takeoff was a real grabber as our bodies experienced 25 lateral G's (25 times the force of gravity) from the force of the catapult. It is impossible to move during the launch, which is why one always sees a slight dip in altitude as the aircraft leaves the deck (until the pilot can assume control and pull back on the stick).

As we were high above the carrier, preparing to land on what looked like a moving postage stamp far below, the pilot commented, "I understand you are a submariner." When I responded in the affirmative, he said, "You couldn't catch me near one of those with a ten-foot pole." To which I replied, "Are you kidding? This is a thousand times more dangerous than a submarine."

We made our approach and because we failed to engage any of the four arresting wires, the pilot applied "full military throttle" to essentially take off again for another try. On the second landing, the plane's tail hook engaged the 4th (or last) wire. As we came to a stop, we were literally peering over the edge of the flight deck.

Later on, I was up on the bridge of the carrier chatting with the Air Wing Commander, who mentioned that his Wing would be participating in an Operational Readiness Exercise (ORE) in Fallon, Nevada the following summer. He invited me to attend and said, "We'll put you through your paces." Thinking back on how much I had enjoyed the aerial acrobatics during Aviation Summer in Pensacola (while at the Naval Academy), I gave him one of the dumber responses of my life, saying, "You can't make it tough enough for me!"

The Reservists passed the tests on *Saratoga* with flying colors, and moved to the next (and final) phase, which included night take-offs and landings on the USS *Ranger (CV61)*, also Forrestal-class, but, based on the West Coast. Although I attended that as well, I did not participate in the actual flight operations, which may have been a wise choice because a jet piloted by the Executive Officer of one of the Reserve Units, who had more than several hundred carrier landings under his belt, crash-landed as the belly of his aircraft hit the edge of the flight deck and plunged into the sea. This was then followed by close to an hour of searching in the dark for the downed pilot.

All that the search-and-rescue helicopter was ultimately able to find was a parachute with a shark swimming nearby. As sad as this mishap was, the overall test was considered a success, and the Naval Air Reserve lived to fight another day. For my part, I came away with even greater respect for naval aviators, who have to be on their "A-game" every minute they're in the cockpit.

Brotherly Love

Finally, while serving in this same capacity in M&RA, an opportunity presented itself for me to do my brother a favor and, in the process, erase whatever lingering guilt I might have felt for trying to force-fit him into becoming a legendary football star or for tricking him into transferring his inheritance over to me (with the exception of the green house and the popcorn popper — so I wouldn't look too greedy). The opportunity arose when Bill Brehm, the Assistant Secretary of Defense for Manpower and Reserve Affairs, (a wonderful and highly capable gentleman, and my boss's boss) asked me to conduct the initial screening of applicants for filling the then vacant position of Deputy Assistant Secretary of Defense for Equal Opportunity. The position itself was higher up the food chain than my own, so it was a bit unusual.

Anyway, a number of highly-qualified applicants applied and during the course of interviewing a candidate from the Environmental Protection Agency (EPA), he made reference to a three-month course on environmental management at the University of Southern California that was offered at no cost to anyone nominated by his agency. The course itself was highly regarded and heavily used by the United Nations, the EPA, and various other federal, state, and city environmental programs. I told him that my brother, who was just about to leave the Navy, had a keen interest in the environment and would find such a course incredibly helpful in preparing for a career in that field. Long story short, Mike was nominated and found the course every bit as good as advertised.

My only misgiving about it all was that the candidate, who secured Mike's nomination, probably did so to enhance his chances of being chosen for the Deputy Assistant position; and that didn't happen. Nowhere along the way did I suggest there might be a *quid pro quo* for the favor, but he may have assumed there was anyway.

After Mike graduated from the USC program, he and his wife moved to the Puget Sound area, where the folks were still living, and applied for a position with the EPA Regional Office in Seattle. He was turned down there, so he applied for a position with the county and worked there for some time as a Natural Resources Planner

A number of months later, I happened to be at a party in Washington where I ran into a gentleman by the name of Stan Legro, who was an Assistant Administrator at the EPA. We immediately hit it off when during casual conversation, we learned that we had both graduated from "Canoe U" (he, the year before me). When I told him that my brother had as well, and that he had attended the environmental course at USC, but then been turned down for a job with the EPA, Stan asked for his name and sent the Seattle office a note. Twenty seven years later, Mike retired after a stellar and fulfilling career in the EPA.

After all that, Mike kept his inheritance.

The Navy Revisited

"Politics is perhaps the only profession for which no preparation is thought necessary."
— Robert Louis Stevenson (1850-1894)

After a year as Director of the new office, I was recruited by then Assistant Secretary of the Navy for Manpower and Reserve Affairs, Joseph McCullen, to become his Deputy Assistant Secretary for Reserve Affairs. Although I was lukewarm to the idea of working full-time on reserve matters, I agreed to apply for the position. As luck would have it, though, the White House intervened and used the position to reward the former Mayor of Charleston, S.C. for his political support of the President.

Not to be deterred, Joe created a new position designed specifically for me, which bore the title Deputy Assistant Secretary of the Navy (DASN) for Manpower. Because of its much broader mandate, I morphed into an enthusiastic candidate. However, Joe's strategy almost came up short, once again because of White House interference, but this time of a different nature. The email exchange below between a Naval Academy classmate and myself on the occasion of my 73rd birthday captures the essence:

> From: EIGIL HANSEN JR
> Sent: Wednesday, November 23, 2011 5:19PM
> To: Doug Johnston
> Subject: Birthday Greetings
>
> Dear Doug,
>
> I wanted to throw in my "two cents" worth in wishing you a great "73rd". You know, I still remember vividly the most unique greeting and conversation I ever had—and it was with you and VADM [Vice Admiral] Jim Watkins, who was CHNAVPERS [Chief of Naval Personnel] at the time. As I remember, you were Asst. to the Navy for Research and Development (I think). Anyway, it was in the 1975-76-time frame: I was over in the Pentagon on business and at the time I was an 0-5 [Commander] and PERS 44a, as Assistant to the Division Director for Officer Assignments.

Anyway, I was winging around the corner on the E-Ring when I ran right into you in the hallway. There was instant recognition. I said "Doug" and you said "Gil", "How are you?" And we began to chat. It was not more than a few seconds later that Vice Admiral Watkins came around the corner. He greeted you with "Good morning, Mr. Johnston" and you responded with "Good morning, Jim". You introduced me to him (although he was my Big Boss, I had never formally met him before), and I said "Good morning, Admiral" and he said "Good morning, Commander". And all three of us chatted for a few minutes with him calling you Mr. Johnston, you calling him Jim, I called him Admiral, he called me Commander, you called me Gil, and I called you Doug. Talk about a crazy example of protocol! I don't think I'll ever forget it. Here's wishing you many more years of serving our Lord and Savior, Jesus Christ. Happy Birthday!!

Gil

From: Douglas Johnston
To: EIGIL HANSEN JR
Sent: Saturday, November 26, 2011 3:00 PM
Subject: RE: Birthday Greetings

Dear Gil,

—Thanks for yours. Until you reminded me, I had totally forgotten about that moment in time. It was probably to avoid such irreverent encounters that the Navy tried to torpedo my appointment to that particular job. A jump from 0-5 to the civilian-equivalent of between 2 and 3 stars was more than naval tradition could bear, so they contacted the White House, which, in turn, contacted Deputy Secretary of Defense Bill Clements (who was on the West Coast at the time) to have him conduct one last interview before I got the job. By then, I had already jumped through the multitudinous normal hoops for approval, including mustering the necessary political support on the Hill; so this did not auger well.

—Clements, was a former Governor of Texas and reportedly tough to the point where Flag officers would sometimes cringe when meeting with him. On top of that, he was known to be strongly opposed to having young men in high places, as evidenced by having turned down two friends of mine who were smooth as silk and incredibly well-qualified, with their Ivy League advanced degrees and the like (one later went on to become Deputy Secretary of the Treasury and the other President of Ford Motor Company). Both of them were 5 years older than me but looked at least 10 years older. It was also the case that the Deputy Secretary of Defense had never before interviewed someone as far down the food chain as me.

—You will appreciate this part. On my way to meet with Clements, I stopped off at the Meditation Room to pray that I'd get the job, which had been newly created for me and which I had come to want (DASN for Manpower). When I left the Meditation Room, I walked out knowing I had the job. I had concluded while meditating that all I had to do was be tougher than Clements during the interview. So, I walked in to find a submarine Admiral at his side, Ken Carr, who I had never previously met. Anyway, Clements started asking me questions (most of which had to have been planted by others, since there's no way he could have dreamed them up himself). After each question, I would calmly indicate that what he had said was one way of looking at it, but then, hit his desk forcefully with my fist and in a raised voice give him what I felt to be a more compelling interpretation.

—During this animated discourse, he learned that I had recently been asked to assess the Navy from the Defense Secretary's perspective, while on a 2-week tour of reserve duty at the CNO Executive Panel (I was working in OSD [Office of the Secretary of Defense] at the time, so the assignment had made sense). Anyway, he asked to see it, so I sent it to him after the meeting. My assessment had been pretty tough on the Navy, since we were just coming out of the Zumwalt years, and there was much to be tough about. He apparently liked it, because I received it back the following day with a "C" in the margin and a note to the fact that I had the job. The whole scenario was totally out of character for me, but it worked. Although the uniformed side of the house didn't make life easy after my appointment, I was able to surround myself with brilliant staff, and we made our mark.

—Sorry for such a long-winded reply, but when I remembered the Meditation Room bit, I knew I had to tell you. Thanks for the birthday wishes. I must say, it's a pretty rarified atmosphere up here.

Warm regards, Doug

Serving in the Navy Secretariat proved to be a labor of love. Joe was a terrific boss; and the opportunity of working with him to have a meaningful impact in a culture I instinctively revered was not to be wasted (Addendum C). Accordingly, I and my team did our level best to improve the management of Navy and Marine Corps military and civilian manpower. Although I only had three staff members, they were a highly talented group consisting of Ing Kiland, Will Story, and Lloyd Embry. Ing was a Navy Commander out of the class ahead of me at the Academy who had recently commanded a destroyer as part of the Navy's famed "Mod Squad", a concept created by Admiral Elmo Zumwalt while serving as Chief of Naval Operations (CNO) to provide highly capable junior officers with an early opportunity for command in Destroyer Squadron 26 (otherwise known as the Mod Squad). In short, Ing was a highly accomplished Navy Line Officer who effectively served as my Executive Officer (or right-hand man) throughout the assignment.

Will Story was also an Academy grad who happened to be one of the more-gifted manpower analysts in the Navy. Rounding out the staff was Lloyd Embry, a superb all-around analyst, who had been the ship's Supply Officer aboard the *James K. Polk* when I served as Engineer.

Two Full Gloves

"The average man's judgment is so poor; he runs a risk every time he uses it."
—Edgar W. Howe (1853-1937)

Not long after assuming my new responsibilities, I received the long-promised invitation to Fallon, Nevada to observe the Operational Readiness Exercise (ORE) of the Air Wing involved in the earlier test of Naval Air Reserve capabilities aboard the *Saratoga*. I accepted the invitation and the day before the exercise was scheduled, I traveled to Reno, the closest major city to Fallon. There I stayed with Carl Gidlund (my friend from OEP of North Beach fame); and because I had never before been to any of the gambling meccas in that part of the world, he and I spent the better part of that night gambling in the local casinos. To cloud one's judgement, these casinos typically provide free drinks as you gamble the evening away. Well, their strategy worked with me (and has ever since); and as I finally left at 4:00 am to drive across the desert for the 6:00 am pre-flight briefing at Fallon, I was both out of money and woefully ill-prepared for what awaited me.

The first two things one is always supposed to do prior to going aloft are to get a good night's sleep and to have a proper breakfast. I had neither, so it was with some trepidation that I overheard the Air Wing Commander (who remembered me from the *Saratoga*) tell the pilot assigned to take me up, "After the exercise, wring him out." My pilot had been an instructor in the F4 Phantom for eight years; and there was little doubt in my mind that I was about to get very wrung.

As we took off, with him in the front seat and me in the rear, I asked where the little brown bag was in the event he should succeed in his assigned mission. He laughed and said, "We don't have such things. Just use your glove." Anyway, as we were observing the exercise, which was a simulated bombing run over Beirut, Lebanon, opposed by F5 ("Mongoose") aircraft, I sensed that I was in real trouble. At the slightest turn, I was breaking out in a cold sweat. Once the exercise was over, he began to wring me out by simulating MIG evasions and SAM (missile) evasions, in addition to any number of other gratuitous acrobatics. Meanwhile, I am feeling totally crushed by the pressure of my "G suit" (a flight suit designed to apply pressure to your body and thereby adjust your blood flow to prevent possible loss of vision during tight turns, inside loops, outside loops, and the like). When doing an inside loop in a G suit, for example, your body can absorb about 9 "G's" (forces of gravity) before the blood leaves your head and you fully "black out" and lose all your vision. Without the suit, it takes far fewer G's to reach that same point.

At one point, I asked the pilot if he could steady out for a bit. He asked if I was all right, and it must have been close to a full minute before I could answer; I was shaking so much from the dry-heaves (having already thrown up everything I possibly could). At one point, I recall actually wishing for a real MiG to shoot me down and put me out of my misery. Anyway, when we finally landed, I exited the aircraft with two full gloves and looking more than a little green around the gills. In my then capacity as Deputy Assistant Secretary of the Navy (DASN), there was no way they were going to miss the chance to fully capture my acute embarrassment, as the photographers merrily clicked away.

When I visited the Post Exchange a few hours later, I ran into a pilot from that same Air Wing, who tried to console me by saying, "Don't worry. Even we experienced pilots get sick in the back seat." As I learned the hard way, the back seat of a high-performance jet is not where you want to be during acrobatic maneuvers, primarily because your body can't anticipate what's coming next. For the next three days, I walked around feeling sore all over from the effects of the G-suit pressing against me during my "wring out."

Taking it to the Edge

Another experience during my tenure as DASN worth mentioning was precipitated by an article I happened to read in *Time Magazine,* while flying home on a commercial jet from the west coast. It was about a Navy Lieutenant who was suing the Navy because he had broken his back during SERE training (Survival, Evasion, Resistance, and Escape). This is training that the Navy provides for its pilots and anyone else who might conceivably get captured behind enemy lines. In any event, the article caused me to think I had best get out in front of the Congress and take a hard look at what was going on to ensure there was no physical abuse taking place.

A few weeks later, I visited our SERE training facility in the California desert and was surprised to find that a classmate by the name of Ted Parsons was in charge. Although I hadn't known him at the Academy, he is a great guy; and we quickly became good friends. With this instant rapport, he showed me the full gamut of what was taking place.

Basically, the process begins by setting the prisoners free in the desert to test their survival skills and ability to evade capture. Because there's really no place to hide, all of them are rather quickly captured and the ordeal begins. The first thing I witnessed up close and personal was a prisoner being "waterboarded," a process in which the prisoner is strapped to a horizontal board, with his head slightly lower than his feet. Then one of the captors begins pouring water over his face, while asking him questions. The prisoner, knowing this is only a training exercise, holds out for a while until he begins having trouble breathing because the flow of water is so intense. At this point, his legs begin to shake; and it is becoming much more than an "exercise." Just when it looks like he can't take it anymore, a wet towel is placed over his face and the volume of water is increased even more. By this time, his legs are shaking rather violently, and he is clearly on the edge. Then it stops, and he's allowed to breath. It should be noted that the gentleman holding the towel is always a Hospital Corpsman, so no one has ever suffered irreparable harm in the process.

All of the prison guards were dressed in East German-style uniforms and talked with a fake accent to add realism to the process. The prisoners were housed in small tiger cages, with no amenities other than a large coffee can, open on one end. However, they didn't get to spend much time in those cages, because of the constant interrogation to which they were subjected, usually sitting tied to a chair with a single light bulb overhead. There was almost no time for sleep in the midst of the never-ending harassment, which often included being slammed around against the corrugated tin walls of the shacks in which they were being interrogated (which generally makes a lot of noise without causing injury).

After several days, the training concluded with the playing of the Star-Spangled Banner over the loudspeakers surrounding the compound. At that point, the prisoners exited their cages and stood at attention, usually with tears streaming down their cheeks. To a man (and there were only men receiving such training in those days), they were glad to have had the experience but absolutely didn't ever want to do it again. As for abuse, I had never in my life seen so much of it. However, in the cold light of day, that abuse seemed more than worth any anguish it might cause.

To get a more balanced understanding of what I had witnessed, I paid a similar visit to the Air Force site for this same kind of training located near Spokane, Washington. The Air Force version was notably milder, and I wasn't surprised to later learn that Navy POWs had generally fared better under duress while imprisoned in Vietnam than had their Air Force counterparts. However, because most of the POW's who returned from captivity in Hanoi felt that their lives had actually been enhanced by the experience suggests that the training had been incredibly helpful for all, regardless of service.

Contributing even more to this remarkable, counter-intuitive outcome was the prison culture forged by Captain Jim Stockdale (Naval Academy Class of 1947), who was later awarded the Medal of Honor and went on to become a Vice Admiral. Indeed, the culture he established promoted the kind of self-awareness, sense of accomplishment, and optimism that later produced five other admirals, sixteen generals, two ambassadors, two college presidents, two senators, two congressmen and numerous political appointees. Yet another indicator of its effectiveness was the 4% incidence of Post-Traumatic Stress Disorder (PTSD) among repatriated Navy POW's vs the 30.6% average for non-POW vets.

Key to it all was an over-riding commitment to return with honor and a stoic resolve to focus only on that which one could personally control. Their code of the west called for absolute honesty in reporting fully to one another "via tapping on the walls" the outcome of their latest interrogation, so that whoever followed could add to the disinformation (or confuse the truth) of what had already been revealed under torture.

Implicit in this approach was a built-in forgiveness that accompanied their recognition that everyone has his breaking point. As long as one did one's best, that was all that was expected. Collectively, the POW's achieved a professional standard of conduct that makes other professionals in tough jobs—even Navy SEALs –look on in awe.[14]

The Kindly Old Gentleman

"It takes less time to do a thing right than to explain why you did it wrong."
—*Henry Wadsworth Longfellow (1807-1882)*

One day, I made a courtesy call on Admiral Rickover, and ended up spending the better part of two hours discussing a range of topics, foremost among which was his strong suggestion that I abolish the Naval Academy. Aside from the fact that we were both graduates of that august institution, and that I had neither the authority nor the desire to do such a thing, we had an animated discussion in which I asked, "What about esprit and elan?" to which he responded, "Oh batshit! Those damn fools (referring to midshipmen) still march to class. In the old days that might have made some sense when the front rank had to kneel while the rear rank fired; but now it makes no damn sense at all." And so it went.

Although the Admiral was notoriously abrupt and as irreverent as one could possibly be, he was referred to in the Submarine Force as the "Kindly Old Gentleman." Despite the range of demeaning adjectives used to describe him by many with whom he crossed swords—boisterous, obnoxious, obstreperous, recalcitrant, rude, crude and unattractive—he was greatly admired by most of us who served in the nuclear submarine service. We worshipped at the altar of success, and he was Mr. Success. We were also keenly aware that the reason Soviet submarines were experiencing major problems with their reactor plants and we were not was because of the rigorous standards to which the Admiral held our nuclear manufacturing industry. In fact, there was a widely-shared joke in the U.S. Submarine Force that you could always tell a Soviet submariner from the Northern Fleet, because he glowed in the dark.

Beyond the personal interview with the Admiral at the outset and the above courtesy call, I had two other encounters with him, the first as a Lieutenant Junior Grade (LTJG) while serving on the commissioning crew of the *USS U.S. Grant (SSBN631)* as the Electrical and Reactor Control Officer. The Admiral made it a practice to ride every new submarine on its initial sea trials; and as we were preparing for ours, our nuclear reactor "scrammed" (shut down) for seemingly no apparent reason. I'm not sure why the sequencing of

---

[14] Additional details of this experience have been brilliantly captured in a book titled, *Lessons From the Hanoi Hilton* by Taylor Kiland, the daughter of my former military assistant, Ing Kiland.

events occurred as it did in the aftermath of that incident, but apparently the Admiral raised the roof when he couldn't get a satisfactory answer for why the scram had taken place, either from the civilian Supervisor of Shipbuilding or our ship's Commanding Officer. Finally, he called in LTJG Johnston, and I explained that I was the guilty culprit. While conducting preventive maintenance checks on the reactor control system with an enlisted technician from my division, we had inadvertently initiated the scram because of an error in the system's official circuitry diagram, which I proceeded to show him. With that, he was satisfied; and we parted company.

The second encounter took place about five years later when I was a Lieutenant Commander (LCDR) serving as Chief Engineer of the Blue Crew on the *Polk*. We were finishing the off-crew phase of our three-month operational cycle (which, as mentioned earlier, consisted of three months aboard ship, followed by three months off), and the Captain and I were concerned about our ability to pass an inspection by the Nuclear Power Examining Board (NPEB), which was scheduled to take place two weeks after returning to the ship for our next patrol. We sent word of our concern ahead to our Squadron Commander in Rota, Spain so that he wouldn't be caught unaware. The NPEB inspections were notoriously difficult, and we were suffering from a "perfect storm" of personnel turnover that left my Department without any experienced Division Officers. Collectively they had spent little, if any, operating time at sea.

As predicted, we failed the exam; and a second examination was scheduled to take place two weeks later during our sea trials following the normal one-month upkeep period alongside a Submarine Tender (during which we repaired any engineering problems that had arisen during the Gold Crew's two-month patrol). In many respects, our odds of passing this second time around were no greater than the first, because we still suffered from the same inexperience at sea. However, there was tremendous pressure to pass the exam and get on with life, because we were scheduled to conduct a test-firing of our missiles during that patrol, the results of which were apparently of great importance back in Washington.

During those two weeks, I spent about 22 hours a day trying to get ready for the next exam, primarily by testing the crew in mock drills that stimulated various engineering casualties. At one point, the ship's doctor confined me to bed rest for a day to address a problem I was having with phlebitis, from being on my feet so much of the time.

Despite our best efforts, we failed yet again as everything that could go wrong did exactly that—problems ranging from loss of the hot-well level control system in one of the main condensers to an inability to properly seat the floating wire antenna in its housing while underwater and any number of other mechanical malfunctions. Personnel performance was not a whole lot better either, as one of my Department's Second-Class Electronics Technicians fell down an open hatch in the Engineering spaces and had to be sent to Sick Bay to recover. In short, a comedy of errors and unprecedented challenges from start to finish.

At that point, the Commander of the Atlantic Submarine Force (COMSUBLANT) decided to have me relieved of my duties as Chief Engineer on the *Polk* and reassigned as Squadron Engineer of Submarine Squadron Two based in New London, Connecticut (in which, ironically, two submarines were already tied up and unable to go to sea because they too had failed their NPEB exams). After I was advised of this decision by the Squadron Commander, Pete Durbin (my skipper) pulled me aside and said the only reason they were taking me instead of him was because I had previously submitted my letter of resignation (which typically took about 18 months to process in those days). I told him not to worry, I fully understood the concept of a "clean sweep" to get things back on track.

A couple of days later as I was preparing to turn the Department over to whoever was going to be assigned to relieve me, I was called to the Commodore's (Squadron Commander's) cabin on the Sub Tender. He asked me to talk to the men in my Department because there was a mild rebellion taking place over my prospective departure. I told him I fully understood the perceived need to replace me and would talk to the crew.

About this same time, Admiral Rickover intervened and in so many words, told COMSUBLANT to shove it. They couldn't relieve me "for cause," because all I had done was work my tail off to fix the problem. I strongly suspect that the Navy Achievement Medal I had been awarded after our previous patrol only added to the political difficulty of making the shift. Anyway, Rickover prevailed, I stayed in the saddle, and we passed the third time around with flying colors. In fact, the Director of the NPEB said it was the highest grade they had ever awarded for one of these inspections. By this time, I was more than a little jaded by the experience; and my only reaction to their accolade was "Big deal. We should have been the best; we took longer than anyone else!" A mountaintop, it was not.

As it turned out, immediately following our experience, a number of other Polaris submarines were also tied up for multiple failures. They too had become victims of the "perfect storm" of personnel turnover, which had been caused by the confluence of (1) termination of the involuntary one-year extension of duty for everyone in the military that had been imposed the year before by the President because of manpower shortages in the Vietnam War and (2) the normal cycle of next-year departures, thus creating in one fell swoop a much greater loss of experience than was normal.

Also exacerbating this problem was a major exodus from the Submarine Force of many of its best and brightest officers because of the negative impact of the NPEB inspections. In its zeal to show that it could be as tough as Rickover's shop had been in previously conducting these inspections, the SUBLANT team under Captain P.J. Early bent over backwards to make the experience as difficult as possible. Even when one passed the exam, that verdict always came at the end of a two or three-page letter that was little short of a scathing indictment from start to finish. There was no such thing as any ship having done a good job when it came to the Engineering Department.

Eventually, the powers that be addressed the problem and assigned Bud Kauderer, a terrific officer with whom I had served earlier on the *Skipjack,* to lead the inspection team. Bud quickly transformed it from a destructive exercise to a highly constructive experience, and the hemorrhaging of officers tailed off accordingly. Bud later made Admiral and eventually served highly successful tours as Commander of all US submarines in the Pacific and later of those in the Atlantic.

In a nutshell, the "Kindly Old Gentleman" had saved my bacon, something I would not soon forget. After passing the exam, I was in the Commodore's Cabin along with the skipper and several others, including Admiral Rickover, reviewing all that had taken place. At one point, it became clear the Admiral was anxious to get back to the States; and I almost keeled over when he picked up the phone and in a rather abrupt conversation with another American Admiral (who was serving as NATO Commander of the Allied Joint Forces Command in Lisbon) said, "I don't give a good G_ _Damn, I want the fastest plane in Spain, and I want it now!" At that, he slammed the phone down. Interpersonal skills were clearly not his strongest suit.

Also contributing to the challenge of our several NPEB exams was the fact that shortly before leaving New London to return to Rota (to relieve the Gold Crew), a general meeting had been called for all nuclear submarine Commanding Officers, Executive Officers, and Engineer Officers in the immediate vicinity. The numbers were substantial, and the meeting took place in the Base Movie Theater. As I recall, the purpose was for Captain Early, then head of the NPEB team, to share his philosophy about the NPEB exams and why they were so essential. After doing so, he opened it up for questions.

At one point, I raised my hand, stood up and expressed my frustration over how little room there was in the Engineering Department for one to be even the slightest bit creative in building a better mousetrap. I noted that when I had reported to my first submarine some five years earlier, the manuals for operating the reactor plant were reasonably succinct and provided a degree of latitude for personal initiative. Now those manuals had become unduly cumbersome and more than a little stifling, as had various other regulations and procedures. Anyway, when I sat down, there was widespread applause throughout the theater, much to Captain Early's embarrassment. Three weeks later, he showed up to conduct our NPEB inspection. He hadn't forgotten.

Pleasant Interludes

While working in the Navy Secretariat was pretty demanding, it wasn't all work and no play. One of the more interesting encounters on the play front stemmed from one day thumbing through a U.S. Veterans Magazine and coming across an article in which a movie starlet by the name of Kathy Kersh was pictured as having recently won a veterans-sponsored beauty contest. I don't recall how I found her address, but hearkening back to my plebe year antics of some 20 years earlier, I wrote her a letter and we ended up getting together on my next trip to California. Although my official reason for going was to inspect the Navy and Marine Corps Training Centers in San Diego, the time in Hollywood was way more fun.

The dating game was always fun and an endless source of interesting memories, some of them quite humorous. One in that category which leaps to mind took place at Ocean Shores, a town on the coast in Washington State. While there with a lady friend, we dropped by a bar one evening where they were providing karaoke as a cheap form of entertainment. Often thinking I had missed my calling while singing in the shower, I thought "here's my one chance at stardom." Knowing I would never again see anyone who was there—at least not in this lifetime—I worked up the nerve to give it a shot. I tried two numbers, the first was an Elvis tune that was quite easy and went reasonably well. However, "You've lost that Lovin' Feelin' " by the Righteous Brothers is much harder than it sounds. Suffice it to say, no one would ever confuse my pitiful rendition with that of Tom Cruise and his sidekick Goose, in *Top Gun*. Happily, and as predicted, I have never again seen any of those poor souls who suffered through listening to me embarrass myself on that fateful night. So, it was back to the showers!

Mingling with Heroes

One of my last acts as Deputy Assistant Secretary was to preside over an annual luncheon of Medal of Honor winners. Ordinarily, that duty would have been assumed by someone higher up the pyramid; but by that time, most senior governmental positions had been vacated, as Ford Administration appointees made way for yet-to-be named Carter appointees. While it was a singular honor to be breaking bread with such a distinguished group of heroes, I couldn't help but notice that most of them were somewhat small in stature. My immediate thought was there must be two dynamics at play here, small targets and a Napoleonic complex.

One hero who wasn't all that short was Rear Admiral Gene Fluckey, a living legend in the submarine force for his exploits as Commanding Officer of the USS *Barb* during WWII. Not only did *Barb* sink the greatest tonnage of any American sub in that war during the five war patrols under Fluckey's command, but it also had the distinction of mounting the only shore-based attack by American forces against the Japanese homeland, when he sent a raiding party ashore under the cover of darkness to blow up a military train with some well-placed explosives. When I had the pleasure of meeting him years later at this luncheon; it was easy to see from his incomparable spirit why he had been such an inspiring leader.

Another of the heroes who, in fact, was short, was an Army Major by the name of Jake Jacobs. During the period I was serving as Director of Policy Planning and Management in the Office of the Secretary of Defense (OSD), Jake spent a summer with my office on detail from his duties at West Point. In those days, at least, most military officers serving in the Pentagon wore civilian clothes to work, except on Wednesdays, when they donned their uniforms. The first time Jake wore his uniform, I was taken aback to see him wearing only a single row of ribbons (military speak for the ribbons that servicemen or women wear above the left breast pocket on their dress uniforms—usually three to a row—with each symbolizing a medal the recipient had been awarded sometime in the past). I knew Jake had served in Vietnam and that those who had typically sported at least four ribbons associated with that conflict. When I looked closer, I saw that the three he was wearing were the Medal of Honor, the Silver Star, and the Bronze Star. In short, only his three highest decorations; the lesser ribbons couldn't compete.

Jake had received his Medal of Honor while serving as a Military Advisor to the South Vietnamese Army, and his heroics were off the charts, including significant hand-to-hand combat. Equally interesting was a story he shared with me about the tickertape parade that was held in his honor when he returned to his home town in New Jersey after the war. At one point, during the proceedings, a stranger complimented him and slipped him a set of keys to a new car. Jake suspected likely ties to the Mafia and a "hot car," but saw fit not to ask and enjoyed what I'm sure must have been countless miles of driving pleasure.

Sharing a lighter moment with Marv Kosters, my boss at the Cost of Living Council (official Department of Transportation photo)

Introducing Acting Director of the FBI (and former submariner) L. Patrick Gray to friends at a Saints and Sinners celebration, at which he was to be "roasted" (used with permission of the House of Representatives Office of Photography-Dev O'Neil photographer)

And with Judge George Boldt, Chairman of the Pay Board (official Department of Transportation photo)

Assessing the volunteer force (official U.S. Army photo)

A real mountain woman

Reviewing Officer for recruit graduation at Great Lakes Naval Training Center in Oct, 1976 (official U.S. Navy photo)

Bidding farewell to Bill as I left the Office of the Secretary of Defense (official Department of Defense photo)

Suiting up for carrier ops (official U.S. Navy photo)

Bob Murray and Bill Brehm, great bosses and incredible friends

Getting woozy (official U.S. Navy photo)

Chapter Six

THE PRIVATE SECTOR

One of the most common characteristics of a person nearing the end of the first half (of the game of life) is that unquenchable desire to move from success to significance.

Bob Buford (1939-2018)

In August of 1976, while still serving in the Navy Secretariat, I attended the inaugural session of a three-week executive program for *Senior Managers in Government* at the Harvard Business School. The Kennedy School of Government, directly across the Charles River, was also a co-sponsor, but because it was new to the world of executive programs, and those kinds of programs had long been among the premier offerings of the Business School, the Business School took the lead.

It was a well-attended, high-quality program; and I greatly enjoyed the experience. The day before it concluded, I was cornered by Professor C. Roland Christenson, a renowned Business School faculty member who had played a central role in the program. He said that whenever he taught a course or an executive program, he always paid tribute to that student whose insights impressed him the most by giving him or her an inscribed copy of a text book he had authored on the case study method of teaching (which I later learned was treated like the Bible at the Business School). In the course of doing this, he suggested that I should consider coming to Harvard to teach after I left government. I don't know what surprised me more, the book presentation or his kind suggestion; but when I pointed out with respect to his teaching comment that I didn't have a PHD, his response was "Oh, Harvard's just arrogant enough to overlook a small detail like that."[15]

---

[15] His answer reminded me of when I was once asked if I knew why Harvard was the only unaccredited institution of higher learning in the country. The answer to which was, "After all, who is worthy to pass judgement?"

Harvard Revisited

"What this country needs are more unemployed politicians."
—Edward Langley (1928-1995)

Fast forward a half year and the country has elected a new President. Because my job with the Navy was a political position, this meant I now had to begin seeking new employment. During this same period, I received a visit from Graham Allison, Dean of the Kennedy School of Government. He said that following the program for senior managers which I had attended, he had received a note from Joe Bower, the Business School professor who had overseen that effort, urging Graham to contact me about establishing an executive program at the Kennedy School. Graham said he was interested in doing so and asked my thoughts on what a program in national security might look like. I told him to give me a week to think it through, and I'd get back to him.

We met again a week later, and I passed him a several page concept paper suggesting that the Kennedy School establish an executive program for Flag-rank military officers and their civilian equivalents, not only from the Defense Department, but from State, the CIA, the Congress and other relevant agencies. My suggestion keyed to the fact that although there were innumerable training programs available for military officers up through the rank of colonel (or captain in the Navy), there was nothing for Flag-rank military officers in the way of continuing education at the corporate executive level. Once one became an Admiral or a General, it was assumed that they already knew all they needed to know. And although they might serve in a Flag capacity for as many as ten or more years, there were no further opportunities available to them for managerial or intellectual refurbishment.

Graham warmed to the idea and asked what role I might play in mounting such a program. I asked him to give me another week, and I would get back to him (Addendum D). In June of 1977, I set sail for Harvard to make it happen.

At this point, I was newly married to my second wife, Norvell, and step-dad to three fine young men: Brint, Chapman, and Pearson. We found a nice home in Wellesley that was about a half hour from Harvard.

The Smoking Raccoon

"Three may keep a secret if two of them are dead." –Benjamin Franklin

Life with Norvell's three strapping teen-agers was both challenging and fun. Brint, the oldest, was at the tail-end of his high school years. Chapman was a couple years behind, and Pearson a couple behind that. They all had their moments, but Pearson's were perhaps the more colorful. Two episodes that leap to mind in this regard were (1) the all-too-frequent phone calls from irate customers on his paper route, wondering where their papers were, and (2) his creative rationale for almost burning the house down.

The mystery of the missing papers cleared up the following spring when the snow melted and revealed the presence of several bundles of old newspapers hidden behind some bushes alongside the house. As for the close-call with the house, one day when I was up in Pearson's room, which was on one end of our semi-finished attic (with Chapman's at the other end), I noticed that a sizeable section of his window ledge looked like charcoal. Something had obviously burned the ledge; and upon looking out the window at the roof below and seeing a number of discarded cigarette butts, it became all-too-apparent what had happened.

When I confronted Pearson with the evidence, he immediately blamed everything on a clever raccoon. There were a number of raccoons in the neighborhood that often woke us up at night with their fighting, and the neighbor next door (a nationally acclaimed economist and highly credible witness) had told us earlier about having walked into his kitchen one afternoon to find a raccoon sitting on their kitchen table eating a banana, which it had actually peeled. Leaning on this as evidence and looking as sincere as he possibly could, Pearson proceeded to fabricate the concept of a smoking raccoon. I don't recall what, if any, punishments he received for those particular misdeeds; but whatever they were, they had little effect.

All three of the boys were incredibly bright, had good hearts, and were the source of countless good memories, some of which took place at sea. While living in Wellesley, I bought a 25 foot sloop, which I moored in Salem Harbor and in which the five of us sailed overnight to Boston Harbor for a close look at the Tall Ships (large topsail schooners, barques, and brigantines from various countries) as they sailed into the harbor the next morning on their way around-the-world. Not much sleep, but a memorable time as we dodged one tall ship after another[16].

---

[16] One night after returning from a day of sailing with Pearson, I pointed to the constellation Orion and told him the middle star in Orion's belt was a shining tribute to my father. I then pointed to Betelgeuse, an even brighter star in that same constellation, and told him that was his. From then on, I called him "Beetle."

A Friend Named Murphy

Another memorable journey at sea took place when Norvell and I sailed down to Marion, Massachusetts, just south of Cape Cod, to visit some friends. On the way back, we ran into a storm; and the waves were such that several fishing boats in the area capsized that day. As for our own boat, those same waves caused two of the six stays (that extended from the deck to the top of the mast to hold it in place) to snap off. Fortunately, they were on opposite sides, so the mast stayed in place. However, it was getting too dicey to continue on, so we headed for shore. The nearest port was Plymouth, and I marveled at the challenge the Pilgrims must have faced when they first landed there. One has to approach from the north to access a relatively narrow channel that takes you into port; and of course, we were coming in from the south.

As we were making our way into port in the dark, I gave Norvell the helm and told her what lights to steer toward, while I took down the sails. Apparently, she lost track, which was easy to do, and we ended up on some good-sized rocks. I was unable to get us off with the motor; and as the tide was coming in, we were being pushed further up onto the rocks. I then took the anchor, got into our dinghy and rowed out to drop it a short distance away. After trying unsuccessfully to pull us off of the rocks by hauling in on the anchor chain, I used the motor to rotate the boat and point it toward the channel. Then I re-hoisted the sails so that as the tide continued to rise, the strong wind would sail us off the rocks and into the channel. This strategy worked, and we spent the night anchored on one side of the shipping channel as we tried to get some sleep. Norvell was able to do so, but I was awake most of the night checking to ensure we weren't being run over by various merchant vessels steaming down the channel.

The next morning, we set sail for Salem Harbor; and although the sun was shining, the waves were every bit as high as the day before. As we passed the breakwater and the sea spray was shooting high in the air, Norvell went below (into the cabin) until we moored some eight hours later. She had had enough, and I couldn't blame her one bit; it had been a rough trip. Thus with the crew having mutinied and no nourishment to be had from the galley, I was effectively lashed to the helm as we fought the waves and made our way north for most of the day. We finally pulled into a peaceful harbor at Scituate (just south of Boston), anchored out, rowed ashore for dinner, then slept on the boat for 13 hours before weighing anchor and finally making our way home.

One thing I learned from that experience and any number of other sailing adventures, whenever you're in a sailboat, Murphy is always at your side. It got to the point where the only times I felt any discomfort was on those few occasions when I returned to port without something major having gone wrong. When I returned to Washington, I bought another sloop, this one a foot longer. And, without even trying, Murphy found his way south to continue our long-running courtship.

The *Coca Cola Girl*

Back on dry land, Norvell and I spent a weekend in Camden, Maine, a charming village on Penobscot Bay nestled between the mountains (at least what passes for mountains in the East) and the sea[17]. Our purpose in going was to visit her mother's cousin, a delightful lady by the name of Kay Aldridge. I had never heard of Kay and didn't know what to expect. But what an enriching experience it proved to be! Then in her 60's, Kay had apparently been famous as an actress in the 1940's, playing the role of the imperiled heroine in various black and white serial productions like *The Perils of Pauline*. She was also the cover girl for Coca Cola and had been featured on the cover of *Life Magazine* no fewer than eight times, allegedly more than anyone else either before or since.

Having dated a range of movie actors, including Errol Flynn, Clark Gable, and Jimmy Stewart, Kay had fascinating stories to tell and tell them she did, with flair and panache, regaling us with one tale after another. She talked endlessly, but everything she said was incredibly interesting; and I can't recall ever feeling quite so thoroughly entertained. At one point, she shared in passing the multiple advantages of dating older women, the fact that "they don't yell, they don't tell, and they don't swell."

Kay lived in a lovely old home on the water, directly across from a charming lighthouse—the first thing you saw from the guest bedroom window when you awoke in the morning. She had been married three times, but her second and third husbands had died on her, so she spent most of her time serving as hostess for any number of activities associated with Camden's rich cultural life. Kay passed away in 1995 at the age of 77, but her memory most assuredly lingers in the hearts of everyone who had the good fortune to know her.

The Field of Battle

Some months later, Norvell's younger brother, Randy, invited me to participate in the Baltimore Decathlon, which he was overseeing that year. Not

---

[17] Rumor has it that at least half of the U.S. intelligence community decided to retire in Camden after conducting rigorous due diligence on charming places to live.

having a clue what I was getting into, I readily accepted and showed up several weeks later to compete in what may have been the most eclectic mix of sporting events ever conceived. It consisted of running a hundred yard dash, heaving a shotput, kicking a football for distance, throwing a baseball for distance and accuracy, a 50-yard swim (half butterfly and the other half freestyle), shooting 20 free throws with a basketball, bowling, shooting pool, playing a round of miniature golf, and one other event I can no longer recall. There were between 20 and 30 of us competing, with each accumulating a total score by adding up the order in which we placed in each event. So, the winner was whoever had the lowest score for the day.

Randy told me up-front that he always fudged on the first event —- the hundred-yard dash —- by running as soon as the starter said, "Get set." True to his word, he did exactly that; but this particular year there was a longer than normal pause between the "Get set" and "Go," so he looked pretty silly running the first few strides all by himself. However, no one thought to disqualify him (after all, he was in charge) so despite his very sheepish look at the finish, he got away with it. As for me, I pulled a hamstring on that event, which undoubtfully impacted my performance for the rest of the day, but not necessarily all for the bad. I have never bowled as high a score as I did with that pulled hamstring.

It was great fun; and although I probably finished somewhere in the middle of the pack, I was pleased to learn at the end that out of a very sizable point total, I had finished exactly one point better than Randy's older brother Buck, who was four years younger than me and a former Green Beret (interservice rivalry and all that stuff). Of course, Randy beat us both; but then again, he should have. In addition to his unrivaled racing technique, he's also one of the nicer guys you could ever hope to meet. The event culminated with a dinner in formal attire at the Maryland Club, where the libation flowed as freely as the exaggerated claims of athletic achievement.

A Star is Born

During our eight years in Wellesley, Norvell was able to explore her God-given talents as an interior decorator; and without any formal training whatsoever, made quite a name for herself. During our first year, she volunteered to decorate a room in the Junior League Show House, an annual affair that attracted numerous visitors and benefitted various Junior League charities. Her room was subsequently highlighted in an issue of *House Beautiful Magazine,* after which the demand for her services became unrelenting.

As for the boys, after graduating from Duke, Brint spent a hitch in the Navy, excelling as a junior officer before leaving the service to attend Princeton Theological Seminary and a career in the ministry. Chapman, who characteristically maxed most of his achievement tests along the way, graduated from the Boston Conservatory with the intent of becoming an actor. As with most good intentions; though, he ended up becoming an ace in Information Technology. Pearson, for his part, focused on the food services business and has served as the General Manager of a parade of different restaurants. For a while, he was planning to become a veterinarian, probably with a specialty in raccoons.

A Challenging Catch

"Fishing is just a jerk at one end of the line waiting for a jerk at the other."
–Tennessee Ernie Ford (1919-1991)

While life with my step-sons was both challenging and a lot of fun, one of my bigger regrets was not spending as much time with my own sons as I would have liked. They were some distance away, but we did have our moments. Several of these related to white water rafting—from the Penobscot River in Maine and the Upper Youghiogheny in the Maryland panhandle to a week on the Middle Fork of the Salmon River in Idaho. The funniest time of all, though, took place on calmer water, while fly-fishing with Keith on a lake in Maine (different from the one where he taught me to play chess).

When I speak to others about this episode, I usually begin by regaling them with a story of how I hooked a 180 pounder, while using only 2-pound test line. As the listeners oooh and aaah, with incredulous, if not disbelieving looks on their faces, I break down and tell them what actually happened. As I was casting my line back and forth (as one does in fly fishing), I hooked myself in the forehead. We were in a canoe and after I unhooked myself and began casting anew, every time I did, Keith would duck and hide his head behind his arm, mirthful grin and all.

I had what I thought would be the last laugh, though, because I was the only one in our party of four to catch a fish that day. But even that became the subject of derisive laughter. I had "foul-hooked" the fish, meaning that I had caught it by its belly rather than its mouth. In my haste to reacquire at least a minimal semblance of dignity, I was quick to point out what an incredible accomplishment it was, asking the others how many fishermen they knew who could replicate such a feat? The only saving grace of this entire episode was the fact that when you do foul-hook one of them, your pole bends almost double as you are bringing it in, making it look like you may actually have a 180 pounder on your line.

Another humorous moment that leaps to mind, albeit on drier land, was when Lance was building an engine for his truck, which was sitting inside a barn. Once built, it reeked of pure power as it roared and strained against its block. Before he finished, we had agreed that he would race it against the turbo-charged Datsun 280 ZX I was driving at the time (as I went about living out my mid-life crisis). Anyway, I was actively rehearsing for the big contest, shifting aggressively between gears and red-lining it at just the right times, when the race was called off. Lance's engine had overheated and exploded. The culprit in all this may have been a pet goat, which ate the instruction manual before he had completed putting the engine together.

Years later and as a matter of pure coincidence, Lance started a private security firm in Eastern Europe on the same day of the same year that I established a Washington-based non-profit to bridge religion and politics in support of peacemaking. Ironically, we were both addressing problems relating to conflict, but coming at them from entirely different directions. The other significant difference was that his enterprise soon grew to a thousand employees, while mine never rose above seven. I liked to say our operation was heavily leveraged.

Breaking New Ground

The decision to mount an Executive Program in National and International Security represented a major shift in priorities for the Kennedy School. In the wake of the Cambodian invasion during the Vietnam War, Professor Tom Schelling had led a contingent of Harvard faculty to Washington to protest that decision with their former colleague Henry Kissinger, who was then serving as President Nixon's National Security Advisor. Receiving no satisfaction from their effort, they returned to Harvard and washed their hands of anything having to do with national security, focusing instead on domestic issues like mass transit, urban planning and crime control.

When I arrived in the summer of 1977, Harvard was still on the Pentagon's "black list" [18] from the Vietnam War; and the students were out front of the faculty in wanting to get back into the national security arena. Sensing this gap, I decided to use the new executive program as a catalyst for closing it

---

[18] *Because of Harvard's perceived support of the New Left's anti-war sentiments and the associated dissolution of its ROTC programs, it was forbidden from any further involvement with ROTC

and getting the university back in the game. To do so, I recruited faculty from the Kennedy School, the Business School, the Law School and the Faculty of Arts and Sciences to teach in the program. The standard model for such programs at the Business School was to use no more than five faculty in any given program regardless of its length (including its widely-heralded, 13-week Advanced Management Program). I deliberately broke that mold by using a total of 14 faculty for what turned out to be a two-week program. To be sure, the challenges of substantive coordination were greater, but it seemed a small price to pay for addressing the larger objective.

Professor Ernest May, was appointed as the Program's Faculty Advisor, and I was delighted with the choice. Ernie was a renown historian who held a joint appointment from the Kennedy School and the History Department in the Faculty of Arts and Sciences. He was a superb teacher (as I had experienced first-hand while pursuing my Master's Degree), and he was every bit as amicable as he was bright. The chemistry between us was great, and we jointly decided on a two-week program, which was about as long as participants at the Flag-rank level could afford to be away. We also settled on "perspective" as the central substantive thread around which all program elements should fit.

A key challenge associated with the program's political/military focus was that of recruiting Admirals and Generals to travel north to the "Kremlin on the Charles" to study national security. In laying the ground work for meeting this challenge, I conducted the modest equivalent of a marketing survey by interviewing a sizable number of military and civilian officials who were well-positioned in Washington policy circles, seeking their advice on what such a program should look like. The more general hidden agenda was to alert the national security community to the program's forthcoming existence.

With a single exception, I ended up recruiting each of the prospective participants on an individual basis, with a goal of securing an inaugural class size of 25. The exception had to do with the Air Force representation. The Chief of Staff of the Air Force was David Jones, who I had gotten to know on a personal level while dating his daughter some two years earlier. Anyway, Dave decided to send a total of seven Air Force Generals, which took us over the top by giving us a class size of 31.

The quality of this class was particularly high since I had recruited them on the basis that this was a pilot effort and their inputs would help determine the shape of all future offerings. Decades later, the program was still going strong; so that early shaping of what was to follow paid great dividends. It also paved the way for a second executive program in State and Local Government, directed by former Governor (and future Presidential candidate) Michael Dukakis, with five additional programs following soon thereafter.

Collectively, these programs significantly enhanced the School's reputation and its financial well-being. Today there are more than 40 such programs for public, corporate, and non-profit leaders.

The financial code at Harvard called for each tub to stand on its own bottom; in other words, for each program to become self-sustaining as soon as possible. This meant that I had to figure out how to support the Executive Program for at least the first two years, until such time as the tuition income became adequate to cover all associated costs. I did this by securing a sizable grant from the Army Research Institute to assess the effectiveness of this kind of training for Army Generals. This was something I would have wanted to do anyway to help improve future offerings, but the stringent requirements of the grant undoubtedly caused me to be more rigorous on this front than I might have otherwise been.

Because the theme of the program was "perspective," that is, viewing the problem at hand through the eyes of one's adversaries or competitors (and adjusting one's own strategy accordingly), I developed a series of ten hypothetical questions that raised difficult questions in different bureaucratic settings as a way of testing the comfort level of the participants in dealing with each of those settings. These ranged from negotiating a treaty with a foreign power to securing Congressional approval for a new program that one was charged with managing (and most everything else in between).

At the end of the program, I asked the participants to assess their comfort level (on a scale from 1 to 10) in dealing with each of these hypothetical situations, both before the program began and after it ended. As would be expected, their comfort levels in most categories increased rather dramatically over the course of the program. Then I sent them the same list six months later, asking for the same feedback. I suspected there might be a dip in comfort level after the post-program euphoria had worn off. Instead, their scores went up even further, suggesting that the program had the enduring value we were seeking.

That first test run of the program provided some interesting and diverse challenges. In addition to monitoring it throughout and doing some of the teaching myself, I also ate meals with the participants. During the second day of doing so, I sensed a mild dissatisfaction with how things were going. There weren't any specific complaints; but after thinking about it a short while, I suddenly recognized the source of the problem. In contrast to the kinds of briefings they were used to receiving in the Pentagon, which always ended with a hard bottom-line, Harvard Professors tended to let students figure out for themselves any "take-away" lessons to be learned. This was particularly true for the case study method of teaching, which a number of Harvard faculty favored. Such sessions almost always tended to fade into the ether toward the end of the class. The next day, I gathered the program faculty together and urged them to devote the last 10 minutes of each session to highlighting the important lessons they felt the participants should assimilate. They did, and the problem disappeared.

Then there were the inevitable substantive challenges. One of these took place when Graham Allison was teaching a class on the Cuban Missile Crisis. Some years earlier, Graham had made a name for himself with the publication of *Essence of Decision* in which he used that particular crisis as the basis for developing the concept of the rational-actor model of decision making as the preferred basis for conducting international relations. At one point during his presentation, he made a point that was challenged by one of the participants. Graham responded to the challenge, but wouldn't back down. At that point, the challenger—a gentleman by the name of Sid Graybeal, who was then serving as Director of Strategic Planning for the CIA—indicated that he had personally briefed President Kennedy on that particular point during the actual crisis. After the laughter subsided, the class voted Graham the foremost *aficionado* on the Cuban Missile Crisis—of those who weren't there.

Indicative of how the theme of perspective played out in the classroom was a session by Kennedy School Professor Al Carnesale in which he invited all of the participants to don Soviet hats and list the problems they would have with the proposed SALT II Treaty (Strategic Arms Limitation Talks) from a Soviet perspective. The blackboards quickly filled with their concerns; and as they filed out of the classroom, one could overhear comments like "Maybe this isn't such a bad deal after all."

Sprinkled throughout the Program (and the others that followed) were a number of social activities that typically included a softball game mid-way through and a trip to our home in Wellesley toward the end, for a catered dinner and group singing around the piano.

All in all, the program was a great success; but frankly, it would be hard not to succeed in that setting—Harvard in the summer, with the unrivaled opportunity to engage intellectually both with one's exceedingly able peers and with some of the brightest faculty on the planet (Addendum E).

The Consummate Odd Couple

During my third year of running the program, I received a call from a reporter for *Boston Magazine*, who was interviewing so-called foreign policy experts on the state-of-play in U.S. relations with the Soviet Union. During the course of our conversation, I mentioned the Executive Program and what it was about. Upon hearing this, he said, "My political editor would really like to talk to you about that." I said, "No problem; have him give me a call." He did call later, and we arranged to go to lunch.

His name was Carl Oglesby and before the lunch, I somehow learned that he had once been head of Students for a Democratic Society (SDS), the left-wing student movement, which among other pursuits, had led protests across the country in the 1960's against the Vietnam War (while I was busy patrolling the ocean's depths in nuclear submarines). Because of its identification with the drug culture and the violence associated with some of its protests, the SDS seemingly stood for everything I was against. Thus, I felt like I was about to dine with the enemy.

As we visited, it became clear that Carl's interest in the Executive Program was more than casual. After taking his measure, I decided to take a chance and said, "Carl, we're going to have another program in the next couple of months; and if you are as interested as you appear, why don't you sit in, play fly-on-the-wall for two weeks, and then write your story?" He did exactly that and produced a six-page article on the program that appeared in the next issue of the Magazine (November 1980). When I read it, I was bowled over; he saw profound dimensions to the program which I had not, and I was the one who invented it. Here, in a single paragraph from that piece, he captures the essence of what it was all about:

> "What the Harvard [national security] seminar appears to work toward as an ideal is a relationship in which the policy elite and the educators alike suffer themselves to be exposed to and challenged by each other. The teachers, flowing with philosophy, learn from the executives of practical affairs that our nation faces genuine external threats and problems, that such threats can blossom in the middle of the night, and that action often must be taken in confusing circumstances in which there is no time for assembling long lists on blackboards in an anxiety-free classroom environment. The officers and officials, flowing with technique, learn from the teachers that the social world either hangs together through broad devotion to social values—including those of fairness and reason—or falls apart, and that if the moment of truth is no time to debate first causes and methodology, then all the more reason to have that debate under one's belt before the moment of truth arrives."

In keeping with his earlier days of protest as head of the SDS, Carl also commented in his article on a small group of demonstrators who had gathered on the front steps of the Kennedy School on the final day of the Program to protest against this unwanted intrusion of militarism on their campus. Although the protestors were wrong in their assumption about what was taking place (Admirals and Generals meeting secretly behind closed doors, "planning the next world war"), their presence provided a poignant reminder of on-campus battles fought a decade earlier over the proper relationship between higher education and the military. Then it was about Vietnam. This time, the stand-off with the Soviet Union. But whatever the national security challenge, it inevitably becomes fair game in raising this same question.

As one of the participants later commented in relation to the protestors, "This summer did a thousand times more good toward lessoning the burden of militarism than any number of actions like this little *pro forma* protest." He was probably right in his assessment, which reminded me of my own misgivings about the self-defeating nature of the University's earlier abolishment of its NROTC Program during the Vietnam era.

Speaking of protestors reminds me of an episode that took place in 1978, two years prior to our Executive Program. The occasion was the dedication of the new Kennedy School complex, the construction of which had just been completed. Among the featured speakers were Senator Ted Kennedy, University President Derek Bok, and Graham Allison; and because of the anticipated size of the audience, it took place outdoors. As the ceremony got underway, a group of demonstrators behind the audience began protesting, loudly enough that it threatened to drown out the designated speakers. In response to this problem, Graham approached the protesters and negotiated an arrangement in which their leader could come to the microphone and voice their grievances, in return for which his followers would remain silent.

The leader was an African-American gentleman, who stepped to the mike attired in black, including a black leather jacket and dark sunglasses. He then voiced his group's concerns, which basically related to the fact that the new building complex would be housing the Charles Engelhard Public Affairs Library. Because Engelhard had made much of his fortune in South African gold on the backs of slave labor and was thought by many to represent the very personification of corporate complicity in the apartheid regime, the protestors had a legitimate grievance. Although the naming of the library had been the *quid pro quo* for a million-dollar contribution from the Engelhard Foundation, it now bears the title "Harvard Kennedy School Library and Knowledge Services."

I don't know when the name was changed, but the presentation by the protest leader was nothing short of incredible. In fact, he was more articulate in his off-the-cuff remarks than anyone else who spoke that day. I just smiled and thought to myself, only at Harvard......

Catching Up with the Sixties

Over the course of some later lunches, I concluded that Carl was actually a patriot, who happened to disagree with U.S. policy relating to Vietnam (and rightfully so, as history would later prove). For example, whenever he traveled to Hanoi or Havana as head of the SDS, he notified the CIA in advance. And some years later when he was approached by the Third Secretary of the Soviet Embassy to help facilitate a Soviet connection to the reopened Congressional investigation of the John F. Kennedy assassination (which Carl had helped to facilitate[19]), he contacted the FBI and kept them fully informed. This episode later became the grist for a fascinating article in the November 1983 issue of *Playboy Magazine* titled, "My Dinners with Andrey: A True Story of the Cold War."

After learning all this, I invited Carl to address the next National Security program and tell them what the 1960's were all about. So, for an hour and a half before an audience of some 80 Admirals, Generals, and comparable-level civilians from the Congress, the Defense Department, the State Department, the CIA and other agencies of government (talk about enemy territory!) he did just that and received a standing ovation. This was followed by a number of invitations from the participants for him to do the same before various other military audiences around the country, including the Service war colleges and the Army Command and Staff College among others. Carl later wrote a definitive book on the anti-war movement of the 1960's titled *Ravens in the Storm*. We remained close friends[20] until he died shortly after his book was published. I miss him to this day.[21]

---

[19] In 1973, a small group of Cambridge writers formed a tax-exempt organization called the Assassination Information Bureau (AIB) to press for renewed investigations of the JFK and Martin Luther King Jr. assassinations. Carl was a co-director of the AIB and moved to Washington several years later when the House, in fact, reopened those investigations by establishing a Select Committee on Assassinations in 1977. Apparently, the Soviets were concerned about the Committee's prospective findings relating to their ties to Lee Harvey Oswald. That connection later proved to be considerably greater than initially thought, so it appears the Soviet concerns were well-founded.

[20] A later chapter in this book describes my thought process leading to the development of a book titled, *Religion, the Missing Dimension of Statecraft*. At the beginning of this process, Carl was the first person with whom I shared the idea for such a book. I found his enthusiastic endorsement particularly encouraging in light of our divergent political views.

[21] One of the more moving eulogies to Carl in the wake of his passing was that offered by Todd Gitlin, a professor at Columbia University and himself a past president of the SDS: "No one I ever met loved America so much as to feel such anguish at what it was becoming. We shall not look upon his like again."

Jousting with Students

In keeping with Professor Christenson's earlier prophecy that Harvard was just arrogant enough to overlook a small detail like needing a PhD to teach, I was invited by the Kennedy School to teach a mid-career (Master's level) course in International Affairs and Security. Because some of the students had already spent a number of years in the State Department, the Defense Department, or the CIA (or their equivalent organizations in other countries), my biggest challenge was not letting them know that in some areas, they knew more about the subject matter than I did. Aside from this larger challenge, the students were a diverse and highly interesting lot (Addendum F).

One was a French civil servant with whom I one day had the following exchange: "Pierre, France is a Catholic country, yet the norm for many Frenchmen is to have a mistress. So, tell me, how do you reconcile the two?" To which Pierre replied, "Oh, zee mistress, zat is love. Zee marriage, zat is business."

Another student was an Israeli Lieutenant Colonel, by the name of Yossi Ben Hanan, who while at a student party to which I had been invited mentioned in passing that he knew Herman Wouk. His comment captured my interest, because I had just finished reading Wouk's widely-acclaimed novel, *Winds of War* and had been mightily impressed. I shared my sentiments with Yossi, and he told me how he came to know Wouk.

In 1973, while on his honeymoon in Nepal, the Yom Kippur War broke out, and Yossi raced back to join his unit. While engaged in fierce fighting in the Golan Heights, he was wounded but continued the fight. A day later, while commanding a makeshift force of Israeli tanks against a superior number of Syrian tanks, he was blown out of the turret of his tank by the explosion of an anti-tank missile. There he laid, severely wounded behind enemy lines, until rescued by Yonatan Netanyahu (the brother of future Prime Minister, Benjamin Netanyahu and a legendary military figure in his own right).

It was while Yossi was undergoing a long-term recovery from his wounds, that Wouk read an account of his bravery in a report by Israeli Defense Minister Moshe Dayan and took it upon himself to seek Yossi out and visit him in the hospital. Other visits followed; and over time, the two became fast friends.

I told Yossi that I was deeply impressed with the breadth and depth of the research that had gone into Wouk's book (I later learned that he had personally spent 15 years in conducting that research). Over the course of the book, Wouk had the reader mentally wearing the hats of such figures as Churchill, Roosevelt, Stalin and Hitler in order to understand the conflict from their perspectives. He also at various times had the reader in the cockpit of an airplane, on the bridge of a ship, and in the conning tower of a submarine. Having personally been in all three settings myself while in the Navy, I was keenly mindful of the physical descriptions and the dialogue that transpired around them, all of which was absolutely flawless.

I mentioned to Yossi that I was thinking about writing Wouk a letter to applaud his masterpiece; and encouraging me to do so, he gave me Wouk's address. Unbeknownst to me, he later spoke to Wouk about my reaction, which undoubtedly accounts for the fact that I received a highly thoughtful reply to my letter when I finally sent it (Addendum G). Yossi mentioned that Wouk typically received an average of 300 letters a day to which he almost never responded (which certainly made his letter to me all the more meaningful). Wouk also sent me through Yossi an inscribed copy of *War and Remembrance,* the sequel to his earlier work.

My involvement with Yossi called to mind a humorous anecdote that took place when a trusted lieutenant of former Israeli Prime Minister Golda Meir was briefing her on a brilliant military caper he had just led. As he did so, though, he spoke in very self-deprecating terms as though he had nothing to do with the victorious outcome. Mid-way through, she interrupted and said, "Don't be so humble; you're not that good."

Well, Yossi was that good; and he earned one of the top marks in the class based on the superb research paper he produced, which only reinforced a theory of mine about the Jewish state of mind (which may or may not be valid). If I were a Jew and was mindful of the centuries of persecution that had taken place against my people, I would ask myself what I could do to avoid being persecuted myself. My inevitable answer would be that I needed to become smarter than everyone else. Hence, I would place a very high premium on education (as most Jews do).[22]

It is the case that all of the Jewish friends I have ever had, male or female, have been exceedingly sharp thinkers and more than able to hold their own in any kind of give-and-take discussion. If they are in fact sharper than most others around them and happen to work in a meritocracy where above-average performance is the key to getting ahead, then they will tend to rise to the top. When they do, those whom they displace often resent it; and if circumstances permit, the cycle of persecution kicks in all over again. Thus, it becomes a *catch 22*, with no good way out. This is clearly an overgeneralization, but to

---

[22] *Perhaps this has been a contributing factor to the disproportionate number of Jews who have been awarded Nobel Prizes: more than 20% of all awardees, although Jews only comprise 0.2% of the world's population.

the extent it has any validity, then it is incumbent upon the rest of us not to let "circumstances permit".

Pushing the Envelope

"All the animals except man know that the principal business of life is to enjoy it." –Samuel Butler (1835-1902)

I had planned to stay at Harvard for two years and then move on (as was my custom); but when the second year wound to a close, Graham asked me to stay longer. With lingering thoughts of the long-postponed PhD in Political Science in the back of my mind, I agreed to stay an additional three years on the condition that they not load me down any more than I already was. Thus, began one of the more intense periods of my life, directing the Executive Program and teaching at the Kennedy School, while pursuing my PhD in the School of Arts and Sciences. Also, because of Harvard's long-established reputation for leaning heavily on psychic income (the privilege of working there) in lieu of adequate monetary compensation, I had from the outset been consulting for a Defense contracting firm outside of Boston. That had to continue as well in order to support my family. Finally, there were the high-priority familial duties of husband and father to be tended to as well. My platter was overfull, so it was one day at a time.

Before embarking on this journey, I had to convince myself of the need for a PhD, which was not an easy calculation, since I had already supervised a number of PhD-holding subordinates during my time in government. I ultimately concluded I needed to do it, if only for my own edification. The opportunity to put an intellectual structure around 20 years of work experience was just too good to pass up.

Although most of the courses I had taken for the Master's degree counted toward completion of the PhD, I had taken them 13 years earlier, so in addition to enrolling in a number of new courses, there was a lot of re-learning to be done as well. All of this needed to be completed in preparation for the "General Exams," a four-hour oral grilling by senior professors from the Faculty of Arts and Sciences. It was an intimidating challenge because one had no idea of where on the vast mountain of knowledge one was expected to have accumulated the panel might start digging.

I was reading so much that I gradually began to lose my eyesight. Adding more lighting around my desk proved inadequate, so I began reading on our back porch where I could see better in the natural light. Unfortunately, it was winter and Boston gets a bit cold in the winter. So, there I sat in a foul-weather jacket, fighting the cold, and, reading my final stack of books. It was only after passing the "Generals" that I was able to find the time to get fitted for a pair of glasses.

Having that hurdle behind me was a huge relief, but there was still a considerable distance to go. At that time (the early 1980's), the statistics relating to earning a PhD were not all that encouraging. Only 12% who embarked on that quest saw it through to completion. And of those who passed their "Generals," only 48% attained actual doctoral status. In short, there were a lot of ABDs (all-but-dissertations) walking around.

Yet another requirement for the PhD was to demonstrate solid proficiency in a foreign language. For me, this meant shaking twenty years of dust off of the several years of Spanish I had collectively taken in high school and later at the Academy. I attempted to do this by auditing a Spanish class on campus during the evenings. I was only able to attend sporadically and was not scoring well on the occasional tests that were being given; but because one could take the doctoral language test as often as desired at six-month intervals, I decided to give it a try to see what it was like.

Although it was only intended to be a practice run, two weeks before the test, I thought why not give it my best shot and try to pass? So, I bought a comprehensive Spanish dictionary and took the test, which consisted of translating a section from a Spanish political science journal within a specified amount of time. The use of a dictionary was allowed and, amazingly enough, I scored well on the exam and no further testing was required. With no little surprise and a great sigh of relief, I gladly accepted their verdict.

I spent much of the next year writing my doctoral thesis, holing up whenever I could in a library at Babson College, a prestigious business school in Wellesley a short distance from where we lived. For my topic, I chose an old favorite, "The Political-Military Implications of Ballistic Missile Defense." I completed it about six months before President Reagan made his famous "Star Wars" speech and remember thinking at the time, "What has he been smoking? The technology for doing what he's suggesting is at least 25 years off." As it turned out, that didn't matter. What mattered is that the Soviets believed him.

With the doctorate now in hand, I was out for a stroll one Sunday afternoon; and although it sounds perverse, I became concerned about being trapped by an idyllic existence – a prestigious job at Harvard, a beautiful home in Wellesley, a nice sailboat in Salem Harbor, and, most importantly, a raft of close, personal friends in the Boston area. At the core of my concern was a fundamental question: "Did I want to spend the rest of my life talking about history, or making a little?" In those terms, it was an easy choice; so I gave Harvard my notice and became a partner in a small, Wellesley-based international management consulting firm until such time as I could find my way back to Washington (Addendum H).

Before leaving the Kennedy School, though, it was necessary to find a replacement. In advertising the position, we leaned heavily on our Executive Program alumni network. By the time that played out, there were a total of 63 applicants, almost all of whom were Flag Rank military officers (serving their last tours of duty or already retired) or high-level civilian executives. After narrowing the list to the top five candidates, I called Bob Murray, my former boss at the Pentagon (who had gone on to serve as Undersecretary of the Navy and who was now heading the Center for Naval Warfare Studies at the Naval War College). I wanted to get his candid assessment of those candidates that he knew. But before we finished that discussion, Bob decided to throw his own hat in the ring. Whereupon I congratulated him on just having become number one on the list. After processing his candidacy with Graham Allison and Ernie May, Bob relieved me and, before long, expanded the Program to include a separate training initiative for officers and civilians at the next level down (but who were clearly on their way up).

My Consulting Gig

"Most of the confidence which I appear to feel, especially when influenced by noon wine, is only a pretense." –Tennessee Williams (1911-1983)

In my new consulting capacity, I found myself involved in a wide range of activities involving a number of different organizations. Two of these organizations were Christian in nature, the first being Prison Fellowship Ministry, the organization founded by Chuck Colson upon his release from Federal prison where he had just served time for Watergate-related offenses. The genesis of this engagement was a lunch with Tom Phillips, then Chairman of the Raytheon Corp., who had personally played a role in introducing Chuck to the Lord prior to his prison sentence.

Tom was concerned that the Ministry wasn't as effective as it could be and asked me to conduct a structural assessment of the organization. I did so and found a number of significant problems, which wasn't all that surprising considering that just about everyone involved in the operation was either a former convict or a former minister. It was my first exposure to a Christian organization (outside of the church), and I found myself a bit shocked to find things taking place in that context that wouldn't be tolerated for a second in the secular workplace. Anyway, the assessment proved helpful in restructuring the operation and enhancing its effectiveness.

My second Christian engagement involved Youth for Christ (YFC), a worldwide movement to help young people become followers of Jesus. The sponsor for this involvement was another businessman by the name of Bob Buford, who owned a television station in Dallas and who nursed a concern similar to Tom's about organizational effectiveness. This effort produced a total of 88 recommendations of which all but two were implemented. One I recall in particular was the fact that YFC's mission statement was seven pages long and more confusing than helpful. To address this finding, YFC brought together all of its national and regional staff and a number of its local leaders as well to develop a new statement. I observed the proceedings, but they did all the work and produced a single-sentence statement that every YFC member around the world could easily remember: "To communicate the life-saving message of Jesus Christ to every young person." It was one of my more gratifying engagements.

Two other assignments related to education, the first to develop the curriculum for a new course at Babson College (the business school in Wellesley, where I wrote most of my doctoral thesis), and the second to do much the same for the U.S. Naval War College in Newport, Rhode Island. This latter engagement was initiated by Vice Admiral Jim Service, President of the College, who had previously attended the Executive Program at Harvard when I was running it. Jim asked me to develop a course for new prospective commanding officers, which proved to be a labor of love, not only because I thoroughly enjoyed the substantive aspects, but because he and I played tennis whenever it was mutually convenient. Particularly gratifying was the fact that the course itself was well-received and had a helpful impact (Addendum I).

And so it went, life as a gadfly—hopping from one assignment to the next. The flexibility was great, but the constant, overriding challenge was the need to maintain some semblance of a steady income. I had a sizeable family to feed. To hedge my bets, I often had as many as five lines in the water at any given time; exploring new opportunities for engagement and hoping that at least one would materialize, all the while fretting that if more than that came in at the same time, one could easily end up overloaded. As luck would have it, I somehow managed to stay fully engaged with interesting tasks—one at a time.

Straying Off the Reservation

I had been consulting for almost two years when I received a call from Morgan Stanley, the Wall Street financial services firm, inviting me down to

New York to meet with Bob Baldwin, the company's Chairman. Baldwin also chaired a small, Washington-based non-governmental organization (NGO) called "Cities in School (CIS)," which was the catalyst for the call. He had previously served as Undersecretary of the Navy during an earlier stint in government, so we spoke some of the same language. Anyway, during our conversation, he persuaded me that as one looked to the future, the problems with our country's youth represented the nation's Achilles heel. About a million kids were dropping out of school each year, and it was the mission of CIS to reverse that flow. By the time we finished our discussion, I had agreed to serve as Executive Vice President and Chief Operating Officer (COO) of CIS for at least two years.

Three days later, I received a call from Joe Jordan, President of the Center for Strategic and International Studies (CSIS)—-thought by most policy makers to be the premier foreign relations think tank in the world—-inviting me to take over as Director of the Center's Political/Military Program. Although this was a dream job for me; I had already sealed the deal with Baldwin and regrettably had to decline.

This was the second time Joe had come after me without success (first to be his assistant in the Pentagon when he was Assistant Secretary of Defense for International Security Affairs, and now this), so he decided to keep a string on me until I had honored my commitment to CIS. He did so by inviting me to various CSIS functions over the next couple of years, and I'm sure that any number of stalwarts from the national security community must have been puzzled to see someone from "Cities in Schools" listed among the attendees at these events.

As it turned out, CIS was the toughest job I ever had. It frequently seemed as though no one in the social services arena had ever heard of basic organizational concepts like structure or team work. Indicative of the difficulty was an incident that took place during my first week on the job. I was sitting in my office when I heard a loud commotion down the hall. Walking down to check it out, I found that the Vice President for Operations, Maurice Weir, had physically thrown Jim Hill, the Vice President for Finance, out of his office and into some boxes that were sitting in the hall. Apparently, Jim had gotten "in his face" while trying to implement a new policy I had just announced.

This encounter ended with Maurice and me standing toe-to-toe about a foot apart, with a more-than-implied possibility of it turning physical, when the organization's president, Bill Milliken, stepped in and defused the situation. In retrospect, he probably saved my life. I later came to learn that Maurice not only had a Black Belt in karate, but was also the Golden Gloves boxing champion in his weight class for the City of New York.

That was only the first of many such problems with Maurice. As an African-American, he felt that such things as getting to meetings on time were "Whitey's rules" and therefore always showed up late, if at all. It was also a major problem getting him to pay back cash advances he received whenever he went on official travel. Despite the egregious behavior, it was all-but-impossible to force a change, since Bill had a real blind spot when it came to Maurice. The two of them were together when Bill first formed Cities in Schools on New York's Lower East Side a number of years earlier, and had been ever since.

After about a year of this, I was at my wit's end and knew I needed to do something dramatically different if I was going to be able to honor my commitment to Baldwin. I somehow concluded that what I needed to do if we were ever going to be able to work well together was to establish a spiritual bond between Bill, Maurice and myself. I don't recall exactly what I did to make that happen; but I did, and it worked. In fact, it worked so well that I actually missed Maurice as a friend when I left CIS after another year and a half.

As our friendship developed, Maurice provided a number of important insights that I found helpful in understanding and dealing with inner-city issues. One had to do with his assessment of the consequences of the slave trade. Slaves who ended up in the deep south of the United States were, for the most part, treated cruelly; and their descendants ended up with an understandable, deep-seated attitude of "Whitey owes me." It was out of this mindset that the Civil Rights movement emerged.

In contrast, those slaves who ended up in the West Indies were generally treated better and consequently developed a strong attitude of self-reliance, assuming that the way to get ahead in life was by standing on one's own two feet. There are undoubtedly any number of exceptions, but examples of the latter who immediately leap to mind are Colin Powell, former Chairman of the Joint Chiefs of Staff, and Louis Farrakhan, former spiritual leader of the Nation of Islam, both of whom trace their roots to the Caribbean.

When I began working at CIS, the organization had programs in five cities across the country. When I left, we were in 23. After another 30 years, CIS is now in more than 200 cities. What that means is that a self-sustaining public/private partnership has been established in each city for the purpose of coordinating human services around the schools in order to serve those youth most at risk of dropping out. At its core, the CIS model calls for a teacher, a social worker, and a recreation worker working together as a team in serving 45 at-risk students in a designated school. Individually, each member of the team is assigned 15 of those kids on a 24/7 call basis— to be there for them whenever they might be needed, much like a surrogate parent.

Beyond these all-important individual relationships, the kids also received tutoring on an as-needed basis; exposure to successful role models who were brought in to inspire them to greater heights; and field trips to ignite their interest in new areas. Sitting over these CIS teams was a CIS-appointed City Director, who answered to a board of directors that typically included the Mayor, the School Superintendent, various corporate sponsors, and others who had a stake in seeing these kids succeed.

Shunn "the One"

A lasting legacy from my CIS experience took root when I had the opportunity to accompany Bill Brock, then Secretary of Labor, to visit our Washington DC program. The CIS National Office received its funding from a consortium of three Federal Departments, the Department of Labor being among them. After Brock addressed a classroom of students at Terrill Junior High School, we mingled with the students over punch and cookies. While doing so, I struck up a conversation with a seventh grader named Shunn Darby. I asked him what he wanted to be when he grew up, and he said, "A dancer."

"That's interesting. Why do you want to become a dancer?"

"Because I'm the best break-dancer in Washington!"

"How do you know? Have you ever been in a contest?"

"No, but I'm the best!"

I admired his moxy and told him that after we were done socializing, everyone would be going down to the cafeteria where the muckety-mucks would give speeches. I said, "After they're done, how would you like to show your stuff to the Secretary of Labor?" To which he replied, "Great!"

All of that came to pass and to this day, Shunn and I have an 8x10 picture on the wall in our respective homes, capturing Shunn in mid-air, while doing a back-flip on bare concrete (and without any music, other than that which he improvised in his head), while Bill Brock and I are both looking on with surprised looks on our faces.

Shunn told me later that he had initially hoped I could be his path to stardom by introducing him to Lionel Richie, a long-time supporter of CIS (who, as it turns out, I have never met). But from that moment in the cafeteria, he and I have maintained a close relationship to this day, a relationship that has made life more meaningful for both of us. Shunn came out of a background that is all-too-common in the inner city: he never met his father; his mother was in a mental hospital most of the time; and he was, for all intents and purposes, raised by his grandmother. Despite the innumerable challenges of an inner-city existence, she imparted a great sense of values in him that has informed his life's journey ever since.

Besides being a fun and inspiring person to be around, Shunn is also a natural entrepreneur. One day while working at the International Club in downtown Washington, he walked outside during his lunch hour and purchased a couple of tee shirts from a Korean vendor. Later that same day, he turned around and sold them for three times as much. Ever since, he has been taking a bus to New York every couple of weeks where he buys "knock-offs" (imitations of well-known brands) and then sells them for twice as much in Washington. He doesn't misrepresent what he's selling, but he does it so well that his customers don't mind that they are buying imitations. In addition to that, he has recently begun selling cars and investing in real estate.

As I thought about Shunn's entrepreneurial gifts, I remembered a movie I had seen quite some time earlier titled, "The Year of Living Dangerously." It was about the communist uprising that took place in Indonesia in the late 1960's; and at one point in the dialogue, the question is posed, "Surrounded by all this poverty, what then must we do?" The answer is to do whatever you can with those with whom you come in contact. Out of that thought process, I concluded that one of the more effective things I could do on the poverty front was to encourage and help empower Shunn to become a role model for other young men in the inner city. His values coupled with his positive attitude and natural talents constituted an inspiring combination well worth emulating. Aside from any such goals, though, my relationship with Shunn has always been special and an end in itself.

After 33 years, Shunn, who used to be a foot shorter than me, is now four inches taller; and we still meet up every month or two for dinner and a movie. On several occasions along the way, he has told me how much it has meant to have someone who believes in him. Undoubtedly true, but I suspect I have benefitted even more by being around him and the insights he has to offer. One day while walking together in downtown DC—me in suit and tie and him in a black leather jacket, jeans, and sunglasses—he said, "Mr. Johnston, I like walking with you; it makes me feel important," I looked at him and replied, "Shunn, I like walking with you; it makes me feel cool."

A Dream Job

After 2 ½ years with Cities in Schools, I was contacted again by Joe Jordan, this time to become his Executive Vice President and Chief Operating Officer at CSIS. I had been keenly aware of Joe's superb personal and professional reputation for quite some time [23] and, as mentioned before, had narrowly missed two earlier opportunities to work for him. So, I was only too eager to seize this chance to make it happen. However, because the compensation for this position was less than I was making at the time, I suggested a *quid pro quo*. Although the entire center would be reporting to me, there was one piece of research I wanted to conduct directly out of my office, that being to examine the positive role that religious or spiritual factors could play in preventing or resolving conflict, while advancing social change based on justice and reconciliation. Joe readily agreed, and we had a deal.

To take my place at Cities in Schools, I recruited John O'Grady, who had been serving as a Vice President in Chuck Colson's Prison Fellowship Ministry. John was Scotch Irish and a former Green Beret who had played a key role in Operation Phoenix during the Vietnam War. This was a secret CIA operation designed to destroy the political infrastructure of the Viet Cong, which, among other things, involved assassinating important leaders in that movement. For his efforts, John ended up as the 4th most-wanted man on the VC's own assassination list and experienced several attempts on his own life before the U.S. pulled out of that troubled country. He was big, smart and tough and seemed ideally suited to do a great job at CIS. He too gave a two-year commitment, but because of the Maurice factor, only lasted eight months before leaving. His departure, however, finally opened Bill's eyes and Maurice left as well soon thereafter.

---

[23] When General Lincoln was asked by President Nixon to head up the Office of Emergency Preparedness, Joe Jordan was selected to succeed him as head of the Social Sciences Department at West Point. And a wise choice it was. Not only was he a superb Army officer and an inspiring leader, but Joe had been something of a legend at the Point. In addition to serving as First Captain of the Corps of Cadets, he graduated 3rd in his class (out of 875) and was an Olympic-class boxing champion as well. He followed that with studies as a Rhodes Scholar and a stellar career in the Army, ultimately retiring as a Brigadier General. He went on to hold a number of high-level positions in government, and on top of all that, was one of the nicest persons you could ever hope to meet. Shortly before he passed away in his mid-90s, I told him I was at last ready to get in the boxing ring with him. With a twinkle in his eye, he said, "You may outlast me, but you would pay a very dear price." I questioned the first part of his response, but had no doubts about the second.

Hobnobbing with Eagles

One of my more delightful duties at CSIS was overseeing its Statesmen's Forums. These were situational gatherings of policymakers, diplomats, academic experts, corporate leaders, and the media who CSIS convened to hear presentations by various heads of state, foreign ministers, defense ministers and other high-level officials from foreign countries who happened to be passing through town. The purpose was to provide these high-level political guests with a forum for presenting their views on critical policy issues and receiving thoughtful feedback from members of the Washington policy community and foreign policy stakeholders. I would typically visit with these notables beforehand, introduce them to the audience prior to their presentations, and then orchestrate the question and answer sessions that followed. It seemed as though every foreign official who visited Washington wanted to speak at CSIS. Thus, these events happened quite often, and it was a great way to get to know a number of highly capable leaders.

Not all of these speakers were from other countries. I recall one occasion in which Senator Robert Dole came over to give his first foreign policy address while campaigning for the Presidency in 1996. Accompanying him to lend moral support were two other Senators, John McCain from Arizona (later to run for the Presidency himself) and Bill Cohen (who went on to become Secretary of Defense under President Clinton). Anyway, while the three of them were standing around chatting prior to the speech, Dole happened to mention someone's name who wasn't present, and McCain piped up, "Yeah, he's a real (expletive deleted)." I was a bit taken aback by the salty language, but no one else batted an eye. That was the John McCain they all knew and liked. I had other visits with John and liked him a lot myself, but was always a bit skeptical of how suitable his temperament would have been for the Presidency.

The Shadow Government

One of the attractions for foreign leaders to visit CSIS was its reputation in some circles as a "shadow government." That was clearly an overstatement, but not by much. CSIS was widely known for its bipartisan impact on government policy, which it achieved in any number of ways. Two of the more prominent, which bear mentioning, were its stable of Counselors and its sponsorship of Congressional Study Groups.

Among its Counselors during my tenure, were former Secretary of State Henry Kissinger, former National Security Advisor Zbigniew Brzezinski, former Secretaries of Defense James Schlesinger and Harold Brown, and others of comparable stature. The intellectual horsepower of these gentlemen was second-to-none; and whenever they made presentations on subjects of national interest, whether it be to public audiences or before Congressional Committees, their views commanded serous attention. In exchange for providing their wisdom and influence, the Center provided them with first-class office space, highly capable research and secretarial support, and a prominent platform for expressing their views.

The Counselors, also provided a touch of humor from time to time. For example, back when terrorism was a growing concern on the world stage in the 1990's, Harold Brown was overheard to say, "The chances of boarding a plane with a bomb on board are one in a thousand. The chances of doing so with two bombs on board are one in ten thousand. Therefore, I always carry a bomb onboard."

As for the Congressional Study Groups, we generally formed such groups around major issues of serious consequence, such as the development of a North American Free-Trade Agreement. To decide if such an initiative was a good idea and, if so, what it should look like, CSIS would enlist the participation of widely-acknowledged trade experts, most from in-town and occasionally some from out-of-town, to form the Study Group. The Group co-chairs would typically consist of two Senators and two Congressmen, split equally between both parties. Each of these chairs in turn, held a key position on a Congressional Committee that had oversight of the topic at hand. These Study Groups would typically meet over lunch on a monthly basis; and as good ideas would bubble to the surface during the course of the meetings, the co-chairs would often assume ownership of these ideas and ultimately translate them into law.

There was never any problem in recruiting the Congressional co-chairs because they clearly benefitted from their participation as they gained important insights helpful to executing their Congressional duties. In 1992, for example, no fewer than 130 members of the Senate and House were intimately involved in CSIS study projects. And, by sponsoring such efforts, CSIS enhanced its mythical reputation for influencing policy. Thus, it was a win-win for all concerned.

Reaping the Whirlwind

Life at CSIS was almost always stimulating and fun. And without exception, it was always challenging. With the ever-changing international landscape, no two days were ever alike in the foreign policy arena.

Perhaps the most out-of-the-ordinary challenge to cross my desk during my 12-year tenure took the form of a visit to my office by a pair of FBI agents to inform me that we (CSIS) had a "fellow traveler" in our ranks. The term "fellow traveler" in political circles means someone who is sympathetic to another's cause. In this case, the cause was that of Cuba and "sympathetic" equated to spying.

The individual in question was a young lady who, although she worked in our African Studies Program[24], had spent time in Cuba at an earlier point in her life and, while there, had developed a strong allegiance to its Communist agenda. Though not her real name, we'll call her Alexandra (Alex) for the sake of convenience. Through a candid exchange with the agents, I learned that rather than arresting her, they wanted to observe her tradecraft—-how she communicated with her "handlers" and what else she did to advance the Cuban cause.

By those in the know, the Cuban intelligence service is thought to be among the best of the best and apparently a cut above the KGB in terms of its procedures and ability to operate effectively in the United States.[25] Hence the Bureau's interest in their statecraft. Thus, whenever Alex went overseas, the FBI had her trailed by the intelligence services of the various countries she visited. To further assist in this process, I recruited a young lady from one of our other programs (who had already demonstrated courage under fire during an uprising in a Latin American country) to befriend Alex and observe her habits from a closer vantage point.

Whenever Alex returned from her periodic visits to Africa, the African Studies Program would often sponsor an event for selected Washington policy makers, journalists, and other interested parties to showcase her observations and findings from the trip. Armed with my insider knowledge, I would listen carefully to her presentations to see if I could detect any bias with respect to Cuban interests. Because there were a significant number of Cubans operating out of Angola at the time, there was indeed a subtle bias in what she had to

---

[24] During my time at CSIS, the Center had a total of 13 programs, most of which were geographic in nature and collectively spanned the globe. The remainder were functional in nature, like the Political-Military Program.

[25] As recently as May 11, 2020, a full 25 years after this episode, an article by a Wall Street Journal reporter titled "How Cuba's Spies Keep Winning," described the role that Cuban intelligence had just played in thwarting a recent attack against Venezuela by a small group of mercenaries and observed that the attack provided "an opportunity to reflect on Cuba's asymmetric-warfare capabilities and the sophistication of its intelligence apparatus, which for more than a half-century has run circles around the U.S."

say and how she said it. Had I not been forewarned, though, I would never have picked up on it. Alex was not just good; she was very good!

This scenario continued to play out as described above until Alex finally left CSIS for work at another major think tank, albeit a step down from the "shadow government." I don't know if she was ever called in by the Bureau, but I suspect they learned quite a bit about Cuban tradecraft.

Geisha Hospitality

As a natural spin-off of running the Statesman's Forums, I was asked to lead a U.S. delegation to the first meeting of a newly-formed U.S./Japan Leadership Council that was to take place in Kyoto, Japan. It was a high-level affair designed to address some of the more pressing challenges in the relationship between our two countries. Because the Japanese delegation included four former Prime Ministers, to save face, I had to come up with at least one former U.S. President for ours. After a great deal of scurrying, I was finally able to recruit President Jimmy Carter; but only if the Japanese agreed to contribute $400,000 toward his campaign to eliminate guinea-worm disease in Africa. I don't know if that payment was ever made, but I do know that President Carter eventually saw his eradication efforts through to completion.

The presentations and discussions of the Council were well-tailored to the challenges at hand, and it was a highly successful encounter. It got off to an interesting start when, at the introductory cocktail session the evening before, I opened by reciting a few stanzas of a Japanese poem relating to the Spirit of Japan, which I had committed to memory. The poem itself was new to me, but the young lady who was serving as my assistant at the time had come across it during her research for the meeting. She sensed that it was something special, and she was right.

From what I can recall, the poem spoke to the soul of the Japanese persona and related, at least in part, to Commodore Matthew Perry's visit to Japan in 1854, which first opened that country to external commerce following a long period of self-imposed isolation. Apparently, the poem itself is not widely known outside of Japan, but I knew it had struck a responsive chord when a number of the Japanese guests surrounded me after I spoke and asked how I had come to know about it.

This being the first meeting of the Council, the Japanese rolled out the red carpet, with seven-course meals served by geisha girls and all sorts of other bells and whistles. During our last lunch at which we were all sitting cross-legged in circles on the floor, I went over to President Carter, told him about the book I was putting together on religion and foreign policy, and asked if he would be willing to write the Foreword. To make it as easy as possible, I told him we would be happy to provide a draft, which he could then change as he saw fit. He said, "I might want to write it myself" to which I responded "All the better."

Two years later when it came time to call in that chit, I sent President Carter a letter requesting the Foreword and included a draft for his possible use. After a very long wait, I received a written reply from his staff, indicating that President Carter never did such things. So, I wrote a second request, reminding him of our conversation in Kyoto and making a less-than-totally transparent reference to the code of honor to which we had both pledged allegiance as midshipmen at the Naval Academy (he fourteen years earlier than me, but little ever changes quickly in our tradition-bound Navy). This one made it past his staff; and within another week or so, I received the draft back with two word changes. Anyway, I had my Foreword and didn't need to spend $400,000 to get it.[26]

Dealing with an Imperfect World

"Success covers a multitude of blunders." —*George Bernard Shaw*

Another of the many opportunities I enjoyed in my position at CSIS was that of participating in or even initiating new substantive projects in which I had an interest. Foremost among those I did initiate and direct was one that focused on America's prospective role in the international arena. The report

---

[26] At an earlier point in the book's development, I had lunch with President Carter at CSIS and asked him if there had been a spiritual dimension to his Camp David negotiations with Israel and Egypt. As I suspected, he said there definitely had been. However, I challenged his answer by noting that Hal Saunders, who he knew well, had told me there was not. Hal, who was on our book's Steering Committee, had been at Camp David working behind the scenes, crafting the accords that were ultimately signed (in his then capacity as Assistant Secretary of State for Near East Affairs). Carter responded by saying Hal was a delightful person and a gifted public servant, but he simply wouldn't have known about the spiritual aspects, because he wasn't present in any of the several meetings at which they were brought to bear. He then proceeded to tell me when each of those meetings had taken place and exactly who was present at each one. Because there were a number of names (and some of them quite difficult to pronounce), I was astounded at his ability to recall such specifics years after the fact and couldn't help thinking how challenging it must have been for him as President to provide visionary leadership for the country, while commanding that level of detail. Without really knowing, I guessed that his penchant for detail must have been at least partially attributable to his engineering experience with Admiral Rickover. Under the good Admiral, one learned to ask why about everything: what were the sizing considerations that went into the design of that particular holding tank? Why does it hold 25 gallons and not 10? etc. etc. It was never-ending.

that was produced, which I had the pleasure of writing, was titled *"Foreign Policy into the 21ˢᵗ Century: the U.S. Leadership Challenge."*

The effort itself, which extended over a two-year period and concluded in 1996, involved 50 of the country's leading foreign policy experts and was co-chaired by former National Security Advisor Zbigniew Brzezinski; Senate Foreign Relations Committee Chairman Richard Lugar; and Lee Hamilton, Chairman of the House Foreign Affairs Committee. All three of them were a delight to work with, but I never fully understood why the leading foreign policy experts in both the Senate and the House came from the great maritime republic of Indiana. Must be something in the water.

After extensive research, discussion, and debate, the final report, which was a consensus document, prioritized U.S. national interests according to whether they were "vital," "important," or "beneficial" and recommended policies for pursuing them. Among the many recommendations was one that I went to great lengths to incorporate which called for establishing a 5,000-person Rapid Reaction Force for the United Nations, which the UN Secretary General could mobilize and deploy on short notice to deal with crisis situations. The French General who oversaw the UN response to the genocide in Rwanda, for example, said that if he had even a small force of that size to command, half a million casualties could have easily been avoided. The proposal itself was first recommended by the Canadians in UN circles some years earlier, and although it had failed to gain any traction, I thought it deserved to be resurrected.

In the absence of such a force, the United States or some other nation will inevitably be forced to go it alone, as happened in the Balkans when, after three years of watching a series of atrocities parade across our television screens, our moral conscience finally kicked in; and we intervened unilaterally. Although we were able to bring NATO along, horrific casualties resulted prior to our intervention. [27]

The Study's importance was captured in Amazon's Book Review:

> *"This policy report represents the culmination of a two-year study on American Foreign Policy. Prompted in the first instance by the absence of any comprehensive U.S. foreign policy agenda for the post-Cold War era, the report describes the kind of world the*

---

[27] There were significant casualties on all sides accompanying the final breakup of the former Yugoslavia, with Bosnian Muslims suffering the greatest losses. More than 80,000 of them were killed at the hands of the Serbs, including the genocide that took place at Srebrenica in Eastern Bosnia in which more than 8,000 Muslim men and boys were massacred within the boundaries of a so-called "UN Safe Zone." Almost immediately thereafter, NATO intervened.

United States should be moving toward and suggests how it should go about doing so......

The report provides a uniquely bipartisan perspective and a much-needed wake-up call at a time of diminished public interest in international affairs."

Feeding the Media

As the beat of the war drums leading up to the Gulf War in 1991 grew louder, CSIS was increasingly called upon by the media to comment on unfolding developments. As one of the world's leading foreign policy think tanks, this was customary fare. What was exceptional this time around was the degree to which CSIS was inundated with requests from the foreign news media as well as our own. Like anyone else at the Center who had a national security background, I was often called upon (usually by television stations) to comment on one aspect or another of what was taking place.

I was opposed to going to war and had not been bashful about expressing that view. Ordinarily, war is a "come as you are" party, but in this instance, we had spent the better part of six months preparing for it. Nor did we launch our attack after exhausting all other options. And that was my principal concern, the fact that we were not going in as a last resort.

In seeking an alternative between attacking, with its potentially severe human and economic consequences, and maintaining the status quo, which would undermine our national credibility in view of earlier ultimatums that had been given, I came up with a siege option—a middle ground approach that would combine limited military action with a more effective exploitation of the UN sanctions that were already in place.

This strategy retained the option of launching a later attack, but at a time when Iraq's military capabilities would have been seriously weakened by siege-induced shortages of critical spare parts and other war-time essentials. Although the idea was picked up by the media, it was unfortunately too late in the game to make a difference, as a full-scale attack was launched only two days later (Addendum J).

As it turned out, we discovered during the course of the attack that Saddam Hussein was much closer to developing nuclear weapons than anyone had thought possible. So, I concluded the Administration had been right after all, albeit for a different and largely unrecognized reason.

An interesting sidebar to this particular conflict came to light when a former CSIS Army Fellow, [28] who was involved in that battle, shared his experience at a CSIS event about a year later. He had been in the lead tank of the lead battalion going up against an Iraqi tank force. Although he and his men were somewhat nervous going in, they soon calmed down after discovering their tanks were superior to the Soviet-made Iraqi tanks with respect to both range and accuracy of fire.

After getting past the opposing tanks, his battalion was conducting a sweep of the battlefield when they overran an Iraqi position. The Iraqis exited their bunkers with their hands in the air; and as they did so, he noticed they were limping and had bloody feet. Upon questioning, it was revealed that the Iraqi officers had ordered the severing of their men's Achilles tendons so they couldn't run from the battle. Then as the U.S. tanks moved in, the officers themselves ran away. As unconscionable as that sounds, it was totally consistent with what I had heard about the example set by their top leadership. [29]

Needless to say, the stakes were often quite high in "getting it right" in some of these media appearances; but CSIS always did a great job of providing (and clarifying for the public) responses to a never-ending stream of complex and challenging questions about current events.

Waxing Nautical

In addition to the Statesman's Forums and my various other duties as Executive Vice President, I also chaired the Center's Maritime Studies Program. This program consisted of monthly meetings at which Navy and Marine Corps officers, civilian officials, and various other maritime-related stakeholders would park their stripes at the door and engage in candid, off-the-record discussions on the topic of choice for that particular month. These always began with a presentation by an expert, followed by a spirited and highly thoughtful exchange among the 30-40 participants. We also presented

---

[28] At that time, each military service customarily assigned one of its up-and-coming officers to CSIS for a year to give him or her broader exposure to the strategic dimension of national security policy.

[29] In a private conversation with former Defense Secretary Jim Schlesinger some months earlier, he told me of a meeting he had recently had with Saddam Hussein in which Saddam asked him where he was going after their visit. Jim named a friend of his who he was hoping to see, but Saddam told him that would be impossible. His friend had been found guilty of a crime for which he had been executed. Jim then said he would like to go see his friend's widow to console her in her grief. As it turned out, Saddam had ordered the killing of the entire family to prevent the possibility of any family member seeking revenge in the future.

an annual award to some deserving individual for extraordinary service to the nation in a maritime capacity, a recognition that commanded significant attention within the naval community.

One of the more notable recipients of our annual award was Admiral Tom Moorer, former Chief of Naval Operations and later Chairman of the Joint Chiefs of Staff. Tom was a CSIS Senior Advisor and a wonderful presence at the Center, who I thoroughly enjoyed getting to know. Beyond the opportunity to honor him with our award, the one other encounter that stands out most in my mind was a visit we had over lunch one day, immediately on the heels of a meeting he had just attended concerning the *USS Liberty AGTR-5*, the U.S. intelligence vessel that was attacked in 1967 by Israeli jets and torpedo boats. At that meeting, approval had finally been granted (close to 30 years after the fact) for the inscriptions on the tombstones of U.S. officers and sailors killed in that attack to include any reference at all to the *USS Liberty*. Tom was absolutely livid over the delay and, more importantly, how the entire affair had been handled.

The incident, which had taken place during Israel's Six Day War with the Arab states and two months prior to Tom taking over as Chief of Naval Operations, had been billed in the media as an "accident," a case of mistaken identity. Tom said there was no way the ship could have been misidentified, since it was very clearly marked as a U.S. vessel and flying the American flag. Moreover, a recording of Israeli communications during the attack supposedly included a transmission from an Israeli pilot saying, "It's an American ship." The response coming back from headquarters, "Sink the ship." Adding further insult to injury was the fact that two waves of U.S. carrier-based jets on their way to defend the *Liberty* were called back by the White House before they got there. Had they not been called back, it is highly likely that at least 25 of the 34 who were killed would have been saved.

Despite suffering a 70% casualty rate, the crew of the *Liberty* performed heroically (one Medal of Honor, 2 Silver Stars, 2 Navy Crosses, 172 Purple Hearts); but even the associated award ceremonies were quietly covered up along with everything else. The details of the attack and ensuing cover-up can be found in an article saluting the heroism of the crew in the June-July 2007 issue of *Veterans of Foreign Wars Magazine*.

Apparently, Israeli war planners feared that Washington would interfere with their imminent attack on the Golan Heights if it became known in advance, hence their attack on the *Liberty* as the most likely source of such intelligence that might give them away. The ensuing cover-up was no doubt driven by Cold War calculations designed to keep the Soviet Union at bay. To be sure, it was hard-ball from start to finish, but failing to come to the aid of one's own forces when under attack has a shameful and lasting ring to it. As far as Tom was concerned, that aspect coupled with the extent of our government's political denial (extending down to the inscriptions on the tombstones), was indicative of how tight the chokehold was that Israel had on U.S. foreign policy at the time.

Tom's acceptance remarks at the award presentation were as inspiring as the man himself, and I know for a fact that he continued to do all he could for the crew of the *Liberty* until his dying day in 2004.

Dancing in the Caucasus

It was out of the above Maritime Studies activity and a couple of in-depth articles I authored on naval arms control for the *Naval Institute Proceedings* that I became a *de facto* spokesman for the George H.W. Bush Administration in opposing the idea of engaging in such controls with the Soviets. As such, I was invited to speak on this topic at various UN conferences around the world. Of course, Soviet spokesmen at these same conferences always provided an opposing point of view; but I felt my arguments were the more compelling, at least from a Western point of view. This was about the same time the Soviet Union was beginning to collapse and its currency along with it. For example, on one UN trip that included speaking engagements in Iceland and Bulgaria, postcards were a dollar a piece in Iceland, while they were 35 for a dollar in Bulgaria. I also paid a dollar for a bottle of 5-star brandy at the airport in Sofia (and have kicked myself ever since for not buying more while I could). A never-ending curse of one's Scot ancestry.

At another UN conference in Sochi, Russia, I took advantage of some free time on the first evening to hire a taxi along with several other participants to take us to Tbilisi, the capital of the Georgian Republic, about an hour away. While there, we visited a night club at a point in time when the government had forbidden the sale of vodka in an attempt to reverse Russia's embarrassing status as the only developed nation in the world in which the average lifespan of its male population was actually decreasing because of excessive alcohol consumption (probably to escape an otherwise debilitating existence). Thus, we were relegated to drinking beer, which actually turned out to be quite good. I also learned a new toast, apparently quite common in the Georgian Republic, *"To your health; we'll buy the rest."*

Although the club didn't have a live band, it did have a very decent disc jockey who played excellent music. At one point, while out on the dance floor, I found myself thinking of how much more pleasant it was to be surrounded by Russians on a dance floor than by Soviet submarines off of Murmansk.

Glasnost was in full swing at the time; and by then, the ruble had totally collapsed against the dollar, so it was a fun and very inexpensive evening.

Another reason I recall my trip to Sochi with a bit of a grin is because everywhere I go around the world that has a coastline, I make it a point to take a swim in the local waters. Sochi is on the Black Sea, so in customary fashion, I donned my trunks and dove in. What I hadn't taken into account was the fact that it was early April at the same approximate latitude as Boston. Although it had felt bearable when I initially tested the water, it turned out to be one of the coldest, fastest swims I've ever had. I still shiver thinking about it.

Another Arrow for the Quiver

Complementing these naval-related responsibilities was my service in the Naval Reserve. When I left active duty in the Navy, I signed up for the Reserves, which consisted of drilling one weekend a month and serving on active duty two weeks a year. The benefits for doing so, once one had served long enough to retire, were payment of a modest monthly salary (a small fraction of that received by an active duty retiree with comparable years of service) and free medical care, both of which kicked in at the age of 60.

There were other, less-tangible benefits as well, such as the opportunities for professional development and networking that arose from one's active duty assignments. For example, three of these assignments included working directly for the Chief of Naval Operations, the Chairman of the Joint Chiefs of Staff, and the President's National Security Advisor—all great opportunities that later proved helpful on other fronts. A case in point: because my candid assessment of the Navy from the standpoint of the Secretary of Defense (which I performed for the Chief of Naval Operations) was reasonably tough-minded, I suspect it may have tipped the balance in securing the final approval of Secretary Clements for my appointment as Deputy Assistant Secretary of the Navy when he asked to see it during my interview.

My task for the Chairman of the Joint Chiefs was to craft the guidance he should give to whichever Presidential candidate prevailed in the 1988 election, Michael Dukakis or George H.W. Bush. The fact that their party platforms on security-related matters were considerably different added to the challenge; but it was a great assignment, which later proved helpful in executing some of my CSIS duties.

Russian Soul

Several years after Sochi, I had another opportunity to visit Russia, while dating a young lady from St. Petersburg. One evening she escorted me to a town square where she and her former husband had stood up against Soviet tanks during the collapse of the Soviet Union. I asked her what the large building was that we happened to be standing in front of at the time. She said it was the City Council and commented that she had never been inside because it was strictly off-limits to the public. I said, "Hang on" and walked her past the guard at the front door, acting as though I owned the place. My ruse worked, and we explored the premises for about 20 minutes before an official of some sort challenged our presence. I explained that we were merely admiring the architecture; and amazingly, he led us out of the building without further comment.

Later, as we were riding the subway back to her neighborhood, I was struck by how foolish my momentary bravado had been. Not knowing a single word of Russian, I could have been squirreled away to the Gulag forever, with no one the wiser for where I was. Oh well, at least she acted impressed.

On my final evening there, she took me to her parents' apartment for a farewell dinner. They were extremely nice and, as pensioners, extremely poor; yet they rolled out the red carpet and served a delicious bowl of homemade borscht and various other treats they clearly could not afford. Although they were well along in years, the spark of romance was still very much alive as Anna, the mother, told me how she had met her husband, Apollo, during the Second World War. She had been working as a nurse in a hospital near the front when he was brought in for medical treatment, having been wounded in the fighting. When she saw him, she instantly thought to herself, "This is my destiny" and never looked back. It was straight out of "Dr. Zhivago".

Anna and Apollo have since passed on, but I will never forget their generous and loving hospitality. Between my experiences in St. Petersburg and earlier in Moscow, I came to appreciate the significance of the concept of "Russian soul", a depth of being that results from constantly focusing inward to escape an otherwise unpleasant reality. They play chess, not checkers.

Know Thine Enemy

On a final naval note, some months after the Soviet Union had disbanded, I was visited in my CSIS office by retired Soviet Navy Captain G.I. Svyatov. Almost immediately, he pointed out that a model submarine mounted under Plexiglas in my office had one too many blades on its propeller. It was a model of my first submarine, the *USS Skipjack*, which had been given to me as a farewell gift when I retired from the Naval Reserve. (At the time, I was stepping down as Commanding Officer of the unit that sits atop the Submarine Reserve, so the gift was both appropriate and appreciated). My Russian visitor, though, was absolutely right in his pronouncement, and I felt a twinge of momentary embarrassment, especially since one of my first tasks after reporting aboard *Skipjack* in 1962 was to help mount the ship's propeller back onto the shaft (from which it had been removed to re-machine the blades). I did this while the ship was undergoing an overhaul at the Portsmouth Naval Shipyard in Kittery, Maine; and remounting the screw included a stint at swinging a sledgehammer alongside several shipyard workers, while tightening it down. So, I had seen that propeller up-close and personal.

After complimenting Captain Svyatov on his keen powers of observation, he thanked me and mentioned that his last assignment in the Soviet Navy had been as the chief designer of its submarines. His task in this capacity, was to meld the best features of their own designs with what they knew of ours (based on their most up-to-date intelligence). He clearly knew his stuff; and we had a fascinating discussion, which culminated with me asking him why it had taken his engineers so long to catch up with ours in the art of submarine silencing. After all, the technical challenge of reducing the noise signature of a submarine was far less demanding than that required to launch a *Sputnik* (their first space satellite). And although his side had eventually built submarines that could run faster and dive deeper than our own; as long as we could hear them before they heard us, we could launch a torpedo at them before they even knew we were there. This was a significant tactical advantage that we enjoyed throughout the Cold War. [30]

His answer was quite interesting and consisted of two parts. First, there was the inertia of their shipbuilding program and an engrained resistance to accommodating new designs and techniques. Second was the fact that their naval tactics were dramatically different from our own, and called for proceeding at top speed toward any new target, while actively pinging on their sonar. [31] In addition to intimidating the target, it also created a lot of noise. U.S. tactics, on the other hand, called for just the opposite, lying in wait, quiet

---

[30] Indicative of this advantage was a Soviet intelligence report that Russian Marshall Akhromeyev is alleged to have handed President George H.W. Bush when President Bush met with Russian President Gorbachev off the coast of Malta in December of 1989: "We have decoded and read every one of your submarine messages for ten years and have been unable to find or kill even one of them. We quit."

[31] Sonar is an acronym for Sound Navigation and Ranging. It works by emitting ultrasonic waves that bounce back from any target that is within range. It determines the distance to that target by measuring the length of time it takes to hear the return echo.

as a church mouse, while passively listening for a target's presence on the sonar—ready to shoot, and almost never actively transmitting on that sonar.

Contributing further to the Soviet submarine noise problem was the fact that all of their submarines had double hulls, which ours did not. For them, it was a tradeoff between increased noise and enhanced survivability. Although our single-hull design is more streamlined and therefore less noisy, it is also more vulnerable to the consequences of a torpedo or depth charge attack. Their double hulled-submarines could theoretically survive such attacks in certain situations, while all it would take to sink a U.S. submarine at deeper depths was a hole in the hull the size of one's thumb.

So, it's different strokes for different folks; and which design one chooses depends on which approach one thinks will be most effective in attacking the other's submarines. I'm not sure that either of us persuaded the other of the superiority of our respective designs, but we had an amicable discussion and parted with me, at least, tremendously impressed with the depth of his knowledge of the U.S. Submarine Force. So much for out-foxing the enemy!

A Time to Reminisce

In April of 1990, during my third year at the Center, I was invited to attend the decommissioning ceremony of the *Skipjack* in Norfolk, Virginia, which turned into a wonderful trip down memory lane. Technically, the ship was already sealed and ready to be towed to Puget Sound Naval Shipyard where the reactor compartment would be removed and carried by barge to Richland, Washington for suitable burial. Then the two remaining sections would be welded together and disposed of elsewhere. However, the ship's Commanding Officer (CO) was kind enough to reopen the boat and give me a last-minute tour prior to the ceremony. There were no lights onboard, so we proceeded by flashlight. Even at that, though, it was a surreal and highly nostalgic step back in time.

The ceremony itself was also quite moving. The CO gave an inspiring address as did the principal speaker, Vice Admiral Ron Eytchison, who had been my roommate on *Skipjack* some 28 years earlier. Approximately 400 officers, enlisted men, and family members showed up for the occasion, which was quite a tribute, since the normal turn-out for this sort of thing is closer to 150. But *Skipjack* was unique. Not only was she the world's fastest in her day, but she was the first of a new class of submarines and represented the wave of the future in terms of hull design and ability to maneuver, setting the stage for all later classes to follow.

The spirit of the occasion was perhaps best captured in a letter from Mrs. Betty Anne Behrens, wife of the late Vice Admiral William Behrens, *Skipjack's* first commanding officer, with which the CO concluded his remarks:

> "Please convey to all the *Skipjack* men present my enduring pride in them and their boat. All those who have sailed in her have added to her honor. *Skipjack* was truly the embodiment of a dream—submariners, designers, engineers—everyone's best effort, every refinement conceived was brought together for the first time. All these high expectations were on the line with a mixture of hope and apprehension.

> I wish I could convey to you that excitement with which she was launched. Bill and his company on board forgot protocol and threw caps in the air; builders and contributors ashore were literally choking back the tears and cheering. It was an unforgettable day. The big question, "How will she perform?" was best answered, I expect, by my husband in one word— "Fabulous!"

> So, to *Skipjack* – the model for every submarine in every Navy in the world, the trail blazer, the record holder, the classiest boat that every sailed – with the cream of the Navy serving in her and loving her every minute—God Bless. When you haul down her flag, a last salute, for I know that every man who ever put his heart and life into *Skipjack* is with her as she leaves."

And as Ron said in his remarks, there is a special bond that exists between shipmates, which transcends just about any other form of comradeship. So, it was great fun reminiscing, particularly with the enlisted men who had served under me, exchanging antidotes and jokes about all that had gone on in the good old days. It turned out to be a very special time, celebrating the memories of one of my more exciting tours of duty. And I must say, after 31 years and more than a million miles of at-sea time, *Skipjack* looked every bit as good as the day I first boarded her.

Into the Pacific

Of my many duties as Chief Operating Officer of CSIS, one of the more interesting was that of overseeing the merger of CSIS with the Pacific Forum, a small foreign policy research institute based in Hawaii. Founded in 1975 by retired Rear Admiral Joe Vasey, Joe had just turned 70 and was concerned that the Forum live on after he was gone, so he approached CSIS about doing a merger. Interestingly enough, CSIS itself had been merged from its inception with Georgetown University until about six months prior to my arrival in 1987, at which time both organizations went their separate ways, largely to avoid future interference with one another in their respective fund-raising efforts. However, a merger with the Forum seemed an opportune way to extend the Center's reach in the Pacific, and I had the task of making it happen.

On one occasion when I was in Honolulu doing due diligence on the Forum's finances and other aspects of its institutional status, I was having dinner with Joe at a restaurant on the beach at Waikiki. As we were socializing over Mai Tais, Joe began sharing sea stories of his exploits during WWII aboard the *USS Gunnell*, while serving as Executive Officer under the command of Lieutenant Commander John McCain Jr., father of then Senator John McCain from Arizona. These included a number of harrowing tales about "close calls" from depth charges following some rather daring attacks against the Japanese fleet.

Beyond the heroics, though, Joe also commented on what a "steamer" the CO had been. This is a term used in naval circles to suggest an unconstrained ability to have a good time when ashore on liberty. He then mentioned a particular occasion in which the skipper had been carried back to the ship in an unconscious state. And according to Joe, he remained that way for the next four days as the sub headed back out on war patrol.

Ordinarily, in peacetime, an episode of this nature would quickly become widely known and carry with it serious legal consequences. In wartime, however, what really counts is how you perform as a warrior in the crucible of conflict. LCDR John McCain Jr. obviously excelled in that environment, as he later rose through the ranks to four stars and command of all U.S. forces in the Pacific. Perhaps even more indicative of this dichotomy in the requirements for effective wartime vs. peacetime leadership was the need to replace more than a third of all U.S. submarine commanders in the Pacific following the attack on Pearl Harbor for "failure to engage the enemy."

At the end of our dinner, I asked Joe if he had ever told Senator McCain any of these stories. He had not, so I told him to let me know the next time he was coming to Washington, and I would set something up so that he could. When that time came, Joe and I met with John in his Senate office; and, with the exception of the steamer incident, Joe told him about his father's exploits on the *Gunnel*. John clearly appreciated hearing the stories; but what was most interesting to me, was how deferential he was toward Joe. John's father had been a giant in the Submarine Force, and Joe had been his right-hand man (and therefore a giant as well). Joe, however, became a giant in his own right as well, having survived no fewer than 21 Japanese attacks over the course of the war. [32]

The merger went well, with the Pacific Forum becoming an autonomous subsidiary of CSIS (Addendum K). Joe lived to be 101, during which time both organizations enjoyed the benefits of synergy and fruitful collaboration. My most important take-away from the merger, though, was the fact that sea stories always tell better over Mai Tais (or some other suitable lubricant).

Long Live the Geriatrics

Finally, the work at CSIS was rewarding in the social sphere as well. Aside from the annual Christmas Party and various other special occasions, foremost among them for me was our annual softball game, which I initiated half-way through my tenure—-between the "Whippersnappers" and the "Geriatrics." As captain of the Geriatrics, I and my mature colleagues were forced to absorb the pain of unmitigated loss for the first three years in a row. At that point and to assuage our wounded pride, we said, "No more Mr. Nice Guy" and took two bold steps. First, we raised the cut-off age between the two categories from 25 years to 30 years, which helped expand our ranks. And second, we actually held a practice session ahead of time.

Most of the youngsters on the Whippersnappers played in a regular softball league against other think tanks and various government organizations around town (Addendum L). We oldsters, on the other hand, just showed up on the day of the game and got our butts kicked. Before the 4th contest, however, we assembled a week before the big game, figured out who was the best player for each position, and conducted a practice.

We then won the next three games in a row. I was the pitcher for our side; but it was slow-pitch, so my contributions to victory were rather minimal (aside from my Lou Gehrig hitting abilities, of course). What made a real difference though, was a gentleman (whose name escapes me) who played shortstop for us. He had once played minor league baseball, and absolutely no one could hit a ball past him.

Beyond having a close to leak-proof infield, we had something else going for us as well. There was a standing rule that everyone who showed up for the game would have a chance to play. That was no problem for us, since we barely had enough players to field a team. However, tons of Whippersnappers

---

[32] The U.S. Submarine Service suffered the greatest attrition of any branch of the nation's military during World War II, with the loss of 52 submarines, 375 officers, and 3131 enlisted men (or about 22% of its total capability).

showed up; and while a number of them played in the regular league, a sizable number did not. So, we took unmerciful advantage of any and all weaknesses as they rotated players.

I left CSIS a year later (Addendum M) and don't know what happened after that. All I do know is that when I left, all Geriatrics, regardless of age, were walking with a bit more bounce in their step.

The new tribe: Brint, Chapman, Pearson, and Norvell

Preacher in disguise

IT whiz

Keith dodges another one

The exploding truck

Raccoon Man aka "Beetle"

Joe Cool's mid-life crisis

Two First Mates?

In calmer waters

The tall ships

Sailing with Carl Oglesby and his wife, Anne

Corralling "The Beetle"

Lance and Keith in earlier times

Trading places 38 years later at a
pub in Edinburgh

Just back from taking their
cousins fishing. To date the
photo, the smallest cousin
is currently a Lieutenant
Commander in the U.S.
Submarine Service.

Tracing ancestral roots on the
Isle of Skye

A lighter moment with staff at
Cities in Schools

Welcoming Defense Secretary
Caspar Weinberger to the 1981
Executive Program in National
and International Security.
(Executive Program photo)

Shunn doing his thing for Secretary of Labor Bill Brock (Department of Labor official photo)

Preparing to introduce Theo-Ben Gurirab, Namibian Minister of Foreign Affairs. (Sylvia Johnson photographer)

Fielding questions for Boutros-Boutros Ghali, UN Secretary General (Sylvia Johnson Photography)

CSIS Counselor Zbigniew Brzezinski responding to Bronislaw Geremek, leader of the Solidarity majority in the Polish Parliament. (Sylvia Johnson photographer)

U.S.- Japan Leadership Council participants (Japan Council photo)

Welcoming Senator Richard Lugar and Ambassador Robert Neumann to a meeting of the post-Cold War Foreign Policy Study Group (Sylvia Johnson photographer)

Presenting Annual CSIS Maritime Studies Award to Admiral Thomas Moorer (Sylvia Johnson photographer)

Sharing a laugh with (l to r) Admiral Jonathan Howe, Deputy National Security Advisor; Robert Hunter, Director of the CSIS European Studies Program; and David Abshire, President and co-founder of CSIS. Many years earlier, Jon and I were in the same Boy Scout troop in Newport, R.I. (Sylvia Johnson photographer)

(official U.S. Navy photo)

A proud occasion

Shunn with Leo Coughlin, my
exceedingly able assistant at CSIS.
(Sylvia Johnson photographer)

Gehrig at bat

Another great victory for the Geriatrics
(note trophy in left foreground)

PART IV
A Loftier Quest

Chapter Seven

A SPIRITUAL ODYSSEY

The destiny of mankind is not decided by material computation. When great causes are on the move in the world...we learn that we are spirits, not animals, and that something is going on in space and time, and beyond space and time.

Winston Churchill

Any attempt to capture one's spiritual journey in words is bound to be a challenging exercise. As I look back on my life, the earliest data point on this continuum probably took place sometime in 1944 around the age of six, while at my grandparent's farm in Brush Prairie, Washington. Both of them almost fell out of their chairs when I crossed myself in the Catholic tradition after saying grace before dinner. They were died-in-the-wool Baptists, and my gesture apparently stemmed from the influence of a Catholic priest who made regular visits to the hospital ward in which I had just spent the previous two years.

Scouting Revisited

"The secret of a good sermon is to have a good beginning and a good ending; and have the two as close together as possible." —George Burns (1896-1996)

Although my folks were not regular church-goers, I somehow found my way to various Sunday Schools wherever Dad happened to be stationed, starting in the 4th grade. Although I can't say what impact they had on my spiritual growth, I do recall specific instances in which I felt a genuine closeness to God. The first such instance took place at the age of ten, while strolling in a meadow beside a Congregational Church in Lemon Grove, California, where I had just attended Sunday service. I can still recall feeling a heavenly connection, while softly singing the tune, "This is My Father's World." Another took place in Newport, Rhode Island a couple of years later, when I was working to earn Scouting's God and Country Award. This involved a range of work-related activities, e.g. cleaning the pews, mowing the church lawn, and any number of other chores. It also involved some challenging memory work as well, like reciting the names of the books of the New Testament and the like. Because of this involvement, I was asked to preach a sermon in that particular church on Youth Sunday. Although that went reasonably well, the only other time I was asked to perform a specific task relating to my God and Country Award was pretty much a bust.

It took place while camping in the woods at a Boy Scout camp near Tillamook, Oregon with Dick Hellburg, the fellow scout from my troop mentioned earlier. In the middle of the night during a severe downpour, several scout leaders visited our tent to make a request. (To this day, I don't know how they found us, since we were in a deep forest in the middle of nowhere). Anyway, they somehow knew that I had earned the God and Country Award and asked if I would be willing to conduct church services the next morning. I readily agreed but didn't have a clue as to what I should do. All I remember is having all of us recite the Twenty-Third Psalm and then asking everyone to sing "Holy, Holy, Holy." Well, I started that particular church hymn on much too high a note. By the time we got to the middle, no one could sing any higher, least of all me, so we abruptly stopped. Thus ended my career as a church choir director.

Because we moved so frequently, I don't recall a lot of church-related activities after that, other than participating in local High Y Clubs, in which those of us in the Club attended a different church once a month. Instead, most of my focus was on the basic adjustments required to keep my head above water in the classroom and on the athletic field at a seemingly endless stream of new schools.

Finally, during my four years at the Academy, we marched to church every Sunday to "Onward Christian Soldiers" and various other Christian tunes played by the Naval Academy band from a gazebo that we passed along the way. Mandatory church attendance was discontinued a number of years later, after which the number of Midshipmen honor offenses increased accordingly.

Despite the above exposure to various denominational mores and traditions and that which I acquired through belonging to different churches while in the Navy, my spiritual commitment could rightfully be described as casual at best. While on submarine duty, for example, I would occasionally play poker all night on a Saturday and proceed directly from there to give the Sunday morning sermon as the ship's Protestant Lay Leader. It was only later, after leaving the Navy and experiencing the distress of a divorce, that I began a more serious spiritual walk.

Getting Serious

"Faith consists in believing when it is beyond the power of reason to believe."
—Voltaire (1694-1778)

During a long-ago conversation with Washington Okumu, a Kenyan Ambassador and good friend, he defined an atheist as "one who has no invisible means of support." And that is probably the principal saving grace of adversity. It causes one to lean on those invisible means of support, as I began doing in the wake of my divorce to Nina. In those days, custody of the children always went to the mother unless she could be proven unfit for the task. She was very fit; so it was a particularly tough time without them, and I lost 25 lbs. in the process. Although I wouldn't recommend it as a way to lose weight, it did inspire me to deepen my spiritual growth.

In my time of need and through a rather circuitous set of circumstances, I found myself drawn to Fourth Presbyterian Church in Bethesda, Maryland and, by extension, to the National Prayer Breakfast fellowship, an involvement that was to have a lasting impact on my life. Before describing that impact, it may be helpful to explain how I came to believe as I do. I attempted to capture that process in a letter to my brother in 2009, which can be found at Addendum N.

Crossing Over

"It would have approached nearer to a miracle if Jonah had swallowed the whale." —Thomas Paine (1737-1809)

In 1974, in my capacity as Director of Policy Planning and Management while serving in the Pentagon, I was assigned to lead a U.S. delegation to a NATO meeting on Euro/NATO training that was to take place in Brussels, Belgium. I decided to also use that occasion to travel to London after the meeting to participate in a gathering of European leaders at Windsor Castle, all of whom were involved in the National Prayer Breakfast leadership network.

The NATO meeting proved highly productive because it provided an opportunity to address what had become a real problem for several NATO countries, i.e. a shortage of opportunities to train their jet pilots for combat operations. Aware of the existence of unused capacity in our own jet pilot training pipeline, I suggested that these countries integrate their training with that of the U.S. by filling available seats in the American program. It was an easy sell, both with the Europeans and our own officials. When I returned to the States, I met with General David Jones, the U.S. Air Force Chief of Staff, to seek his support for the idea. He instantly agreed, and the motion was carried. The quickness of his response was undoubtedly influenced by the fact that we already enjoyed a personal relationship, stemming from that earlier time when I had dated his daughter.

Beyond the economic benefits that flowed from the new, joint jet pilot training arrangement, I developed a close friendship with Bob Fiss, an Army Colonel from the Office of International Security Affairs in the Pentagon, who was assigned to assist me in preparing for the NATO meeting. Bob was a 1943 graduate of West Point, exceedingly well-versed in NATO-related affairs, and as pleasant as one could be. Although that was my only official foray into the NATO inner sanctum (because of a change in jobs a few months later), Bob stayed with it for several more years, visiting some of the nicer locations on the planet with his wife, Barbara, as the various NATO countries took turns hosting the meetings.

While the NATO meeting was professionally satisfying, the later meeting at Windsor Castle proved even more memorable. After landing in London, I headed off to meet with a few friends at a pub a few blocks from the downtown airport bus terminal. Shortly after exiting the terminal, I was hit by a car while crossing the street.

The impact from the car, which was going about 40 miles an hour, crushed the American Tourister suitcase that I was carrying in my right hand and catapulted me through the air for about 12 feet. I landed on my left forearm and immediately experienced two sensations. The first was total surprise. Although I had looked in the correct direction as I was crossing the street, I wasn't aware that Londoners sometimes drive without their lights on at night, if they think the street lamps provide sufficient visibility.

The second sensation was an overwhelming sense of peace that coursed throughout my body and instantaneously caused me to realize that there, but for a stroke of good fortune, I would not have been around to worry about all the silly little things I normally worried about. That realization triggered an immediate reordering of priorities, which lasted all of two weeks before I reverted to form.

This incident also alerted me to the fact that there were others who had undergone a similar experience, as documented in the work of a Swiss psychiatrist about a year later who interviewed a number of people around the world who, after being pronounced "clinically dead," had returned to life. Her findings revealed that most of them had experienced the same total sense of peace, had seen a blinding white light (I hadn't made it that far), and in some cases had met Jesus and/or close relatives who had gone before. After my own experience, I could readily understand why many of those interviewed said they were no longer afraid to die. In fact, a number of them expressed resentment at having to "come back".

Anyway, as I was picking myself up after the collision, I was amazed to find that a bottle of Old Grandad bourbon, which I had purchased at a duty-free shop in the airport, had survived the crash intact inside my crushed suit-case. About that same time, a plain-clothes policewoman, who happened to be walking by at the time of the crash, heard the thud, observed me flying through the air, and hurried over to help me back on my feet. She asked if I was all right, and I told her I thought so. I was careful in how I responded because of what a friend had experienced when recently hit by a Volkswagen back home in Virginia. When asked that same question, he indicated that he was fine, and the VW drove off. Several weeks later, he was in the hospital because of delayed problems resulting from the accident.

I later wrote a letter to the President of American Tourister, describing my experience, complimenting the company on the durability of its luggage, and all-but-outright asking for a new suitcase to replace the old. The attempt failed, but I did receive a nice letter back, indicating that the company typically received several hundred letters a day, with almost all of them complaining about one thing or another. On rare occasions, though, they received a letter such as mine, which "made their whole day."

After the policewoman helped me to the pub, I hooked up with my friends and shared my experience over a double shot of Single Malt. About 30 minutes later, the policewoman returned with a "bobby" to capture the details of the incident. As I'm sitting with the two of them in the bobby's car, he asked me the time of the accident. The policewoman said "10:30 pm", and I challenged her response because my watch showed the time to be 10:30, and I knew it had been at least 30 minutes earlier. The bobby noticed that my watch was broken and exclaimed, "Aha, the time of the crime." To which I replied, "Sherlock!"

He then asked if I was all right. I said I thought so, but wasn't altogether certain, since I had experienced some difficulty in holding my drink at the pub. He said, "You should go to the hospital and have your hand x-rayed. It's free, you know." I said, "Really? I thought that was only for native Englanders." He responded, "We do it for every bloody bloke. That's why we're no longer Great Britain!"

I did as he said and ended up with a cast on my arm for the next six weeks. More to the point, though, this experience only added to my conviction that there is far more to life than meets the eye.

The discussion at Windsor proved very rich and became the source of several new friends. One evening after a full day of meetings in the Castle, I visited a pub in town with another conference participant by the name of Nathaniel Lorch. Nathaniel was Secretary General of the *Knesset*, the Israeli parliament, and a stimulating conversationalist. On our way back to the castle, I asked him if he knew who was most responsible for America's support of Israel. He said, "Of course." I said, "Who?" And he said, "Leon Uris." I was bowled over by his response, because that was precisely who I was thinking of, but had assumed that the answer to such a question would be so subjective as to command a different response from everyone who answered. In my own case, it was my reading of *Exodus* by Uris that had inspired my sympathetic leanings toward Israel.

As it turned out, it was Nathaniel who had persuaded Uris to write the book. He did so because he (Nathaniel) had been captivated by *Battle Cry,* Uris's first novel. Although that became a widely-acclaimed book, a successor novel by Uris had bombed, and most critics wrote him off as a one-trick pony, a single-success author. However, Nathaniel, saw beyond that and invited Uris to write a novel that told the story of the founding of modern-day Israel. Uris agreed to do so on the condition that no one could change anything he wrote. Nathaniel agreed, and *Exodus* resulted, as did *Mila 18,* a later volume that focused on the uprising of the Jewish ghetto in Warsaw against the Nazis during World War II. Both of these attracted global acclaim and put Uris on the map as a serious and highly capable author. Nathaniel's instincts were clearly on the money.

One of the many other interesting gentlemen I met during that weekend was George Thomas, Speaker of the British House of Commons. He was a very affable fellow, who in the course of a longer conversation shared with me how he had spent 30 years plotting and scheming to become Speaker. But when the actual time came for the Bailiff to escort him from his normal seat to the Speaker's seat, tradition required that he feign resistance by physically resisting the advances of the Bailiff. Apparently, a number of Speakers over the course of the country's history had been beheaded when the King or Queen "shot the messenger."

A Life-Changing Experience

On a trip to visit my folks following my divorce, I met Wes Trucker, pastor of Harper Free Evangelical Church, the only church in Southworth. The meeting, which took place one Sunday after church, led to a later stroll along the beach, an extended conversation, and the beginning of what became a long-lasting friendship. He was a very pleasant fellow, and we agreed to stay in touch.

Some months later, I received a call from a friend of his by the name of Bob Andringa, who told me over the phone that Wes had asked him some months earlier to introduce me to the National Prayer Breakfast fellowship.[33] Bob said Wes was coming to town in another couple of weeks, and he felt obliged to make good on his commitment before Wes arrived. So Bob picked me up at my home in Northern Virginia and drove me over to Fellowship House in the embassy district of Washington. It was there that he introduced me to Doug Coe; and the rest, as they say, is history.

Doug was the key facilitator of the National Prayer Breakfast (NPB), an annual event in Washington D.C. that brings together about 4,000 people from around the world in the spirit of Jesus to promote peace and serve the poor. The NPB has not only inspired the replication of similar breakfasts in other countries, but it has also promoted the formation of countless small, locally-based fellowship groups in the United States and overseas that meet weekly to give practical expression to these noble goals. Those involved in these activities are collectively referred to as "the fellowship" or "the family" and are generally devoted to replicating the sense of mission and inclusiveness mirrored in the life and teachings of Jesus.

Doug had a unique ability to inspire fellow believers to convert their faith into action by serving others, either in their own communities or in other parts of the world —- all in the spirit of Jesus. Indeed, there was a longstanding joke among those who became involved in such efforts: "God has a plan for your life, and Doug Coe will tell you what it is." Anyway, I too became caught up in fellowship-related activities, and the following are representative of the sorts of initiatives I found myself pursuing because of Doug's influence. In

---

[33] As it turned out, Wes was then serving as the Fellowship's point man in the Pacific Northwest, coordinating all of its activities in that region; and Bob, who was then serving as Staff Director of a committee on higher education in the House of Representatives, was also deeply involved with the Fellowship. Wes went on to become a key figure in the Salvation Army, and Bob became President of the Council for Christian Colleges and Universities. I had the good fortune of becoming life-long friends with them both.

my particular case, though, that influence was a bit more indirect in nature than that experienced by most others.

At one point, Doug wanted to groom me to take over the fellowship activities in Europe, but I begged off after concluding it wouldn't be a good fit. On another occasion, he asked if I would be willing to chair the International Foundation Board, [34] which provides legal oversight over the fellowship's numerous non-profit activities. Again, I declined, because I didn't have the time to do it justice. Offsetting this rather poor track record of negative responses, though, were the various initiatives I did pursue that flowed out of other, more casual, conversations with Doug.

For example, in 1974, Doug mentioned in passing that he had been praying for years for a small fellowship group at the top of the Pentagon. As luck would have it, I was working there at the time and between me and my two bosses, Bob Murray and Bill Brehm, we collectively knew the three Service Secretaries (Army, Navy and Air Force) and the four military Chiefs (the Chief of Naval Operations, the Commandant of the Marine Corps, and the Chiefs of Staff of the Army and the Air Force). We approached them about forming a fellowship group consisting of as many of them as were inclined to participate that would meet every other Tuesday morning. Most of them agreed, and we were off and running.

At the initial meeting of this group, I invited Doug to attend. He did and brought with him, Senator John Stennis, an arch-conservative Republican from Mississippi, and Senator Harold Hughes, a tough-talking, truck-driving liberal Democrat from Iowa. They shared with the group how they often strongly opposed one another on the floor of the Senate; but when they emerged from the weekly meetings of the Senate Prayer Breakfast Group, it

---

[34] *The foundation had historically been called The Fellowship Foundation until a board meeting in the late 1970's, at which Dick Halverson, then Pastor of Fourth Presbyterian Church and a central figure in the National Prayer Breakfast fellowship, proposed to the Board that the word "Fellowship" be dropped from the foundation's title, because the capital "F" in the word suggested an exclusiveness that was inappropriate. I was serving on the Board at that time, and in response to Dick's suggestion noted that the most exclusive country club in Boston was called "The Country Club" and said we should avoid falling into that same trap by becoming "The Foundation." After a few laughs, the proposal was tabled for future consideration.

A few days after returning to Boston where I was living at the time, I received a call from Doug to discuss the matter further. After he essentially repeated the same rationale as Dick, I said "Doug, I don't have a problem with renaming the Foundation. I just think we need a word to substitute for "Fellowship." He said, "Like what?" "I don't know, how about 'international'? He said fine, and the ayes had it.

was always arm-in-arm as brothers in Christ. The whole idea, of course, was to inspire this same approach in the newly-formed Pentagon Breakfast Group.

In addition to the deeper bonds of friendship that formed over time, members of the Pentagon group would often invite a guest to attend. Typical of such guests was Jeremiah Denton, a Navy Captain who had just returned from close to eight years of captivity in North Vietnam.[35] In the meeting, Jerry didn't speak about his time as a prisoner but rather of his shock at how much America had changed during his absence. He indicated that he was thinking of leaving the Navy so he could speak out against the moral decay that he saw taking hold in American culture. During the discussion, he mentioned in passing that his wife was concerned about him leaving the Service; and as the meeting was breaking up, I privately suggested that he take her feelings into serious consideration.

The next day Jerry called me and said that his wife had, in fact, threatened to leave him if he left the Navy. I suggested that he owed both her and the Navy his continued allegiance for at least another two years (for standing by him throughout his ordeal), after which he could reevaluate his situation once things had settled down a bit. Jerry did so; and as luck would have it, he was promoted to Rear Admiral, saved his marriage, and later became a U.S. Senator from Alabama, with the best of all platforms to speak out on the issues.

Another guest was a political leader from Turkey; and through the influence of the breakfast, we were able to persuade him that his country would have to improve its treatment of political prisoners before the Pentagon would consider his country's request for additional armaments.

There were other guests as well, and there seemed no end to the good that could be accomplished when interacting with others on a spiritual rather than strictly political basis. The group continued for a total of twelve years, which was a surprising longevity in light of the frequent turnover in these top military and civilian positions—probably about 18 months on average. I myself moved away after a couple of years to Boston; and the glue that ultimately held things together was the strong commitment (and continuing presence) of General David Jones, who served for a full term as Air Force Chief of Staff followed by two terms as Chairman of the Joint Chiefs of Staff.

---

[35] While a POW, Captain Denton was forced by his captors to participate in a 1966 televised propaganda interview that was broadcast in the United States. While answering questions and feigning trouble with the blinding television lights, he blinked his eyes in Morse Code, spelling the word "torture." This provided the first confirmation that American prisoners were being tortured.

Changing Direction

During yet another conversation with Doug, he indicated that after he was gone, he didn't see any need to replace himself, because of all the seeds (of fellowship) that had been planted around the world, which he felt could collectively sustain the effort over time. I didn't argue the point; but I also didn't buy it, not for a second. Doug was clearly the glue that held everything together, both in terms of the innumerable individuals involved (many at the highest levels of influence in the public or private sectors of their respective countries) and in terms of their inter-related efforts to do good in the world.[36] Although I kept these reservations to myself, that exchange caused me to mentally ask myself what I might do to affect our system (of government) in such a way that this kind of work would continue, even if the fellowship were to one day fade into the ether for lack of effective leadership. Thus, did I unwittingly open myself to a complete change of direction in my life's journey.

Several years later, while discussing nuclear doctrine in a course I was teaching on International Affairs and Security at Harvard, it occurred to me that while we and the Soviets were spending billions of dollars and rubles on advanced weapon systems, the sole purpose for which was that they not be used (because we were enhancing deterrence), a sizeable fraction of the rest of the world was literally starving to death. This struck me as more than a little ludicrous. Wearing this same security-related hat, I also concluded that while we were probably second to no one in history in terms of our ability to mount a strong defense to keep the peace, I felt we were woefully inept at making peace.

Then, donning an entirely different hat – that associated with my long-standing involvement with the National Prayer Breakfast – I thought about instances in which individuals operating on the basis of their personal religious faith had been able to reconcile differences between people or factions—sometimes bringing wars to a halt — with no one the wiser for how it had taken place (because it was almost always done in strictest confidence). It occurred to me that if I could capture this kind of activity in a compelling manner and make it known to policymakers and foreign policy practitioners it might be possible for government to reinforce it and build upon it (but never try to own it, lest it become tainted with the government's political agenda)— in short, to create a synergy for peacemaking that didn't otherwise exist.

---

[36] Hillary Clinton in her 2003 memoir titled *Living History* referred to Doug as a "genuinely loving, spiritual mentor and guide to anyone, regardless of party or faith, who wants to deepen his or her relationship with God and offer the gift of service to others in need."

Wearing both hats, I also predicted there would probably be a strong need for such synergy once the Cold War ended, as deep-seated religious and ethnic antagonisms, long suppressed by the bipolar confrontation between the super-powers, boiled over and become a new source of conflict in different parts of the world. Because the overriding challenge for the United States during the Cold War was to contain the "godless" Soviets, religion had been totally off the policymaker's screen. Hence, the need for new tools to address the kind of identity-based conflicts that loomed on the not-so-distant horizon.[37] It took another five years before I had an opportunity to put thought to action; but in the meantime, there were other fish to fry.

We Are the World

In 1984, the country of Ethiopia was undergoing a severe famine that commanded world-wide attention when its first-hand consequences were graphically portrayed in a BBC television special. As I was saying grace before dinner one evening, with Ethiopia on my mind, I prayed as was normal around our table, that we be "mindful of the needs of others." Reflecting on that prayer a bit later, I thought to myself, "Talk is cheap. I need to do something meaningful to address this problem." This thought process ultimately led to the idea of sending a plane-load of critical food and medical supplies to Ethiopia as a Christmas gift from the city of Boston. With this as the goal, I took time off from work to make it happen and teamed up with a kindred spirit by the name of Tom Moore, a local attorney, who shared similar sentiments about wanting to help.

The first challenge was to raise sufficient funds (about $85,000) to charter a DC8 to transport the desperately-needed supplies. Never having done anything like this before, I approached Tom Phillips, Chairman of the Raytheon Corporation and a good friend, to see if Raytheon would contribute to the cause. Tom readily agreed to put up $10,000 to get us started. Because of the company's stellar reputation and its stature as the single largest employer in the state of Massachusetts, Raytheon's contribution provided the credibility we needed to elicit contributions from other companies. A number of them gave, and a contribution from Data General eventually took us over the top,

---

[37] This assumption was later borne out as religion did, in fact, play a role in an increasing number of conflicts. Dr. Isak Svensson, Professor in the Department of Peace and Conflict Research at Upsalla University in Sweden, documented in his 2012 book titled, *Ending Holy Wars: Religion and Conflict in Civil Wars*, the fact that religion in some form was involved in global conflict 3% of the time in 1975, 18% in 1989, and 49% in 2008.

as they gave one dollar for every employee they had on their global payroll as of Christmas day (which equated to $18,504).

Meanwhile, we were able to get a local television station to challenge the viewing public to fill the aircraft with the needed supplies through their financial contributions. So, every evening, Channel 4 would flash a profile of the aircraft on its screen, indicating how much fuller it was becoming from day to day.

Because Ethiopia was under Communist rule and setting political conditions on any food it provided to the population (of either supporting the regime or starving), we needed an alternate conduit for ensuring the supplies actually reached their intended target. Accordingly, we chose to work through Oxfam, a non-profit organization that wanted to help and which had an on-the-ground capability for reaching the people directly.

Things were proceeding well until World Vision, another Christian non-profit with ties to Ethiopia, offered to donate 17,000 oral rehydration kits, which were stored in a warehouse in Kansas. Starving people are generally unable to digest food properly without first consuming a mixture of sugar and water as provided by these kits. I was grateful for their offer and planned to have Channel 4 televise the arrival of the kits on the tarmac at Boston's Logan Airport, when Oxfam strongly objected to accepting anything at all from World Vision. Their problem was purely political in nature. While Oxfam was quite vocal in its criticisms of the Ethiopian government, World Vision was more circumspect, because it had seven major feeding stations sprinkled across the country and didn't want to risk having them shut down.

To address this "holier than thou" attitude on Oxfam's part, I met with the head of their U.S . operations and his staff to discuss the matter. At the end of a fruitless discussion, I said, "Do you mean to tell me that in a situation where even our geopolitical arch-enemy has agreed to cooperate with us in feeding Ethiopia's starving population (by delivering U.S. grain from Soviet helicopters) that you can't bring yourself to cooperate with another Christian organization that is every bit as committed to alleviating hunger as you are?" Despite their obvious discomfort, they didn't back down; and we were forced to purchase the kits from commercial sources. A poignant example of letting petty instincts triumph over the better angels of our idealism.

Despite the numerous hurdles, the DC8 flew over on January 21st. Although we missed our Christmas target, the timing was none the less fortuitous. The supplies arrived during a lull between the arrival of the immediate air-borne assistance provided by the U.S. and other countries and the major humanitarian relief that was coming later by sea. A television crew flew over with the supplies, so the citizens of Boston were able to see first-hand the impoverished Ethiopians receiving the 36 tons of supplies which their contributions had made possible.

A week later, more than 40 of America's top recording artists gathered in Hollywood to record "We Are the World," a song written on the spot by Lionel Richie and Michael Jackson, which swept the country by storm as it helped raise awareness and funds for alleviating hunger in Africa. That song still stands as a classic example of the power of music to inspire people to rise above themselves in serving a greater cause.

On a personal level, this experience confirmed what I had long suspected: (1) that anyone can make a difference, once they put their shoulder to the wheel, and (2) that financial gain rings hollow when compared to the satisfaction that comes from serving others.

Getting Real

One of my more telling lessons in humility occurred when I was heading the Policy Planning and Management shop in Manpower and Reserve Affairs at the Pentagon. As previously mentioned, it was a new office and with it came the opportunity to hire an entirely new staff of twelve individuals. I was determined to hire the best people I could find, and that is what I did, with one exception. My boss leaned on me to hire a gentleman named Jim Whittaker, who he had met at church and with whom he was highly impressed, albeit for reasons unrelated to the job. I soon found myself leaning on Jim a good bit to improve his work performance.

One day, he entered my office and said he wanted to share something with me. I invited him to do so, and he started by telling me he had grown to resent the pressure I had been putting on him. Then he asked my forgiveness for his negative attitude and said he wanted to clear the air and get things on a better footing. He then gave me the Jerusalem Cross that was hanging around his neck. I was totally taken aback by the spiritual nature of his gesture, but I accepted the cross and put it around my own neck (where it hangs to this day, some 46 years later).

Although I continued to lean on him because we had a job to do, it was done in an altogether different spirit. My limited understanding of human nature would have expected that he would be the one wanting an apology from me; but experiencing the reverse was a real growth experience for me on the learning curve of loving one's enemy. That's an overstatement of what this represented, because there never were any hard feelings on my part; but it opened my eyes to a whole new way of thinking and the associated lesson in humility that it conveyed.

Years later, I hadn't seen Jim since our days in the Pentagon, but I somehow learned he had been hit by a car that had jumped the sidewalk and broken both of his legs. When I visited him in the hospital, I was once again humbled by his inspiring spirit. Although in a great deal of pain himself, he was grateful for the experience because it had enabled him to encourage others in the hospital who were also undergoing difficult recoveries. What a rare individual and what a living example of walking the talk of one's beliefs!

A Critical Insight

Another important insight I encountered on my life-long, often intermittent spiritual odyssey was that offered by a 19th century Algerian freedom fighter, Emir Abd el-Kader ibn Muhieddine, who once wrote:

> *...If you think God is what the different communities believe—the Muslims, Christians, Jews, Zoroastrians, polytheists and others— He is that, but also more...None of His creatures worships Him in His entirety...No one knows all God's facets. Each of His creatures worships and knows Him in a certain way and is ignorant of Him in others.*

In other words, no one person or group has a complete understanding of the Creator, no matter how many "disbelievers" they may have slain along the way. As my good friend John Kiser, a gentleman farmer and accomplished author, who wrote a widely-heralded biography of the Emir, succinctly summarized it, "The Kingdom of God is bigger than the Church; salvation is ultimately a mystery." Or, as Fredrick The Great expressed much the same in 1740, "All religions must be tolerated.......every man must go to heaven in his own way."

In important respects, the Emir's message can be seen as complementing that of *Isaiah 55, verses 8 and 9:*

> *For My thoughts are not your thoughts, neither are your ways My ways, declares the Lord.*
>
> *For as the heavens are higher than the earth, so are My ways higher than your ways and My thoughts than your thoughts.*

Compassionate both on and off the battlefield, Abd el-Kader went on to become one of the most admired figures of the 19th century, one to whom President Lincoln, Queen Victoria, and the Pope alike paid tribute. Internalizing the essence of Abd el-Kader's insight essentially frees one up from any overpowering need to impose one's own beliefs on others. And the world becomes a much friendlier place.

All that lives must die, passing through nature on its way to eternity.

—Hamlet

Chapter Eight

CAPTURING THE VISION

The mark of an educated man is his capacity to discuss the person of Jesus without adolescent embarrassment.

Nathan Pusey
President, Harvard University (1953-1971)

Although I had the necessary license from CSIS to proceed with the Religion and Conflict Resolution Project, I was mindful of the Center's conservative donor base and decided to label the project "Religion and Conflict." This was long before the wake-up call of 9-11, when religion's relevance to international security became apparent to all. However, until that unhappy episode, "conflict resolution" was instinctively equated with pacifism, and "religion" was thought by most political scientists and foreign policy practitioners to be soft, irrational, and irrelevant. Consistent with this mindset, the State Department was tightly bound in a longstanding, institutional straight-jacket of dogmatic secularism.

For the first three years, I was only able to secure minimal funding for the project in the amount of a $35,000 grant from the U.S. Institute of Peace. However, when the Berlin Wall came down in 1989, that abruptly changed. The role of the church in that transformation was all-too-apparent, ranging from the influence of the Pope in Poland to the role of the Lutheran Church in East Germany and other Protestant churches in Romania. At that point, I came out of the closet and re-named the project "Religion and Conflict Resolution." With this new awakening to religion's potential role in resolving conflict, we were able to secure a collective total of $354,000 from five foundations to produce a book that captured this potential.

I initially thought that such a book would be a single-authored volume, but soon determined that the complexities surrounding the intersection of religion and politics were probably beyond the grasp of any single individual or academic discipline to address. Accordingly, I recruited a stable of accomplished scholars from nine different disciplines, ranging from theology on the one end to military strategy on the other — and everything in between.

I also concluded early-on that the most effective approach for proving religion's role in different settings would be to capture its influence in a series of case studies. At first, the intent was to do so by using examples from a number of different faith traditions; but at the end of the day, we were relegated to Christianity largely by default. To be sure, the peacemaking mandate in Christianity is more prominent than that found in most other religions; but after closely examining those other faiths, we were unable to find good examples of the spiritual dynamics we were seeking to describe. That doesn't mean they didn't exist; only that we were unable to find them.

In addition to engaging a range of gifted researchers from different disciplines, I established a Steering Committee of world-class scholars and diplomats to provide direction and informed insights as we undertook the research and eventually compiled it into a cohesive whole. This generally took place over a series of lunches during the initial and final phases of what turned out to be a seven-year effort. Among the luminaries involved in this process was Edward Luttwak, widely acknowledged to be one of the brighter scholars and strategic thinkers in the world today. Ed commented to me on more than one occasion that those luncheon discussions were the most intellectually stimulating exchanges in which he had ever taken part.

The substance of the book in its final form included seven case studies that spanned the globe, with examples from Europe, Asia, Africa, and Central America. These included (1) Franco-German reconciliation following World War II; (2) religious reconciliation between the Sandinistas and the East Coast Indians of Nicaragua in the 1980's; (3) the role of the Quakers in ending the Nigerian Civil War in the late 1960's; (4) the facilitation of East Germany's opening to the West by the Lutheran Church; (5) the role of Cardinal Sin and the Catholic Church in the overthrow of the Marcos regime in the Philippines; (6) the complicity of the Dutch Reformed Church both in the initial justification of apartheid and in its later overthrow; and (7) the role of Moral Rearmament and the Quakers in facilitating a peaceful transition from the state of Rhodesia to that of Zimbabwe in 1980.

As one might imagine, capturing the spiritual dimension of change can be a challenging proposition. How does one prove the influence of something that cannot be seen or precisely measured? Attempting to do exactly that, we sent our scholars to the relevant locations for extended periods of time to conduct the necessary research. Unsurprisingly, the book that finally resulted provides an unusually rich lode of primary source materials based on extensive inquiries about previously unexamined topics.

Included among the several chapters that I authored was one on the role of the church in establishing and later abolishing apartheid in South Africa. My research on this was facilitated by a personal invitation from the South African Ambassador to visit his country as part of a government program to expose opinion leaders from around the world to the on-the-ground realities in South Africa. The underlying assumption was that this first-hand exposure would lead to a more informed understanding of the difficult challenges facing that country. Such a visit could take place either under the sponsorship of the government itself or of a consortium of private South African companies. I opted for the latter, and my ten-day visit proved to be a rather sophisticated soft-sell from start to finish. They arranged for me to meet with anyone I wanted regardless of how radical that person might be and to do so either with or without a government official present, according to my preference.

I still remember the terrible case of jet lag I had after landing in Johannesburg. Without any sleep on a plane ride that took forever nor during the first night I was there, I had to fight hard to stay awake for the next day's appointments. My first meeting was with Byers Naude, a widely-respected minister and elder of the Dutch Reformed Church (DRC), who chaired the Christian Institute (an ecumenical organization that promoted nonracial Christianity and the training of black theologians). In this latter capacity, he had long been a thorn in the side of both the DRC and the government. He was also a critical source of information for my research. So, there I was in his living room, sitting on the edge of a chair and feigning rapt attention, with mental toothpicks striving to keep my eyelids open. A rich discussion, but not my finest hour!

My first weekend in South Africa found me in Capetown with free time on my hands. Thinking back to an earlier time when I collected stamps as a kid, I remembered how intrigued I had been by pictures of the Cape of Good Hope on various South African stamps. So, I rented a car to drive down to see the Cape. Along the way, I picked up a young Dutch hitchhiker and gave him a ride to Sandy Beach, which was about a third of the way to the Cape. As I dropped him off at the trail leading to the beach, he told me it was a nudist beach and invited me to come take a peak, indicating that I could leave my swimsuit on if I wanted. I thanked him and declined the invitation. As I was driving off, I had gone about a block and a half before I thought to myself, "Wait a minute. I'm 52; the future is now." I never saw the hitchhiker again, but I can personally attest to the fact that the mountains and the sea are not the only things of beauty in South Africa.

A Sanity Check

At the point when we had a rough draft of the book manuscript, I made arrangements to present our preliminary findings to a diverse audience of about 600 individuals who had traveled from all over the world to Caux, Switzerland, to participate in the summer programs sponsored annually by Moral Rearmament (MRA), a global spiritual and moral network (later renamed Initiatives of Change). They do this in a grand old hotel overlooking the Alps and the eastern end of Lake Geneva (the same hotel in which they facilitated Franco/German reconciliation following World War II). Eleven scholars and practitioners from the book's steering committee accompanied me and participated in the presentation of our findings, first to the larger audience of 600 and later to a smaller group of 32.

The smaller group session ran considerably longer than the plenary presentation in order to provide adequate time for in-depth feedback. This group included a number of current and former high-ranking officials from other countries, ranging from the Foreign Policy Spokesman for the British Parliament to the former leader of the guerilla forces in Sudan's first civil war following independence.

As it turned out, the feedback at Caux proved even more valuable than I had anticipated; and, among other suggestions, we dropped one of the case studies we were planning to include. Under the tough-minded scrutiny of the smaller group, it became apparent that spiritual factors had played less of a role in mediating a successful outcome in that particular conflict than we had initially thought.

Because the book was plowing new ground in a difficult arena, it was critically important that we accurately capture the relevant facts in each of the case studies and that we be extraordinarily careful in developing our associated findings. MRA played an important role in that process along with many others. As former Assistant Secretary of State Hal Saunders, principal architect of the Camp David Accords (which established the current peace between Israel and Egypt) and a member of the book's steering committee, commented at one point, "In my experience, the collaborative nature of this project is unprecedented."

Making A Difference

"The American temptation is to believe that foreign policy is a subdivision of psychiatry." —Henry Kissinger

When *Religion, the Missing Dimension of Statecraft* first appeared in 1994, the role of religious influence was an under-appreciated ingredient in international affairs. More specifically, most diplomats either misunderstood or ignored the positive potential of that role. To the extent they did think about religion, it was almost always viewed as a negative influence. Although the absolutism that often accompanies deep-seated religious convictions doesn't always lend itself to compromise, and the virtue to be found in those convictions is sometimes too weakly-rooted to prevent its cooption by power politics, there is nevertheless a second edge to this sword; and it was totally off the policymaker's screen. So, while there is clearly a need to deal with religion's confrontational aspects, there is an even greater need to capitalize on its harmonizing elements and bridgebuilding potential.

The time is past due for religion to be treated as a serious variable in the foreign policy equation. No longer can we afford to treat it as a geopolitical orphan when its purposeful exclusion leaves foreign policy practitioners with an inadequate frame of reference for dealing with problems of communal identity like ethnic conflict, tribal warfare, and religious hostilities.

The purpose of the book was to address this omission and to help facilitate the incorporation of religious considerations into future U.S. foreign policy calculations. In doing so, it had two principal targets. First, and most immediate, was the U.S. Foreign Service Institute, which trains our country's diplomats. Second, were universities, colleges, and seminaries out of a conviction that it is the next-generation that will be best able to run with these new ideas. Teaching old dogs, like me, new tricks is simply too difficult. Toward this foreign policy goal, the book provided the first systematic account of modern situations in which religious or spiritual factors had been instrumental in preventing or resolving conflict, while achieving nonviolent social change. As mentioned earlier, the cases themselves spanned the globe and additional essays summarized the findings to bring out their implications for the foreign policy and religious communities.

The book, which was published by Oxford University Press, struck a responsive chord and almost immediately began receiving global acclaim. I can speak immodestly about this aspect, because most of the credit for the accolades rightfully belongs to the impressive array of scholars and researchers who participated in the effort. On the diplomatic front, the book quickly became required reading at the U.S. Foreign Service Institute; and within academia, it was soon incorporated as a required text in a number of graduate and undergraduate courses across the land.

The book was also the subject of favorable reviews in more than 60 prestigious journals and periodicals during the first year following its publication, including *Foreign Affairs,* the *New York Times,* the *Washington Post,* and the *International Herald Tribune.* It received half a page of commentary in the London *Financial Times* and a full page spread in the *Washington Times.*

In 1999, the book was selected by *Sapio* (Japan's equivalent of *Time Magazine*) as one of the twelve most important books to read in preparing for the 21st Century. At first, I was hard-pressed to understand why a country with 50 years of crass materialism superimposed on a base of Shintoism and Buddhism would become so enamored with a book that was largely Christian in its content. Then it hit me. Having suffered first-hand the devastating consequences of nuclear attack, the Japanese have an abiding interest in resolving differences through non-violent means.

At last count, the book was in its 12th printing and has come to be viewed as a seminal work in the field of religion and international affairs. In October of 2014, Georgetown University sponsored a major event celebrating the 20th anniversary of its publication, and CSIS did the same on its 25th anniversary in February of 2019. Some of this recognition was no doubt attributable to the three-part strategy that underpinned the book's development and its later outreach, a strategy that was designed to ensure the widest, relevant readership for the new ideas.

First, having the book come out under the auspices of CSIS made it more likely to resonate with policymakers because of the Center's long-held reputation for tough-minded scholarship—scholarship that generally reflected a Cold War, steely-eyed, political/military bent to foreign affairs and the clear implication that the most effective way to resolve conflict was by defeating the opposing side. Second, having the book published by Oxford University Press—- thought by many to be the best of the best—would give it considerable cachet within academia. Finally, a concerted attempt was made throughout the book to purposely understate the significance of the findings.

Because the theme of the book would be a difficult sell to the "realist" school of international relations, it was absolutely crucial to avoid even the faintest hint of exaggeration anywhere along the way, lest it invite criticism and risk undermining the credibility of the basic argument. This aspect didn't escape the scrutiny of Francis Fukuyama (of *End of History* fame), when he reviewed the book for *Foreign Affairs,* the leading scholarly journal for foreign policy practitioners: "The editors' concluding comments try not to overstate the positive role of religion, but the book brings badly needed balance into the discussion of religion and international affairs."

On a more practical note, the book's success probably also related to an assumption I made at the outset that the only way for any single book to attract attention in the midst of a sea of competing volumes was for it to have an exciting cover [38] and an intriguing title. Then, and only then, might the casual observer actually open the book to examine its contents. In addition, I sought the advice of Walter Laqueur, a prolific and widely-published CSIS scholar; and he advised that I not lean solely on the publisher to promote the book, since they typically don't do much on that score. Armed with this advice, I was able to secure a foundation grant in the amount of $10,000 a year for three years to support a personal push in marketing the book, largely through public speaking engagements, radio interviews, and television appearances across the country and overseas.

The Essence

It has been said that the art of diplomacy is letting someone else have your way. To the extent this is true, it becomes easier to achieve if diplomats have a nuanced appreciation for the positive role that religious leaders and institutions can play in advancing diplomatic interests. As illustrated in the book's case studies, religious leaders and institutions can, and often do, play a role in addressing political differences that would otherwise result in conflict. Under the right circumstances, their credibility as independent sources of moral authority enables them to build trust and bridge differences between adversaries. Moreover, in selected instances, they are also able to capitalize on the transcendent aspects of an adversary's personal religious faith in overcoming the secular obstacles to peace (by effectively shifting one's accountability to God rather than to some ideology, political movement, or ethnic agenda). This, in turn, often elicits better behavior as well.

The situations that most lend themselves to religious mediation are those in which a mutually debilitating impasse has been reached or where the major political, economic, and security issues have largely been resolved (thereby clearing the way for a breakthrough at a higher level of trust, which the religious third party brings).

The challenge, however, increases significantly if opposing religions are involved. When reconciling disaffected religious factions, interfaith dialogue is often offered as a suggested remedy. However, its perceived worth is probably overrated, if it only amounts to *ad hoc* meetings and a sterile exchange of views about one another's belief systems. If, on the other hand, it includes a mandate for action and a commitment to meet on an ongoing basis, then the

---

[38] The cover that I chose was a fresco by Raphael found in the Apostolic Palace in Rome, which depicts Pope Leo I meeting Attila the Hun in 452 AD in order to dissuade him from sacking Rome (successfully, as it turned out).

relationships that result will likely lead to increased trust and an ability to go much further in reconciling differences.

In the larger picture, though, the strategic premise is that religious peacemakers, when properly trained and supported, can add a critically important dimension to the work of diplomats in dealing with problems of communal identity that often exceed the grasp of traditional diplomacy[39]. In some situations, this added capability can make the telling difference between failure and success by providing (1) an improved ability to identify and deal with any religious issues and (2) a transcendent environment for dealing with deep-seated differences.

Just as religious leaders have major contributions to make in the field of diplomacy, so too do diplomats have a great deal to offer to religious peacemaking. First and foremost, they can bring the secular assets of their governments to bear in useful ways that can reinforce or build upon the efforts of religious peacemakers. This, however, needs to be an arms-length kind of activity, lest any perception of government ownership of the process undermine the very initiative it seeks to support (by destroying the perceived neutrality of that process with the intrusion of the government's own political agenda).

An excellent illustration of how this works can be found in the role played by the governments of Italy and the United States in concert with the lay Catholic Community of St. Egidio as they collaborated in resolving a long-running civil war in Mozambique in the 1990s. The final breakthrough to peace evolved from the Community's recognition that it needed to do something to resolve the conflict if the humanitarian assistance it was providing was to have any useful long-term impact. Accordingly, it took steps to win the trust of both sides and then engage them in a round of peace talks. In the final stage of those talks, the Community included diplomats from Italy, the United States, Portugal, France, and the United Nations in the process. They, in turn brought the resources of their respective countries to bear in overseeing the signing of the peace agreement, monitoring the cease-fire, and guaranteeing fair elections. Throughout this entire process, Italy and the

---

[39] Years later when commenting on her own book, *The Mighty and the Almighty* during a public presentation, former Secretary of State Madeleine Albright paid tribute to *Religion, the Missing Dimension of Statecraft:* "About a dozen years ago, when I was just beginning to think about writing a book on religion and foreign policy, I discovered in my research that Doug had already written it. So, I did what any self-respecting author would do and borrowed from him as many ideas as I could short of outright plagiarism. To be clear, I had his permission and it helped that we were thinking along the same lines."

United States played helpful, but largely invisible, roles behind the scenes in facilitating the Community's efforts.

Collectively, the above actions led to peace in Mozambique under a democratically-elected government, with an economy that, until later devastating natural disasters, was on the rebound and outperforming the rest of the continent—all because official diplomacy was able to reinforce and build upon the trust developed by a religious third party.

Translating Theory to Action

"Peace is not the absence of conflict; it is the ability to handle conflict by peaceful means." —Ronald Reagan

When I began my efforts, I viewed the book as an end in itself; but because of its surprising impact, I became inspired to walk the talk by establishing a new Program in Preventive Diplomacy at CSIS. To lead the program, I hired Joe Montville as the program director and David Steele as his deputy. Joe is a retired foreign service officer who had served on the Steering Committee for the book and who was the first person to have coined the term "Track Two Diplomacy" (unofficial diplomacy) in an article he authored in 1981 for *Foreign Policy Magazine*. David is an ordained minister in the United Church of Christ, who left the ministry to work in the field of conflict resolution and who had conducted valuable research on two of the chapters in the book. In addition to my other Center duties, I chaired the program, and we hired a couple of additional staff as well.

The program's first initiative consisted of training religious clergy and laity in the Balkans on the principles and techniques of conflict resolution. Because this was our first attempt to operationalize some of the concepts described in *Religion, the Missing Dimension of Statecraft*, it warrants a fuller explanation. First and foremost, because war was actually being waged on multiple fronts between the various religious and ethnic groups, the purpose of our workshops was to encourage and empower the religious communities in the former Yugoslavia to assume a leadership role in sponsoring peacemaking and conflict resolution initiatives. Toward this end, the workshops were inclusive in nature, with representation from the Catholic, Orthodox, Muslim, Protestant and Jewish faiths in Serbia, Croatia, and Bosnia & Herzegovina. They also included a tiered approach to the training that focused first on people, then problems, and finally systems.

At the outset, it was unreasonable to expect participants to engage in joint problem-solving with others who they didn't trust and with whom they had no prior relationship. To overcome this hurdle, we began the process by giving individual participants the opportunity to express their grievances. As each of them shared the tragedies that had befallen them or their families at the hands of another ethnic group seated around the table, empathy slowly began to take hold; and after the first few presentations, the atmosphere changed accordingly. Helping them to recognize that today's aggressors were often yesterday's victims frequently resulted in a reevaluation of the roles (both helpful and unhelpful) that each ethnic group had played in the near and distant past. This walk through history, in turn, led to some amazingly open acknowledgements by individual participants of the transgressions committed by their own ethnic groups.

We then examined the psychology underlying the transition from being a victim of aggression to becoming an aggressor one's self, with an eye toward identifying those points in the cycle where intervention aimed at forgiveness and reconciliation might be possible. The concept of forgiveness was presented, not in terms of letting an aggressor off the hook, but in terms of healing one's self. Its purpose was to enable victims to let go of their hatred and any corresponding need to get even. With the act of forgiving, one does not forget the past, but rather opts for a new tomorrow by consciously breaking the cycle of revenge. In this context, the justice that one seeks is restorative, rather than retributive in nature.

The second-level seminars, in addition to continuing the focus on attitudinal change, were designed to impart the problem-solving capabilities that would be needed to mediate differences and settle local disputes. This included developing effective communication, problem-solving, and mediation skills. Some of the participants later became involved in negotiating local disputes; and, in at least one instance, provided back-channel communications in support of higher-level, formal negotiations.

The third-level seminars focused on identifying creative roles that religious communities could undertake to support positive social change and develop improved relations within and between neighboring republics. They drove home the point that all such conflict resolution initiatives should be geared toward achieving the larger goal of building a harmonious civil society. In this case, that meant empowering enlightened people of faith to promote democratic pluralism and social justice, as well as peace.

Several additional aspects of this effort are also deserving of mention:

- Selection of the right target audience for the workshops was extremely important if the training was to have its desired impact. Above all, this meant recruiting individuals who could effectively leverage what they had learned, such as teachers and journalists.

- Diversity of staff was also a major contributor to the project's success. The conflict resolution team consisted of an American, a Russian woman, a Pole and a Dutchman; and it collectively included expertise in theology, psychology, sociology, anthropology, cross-cultural communications, and political analysis (in addition to conflict resolution). With this international flavor and professional breadth, the team was able to provide a global, multi-disciplinary perspective that avoided the problem of "Here come the Americans, telling us what to do again." By the same token, it sometimes complicated the task of achieving a smooth and well-integrated flow.

- Ongoing support at the local level was also essential, which required the engagement of on-scene, partnering institutions to reinforce critical aspects of the training and to initiate follow-on projects that could address the systemic problems relating to social structure.

It should be noted that every one of these workshops concluded with the participants developing an action agenda which they resolved to pursue on a joint basis. These action items ranged from taking steps to influence their political leaders in positive directions to publishing and distributing multi-faith newsletters in their communities to implementing helpful initiatives in the schools. Although some of these efforts didn't always prove feasible, they often led to others that did. Significantly, these action agendas were developed without any prompting from the workshop facilitators.

Finally, one needs to understand what there is about religious reconciliation that provides its unique potential for addressing identity-based conflicts. Briefly stated, the moral and spiritual nature of religious involvement brings with it a long tradition of teachings based on neighborly concern and the betterment of humanity. Even if the predominant expression of any given group's religiosity may have been distorted by excessive nationalism, that doesn't necessarily pervert the entire core of its tradition. Indeed, even in these compromised situations, it is not unusual to find strong voices of dissent from within the faith, challenging any sectarian tendencies as they arise.

Local religious leaders also frequently enjoy high esteem and influence at the grassroots level. In the former Yugoslavia, for example, there are any number of priests and imams who enjoy greater credibility with their people than do the politicians. Most of the latter are either "reconstructed" communists or newcomers to positions of social prominence. Clergy, on the other hand, have typically enjoyed a long-term relationship with the people and a history of resistance to communism. Consequently, they are usually better-positioned to mediate or negotiate differences from a posture of neutrality and compassion.

One of the more unfortunate aspects of the conflict was the degree to which religion was being manipulated by the politicians to promote nationalistic goals. Among the more egregious examples were those perpetrated under the auspices of the Serbian Orthodox Church.[40] On more than one occasion, Serb soldiers proceeded directly from partaking in holy communion to massacring Muslim "enemies" and carving crosses on their bodies.

An Orthodox priest in one of our seminars told of a Serb commander who ordered the killing of everyone in a Bosnian village and then oversaw its execution. He later asked this priest if he could ever be forgiven. To be sure, there were also acts of love by Orthodox priests toward their neighbors and, in some cases, their enemies, but they were sadly few and far between.

What is not widely known is the fact that many of those who participated in such massacres later committed suicide, particularly those who had participated against their will. This ability to manipulate the Serbian church faded with time as church leaders eventually found the courage to stand on religious principle in resisting such efforts. Thus, religious communities, even when they may have been compromised politically, are capable of generating constructive initiatives in reconciliation and peacemaking when they put their minds to it. Indicative of this potential is an exchange that took place between Peter Kuzmic, a good friend who leads a Pentecostal Seminary in Osijek, Croatia, and the Muslim Mayor of the Bosnian town of Bihac:

> *"During our visit, I asked the mayor, "How is it that we get along so well? You are a Muslim and I am a Christian." He smiled and said, "That's because I am not the kind of Muslim your friends from the West think about when they hear the word Muslim, and you are not the kind of Christian that Muslims think about when we hear the word Christian."*
>
> *I have a Muslim name, I am culturally Muslim, but I'm not really a devout Muslim. I don't pray regularly, and I don't know*

---

[40] Because Bosnia was assimilated into Ottoman culture to a much greater degree than Serbia when both were conquered by the Ottoman Turks in the 14th century, including their religious conversion to Islam, Serbs typically look down on Bosnians, considering them to have been "Turkified." Hence their attempt to eradicate all signs of Bosnian culture in the most recent war, including a purposeful targeting of Bosnia's National Library, in which more than 700 priceless manuscripts went up in smoke.

what my level of commitment to Mohammed is. But I am now very much interested in your Jesus because of what your organization has done to alleviate human suffering and bring the word of hope and life into this situation of despair and death.

You are not the kind of Christian that fits the mental image we have of Christians, because you have not come for territorial gain or with a political agenda or ethnic propaganda. Instead, you have loved us without pushing your religion down our throats." Then he added something that amazed me: "You have credibility with us because of your vulnerability with us. Because you became vulnerable with us and helped us."

During the latter stages of our involvement, we were invited to participate in a series of White House meetings to coordinate the separate efforts of NGOs in the rebuilding of Bosnia. During these sessions, I pressed hard for the creation of multi-ethnic reconstruction teams as a way of incorporating reconciliation as an integral part of the reconstruction process. My assumption was that if a Bosnian observed a Serb helping to rebuild his home (which other Serbs had destroyed), that might prove helpful in rebuilding relationships as well. It seemed clear that any good will generated by bricks and mortar accomplishments were likely to prove short-lived in the absence of mended relationships. I don't know what, if anything, came of my suggestion, but I think the logic was sound.

The training we provided in the Balkans took place while war was being waged; so, there was considerable risk involved, both for us and for the trainees who participated. It was in response to this risk that David Abshire (who by this time had re-claimed the presidency of CSIS) advised me that the Center's board was concerned about its fiduciary liabilities if something should happen to one or more of our staff and suggested that we refrain from going into war zones.

At one point, our training team had been trapped in Sarajevo while the city was under siege from Serb gunners in the surrounding hills. The team finally escaped on foot over a mountain, after paying a local youth to show them the way. So the board's concerns were well-placed; but when I conveyed Dave's suggestion to the program staff, David Steele responded by saying, "The Lord has instructed me to work in these settings." My response was "Maybe so, but He told me to tell you to lay low for a while."

It was this development that started me to thinking about the need for a different kind of organization to sponsor our efforts, one where board members would know from day one that going in harm's way was part of what we do. So, on August 1 of 1999, I left the think tank to form a "do tank," the International Center for Religion & Diplomacy.

The Birth of a Dream

"We learn from history that we do not learn from history."
–George Wilhelm Friedrich Hegel (1770-1831)

As noted earlier, religion was totally off the U.S. policymaker's screen for most of the 20th century. Indeed, it was barely mentioned in Hans Morgenthau's *Politics Among Nations* published in 1948, which had served as the bible for foreign policy practitioners since the beginning of the Cold War. Because the overriding challenge of that war was to contain the "godless" Soviets, there was little reason to miss its absence.

Going back even further, though, for more than two hundred years, the influence of Enlightenment prejudice worked to purge religion from the Western policymaker's calculus on the basis that religion was to have a diminishing influence in the affairs of humankind as secular humanism took increasing hold. Yet, at any given point in time, there are typically somewhere between 30 to 40 major conflicts taking place in different parts of the world, with about half of them incorporating religious dimensions of varying degree. Whether religion is the root cause of a particular conflict or a mobilizing vehicle for ethnic or nationalist passions (or merely a badge of identity), it is clearly central to much of the strife that is currently taking place. We live in an age of rage; and although the majority of religious movements are peaceful, errant ideologies in some are exacerbating that rage by justifying and encouraging violence.

Consistent with the fact that ideologies need to be countered with better ideas, those steeped in religion have to also be challenged on religious grounds. When one considers the fact that human nature instinctively aspires to a higher order of things (with close to 84% of the world's seven billion inhabitants deriving their reason for being from their religion) and that religion has long been a driving force in personal and group behavior, its past neglect in the conduct of foreign policy has been more than a little strange. Ironically, its purposeful exclusion was not the product of rational analysis but rather a predictable outgrowth of dogmatic secularism coupled with economic determinism. Whatever the reason, religion's role in today's conflicts is clearly too important to be marginalized. It was to rectify this glaring oversight that the International Center for Religion & Diplomacy (ICRD) was born.

On a Wing and a Prayer

"Ah, but a man's reach should exceed his grasp. Or what's a heaven for?"
—*Robert Browning (1812-1889)*

For at least a year prior to establishing ICRD, I thought I should wait to make it happen until I had raised at least three years of operating costs, so it could begin on a solid financial footing. After a while, I realized how unrealistic this was, and eventually launched the enterprise in August of 1999 with a sum total of $10,000 donated by David Vander Mey, a close friend who later served—and continues to serve— with distinction on ICRD's board of directors. Even though I didn't take a salary during the first year, $10,000 is not a lot of money. Fortunately, another good friend by the name of Dick Ruffin, who was then serving as Executive Director of the U.S. chapter of MRA, let us use two rooms in his office suite on a rent-free basis for our first year of operations. Further, another former naval officer by the name of Bob Bovey, who I had known from submarine days, volunteered to serve as the Center's Executive Vice President on a *pro bono* basis. Beyond that, an incredibly able young scholar by the name of Jonathan Eastvold served as our research assistant and Tonya Leyman as our administrative assistant.

When interviewing for the research position, Jonathan commented that he had dreamed of working for an organization like ICRD since the age of three. I remember thinking to myself at the time, "I don't know what I was doing at the age of three, but it certainly wasn't dreaming about this Center." As it was, I was only able to pay him subsistence wages, and a very meager subsistence at that. Despite the bare-bones nature of our beginning, we immediately hit the ground running as we undertook our first project in the Sudan.

The Way Ahead

When I first established the Center, I had in mind forming what one might call an "insider's club" — a small, but highly effective organization on which governments, the UN, and others could call to handle important but highly difficult tasks. To make this vision a reality, though, would require that those who subscribed to the *Realist School* of international relations be persuaded that under the right conditions, religious leaders and institutions can play a critical role in advancing peace in situations where other forces cannot. To convince the doubters and promote the future inclusion of religious considerations in the practice of U.S. foreign policy, I leaned heavily on my political/military credentials to craft the following argument.

Selling the Concept

For a number of years, defense planners have been wrestling with the challenges of "asymmetric threats," a term associated with creative, unconventional attacks by disadvantaged opponents against more powerful adversaries—-much like that used by Bin Laden on 9/11 to rock the United States back on its heels. In response to this challenge, the Pentagon came up with a new strategy called "Irregular Warfare," which requires a much tighter coordination between defense, diplomacy, and development. This is all to the good, but there are simply not enough resources in national treasuries to protect any given country against the full spectrum of possible asymmetric threats. What is needed instead, is an asymmetric counter to these threats, one that addresses the ideas behind the guns. This sounds reasonably straightforward, but it is complicated by the religious nature of those ideas.

As has been abundantly clear from our recent military interventions in Iraq and Afghanistan, the United States has little ability to deal with religious differences in hostile settings or to counter demagogues like Osama Bin Laden—and, before him, Slobodan Milosevic—who manipulate religion for their own purposes. It is no small irony that one of the most religious nations on the face of the planet is finding it so difficult to deal with the religious imperatives that all-but-dominate today's geopolitical landscape.

Among the reasons, three stand out. First has been our long-held commitment to the rational-actor model of decision making that has governed America's practice of international relations for as long as I can remember. This model considers religion to be irrational and therefore outside the policy maker's calculus. In other words, we simply don't know how to deal with it. Second is the fact that we have let our separation of church and state serve as an excuse for not doing our homework to understand how religion informs the worldviews and political aspirations of others (who do not similarly separate the two).

Finally, there are the operational constraints stemming from the political ambiguities surrounding our separation of church and state, which hinder our ability to respond effectively. Because religion in the West is so compartmentalized, government and industry have typically run for the hills whenever they have heard the word, for fear of being accused of favoring one faith tradition over another. The extraterritorial extension of this mindset, in turn, has caused many of our political and military leaders to ignore the religious dimensions of the threats they are facing. Consequently, we often end up fighting with one hand tied behind our back.

Faith-Based Diplomacy: An Asymmetric Counter

The specter of religious extremism married to weapons of mass destruction only adds to the urgency of bridging this gap. One approach for doing so that has shown unusual promise is a new form of engagement called "faith-based diplomacy." At the macro level, this term simply means incorporating religious considerations into the practice of international politics. At the micro level, it equates to making religion part of the solution to some of the intractable, identity-based conflicts that are posing such a problem for traditional diplomacy. Since its inception, ICRD has been practicing this form of diplomacy in selected trouble spots around the world as it seeks to address "the ideas behind the guns." Examples of how we have done this in such places as Sudan, Kashmir, Pakistan, and Saudi Arabia are provided in later chapters.

An Important Caveat

"My life is my message." –Mahatma Gandhi

The innovative dimension of this work is its reliance on commonly-held religious values as a catalyst for positive change. Religious reconciliation has great potential to combat religious extremism, and act as an "asymmetric counter" to that particular threat. In other words, the best antidote for bad theology is good theology. That said, it is important to recognize up-front that faith-based diplomacy is not well-suited for government practitioners. In the West, the legal constraints relating to church/state separation get in the way. The same holds true for a government's political agenda, which inevitably compromises the balanced neutrality normally required to mediate serious differences between adversaries. Not only do religious leaders and NGOs have neither of these constraints, but they often enjoy a unique maneuverability that enables them to sidestep obstacles that would otherwise stall more traditional actors.

Thus, the task must fall to religious leaders themselves or to NGOs like ICRD that are equipped to take it on. Whoever is carrying the torch, it is challenging work; and success doesn't come easily. First, in addition to requiring a special set of skills, it is physically, emotionally, and psychologically draining. It also carries no small degree of risk, since more than a few spiritually-minded peacemakers have paid the ultimate price for their efforts – Mahatma Gandhi, Martin Luther King Jr., Anwar Sadat, Yitzhak Rabin, the list goes on. But despite the risks and whatever discomfort one may feel in navigating the relatively uncharted waters of spiritual engagement, the stakes are simply too high for us not to give it our best effort.

The Ultimate Challenge

For the better part of human history, war has been the norm. According to the University of Oslo and the Norwegian Academy of Sciences, there have been no fewer than 14,000 wars in the world since 3500 BC; which means the world has been relatively peaceful for less than 5 percent of the time over the last 5600 years.

It has never ceased to amaze me how quick people are to romanticize the idea of going to war whenever they feel offended or in any way threatened by some other group or country. Yet those who survive the horrors of that experience seldom, if ever, want to talk about it. One trip around the orthopedic ward of a military hospital suggests why.

War is the ultimate indictment of the human race, and we will need to find better ways to resolve our differences if humankind is ever to realize its full potential. Hopefully, faith-based diplomacy coupled with religious reconciliation can help pave the way as a force for good in our increasingly troubled world.

"Given American intellectual history, it is in a sense not at all surprising that Americans should think about foreign policy in religious terms…Religious revivals are what the United States seems to have instead of revolutions; it is a land of prophets, not philosophers…"

Frances Fitzgerald
New Yorker Magazine
November 11, 1985

Chapter Nine

EXPANDING THE BASE

Do all the good you can, by all the means you can, in all the ways you can, in all the places you can, at all the times you can, to all the people you can, as long as ever you can.

John Wesley

In addition to operationalizing the concept of faith-based diplomacy, it was also necessary to establish the intellectual basis for the varying stages of its practice along the way. *Religion, the Missing Dimension of Statecraft* made a strong case for empowering religious clergy and laity as third-party mediators in conflicts where a higher level of trust was essential to achieving a breakthrough to peace, and it was having an impact.

> *"I urge anyone concerned about conflict in today's world, in reading this book, to take into account the import of its message."*

Jimmy Carter
from the Foreword of
Religion, The Missing Dimension of Statecraft

None of the conflicts examined in this book, however, were precipitated by religious differences. To deal with those that are, we published *Faith-Based Diplomacy: Trumping Realpolitik* in 2003.

Religious Disputes

"Let there be no compulsion in religion." —*Quran, Surat Al Baqarah verse 56*

This second book was also an edited volume published by Oxford University Press, and it focused on how the peacemaking tenets of different religions could be brought to bear in ongoing conflicts in which those religions were actively engaged. For Hinduism, the conflict in question was Kashmir; for Buddhism, Sri Lanka; for Judaism, the Middle East; for Christianity, Bosnia and Kosovo; and for Islam, the Sudan.

This was no small undertaking in light of the conventional wisdom that religious-based conflicts are inherently intractable owing to the absolutism that often accompanies religious convictions. Or, so it is assumed. This has undoubtedly been the thinking behind the fact that religion has never been at the table (not even in a one-off capacity) in any of the past Middle East peace initiatives. Despite the fact that most policymakers assume religion to be part of the problem (and therefore tend to neglect its peacemaking potential), a strong case can actually be made for making it part of the solution. In the Middle East, for example, having religious leaders involved in the peace process could prove advantageous on three possible fronts.

First, it would enhance the moral authority of the deliberations. The conclusion of the first civil war between the Islamic north and the Christian/African Traditionalist south of Sudan following its transition to independence in 1955 was mediated by the World Council of Churches and the All-African Council of Churches. Then, as now, the Muslims held 90% of the power; but when I queried high-level Sudanese Muslims who were involved in those negotiations as to why they let these two Christian organizations mediate the peace, they said "it was because of the moral authority that they brought."

Second, the presence of religious leaders in future Middle East peace initiatives would provide a capability for dealing with religious issues, which past lineups have not. In the wake of the failed 2000 Camp David Summit, for example, Dr. Ronald Hassner, a Berkeley political science professor, concluded it was the failure to include religious leaders in the process or even to consult with religious experts prior to the negotiations that led to the collapse of negotiations over the final disposition of Jerusalem. As he put it, "Both parties seem to have assumed that the religious dimensions of the dispute could be ignored. As a result, neither party had prepared seriously for the possibility that the Temple Mount issue would come to stand at the heart of the negotiations."[41] Further, political scientist Dr. Menahem Klein, who advised the Israeli government during those same negotiations, confirmed

---

[41] This insensitivity to religious concerns in one of the most religiously-attuned parts of the world is all the more puzzling when one considers the central role America has played in past Middle East peace negotiations. Not only has this region been crucial to U.S. national security; but in its capacity as one of the more religious nations on the face of the planet, the United States should understand better than most how forcefully faith can drive action.

that "The professional back channels did not sufficiently treat Jerusalem as a religious city..."

Finally, if one wants whatever political settlement emerges from such deliberations to be lasting in nature, religious leaders will need to feel a sense of ownership in that process because of their unrivaled influence at the grassroots level. Absent that, the settlement is likely to be viewed as an agreement between elites that won't necessarily resonate with those on the receiving end of its provisions.

> *"What is needed is an effective strategy of cultural engagement that incorporates religion as a tool for preventing problems from reaching the crisis stage. This book does an exemplary job of pointing the way toward constructing such a strategy."*
>
> Lee H. Hamilton
> former Chair, House Foreign Affairs Committee
> from the Foreword of
> *Faith-Based Diplomacy: Trumping Realpolitik*

Internal Adjustments

"Oh, it is excellent to have a giant's strength. But it is tyrannous to use it like a giant." —William Shakespeare (Measure for Measure)

Whenever I made presentations on the first book to the State Department or other diplomatic audiences, I was somewhat critical of our Foreign Service, accusing it of being largely indifferent to religion's influence. In response— and to their credit—the Foreign Service Officers in these audiences didn't get defensive. In fact, they readily admitted to having a blind spot.

As I looked around some 15 years later, noting that next to nothing had changed, I concluded the Foreign Service either didn't want to fill that blind spot or it didn't know how. Assuming the latter, I set about producing a third book that would address the organizational and legal adjustments that would be required for the U.S. government to deal effectively with the religious dimensions of today's conflicts.

In addressing this need, *Religion, Terror, and Error: U.S. Foreign Policy and the Challenge of Spiritual Engagement* sought to accomplish three important tasks. First, to show how religious considerations can be incorporated into the daily practice of U.S. foreign policy. Second, to provide a successor to the rational-actor model of decision-making that accommodates so-called "irrational" factors like religion and non-state actors. And finally, to offer a new paradigm for U.S. leadership that is better suited to an evolving multipolar world, one in which America leads more by example than by force. In spiritual terms, one might think of it as *servant leadership* at the international level.

Creating Buzz

To create increased awareness in Washington policy circles once the above book was published, we held a major book event at the National Press Club, which attracted a standing-room-only crowd. The event itself was moderated by Sally Quinn, a renown columnist for the *Washington Post,* and involved a panel of noteworthy commentators: Edwin Meese, former U.S. Attorney General in the Reagan Administration; James Glassman, former Undersecretary of State for Public Diplomacy and Public Affairs in the George W. Bush Administration, and the Reverend David McAllister-Wilson, President of Wesley Seminary.

Sally kicked off the proceedings with a warm welcome, after which I gave an overview of the book and its findings. This was followed with short presentations on various aspects of the book by each of the panelists; and then, with Sally moderating, we collectively fielded questions from the audience.

The event was billed as "a game-changer for effective engagement with the Muslim World;" but it actually encompassed a much broader mandate, citing past errors in American Foreign Policy with respect to its neglect of (or inappropriate response to) religious imperatives and explaining why the United States needed to rethink old assumptions, reject past practices, and create a new paradigm for U.S. leadership in the world.

Aside from the great turn-out (facilitated by Jan DuPlain, a good friend and terrific events coordinator), the rich discussion that ensued, and the considerable book sales that followed, most gratifying to me was Jim Glassman's tribute to our faith-based approach to diplomacy and Ed Meese's strong endorsement of the book's treatment of our country's separation of church and state. The latter included not only an interpretation of original intent (of the Founding Fathers), but a recommendation on how the existing political ambiguities surrounding its practice can be effectively addressed. He said it was as good as he had ever seen; and with his reputation as a formidable constitutional scholar, it was a meaningful endorsement.

Encountering Islam

One has to wonder why Christianity and Islam—two world religions that share more in common theologically than any other two—either talk past one another at best or, alternatively, resort to conflict to settle their differences. At least part of the answer lies in the fact that we speak two different languages. The Christian West speaks the language of secularism, while Islam speaks the language of integration (of religion and politics). When we in the United States use the term "secular", for example, Muslims hear "Godless", while what was intended was "freedom to worship as one pleases". Similar differences in interpretation apply to other terms as well, such as "crusade" and "jihad."

Contributing to the "Godless" interpretation of secularism is the unfortunate cultural image we sometimes project overseas. Far too often, when I find myself in some remote part of the world and turn on the television (if they have such a thing), the American program that fills the screen is the Jerry Springer Show, which is as offensive to us as it is to them, yet we seem powerless to do anything about it. Perhaps it is time for an amendment to the First Amendment.

Adding to the difficulties of differing interpretations of individual words are the choices of religious scripture used to inspire adherents in untoward behavior. When religious scripture is retrieved selectively and applied situationally, it can become a powerful tool for justifying the unjustifiable. In a context in which religious legitimacy trumps all, Al-Qaeda often leans on Surah 4, verse 89 of the Qur'an to justify extremist activities: "Slay the enemy wherever you find him." In isolation, this verse appears to promote an aggressive spirit of violence. However, if one continues on to verse 90, one finds the opposite to be the case: "If they leave you alone and offer to make peace with you, God does not allow you to harm them." Of course, this verse is never cited. The problem is that if religious terrorists, can point to a "precedent" in sacred scripture or tradition, opponents will find it difficult to dispute its morality, despite its obvious contradiction with the overarching spirit of the religion.

Beyond any considerations of language, though, Muslim grievances with the West are deep-seated and extend back in time to the Crusades, European colonialism and the loss of the Caliphate following World War I.[42] The West, on the other hand, is more concerned with the current surge in terrorism and the future demographic implications of Muslim immigration coupled with the wide disparity in European and Muslim birthrates. Many in the West feel that Muslim immigrants are taking undue advantage of Europe's hard-won tolerance and social liberties and are fearful that a continuation of this trend will ultimately threaten European cultural identities. Superimposed on all of this is the ongoing collision of globalization with traditional values, often embedded in religion. This third book examines the concerns of both communities in greater depth and explores the possibilities for finding an acceptable way forward.

The above realities contribute in significant measure to the fact that of the dozen-or-so conflict situations in which ICRD has been involved, all but one has had an Islamic interface. Although each of these interventions has required a unique approach tailored to the specific needs of that particular engagement, more general initiatives have also proven helpful.

For example, during ICRD's simultaneous involvements in Sudan and Kashmir, I invited four prominent leaders from the Sudan and two from Kashmir to attend the National Prayer Breakfast held annually in Washington. Included among them were the Foreign Minister of Sudan, a former Prime Minister (and now head of Sudan's leading opposition party), the Secretary General of the International People's Friendship Council (a co-sponsor of our project work in Sudan), and the General Secretary of the Sudan Council of Churches (also a co-sponsor). The Kashmiris included the President of the Kashmir Foundation for Peace and Development Studies (and former leader of a two-million strong Muslim militant movement) and a former leader of human rights initiatives in Kashmir. When it was over, all five of the Muslim participants expressed great surprise at the extent to which religious faith underpins our democratic process in the United States. They also commented that they felt much closer as a result. Clearly, personal interactions of this nature have a role to play in widening the bridges of mutual understanding.

---

[42] Yet another point of contention is captured in this statement by an unknown Islamic commentator about the influence of Franciscan monks in the Middle East: "The only missionaries we fear are the Franciscan monks. For 700 years they have given us fits. Our approach is to persuade potential converts with apologetics. We're great at arguing, but that doesn't work with the Franciscans. Instead of engaging us, they quietly go about our cities, serving everyone. Once people are served, they become interested in Christianity, and the next thing you know they've become followers of Jesus. Those Franciscan Christians don't fight fair with us."

Needed Realignments

In describing how the government should realign itself to deal more effectively with the causal factors underlying religious extremism, the book explains how existing capabilities could be redirected to respond to that challenge and then identifies additional capabilities that would be needed to complete the task. Included among the former are (1) an expanded role for military chaplains in preventing conflict; (2) development of a closer partnership with the American Muslim community that will enable policy makers and diplomats to capitalize on the extensive paths of influence which that community enjoys with Muslim communities overseas; and (3) closer coordination between our diplomatic and military efforts on the one hand and relevant Non-Government Organizations (NGOs) on the other. The latter often enjoy a longstanding credibility with the populations in question and at times command an unrivaled social space, extending from local organizations and civil society leaders to national governments and the United Nations.

Among the new capabilities that would prove helpful are (1) development of a proactive conflict-prevention capability in the form of Conflict Prevention Research Teams (consisting of regional experts, social science professionals, and situational combinations of professional practitioners from other disciplines) that could be deployed to unstable areas where conflict threatens and advise the U.S. government and other relevant organizations on measures that should be taken to defuse these situations; (2) establishment of a *religion attaché* as a new position in the Foreign Service that would be assigned to US missions in countries where religion has particular salience; and (3) the active promotion of *organic suasion* as a vehicle for promoting "peace from within."

The challenges to developing an effective prevention capability include three generic obstacles that must first be overcome. First, there is the need to think beyond one's "in box" in order to shape events, rather than merely react to them. In short, one has to move beyond the "crisis of the immediate." Second, is the difficulty of demonstrating one's effectiveness by proving a negative. In other words, how do you prove something didn't happen because of something that you did. Finally, and overriding all else, is the challenge of mustering the political will to act when most politicians are disinclined to sacrifice anything in the present to serve a larger goal in the future (when they may no longer be in office). Compounding this latter difficulty is the fact that democracies typically need a crisis before they can achieve the political consensus to act.

Religion attachés could provide Ambassadors with valuable insights and advice on developing religious trends and assist them in dealing with the complex religious issues that inevitably arise. Organizationally, they could be integrated within the Political Section of the Embassy staff (much like Political/Military Officers) to ensure their ongoing ability to have a meaningful impact. In short, their presence could go far in helping the United States avoid uninformed policy choices such as those it has made in the past in Vietnam, Iran, Lebanon, and Iraq.

It is estimated that a cadre of 30 such attaches could handle the country's global needs in this arena at an annual cost of $10 million. An expense of this magnitude for an improved ability to deal with the causal aspects of events like 9-11, pales in comparison to the billions being spent on symptoms (for baggage inspectors and the like).

Organic Suasion

Organic suasion is an important concept that deserves fuller explanation. Often the human body's best weapons against disease are its own internal biological defenses. Similarly, in a context where religious legitimacy trumps all else, the best antidote for religious ignorance is religious understanding. This is the basis for a concept in which religious extremism is moderated through organic interaction with members of the same faith tradition who are committed to living out the peaceful tenets of their theology. Ironically, demagogues like Bin Laden, who misappropriate religious scripture to justify their violent actions, unwittingly open the most effective avenues for countering such actions. This should come as no surprise in light of the fact that the core principles of most world religions, including Islam, are about peace, neighborly concern, the betterment of humanity, and one's relationship with one's Creator.

An early example of organic suasion took place in 2002 when a Yemeni judge, Hamoud Abdulhamid al-Hitar, and four of his friends challenged five al Qaeda prisoners to discuss the appropriate interpretation of the Qu'ran in relation to violence. In this high-stakes theological poker, the judge offered to join the prisoners' cause if the prisoners could convince him and his friends that their interpretation was correct. If, on the other hand, the judge and his friends prevailed, the prisoners were to renounce violence and work for peace. Several years later, those prisoners and several hundred others who followed had been released and were actively engaged in peacemaking. According to the judge, and as subsequently affirmed by European diplomats, the approach was highly successful— as least until later prisoners began abusing the opportunity by faking their newly professed convictions. Early on, however, some of the former militants led authorities to weapons caches and even provided advice on tracking former terrorist colleagues.

Other examples of this concept would include the approaches taken by ICRD in (1) promoting a cooperative spirit among next-generation leaders of the different religious communities of Kashmir, (2) securing the release of Korean missionaries held hostage by the Taliban, and (3) reforming the madrasas (religious schools) in Pakistan, each of which is described in later chapters.

Rules of Engagement

To illustrate how one might go about redirecting existing assets and taking the chaplains as an example, in early 2001 — months before the events of 9-11 — the U.S. Navy initiated a training program on religion and statecraft for all Navy, Marine Corps, and Coast Guard chaplains. The purpose of this training was to enhance the conflict-prevention capabilities of the sea service commands, which are typically at the cutting edge of our country's overseas involvements.

In addition to the favorable impact on book sales (as the Navy bought all 1300 chaplains a copy of *Religion, the Missing Dimension of Statecraft*), this training explored in considerable depth the benefits that could accrue from military chaplains establishing relationships of trust with local religious leaders when they are stationed overseas. It also examined the potential benefits of chaplains serving as advisors to their military commanders on (1) incipient threats to stability posed by local religious frictions, and (2) the religious (and cultural) implications of command decisions that are either being contemplated or may have already been taken. Finally, chaplains can also provide a reconciling influence in addressing any misunderstandings that might arise between their military commands and local religious communities.

I had the pleasure of leading the four-person team that conducted this training, which also included Donald Shriver, President Emeritus of Union Theological Seminary; Joseph Montville, Director of the CSIS Preventive Diplomacy Program; and Richard Ruffin, Executive Director of the US wing of MRA. All three of these gents were exceedingly able and a real pleasure to work with. Don was a giant in his field and had recently authored *An Ethic for Enemies,* a highly acclaimed book that makes a compelling case for incorporating forgiveness in politics as the most effective way to break the never-ending cycles of retaliation and revenge that all-too-often plague relations between nations. Joe was a retired Foreign Service Officer, a pioneer in the psychological aspects of conflict resolution, and an ardent champion of Track II Diplomacy.

Dick was a Rhodes Scholar and probably the most effective trainer of the four of us. He also has a fascinating pedigree. His forebearers founded the city of Richmond, which later became the capital of the Confederacy; and he is a direct descendant of Edmund Ruffin, a wealthy Virginia planter and slaveholder, who discovered he could increase the yield of his cotton fields by 40% if he fertilized them with calcium-rich soil from the Tidewater flats. Unfortunately, the digging, transporting, and spreading of that soil was a highly manpower-intensive operation, and Edmund became an even greater champion of slavery than he already was and a leading spokesman for seceding from the Union. In fact, he did all he could over a 20-year period to persuade southern governors to go this route and, although a civilian, was given the honor of firing the first shot of the Civil War. When the war was over, he wrapped himself in a Confederate flag and killed himself by firing what was probably one of the last shots of that ill-fated rebellion.

Dick, himself, is a deeply-caring person on whom the legacy of his slave-holding lineage weighs heavy and who is strongly committed to doing what he can to heal the wounds of America's racial history. Shortly after the turn of the millennium, he helped launch an MRA program titled "Hope in the Cities," which sponsored an event in Richmond for 500 of its citizens (from all stations in life) who jointly walked a significant slice of that city's history.

Among other destinations, this included visits to (1) the old slave auction block where slave ships disembarked their unfortunate cargo; (2) the platform on which a modern-day Patrick Henry, dressed in colonial attire, issued forth his famous challenge to "Give me liberty or give me death;" and (3) a well into which a black woman had just jumped to her death with her 21st and 22nd babies under her arms, not wanting to see them forced into slavery as all of their siblings had been (giving a slightly different twist to Henry's challenge). Although the walk took place on the hottest day of the year, it had a therapeutic effect on the participants, imbuing them with an empathy and respect for one another that had not previously existed.

The chaplains training, which took our team all over the world, was well received by the chaplains, with about a third of them enthusiastic about the possibility of an expanded mandate, another third quite willing to give it a try, and the remainder protesting that it wasn't why they had "signed up." Based on their performance during the program, it became obvious that with the right kind of training, the two-thirds who were supportive represented a formidable capability that could potentially be brought to bear to good effect, especially in situations where religion is an influential ingredient in the security equation. Capitalizing on this capability, however, would require two important steps. First, the line officer community would need to expand the rules of engagement (ROE) for its chaplains to include these new functions. And, second, the Chaplain Corps would have to adjust its personnel policies to support the new ROE by providing chaplains who wanted to participate in this manner with the opportunity to do so, perhaps through the development of an appropriate training subspecialty within the Corps.

Although the stakes skyrocketed with the attacks of 9/11, neither of the above measures has proven easy to address. During the course of the 2001 training program, for example, it became clear during visits to the various military commands that even if the chaplains were willing to take on the added functions, the line community was going to take further convincing. To address this aspect, I authored an article for the *U.S. Naval Institute Proceedings,* titled "We Ignore Religion at our Peril" in which I described the training that had taken place and made a strong case for capitalizing on the formidable potential of military chaplains to contribute to the nation's conflict prevention agenda.

The article had no apparent effect at the time, but it has been encouraging to note the progress that has taken place since then. For example, a later revision to the official publication that spells out the role of military chaplains in joint operations, expands their mandate to include engagement with local religious leaders and to serve as the chief religious and cultural advisors to their commanders.

At the end of the day, however, and as suggested above, the enlightened use of military chaplains is a function of the military commander's discretion. And here there is a bit of a problem. Little in the way of religious education is provided to prospective or current military commanders either at the Service Academies, the Command and Staff Colleges, or the various War Colleges. As a consequence, commanders in the field are essentially "winging It." To address this weakness, Pentagon planners should review the current training requirements for military officers, with an eye toward determining what additional training in religion and culture should be added at each stage in an officer's development to ensure that he or she can think both strategically and tactically about the influence of religious factors in their respective areas of responsibility. The stakes for getting this right can be very high.

Although much of the progress that has been achieved to date in empowering military chaplains for these new functions has been *ad-hoc* in nature and remains incomplete, the goal of enabling them to play an important role in preventing conflict (rather than solely dealing with the human casualties after it has erupted) makes sense for two important reasons. Not only will it give chaplains greater peace of mind, but the cost of avoiding conflict in the first instance will always pale in comparison to the loss of blood and treasure incurred in going to war. That alone should inspire us to give conflict prevention our absolute highest priority as we move into the future.

Perhaps the most telling hurdle that stands in the way of equipping the U.S. government to deal effectively with religious imperatives is the need to address the political ambiguities surrounding our separation of church and state. As mentioned earlier, it is these ambiguities that inhibit many of our political and military leaders from addressing the religious dimensions of the threats they may be facing. The book examines this challenge in considerable depth and explains how it could be readily overcome if the political will existed to do so.

Although, the book gets a bit technical in dealing with such things as alternative bureaucratic structures within the State Department to address certain aspects of the problem, it received the Book of the Year Award in 2011 from Foreword Reviews, the rating agency for universities and independent publishers. It placed first in the political science category and third in religion. I had to smile when I learned this, thinking it made perfect sense in light of my doctorate in Political Science and total absence of schooling in religion.

A Toe in the Water

Thus far, the State Department has taken a limited step forward through its establishment of a Religion and Global Affairs Office (RGA) in 2015 that originally reported directly to the Secretary of State. During the succeeding Administration, however, it was effectively marginalized through a loss of staff and influence and remains so to this day. At the same time, though, the long-established Office of International Religious Freedom has grown in prominence and stature (as a signature concern of the Evangelical community, whose influence weighed heavy in the political process during those years).

Establishment of the RGA Office resulted from a recommendation by a Working Group on Religion and International Affairs co-chaired by the White House and State Department and in which ICRD played a central role. Ironically, this development trailed by five years the establishment of a similar office in the French Ministry of Foreign Affairs. Even the authors of secularism understood the need to deal with religious influence in an enlightened manner. [43] Although the RGA represents a band-aid fix where major surgery is required (as outlined in *Religion, Terror, and Error*), it was clearly a step in the right direction.[44]

> *"This is a visionary approach that goes beyond the whole-of-government effort and which expands the current definition of smart power. From my two decades of experience in the Islamic world, I am convinced that the vast majority of Muslims would embrace this approach as a means of clearly expressing their beliefs and enabling them to understand ours."*

> General Anthony Zinni, USMC (Ret)
> former Commander-in-Chief, U.S.
> Central Command and former
> US. Special Envoy to the Middle East
> from the Foreword of *Religion, Terror, and Error*

Responding to a "dirty bomb" detonated in an American city would be an urgent matter. Proactive steps to prevent such a catastrophe should command the same degree of urgency.

---

[43] Another manifestation of French awareness took place during Algeria's struggle for independence. Whenever French forces found themselves in a precarious situation and were looking for a way out, it was their military chaplains that they sent out to negotiate with the Muslim insurgents.

[44] To some extent, the British beat everyone to the punch twenty years earlier by establishing within its Foreign Office a unit on preventive diplomacy and the role of NGOs in that context.

Representative Endorsements

1. *Religion, The Missing Dimension of Statecraft*

"While religious differences often stimulate or worsen confrontation, paradoxically the spiritual commonalities deep within all faiths promise a way to reconciliation. This book should serve to promote inter-religious understanding and add to the tools that diplomacy can employ for peace."

Boutros Boutros-Ghali
Secretary General, United Nations

2. *Faith-Based Diplomacy: Trumping Realpolitik*

"In a world that is burdened by an ever-widening gap between rich and poor, deadly conflicts of identity, permeable international borders, weapons of mass destruction, and suicidal terrorism, Faith-Based Diplomacy is a compelling and intellectually sound piece of work that bravely points the way toward a more promising future."

Zbigniew K. Brzezinski
former U.S. National Security Advisor

3. *Religion, Terror, and Error: U.S. Foreign Policy and the Challenge of Spiritual Engagement*

"This is the most important foreign policy book I have read in recent years. This book pulls off the huge accomplishment of turning the game completely around."

Dr. Stanton Burnett
CSIS Director of Studies;
former Counselor and Director of
European Affairs, U.S. Information Agency

Chapter Ten

FIRST BITE AT THE APPLE

Since acquiring independence from Britain in 1956, the Republic of Sudan had been ravaged on and off by protracted conflict between the Arab, Islamic north, and the rebellious Christian/African traditionalist south. The toll of this struggle was severe, totaling more than two million dead and 4.5 million displaced. The conflict, while fundamentally about political power and an inequitable distribution of resources, was cloaked in religious overtones.

My decision to establish the new Center was based in part on a desire to capitalize on the numerous relationships of trust that had been established around the world through the Prayer Breakfast fellowship (and selected other networks) by systematically bringing them to bear in promoting peace in trouble spots where conflict threatened or had already broken out. When I shared this idea with Doug Coe, he immediately lit up and said, "This has been the missing piece. We've always had the spiritual and relational dimensions, but we've never had the professional."

Soon thereafter, I also shared the vision with those involved in a weekly Ambassadors' Prayer Breakfast, which I had been attending for quite some time. After doing so, I was approached by Abubaker Ahmed, a member of the group and former Political Director in the Office of the President of Sudan, to see if our new Center could help bring an end to the civil war that had been raging between the Islamic North and the Christian/African Traditionalist South of his country for the past 16 years.

The Low-hanging Fruit

Normally, when launching a new enterprise, one goes for the low-hanging fruit, the easier challenges, in order to gain experience and establish credibility. Sudan represented quite the opposite—a seemingly intractable and highly complicated conflict that had already claimed two million lives and displaced more than four million others, and to which there would be no easy solution. Moreover, at that point in time, the country had been at war for a total of 33 years out of the 44 since achieving independence in 1956.

Breaking the Ice

In April of 1999, I traveled to Sudan with Abubaker to assess the situation and lay the groundwork for our possible future involvement once the new Center was established. With Abubaker's prior Ambassador-rank status, all doors to government officials were open, including that of the Foreign Minister, Mustafa Ismail. Mustafa was the first high-level official with whom I met; and our conversation was meaningful, if not a bit testy.

I told Mustafa there was a movement underway in the United States that was seeking to impress on the consciousness of all Americans the plight of South Sudan, much like Kosovo had been during the recent conflict in the Balkans. The movement itself was being spearheaded by several Senators and Congressmen who were attempting to rally U.S. support in opposing the inhumane tactics which the North had allegedly been using against the Christian South. I noted that this did not auger well for the North and suggested that to counter it, the regime should seize the moral high ground by announcing a bold stroke for peace. Although predictably defensive about the basic allegation, Mustafa asked what a "bold stroke" might look like. I asked him to give me a day to think it over, and I'd get back to him.

The next day I phoned Mustafa and suggested that within the next few months, the North should announce a date certain three years in the future on which the government would hold a country-wide referendum on granting independence to the South. Then use those three years to build desperately-needed infrastructure in the South, so that when the vote was finally taken, a majority of southerners would opt to remain unified with the North. I told him this was exactly what President Kenyatta had done in 1963, when Kenya achieved its independence. At that time, the upper third of the country wanted to break-off and become a part of Somalia, with which it shared a common border, religion, and ethnic roots. Kenyatta agreed to hold a referendum in three years and then used that interval to improve conditions in the north—to the point where they greatly exceeded those of Somalia when the final vote was taken. At that point, no one wanted to leave. Mustafa agreed to give it consideration, and we left it at that.

Although there were a number of NGOs working in Sudan when I made that first visit, almost all of them were engaged in the South, bringing needed relief to those who were suffering in the zones of conflict. With our unimpeded access in the North, however, I opted for a different strategy. Rather than dealing with the symptoms of the conflict, I decided we should address its causal aspects by establishing relationships of trust with the Islamic regime and from that vantage point, inspire it to take steps toward peace that it wouldn't otherwise consider.

Building Trust

A watershed moment in this strategy came in November of 2000 when ICRD in partnership with the Sudan Council of Churches (SCC) and the International People's Friendship Council (IPFC—the Sudanese equivalent of a Western Chamber of Commerce, with loose ties to the government) convened a meeting of 30 religious leaders and scholars from the Muslim and Christian communities to address the religious aspects of the conflict (and selected other religious issues that were contributing to social tensions more generally).

Because the stakes were high and we were feeling our way in developing this new form of diplomacy, I will describe in some detail exactly how we went about making something useful happen. So, reader, please excuse if any of this strikes you as a bit ponderous.

The greatest challenge leading up to the meeting was that of securing the Christian participation, because of their disillusionment stemming from three earlier inter-religious dialogue conferences the government had convened over the previous decade. These were international conferences involving a number of different countries; but in none of them, had the Sudanese Christians been able to voice their grievances. In fact, when they attempted to do so, they were deliberately drowned out. Based on this past experience, they had three principal concerns: that their views would not be heard, that nothing useful would come of it, and that it would once again provide PR benefits to the government at their expense.

These concerns were largely (but not totally) allayed by my assurances that (1) the basic purpose of the planned meeting was to develop action recommendations designed to benefit non-Muslim minorities (meaning that it would therefore be smaller in size and practically focused), (2) their concerns would, in fact, be heard because of their prospective leadership role in the meeting, and (3) the meeting would be off-limits to the media. In my spirited discussions on these matters with Enock Tombe, General Secretary of the Sudan Council of Churches (SCC), I rather unfairly trumped his concerns by noting that he, as a Christian, was called to be a peacemaker. Because the meeting was about achieving peace, he had no alternative but to attend. So he did, along with other Christian colleagues, albeit with their heels dragging.

Approach

To produce recommendations that could lead to meaningful change, a staged approach was adopted, in which a list of the specific issues to be addressed was developed and agreed to by the relevant parties in advance of the meeting. Qualified scholars were then engaged to prepare papers on over-arching themes that collectively encompassed all of the listed issues.

The prescribed format for each session of the meeting called for an assigned author to briefly distill the essence of his or her findings, after which a discussant would provide an alternative point of view (the Christian perspective, if an Islamic scholar had presented and vice versa). This was then followed by extensive discussion and debate. At the end of the second day, draft recommendations on each of the pre-approved issues, which were generally succinct and hard-hitting, were passed to the participants. They were then invited to consider these at their leisure, with an eye toward suggesting improvements or providing better ideas on the final day of the Forum. Additional recommendations relating to unanticipated issues that arose during the dialogue were also to be addressed on that final day.

Participants

The goal with respect to participation was to keep the size of the group to manageable proportions, with an equal split between Sudanese Muslims, Sudanese Christians, and international attendees from both faiths. Happily, that goal was met, with the 30 participants more or less equally divided between the three categories. In addition, several others also attended as special guests, including an American Episcopal Bishop, and an American businessman (both of whom were testing the waters with respect to possibly becoming members of our Center's board). Repeated attempts to secure the participation of an English-speaking, Sudanese African Traditionalist proved unsuccessful. The ranks of the "Traditionalists" were simply too splintered for any single member to be able to speak for the whole. Accordingly, a Southern scholar with academic expertise on that perspective provided input on a surrogate basis during the deliberations.

Proceedings

Each session was chaired by a figure of significant stature (to lend added weight to the occasion) and co-moderated by designated representatives from ICRD, the SCC, and the IPFC. All participants who took part did so in their religious or scholarly capacities, even though a number of them wore other hats as well.

Because Islam is so decentralized, religious scholars often have a broader influence over religious matters than do individual imams, whose reach beyond their respective mosques is often quite limited. One such scholar, who played a key role in the conference and with whom I formed a strong friendship, was Dr. Abdul-Rahim Ali M. Ibrahim. In addition to his formidable scholarly credentials, he also chaired the Shura Council, the governing body of the ruling party (serving as an ongoing force for good in an otherwise questionable regime).

Government officials participated in those sessions in which subjects within their respective areas of responsibility were being discussed, both to provide the government's perspective on existing policies and procedures and to hear first-hand any problems these policies might be causing and what might be done to address them..

Each evening, a prominent Sudanese political figure addressed the participants (and an expanded public audience) on a topic relating to the substantive agenda for that day. These included presentations by (1) Abel Alier, a widely-respected southern lawyer, who spoke on "Religious Tolerance and Co-existence in a Multi-ethnic Society", (2) Dr. Hasan al-Turabi, then Speaker of the Parliament, who spoke on "Shari'a (Islamic Law), Democracy, and Human Rights", and (3) Dr. Ibrahim Ahmed Omer, then Secretary General of the National Congress Party (the ruling party) who spoke on "Non-Muslims and the Shari'a".

Outcome

Although the meeting had incendiary potential in light of the deep grievances involved, it produced a genuine breakthrough in communications between the two sides and yielded 17 consensus recommendations that were designed to support interreligious cooperation on matters relating to human rights, education, employment, and humanitarian assistance (all areas in which religious minorities felt some degree of discrimination). Even more significant were the personal relationships that were established. What started out in frosty silence, ended with back-slapping, joking, and laughter.

The quality of the dialogue was unusually rich, both in its candor and in the thoughtfulness of the exchanges that transpired. Local Christian leaders commented that this was the first time they had ever been heard. A prominent Islamic scholar, who also served as an imam, remarked that he was totally unaware of some of the problems that had been discussed. And an elder statesman (a retired Sudanese diplomat) stated categorically that this was the first time in the history of the country that Northerners and Southerners had spoken to one another from the heart. He also said he had never before seen so much intellectual horsepower assembled in any single gathering as that which existed on the Muslim side in the meeting.

This Muslim makeup was not by accident. We were attempting to address a very basic question: what steps could an Islamic government take to alleviate the second-class status of non-Muslims in a Shari'a context? If we could come up with sound answers to that question and had highly credible Muslims around the table, then perhaps those answers could resonate in other Muslim-majority countries like Indonesia and Pakistan, where similar tensions existed.

The credibility of our effort was considerably enhanced by the political endorsement of Dr. Ali Osman Taha, the First Vice President of Sudan (and second in command), who in the aftermath also reviewed the recommendations, with an eye toward early implementation. Further, a report on the results of the meeting was forwarded to the Inter-Governmental Authority on Development (IGAD—a consortium of East African countries officially charged with mediating the Sudanese conflict). For quite some time, religious issues had contributed to a stalemate in the IGAD's deliberations. The hope behind our initiative was to complement that body's efforts by engaging religious experts to deal with the religious issues and in so doing, free up the IGAD to achieve closure on other fronts.

Faith-based Diplomacy

The success of the meeting was attributable to the fact that it (1) engaged as co-sponsors credible indigenous institutions, representing the differing points of view that would need to be accommodated; (2) recruited balanced representation from both sides in terms of numbers and stature; (3) determined in advance the desired outcome, and devised an effective strategy for achieving it; and (4) found ways to incorporate a meaningful spiritual dimension in the proceedings. On balance, it was the last factor, the faith-based nature of the undertaking, that probably weighed the heaviest in contributing to a successful outcome.

Each day the proceedings began with prayers and readings from the Bible and the Qur'an. This was preceded earlier in the morning by an informal prayer breakfast for the international participants and local Muslim and Christian religious leaders (on a rotating basis). Finally, and perhaps most importantly, we brought with us a prayer team all the way from California—halfway around the world—whose sole purpose was to pray and fast for the success of the deliberations during the four days of the meeting.

The prayer team was led by Brian Cox, an Episcopal priest from Santa Barbara, who was voluntarily serving as ICRD's Vice President for Dispute Resolution Training. When he called me from California to ask what I thought about him bringing a prayer team, I said, "I can't imagine that folks who pray five times daily are going to get upset if we bring a prayer team" and strongly encouraged him to do so. The prayer team's efforts were buttressed by an equal number of Sudanese Pentecostals who also joined in the effort.

Over the four days of the meeting, one could see members of this joint prayer team slipping into the proceedings and sitting quietly on the sidelines to determine exactly what to pray for, then returning to the team to better focus its efforts. These activities coupled with appropriate breaks in the proceedings for Muslim prayer times provided a transcendent environment that inspired participants to rise above their personal or religious differences and to begin working toward a common good. From start to finish, the dialogue was cordial and respectful (Addendum O).

Another aspect of this faith-based undertaking took place in the months leading up to the November meeting during the various conversations I would have with high-level Sudanese officials. These would typically be *realpolitik* discussions in which I would be trying to persuade them that what we were suggesting was in their own best interest to do, but all the while looking for convenient opportunities to make a helpful reference to the Qur'an or to what the Prophet (PBUH) might have done or to how Jesus might have reacted. I found that integrating faith into the discussions inspires Muslims to open up, because they feel inherently more comfortable operating within a spiritual framework than they do in dealing with purely secular constructs. This is true even when it involves faiths other than their own. It is their comfort zone.

Implementation

Implementing the recommendations of the November 2000 meeting became the focus of our efforts over the next two years, especially those that we thought could have the greatest impact. The most far-reaching of these was the task of establishing an Inter-Religious Council that would bring top

Muslim and Christian religious leaders together on a monthly basis to address the religious aspects of the conflict, ease social tensions more generally, and formulate policy recommendations to alleviate the second-class status of non-Muslim minorities. Forming such a Council would also constitute a meaningful first-step toward implementing a number of the other recommendations that emerged from the meeting.

Establishing the Sudan Inter-Religious Council (SIRC) took much longer than it should have for several semi-related reasons: the intense sensitivities involved; the formidable bureaucratic hurdles to be overcome in giving it proper legal status; the need to recruit religious leaders for the Council who not only enjoyed considerable influence, but who were open to thinking in new directions; and the overriding need for a gifted leader who commanded the respect of both faith communities and had the managerial and inter-personal skills to pull it all together.

Adding to the above challenges was the absence of a constant ICRD presence. We didn't have sufficient resources to open a local office; so whenever Abubaker and I left town, any forward momentum we had been able to establish came to an abrupt halt. This paralysis derived from the fact that our interactions with Sudanese officials had generally been confined to top decision-makers. In our absence, the second and third-tier officials, who actually make things happen, deliberately stalled out of a concern that any changes resulting from our efforts would likely benefit the Christians at their expense. So, including these levels of leadership in future top-down efforts became an important lesson to carry forward.

Yet another lesson, albeit of a more humorous nature, was the need to keep pace with one's resources; that is, don't undertake activities with inadequate funding to do so. Leading up to the formation of the Council, we felt a need to conduct a faith-based reconciliation seminar for the Sudanese Muslim and Christian religious leaders. However, because of the economic sanctions imposed on Sudan at that time by the United States (relating to its support of terrorism), we were tightly constrained in our ability to receive any kind of funding from Sudanese sources—despite the fact that we had secured a waiver from our Treasury Department to do business within its borders. As a result, we were operating in a very hand-to-mouth mode throughout our involvement and at this particular point in time had very little funding for the seminar. Accordingly, we rented the only facility we were able to afford that could accommodate such an event. This turned out to be an old, run-down hotel that was no longer functioning. In fact, the building was condemned and hadn't been used for the better part of a year.

Although we were able to spruce up the downstairs sitting area to make it respectable enough to hold the seminar, the upstairs rooms in which ICRD staff and yet another prayer team from Santa Barbara stayed was God-awful in every respect imaginable. Deep dust, no hot water, no fans, numerous mosquitoes (with malaria season in full-swing), and endless other shortcomings contributed to what could only be described as pitiful conditions—to the point where it actually became comical. To this day, whenever Brian Cox (who conducted the seminar) and I mention The Green Hotel, we break out laughing. The whole experience gave new meaning to the age-old maxim that you get what you pay for.

As might be expected, the relational aspects of the Inter-Religious Council's formation were of overriding importance. Above all, if the Council was to have its desired impact, its members would need to develop a keen sense of trust with one another. Thus, securing the right personalities was a key challenge. Even more challenging was choosing the right leader. Once that leader was identified, it took an additional five months to secure the government's approval of our choice.

Al-Tayib

Dr. Al-Tayib Zein Al Abdin was a highly respected college professor who had been a prominent figure in the Islamic movement in Sudan; but when the Bashir regime took over in a coup in 1989, he distanced himself from the government and, in effect, became a thorn in its side. This usually took the form of periodic criticism of the regime in his weekly column in a prominent Khartoum newspaper. Because his moral authority was without peer, he was thought to be the only person who could openly criticize President Bashir by name in the newspapers and not go to jail. He had also been the Political Science Professor for a least half of the President's Cabinet, so there was a significant love/hate relationship that needed to be traversed in securing the government's acquiescence to his appointment as the first Secretary General of the SIRC. Ergo the five months it took to get him in place. Along the way, the government tried to extract certain concessions from him (like discontinuing his news column). Consistent with his reputation as a man of principle unafraid to speak truth to power, he refused; which only added to the delay.

Once Al Tayib and the other members were in place, though, things moved quickly, as the Council implemented more concrete measures to benefit non-Muslims in the first four months of its existence than the churches had been able to achieve acting alone over the previous 15 years.

Among the Council's early accomplishments, it (1) secured permits and the necessary land (valued at $326,000) from the Sudanese government to build three new churches in Khartoum, the first new churches to be built in 25 years; (2) defused a highly-charged political/legal confrontation between the Episcopal Church and the Government of Sudan; (3) secured $230,000 from the government (in the form of land and cash) as compensation to the Catholic Church for the government's illegal confiscation of a major Church property in 1997, thereby removing an ongoing obstacle to Catholic cooperation with Muslim religious leaders; (4) secured increased national media time for Christian programming; (5) facilitated a ban on commercial development adjacent to Christian cemeteries; and (6) conducted a three-day training workshop for 30 next-generation Christian and Muslim leaders on "Protecting Religious Freedom in the Sudan."

Leading into the North/South Peace Agreement that was finally signed in 2005, the Council also conducted a major conference for 600 Muslim and Christian leaders on "The Role of Religious Leaders in the Peace Process." In addition to discussing how to involve religious leaders in that process, the conference focused on providing freedom of movement for religious leaders to perform their duties in the zones of conflict and on protecting holy sites on both sides from destruction or desecration. This was a major event that attracted the attention and participation of top political leaders and inspired extensive press coverage.

Aftermath

Of the Council's many achievements, perhaps the most dramatic was the role it played in September 2005 (again, after the peace agreement was firmly in place), when widespread rioting broke out following the death of John Garang, former leader of the guerilla forces in the South, who was killed in a helicopter crash under somewhat suspicious circumstances. Working through the mosques and the churches, the Council was able to arrest the rioting within a few days, saving untold lives in the process.

A Note of Disillusionment

To complement and, in important ways, reinforce the activities of the SIRC, I approached the British Embassy for funding to support the formation of a Committee to Protect Religious Freedom in the Sudan. Until then, there had been no mechanism for investigating alleged violations of religious freedom to determine the truth of what had actually taken place. Nor had there been any capability to rectify a problem once it became known. Thus, this independent committee would bring accountability to a highly sensitive area through fact-finding teams and associated recommendations to the concerned parties and governmental authorities.

The total funding required to establish and operate this team for its first year was only $32,000, and it was to be a straight pass-through from the Embassy to the Committee itself. The British ultimately provided the funding, but not without a disquieting note of concern along the way. During my next trip to Sudan after first proposing the idea, I visited the Embassy to determine our proposal's status. They said they had not yet approved my request because in the process of conducting their own due diligence, they learned that the Sudan Council of Churches (then under new leadership) was opposed to the idea. I was more than a little taken aback because it was the Christians who stood to benefit the most from the activities of such a Committee.

When I followed up with the SCC to determine what had gone wrong, I was mortified to learn that the resistance stemmed from a concern on the part of Christian pastors that such a committee might shine too much light on alleged atrocities (by providing more truthful representations of what had actually taken place) and cause funding from American churches in response to these atrocities to dry up. With more than a little embarrassment on its part, I persuaded the SCC to change its stance; and the funding was soon forthcoming.

Implications

The significance of the Council's formation for ICRD was that it solidly confirmed the wisdom of "respectful engagement" as a strategy going forward. In this case, it resulted in the establishment of two independent bodies whose tasks, in part, were to hold an Islamic dictatorship accountable for its religious policies. Not only did the regime permit their establishment, but it also agreed to give serious consideration to their recommendations. Happily, the government subsequently honored that commitment, even though doing so cost considerable sums in the process.

Al-Turabi

Among my more pleasurable experiences in Sudan were the numerous visits I had with Hasan al-Turabi, who in addition to serving as Speaker of the Parliament was known to be the leading figure in promoting militant Islam across North Africa and beyond. Despite his rather sordid reputation, he was a delightful conversationalist who knew the West well, having been educated at the University of London and the Sorbonne in Paris.

Turabi had also spent a cumulative total of seven years behind bars as a political prisoner. When discussing that experience, he said he hadn't found it so bad—three meals a day, a roof over his head, and the opportunity to read a thousand books. Based on the content of our lengthy and often fascinating discussions, I think he must have remembered most everything he had read.

I also found it interesting that in spite of his militant credentials, Turabi had long been a champion of women's rights dating back to the 1970's (possibly owing to his wife's influence). When I discussed that aspect of his reputation, he confessed to being guilty as charged. He said that when he sought to promote "women's lib" in Sudan, he would have failed miserably had he attempted to use a Western model. But all he had to do was point out how the Prophet (PBUH) had treated women, and that carried the day.

This helped explain my initial surprise during my first trip to Khartoum at not seeing any women wearing a veil and learning that (1) there were more women than men in the universities, (2) there was a specific number of seats in Parliament that were specifically reserved for women, and (3) a Catholic woman was serving in the President's Cabinet as the Secretary of Labor (who was quite vocal about her Catholicism). In short, a reality far different from what I expected.

Al-Shifa

Another memorable experience was my trip to the Al-Shifa pharmaceutical factory outside of Khartoum. In response to the bombing of the U.S. Embassies in Kenya and Tanzania by Al Qaeda in 1998, President Clinton ordered the destruction of the Al-Shifa facility and of suspected terrorist training camps in Afghanistan. The former was based on the supposedly "informed" assumption that Al-Shifa was producing ingredients for chemical weapons (specifically agents for making nerve gas). When that assumption was later disproven, the back-up rationale became Osama bin Laden's alleged financial ties to the facility. When that too was found to be false, the actual owner of the factory was labeled a terrorist; and his assets were frozen.

I happened to be in Sudan shortly after the attack and was the first Westerner to tour the destroyed facility. I did so in the company of the plant manager who had witnessed the destruction as it was taking place on his closed-circuit television at home. He said it broke his heart to see it happen, because the plant had been his pride and joy. For him, managing that facility had been a life-long dream. During my tour of the ruins, I learned that the factory had previously undergone periodic UN inspections to ensure the quality of its animal husbandry products and the like. It was also an unguarded facility, other than the several watchmen assigned to patrol the premises at night. As I waded through the pharmaceutical waste, sometimes up to my knees, it seemed clear that the attack had been a huge mistake.

At one point, I couldn't help but mentally put on my former national security hat and marvel at the incredible accuracy of the 16 Navy cruise missiles that had flattened the block-long facility. Within that square, total destruction; outside the square, totally untouched. Fortunately, only a few people were killed because the plant manager for reasons I can no longer remember, had chosen not to run a second shift on that particular day.

On a later trip, I had dinner with Salah Idriss, the Saudi national who actually owned the factory. He shared with me the fact that he had engaged a high-priced Washington law firm to unfreeze his assets; and it had succeeded in doing so. At that point, he switched from that firm to Laurence Tribe, a Harvard Law professor considered by many to be the leading expert in the country on U.S. constitutional law, in order to sue the United States government for financial restitution, including lost revenues and the cost of building a new facility. I was impressed with his logic for changing lawyers. He wanted to avoid the possibility of the same judge looking at the same lawyers and thinking, "I already gave them an earlier victory on the assets, so maybe I'll rule differently on the restitution." Idriss felt confident he would prevail in the courtroom and that the U.S. government would be made to pay, most probably out of the public eye in order to save face.

I never heard the final legal outcome, but the public health consequences were undeniably severe. At the time of the bombing, Al-Shifa was producing most of the country's pharmaceutical products. It also specialized in anti-malarial drugs and was the only plant in the country producing (1) affordable drugs to combat tuberculosis (for more than 100,000 patients) and (2) veterinary drugs to kill parasites that passed from herds to herders, one of the country's leading causes of infant mortality.

As recently as last year, the plant had not been rebuilt; and without the lifesaving medicines that it produced, it is highly likely that thousands of Sudanese either suffered or died as a result. Soon after the attack, the Clinton Administration vetoed Sudan's request for a UN inspection team to examine the destroyed facility and determine the truth of what had taken place, undoubtedly to avoid the global embarrassment of revealing sloppy U.S. decision making.

Religious Freedom

Another important lesson I took away from the Sudan experience was how easily facts can become distorted by the judgements of commentators who haven't actually witnessed what it is they are judging. Such was the case when I returned from a trip to Sudan in 2000 to find a pronouncement by the U.S. Commission on International Religious Freedom that Sudan was the most violent oppressor of religious liberty in the world at that time. As far as I was able to determine, none of the Commission's members had ever set foot in Sudan; but this was their verdict.

I, on the other hand, had just returned from Khartoum where an Easter Gospel Campaign led by the late German Evangelist Reinhard Bonnke had been underway in the heart of the city. Over the six days of that campaign, the cumulative total of those who participated numbered about 735,000, the majority of whom were Muslims (primarily because Bonnke's was a healing ministry). In addition to the fact that the Campaign had all-but-frozen the local transportation grid, it also raised questions in the minds of many Muslims about the propriety of holding a Christian crusade in the middle of an Islamic capitol.

A group of these concerned Muslims visited President Bashir to voice their concerns. The Pentecostal pastor who had been involved in inviting Bonnke in the first place (and who I knew quite well), accompanied the group and later shared with me Bashir's response to the group's petition: "You know, the Christians were here before us; and they have every right to celebrate Easter." Getting no satisfaction there, they took their complaints to Hasan al-Turabi; and his response was, "I have been watching this very closely and they are not attacking Islam. They are merely celebrating their religion. Why don't you celebrate your religion and see how many Christians complain?" President Bashir also went on national television to defend the event, calling it an important example of religious freedom in Sudan.

Although Sudan was attempting to win favorable international trade agreements by show-casing its accommodation of Christians and their practices, it would be quite a stretch to conclude that Sudan was the most violent oppressor of religious liberty in the world, especially when contrasting its treatment of Christians with that of other Muslim-majority countries like Saudi Arabia (where the Archbishop of Canterbury couldn't even exit a plane in his vestments). Sweeping generalizations based on inadequate evidence are seldom helpful and almost always prove counter-productive.

Other Factors

There were several other factors that also contributed to our success in important ways. First, Doug Coe was actively working through National Prayer Breakfast channels with President Bashir and Dr. John Garang, leader of the Sudan Peoples Liberation Army in the South, to help reconcile their differences.

Second, consistent with Doug's efforts and our own mission of bridging religious and political considerations in support of peacemaking, we helped arrange informal, off-the-record meetings between the Sudanese Foreign Minister and the U.S. Assistant Secretary of State for African Affairs to address the non-Muslim aspects of the conflict.

Third, our commitment to integrating the religious with the political proved helpful at a deeper level as well. On one of my more than a dozen trips to Sudan, I spent an evening with Ahmed al-Mahdi, the spiritual leader of an estimated ten million Muslims. Referring to former Senator (and Episcopal rector) Jack Danforth, who was then serving as U.S. Special Envoy to Sudan, al-Mahdi said, "It was in his capacity as a man of God that Senator Danforth opened my eyes and those of my colleagues to the need for us to reach out to the Christians."

Senator Danforth was also a strong supporter of our Center's work in addressing the religious aspects of the problem. On one of his trips to Sudan, he went out of his way to meet with the newly established SIRC, a move that didn't escape wider notice. Indeed, one of the leading newspapers made a big point of the fact that he met with the Council before meeting with any state officials.

Finally, and although difficult to measure, another ingredient in the mix was the fact that my recent role at CSIS commanded considerable respect— probably more than it deserved—from Sudanese government officials, and most particularly, the Foreign Minister. Sudan was anxious to escape the bonds of U.S. economic sanctions, which had been imposed in 1993 because of its terrorist-related activities. And because of CSIS's reputation, they appeared to think I had greater influence with the U.S. government than was probably the case. This, in turn, may have provided added incentive for them to appear as cooperative as possible in supporting our agenda.

On a Personal Note

During my many visits to Sudan, Abubaker was always with me; and much of the credit for our success rightfully belongs to him. Not only did we become good friends in the process; but because we assiduously worked around his need to pray five times daily, I came to admire the discipline of his commitment, and we became spiritual brothers as well.

> *"The reason the government of Sudan supports the work of ICRD is because they came to make peace and they have no hidden agenda."*

Quitbe al-Mahdi
Political Advisor to
the President of Sudan
and former Director of Intelligence

Chapter Eleven

KASHMIR

In 1947, the British partitioned India, thereby creating the new nation of Pakistan to serve as a homeland for Muslims who were uncomfortable with the idea of living in an independent India that was primarily Hindu. Most Kashmiris assumed that Kashmir, a predominately Muslim area lying along the line of partition, would go to Pakistan. However, when the Hindu maharajah of Kashmir hesitated in acceding to either Pakistan or India, Muslims revolted and the maharajah agreed to cede control to India in exchange for Indian military assistance to contain the uprising. Pakistan refused to recognize this accession and campaigned to reverse the situation. These events evolved into a bitter dispute between India and Pakistan over Kashmir that lasts to the present and has led to two major wars and numerous border skirmishes along the way.

About a year after our Center came into being, I called Brian Cox, who by this time had been promoted to Sr. Vice President, and told him I was concerned that no one seemed to be doing anything to address the tensions between India and Pakistan over their competing claims to Kashmir. Two wars had already been fought because of their zero-sum competition over that troubled state, and both sides now had nuclear weapons. Although it was the leading nuclear flash point in the world, no one was addressing it. I said we needed to do something about that and asked him to take it on. He agreed and through the helpful connections of a good friend and member of our board, former National Security Advisor Bud McFarlane, Brian was able to secure the necessary introductions to get things started.

After considering the situation more closely, it became clear that a top-down approach like that which we used in Sudan was out of the question owing to the political gridlock that existed at the national level. Moreover, the seeming intractability of the dispute had created a sense of timelessness about the conflict in the halls of power and mountain passes alike, with Muslims and Hindus staring nervously at one another through the cross-hairs of their rifle sights or, more ominously, their nuclear delivery systems. Further, I suspected from the outset that neither country really wanted to resolve the dispute, because Kashmir essentially serves the same purpose for them as Palestine does for Arab leaders—- a convenient escape valve to divert public attention from domestic problems by channeling their passions toward increased tensions in Kashmir (which they calibrate on an as-needed basis).

Peace from Within

With this understanding, a deliberate decision was made to work with next-generation leaders to promote peace from within by changing the spiritual, political, and social dynamics of the region and thereby set the stage for a resolution of the impasse that had prevailed since India's partition in 1947. In practical terms, this equated to developing a cooperative spirit between these prospective leaders across the existing religious, ethnic, and geographic divides (including the Line of Control that separates the Indian and Pakistani sides of the disputed territory). The term "next generation leaders" did not apply so much to age as it did to success and upward mobility. In other words, these were lawyers, journalists, college professors, and others who were on their way to becoming leaders of civil society. It was also important that they be able to leverage their ICRD training with others.

To meet this challenge, Brian leaned on a faith-based reconciliation process, which he had developed over a number of years through his work with disaffected parties in the Balkans and elsewhere. Through faith-based reconciliation workshops he was able to go deep in examining participants' understandings, perceptions, and attitudes toward others. Perhaps the most sensitive of the various elements included in these sessions is that of addressing any unresolved wounds of history, particularly those that have led to seemingly endless cycles of revenge.

Testing the Waters

To better understand the potential of these Faith-based Reconciliation Seminars, I participated in one that Brian conducted in Newport Beach, California, which was specifically tailored to promote reconciliation across the conservative and liberal divisions within the Episcopal Church relating to sexual orientation. It was a controversial topic, but Brian was an Episcopal Priest and enjoyed a stellar reputation as a reconciler, so it made sense for him to take it on.

There were 93 participants in attendance, and at one point in the several-day session, we broke into nine working groups and were asked to list any unresolved wounds of history that America had endured over the course of its history. As one might suspect, heading such a list would be the past treatment of Native-Americans, African-Americans, and Mexican-Americans. However, dwarfing these and all other predictable suspects, at least in the collective judgement of this particular group of participants, were the wounds that still festered from the Vietnam War, which had taken place some 30 years earlier.

I was surprised that this was the case, but the point was driven home rather dramatically in a story told by a head of one of the other working groups, who was reporting his group's findings to the larger audience. He was tall, solidly built, and sported a crewcut—the very image one would associate with a Marine Veteran, which he was. He told of an incident that had taken place just prior to completing his last tour of duty in the jungles of South Vietnam. His unit had recently captured two Viet Cong (VC) and was taking them back to the unit's base camp for further interrogation. At one point, the captives attempted to escape, but were brought down by machine gun fire from one of the Marines. When the second VC was shot, he collapsed like a punctured balloon, which at the time struck our veteran as a bit comical; and it caused him to laugh. Almost immediately afterward, though, he began to cry as he realized the extent to which he had been dehumanized by the war. One could tell the emotions were deeply felt by the tears flowing down his cheeks as he told his story.

During the ensuing discussions around that topic, I became aware of the extensive pain that was still being felt by just about everyone associated with that conflict, from those who did the actual fighting and felt unwelcome upon their return home, to those who ran off to Canada and still felt the guilt, to the loved ones left behind by those who were killed or missing in action and their eventual feelings of betrayal by their government. The list goes on, but I suspect the reason I was somewhat insensitive to most of this was because I was submerged in various submarines for most of that war, with a singular fixation on the Soviet Union.

The Vietnam episode was particularly instructive to me and it, combined with all else that transpired during the remainder of the seminar, demonstrated how deep-seated the challenges of reconciliation can be and how critical the concept of forgiveness is to meeting them.

A Higher Accountability

"Forgiveness is a facing of the past that frees us from the past." —Irene Hannah

In many respects, these workshops are designed to engage the transcendent aspects of a participant's personal religious faith in overcoming the secular obstacles to peace. At their conclusion, it is not unusual to find former adversaries embracing one another and, on some occasions, even shedding tears.

What sets these workshops apart from others is the degree to which they transform hearts as well as minds. This aspect was graphically illustrated during a meeting I attended with the core leadership group Brian had recruited to lead the initial effort with the Kashmiri Muslims. Of the 12 Muslims sitting around the table, two of them spoke up and said that because of the ICRD workshop they had attended, they were now able to forgive the perpetrators who had killed members of their immediate families. In one man's case, it was his son who had been killed, and tears rolled down his cheeks as he spoke.

I was stunned by their testimonies, because forgiveness is not the first thing that leaps to mind when thinking of Islam. And I wondered how many Christians like myself, who purport to be about forgiveness, could internalize the concept to the degree these two Muslims had. I'm not absolutely certain that I could, until put to a similar test. The core group was later expanded to 23 members, to include female representation as well as representation from other religious communities. Its principal function was to provide leadership at the local level and to recruit suitable candidates for the workshops.

For the workshops to be effective, a graduated approach is usually required in which the initial sessions are devoted to training moderate leaders from a single religion. After sufficient traction is established in promoting a reconciling spirit among these leaders, recruitment for the next round of workshops is expanded to include a modest number of extremists as well—again, from the same religion. This same process was repeated for each of the three religions involved, until sufficient groundwork was laid to bring together selected graduates from all of the religious groups in a final round of workshops.

Even with this gradual approach, tensions typically ran high in the later sessions as longstanding adversaries confronted one another for the first time. Despite any initial discord that arose, the workshops confronted the problems of alienation head-on and, in the process, inspired participants to rise above themselves as they began to feel accountability to a "higher religious calling"[45] rather than to some ideology or political movement.

An interesting side-bar to these workshops is the fact that those partici- pants, who at the outset are the most vocal in their criticisms of ICRD, later become some of our greatest champions. This usually results from a dis- arming realization that we are neither missionaries nor CIA agents, as they initially suspected, but merely boy scouts attempting to do a good deed.

The Problem

When India was being partitioned in 1947, the guidelines formulated by the British (who had exercised colonial rule over the region for the previous hundred years) called for inclusion in the new state of Pakistan all contig- uous, Muslim-majority areas. The situation in Kashmir, however, was com- plicated by the fact that it was being ruled as an independent principality by Hari Singh, a Hindu Maharajah. Although Kashmir was an overwhelmingly Muslim state, Pakistan feared that its Hindu ruler would side with India, so it launched a covert operation to infiltrate the Valley and overthrow the govern- ment. Singh appealed to India for military assistance and, in return, pledged to become part of the Indian union. This, in turn, provoked a war with Pakistan that ended with a cease-fire brokered by the UN in 1949, which established a cease-fire line, later renamed the Line of Control (LOC), on one side of which two-thirds of Kashmir would be controlled by India, with the remaining third controlled by Pakistan.

As part of the cease-fire, a UN resolution was adopted that called for a "free and impartial plebiscite" to decide the state's future. In other words, let the population decide for themselves whether their state should go with India or with Pakistan. Apprehensive of the likely outcome of such a referendum, India has never permitted it to take place; and the stalemate across the LOC continues to the present.

Our Approach

Of all the trouble spots where we have been involved, Kashmir was the one most likely to respond to a strictly faith-based approach, if only by default. Because of the longstanding nature of the dispute, almost every other approach to resolving the matter had been tried and found wanting. When we

---

[45] In the case of Buddhism, this calling is their submission to dharma (the ultimate law of all things). The same holds true for Hinduism, as exemplified in the work and teachings of Mahatma Gandhi.

showed up with a strategy of making religion part of the solution, the general attitude was, "Why not? We've tried everything else." (This called to mind my earlier experience at Cities In Schools, when the only approach that worked in my dealings with Maurice Weir was also spiritual in nature).

Our first effort to unfreeze the stalemate and create movement in the region began with a faith-based reconciliation workshop for Kashmiri Muslims and Kashmiri Pandits (after first conducting a preliminary workshop). The Pandits are a Hindu Brahmin community from the Kashmir Valley that was driven out of the Valley in 1989 by a militant Muslim movement, which had formed earlier that same year in response to the general mistreatment of Muslims. Most of the Pandits resettled in refugee camps outside of Jammu, the winter capital of the Indian-controlled area, where they generally lived a meager and challenging existence.

In July of 2002, we brought them together in Gulmarg, a city in the Kashmir Valley about two hours from Srinagar, the summer capital of Indian Kashmir. The tensions ran high, particularly for the Pandits who had not set foot in the Valley for 13 years and who, as Brian described it, "felt they had been forced to leave a land that was a part of their very soul."

Notable progress was made both at this first joint workshop and at a later, significantly larger one that followed. A notable breakthrough occurred in the second workshop when in response to an inflammatory diatribe at the outset by a Hindu Pandit directed against the Muslim community, the Muslim members of the leadership core, who had already apologized for their part in forcing the Pandits out of the Valley, decided to listen attentively, absorb the pain, and resist the temptation to respond in kind.

On the last day, that same Pandit stood up and apologized for the Pandit insensitivity to Muslim suffering that had taken place under earlier Kashmiri regimes in which the Pandits had enjoyed significant influence. This was the first time a Pandit leader had ever publicly apologized to the Muslim community. It was also the first seminar in which the indigenous Muslim leadership core assumed a significant role in conducting it.

These workshops were followed in October with an invitation-only meeting in Srinagar of 70 Kashmiri Muslims, representing a broad cross-section of civil society. Over the course of this day-long meeting, I was surprised at how forthcoming the participants were. Not only were they willing to have the Pandits return, but they actually wanted them back. They felt they had lost an important part of their culture when the Pandits left. As it turns out, I shouldn't have been surprised, because before the partition challenge, Kashmir had long enjoyed a rich cultural tradition known as "Kashmiriyat," a uniquely hospitable assimilation of Islamic, Hindu, Sikh, and Buddhist influence. In many respects, it was this kind of pluralist society we were seeking to re-create through rebuilding relationships of trust across the religious and regional divides. [46]

The civil society meeting was followed by a fact-finding trip to the Pandit refugee camps in January of 2003, to see first-hand how they were living and to test their willingness to return to the Valley. The living conditions were pretty terrible, and while most longed to return, some had already established deep roots in the Jammu area, which prevented them from leaving. Others were fearful of an uncertain future back in the Valley.

These ICRD activities paved the way for the Pandit's return, which gained increasing traction over time and eventually led to a change in Indian government policy, which supported the idea.

The Bottom Line

After six years of working with the core group leaders and a number of cell groups that had also been formed, the effort concluded with a meeting in Nepal at which Muslim, Hindu, and Buddhist participants from both sides of the LOC committed to (1) working together to help facilitate a peaceful resolution to their longstanding conflict (including support for a return of the Pandits to the Valley) and (2) rebuilding a civil society that equally served the interests of all. Thus, our immediate goal of promoting a cooperative spirit across the various divides, including the LOC, was achieved (as captured in a Memorandum of Agreement signed by all of the participants—Addendum P).

When we first began the project, a peace process between India and Pakistan relating to Kashmir was just getting underway; but by the time we achieved our goal, that process had become a distant memory. Because of this failure at the top, we were unable to find a way to capitalize on our newly-created good will at the national level. That good will, however, did prove instrumental in facilitating the return of the Pandits.[47]

---

[46] It was during this day in Srinagar that I paused long enough to enjoy the beauty of the place. Set in the Kashmir Valley about a mile above sea level, with the Himalayas in the distance, Srinagar lies on the banks of the Jhelan River (a tributary of the Indus) and adjacent to Lakes Dal and Anchar. It serves as the summer capital of the Indian Union Territory of Jammu and Kashmir and is a favorite vacation spot for British and other foreign tourists with its gardens, waterfronts, and houseboats.

[47] As of 2016, about 2,000 Pandits had returned to the Valley.

Both India and Pakistan claim to want a lasting peace, but their actions seem to suggest otherwise. While Pakistan gives lip service to Kashmiri independence, it seems clear they want to annex the whole state for themselves. By the same token, it is the impasse over Kashmir that enables the Pakistani military to command a disproportionate share of that country's resources. India, for its part, is fearful that if they let Kashmir go, other independent-minded states could soon follow, thereby threatening the solvency of the entire nation.

Throughout our work in Kashmir, we collaborated with two indigenous organizations: the Kashmir Foundation for Peace and Developmental Studies on the Indian side of the LOC and the Kashmir Institute for International Relations on the Pakistani side. This collaboration was quite extensive and encompassed the planning, execution, and evaluation functions. Significantly, the Kashmir Foundation reached the point where some of its senior staff were able to conduct substantial portions of future workshops. And as previously mentioned, we helped cement these relationships along the way by hosting the leaders of both organizations at the National Prayer Breakfast in Washington.

Over the course of this project, I made a few on-scene cameo appearances to (1) meet with high-level Kashmiri officials to bolster Brian's efforts, (2) to speak at the Civil Society meeting, and (3) provide added encouragement to our indigenous partnering institutions. I also capitalized on my connections at the State Department to seek U.S. government support for what we were doing. That effort was making a degree of headway when at one point, a team from State, which was about to fly to India to conduct an on-the-ground assessment of our progress (prior to possibly providing financial support for the effort), was called back at the last minute when India withdrew the team's visas—consistent with their longstanding refusal to permit third-party involvement of any kind in resolving the dispute over Kashmir.

Although ICRD's funding to support additional work in Kashmir dried up following the meeting in Nepal, the Foundation and selected graduates of the workshops have continued to work for peace as they are able. At one point, they were attempting to develop a model community based on faith-based reconciliation in Boramullah, a mountainous village on the Indian side of the LOC that was once known as the seat of the Islamic militant movement. Toward this end, classes in faith-based reconciliation were being taught in the schools, and a number of cell groups had been formed to advance their outreach beyond the immediate area.

Despite these impressive gains at the local level, further progress toward resolving differences at the national level has been halting at best. In fact, one might say it suffered a major setback in the summer of 2019, when India revoked Article 370 of its Constitution, which had granted a unique measure of autonomy to Kashmir as a precondition for Kashmir's accession to India during the 1947 partition. Among other things, this article allowed the state of Jammu and Kashmir to have its own constitution, a separate flag, and the right to establish its own laws other than those relating to defense, foreign policy, and communications. Further, beyond this dubious license taken with the Constitution, steps were also announced to split the state into two more centrally-governed "union territories."

Although the future for Kashmir remains unsettled, one can only hope that over time, the improved relationships at the local level based on faith-based reconciliation will have a broader and lasting impact.

> *"In Kashmir, none of the 'old hands' would have imagined that you could have achieved the measure of reconciliation you have already established."*

Robert McFarlane
former U.S. National Security Advisor

Chapter Twelve

IRAN

In 1951, Iranian Prime Minister, Mohammed Mossadegh, nationalized his country's oil industry and expelled the Anglo-Persian Oil Company. With the popular support of the Iranian people, he was seeking greater independence from Western influence. Anxious to recoup its influence and fearful of the possibility of a prospective Iranian alliance with the Soviet Union, British intelligence, with the CIA's assistance, engineered a coup in 1953, and cleared the way for a past ally, Shah Mohammed Reza Pahlavi, to assume power. The Shah later established a State Information and Security Organization (SAVAK), which functioned as his secret police. Its brutality, in turn, contributed to the fall of the Shah in 1979 and a takeover by Ayatollah Khomeini. The associated seizure of the U.S. Embassy and its personnel by Iranian college students created a rift between Iran and the United States that lasts to the present.

While Kashmir was in process, we also became involved in Iran. There, I had the pleasure of being part of a nine-member, Abrahamic delegation which visited that country in 2003 under the leadership of Cardinal Theodore McCarrick, who was serving as Archbishop of Washington at the time. By "Abrahamic", I mean that it included Jews, Christians, and Muslims, all of whom trace their roots to the patriarch Abraham.

While in Iran, we met with a number of religious and political leaders, including several Grand Ayatollahs, the President, the Foreign Minister, the Chief Justice of the Supreme Court, the head of Parliament, and various university faculty and students. In each of these meetings, the Cardinal asked the host's permission to begin with a prayer, which was always granted (and seemingly very appreciated). Through respectful engagement, we were able to build an initial degree of trust that we hoped could help provide a future basis for cordial relations between our two countries.

The Axis of Evil

Of all the other countries I have ever visited, none has impressed me as much as Iran with respect to the richness of its cultural heritage. The legacy of the Persian Empire lives on, especially in the reverent homage paid to its poets. Rumi, a thirteenth century Persian Poet, who has ranked as the most popular poet in America for more than two decades, is but one among many whose works Iranians celebrate. When I commented to an Iranian philosopher that every Iranian must be a poet at heart, he replied, "From birth!"

The architecture was stunning as well. I recall admiring the beauty of the mosques in Isfahan, with their uplifting patterns of gold filigree painted on pale green domes, supported by inspiring, often breathtaking, mosaic structures and thinking to myself, "I always thought Washington was a pretty city; but next to this, it's not even a close second. Above all, we must never bomb this place."

Our meetings were many and varied. In one such meeting, the Grand Ayatollah with whom we were visiting, commented that any attempts to reconcile the differences between our two countries would inevitably prove fruitless in the context of political pronouncements such as that recently voiced by then President George W. Bush, in which Iran was declared to be part of an "axis of evil." I thought to myself, "Neither does 26 years of The Great Satan" (as the United States is commonly referred to by Iranian political and religious leaders). I chose not to give that thought verbal expression, but was amazed at the seeming incongruity of how warmly we were received wherever we went (and at all levels of society) versus the steady drum-beat of anti-American rhetoric that typically characterizes their Friday sermons and political rallies. Indeed, prominent on tall skyscrapers in downtown Tehran are gigantic murals showing bombs dropping on a silhouette of the United States. At the end of our visit, Kamel Kharrazi, Iran's Foreign Minister, said that ours was the highest-level American delegation to visit Iran since its revolution in 1979. If true, it was a sad commentary.

This emotional disconnect only becomes understandable when one distinguishes between a people and their government, which is probably why I found it so easy to be friendly with every Iranian I met, while, at the same time, feeling total disdain for their governing theocracy and its treatment of the Bahai's.[48] I was further struck by the irony that the one Muslim country the United States was most likely to bomb next (for geopolitical reasons) was

---

[48] The Bahai Faith, which originated in Iran in the 1840s as a reformist movement, is viewed by the government as a heretical, "counter revolutionary" Muslim sect and suffers mightily as a result.

the only Muslim country in the world where there was such a widespread affection for Americans.[49]

Fundamental to the geopolitical angst that exists between our two countries is Iran's quest for regional preeminence (Ayatollah Khomeini picked up where the Shah left off in this regard) and its premise that resistance to the United States will be the *sine qua non* for preserving its revolutionary edge. Further complicating the relationship are two unresolved wounds of history dating back to 1953 in the first instance, when we assisted the British in the overthrow of Mohammad Mosaddegh, Iran's democratically-appointed Prime Minister, and more recently, to the 1979 seizure of the U.S. Embassy and its personnel by Iranian revolutionaries, which stretched out for 444 days before Iran let them go. Because the latter took place in reaction to the excesses of the Shah's secret police and the Shah himself assumed power as a result of our toppling of Mosaddegh, one might say these wounds are directly linked. Either way, until they are effectively addressed, it seems unlikely that sufficient grounds for a cordial relationship will ever be found.

An important tangential take-away from the trip for me was how important it is to crosscheck (to the best of one's ability) how the media characterizes important events overseas. During the course of our trip, for example, widespread protests erupted on Iranian university campuses, which were interpreted in the Western news media as students revolting for a more democratic form of government. In actuality, the protests were a reaction against the government's decision to privatize various functions, including education. This meant that from that point onward, students would be required to pay tuition, some of whom could afford it, while others could not. The students felt this dishonored the spirit of the revolution (of 1979). They didn't want to start a new revolution; they merely wanted to honor the old.

Thinking Anew

Another meaningful take-away for me was the opportunity that the trip provided to get to know Cardinal McCarrick better. Although he had served on our Center's Advisory Council since its inception in 1999, he was Archbishop of Newark for much of that time, and we had not had many opportunities to interact. At one point on this trip, however, he and I were alone in a car riding from one meeting to the next. While chatting about various topics, I brought up the subject of priests who had recently been found guilty of pedophilia and

---

[49] That affection has undoubtedly abated in the wake of America's withdrawal from the multilateral nuclear agreement with Iran and the subsequent imposition of harsh economic sanctions in its stead.

how heinous I thought that was. Such a grievous violation of trust not only subjected young victims to the criminal nature of the act itself, but also to the likely destruction of their spiritual beliefs, probably for life. The Cardinal expressed his agreement, and we moved on to a different topic.

Little did I dream that 15 years later Cardinal McCarrick would be disgraced by similar misdeeds from his distant past that had recently come to light. As a result, he was subsequently dismissed from the priesthood. I found this more than a little difficult to process, because I had felt tremendous respect for him both as a very likeable priest and as a superbly capable diplomat. On more than one occasion, I had expressed my personal view to others that everything good they had ever heard about the Catholic Church could be found in this one man. Thus, it was doubly disillusioning for me to see the valleys in this gifted man's life so overwhelm the mountaintops that his impressive diplomatic achievements would be all-but-totally forgotten in the cold glare of scandalous revelations.

Having thought about this problem a bit, I think it is past time for the Church to think anew. For the first thousand years of its history, priestly celibacy was not required in the Catholic Church. A degree of continence was, but not complete abstention. Over time, though, the requirement evolved to one of total abstinence. The spiritual basis for this evolution was a desire to emulate the totality of commitment modeled by the Apostles of Jesus.

Planned or unplanned, a less-spiritual side benefit was that of keeping all resources within the Church (by not letting them get frittered away through family inheritances and the like). Ironically, to the extent the celibacy standard may have contributed to deviant behavior, the resources are now flowing out of the Church in all-too-great abundance through private payoffs and legal settlements.

The Catholic Church already accepts into its priestly ranks married pastors from selected Protestant denominations without requiring them to leave their wives. Before the sky falls completely, perhaps it is time for that exception for outsiders to become the rule for all.

Sharing Insights

About six months after we returned from Iran, our Center sponsored a presentation on Capitol Hill for members of Congress and their staffs on "The Role of Religion in Iran". The speakers were Cardinal McCarrick and Ayatollah Ahmad Iravani (who was teaching at the Catholic University Law School and who had coordinated our earlier trip to Iran). They did a splendid job of conveying a number of important insights; and when it was over, some in the audience stayed behind for further discussion. Among them was Senator Hillary Clinton, with whom I chatted for quite some time. Going into this discussion, my attitude toward her was that of the average Republican, wary at best. However, I soon changed my mind, as I found her to be exceedingly bright and a charming conversationalist. I recall thinking at the time how foolish it is to be overly judgmental about someone before you get a chance to know them. It's probably not a good idea to be judgmental in any event, but that's a different conversation.

Returning the Favor

Two years later, our Center raised the funds to sponsor a reciprocal visit of high-level Iranians to the United States. It too was Abrahamic in its makeup, included nine participants, and lasted for a period of ten days – in other words, total reciprocity on all fronts. One of the highlights of that visit was when we sat the delegation down with eight well-informed Congressmen and addressed all of the hot-button issues. At one point, one of the Congressmen pointed to the young, but highly poised, Ayatollah who was leading the group and asked, "Tell me, do you think Israel has a right to exist?" The Ayatollah leaned back in his chair, gave a slight chuckle and said, "Of course Israel has a right to exist; just as we have the right not to recognize it." Such was the level of repartee.

If I were asked to grade the two sides, I would have had to give the Iranians the higher marks, if only because of the inherent difficulty of defending the double standards to which our country so often resorts. We come down hard on Iran on the nuclear question, yet turn a blind eye to Israel, (which, unlike Iran, hasn't even signed the Nuclear Nonproliferation Treaty). We levy similar criticisms with respect to Iran's treatment of religious minorities, while all-but-totally ignoring Saudi Arabia, where the plight of religious minorities is far worse. In fact, Iran is the only country in the entire region that protects minority religions in its constitution, specifically Christians, Jews, and Zoroastrians.

Iran also has the only sizeable Jewish population in the region, which, at the time of our visit, numbered close to 25,000. In speaking privately with the Jewish member of Parliament and the Christian Archbishop who were part of the Iranian delegation, they indicated that each of their respective religious communities had just received one million dollars from the President's budget to repair their synagogues, churches and hospitals. The following year, that amount was to be increased to two million dollars and would be funded directly by the Parliament. This level of funding would then continue on a yearly basis. Although it may have changed since then, at the time of our trip,

Iran was treating its Jewish population considerably better than its constant invective toward Israel might have suggested.

Another highlight of their visit was a luncheon that we co-sponsored with the U.S. Institute of Peace, which in addition to the Iranians, included an impressive cross-section of American Muslims. The two groups engaged in a stimulating discussion of *ijtihad,* a long-dormant Islamic concept in which the application of religious principles to contemporary life is periodically reexamined in light of significant changes in the external environment. Although the concept was widely applied when Islam was at its peak, it faded into disuse as the religion grew increasingly defensive and protective of traditional values under the onslaught of colonialism and various other outside forces. Thoughtful input was provided by both sides, with the American Muslims making a strong and seemingly persuasive case for why the concept should be revived.

Both of the above discussions represented significant steps forward in terms of establishing relationships, clarifying perceptions, and providing a better understanding of the issues that divide. In short, the stage was set for taking future engagement to a higher level.

Trumping Realpolitik

Two other aspects of the visit that should be mentioned were a bit more spiritual in nature. During their stay in Washington, we were able to house the Iranians at the Cedars, the tastefully-appointed mansion on the Virginia side of the Potomac River that serves as the base for the National Prayer Breakfast fellowship. Consistent with that purpose is the unassuming "Spirit of Jesus," that permeates throughout.

On the first evening of their visit, the President of the University of Tehran was overheard saying, "I can't wait to get out of this godforsaken country." Upon his return to Iran, though, he called his son, who was planning to conduct his graduate studies in the United Kingdom and urged him to do them instead in America. It was inspiring to see the attitude of the Iranians grow warmer over the course of their visit as the spiritual ambiance of the Cedars and its support staff worked its magic.

The second noteworthy aspect related to the fact that in America it is the people who decide when and where to build their churches, mosques, and synagogues and who then raise the required funds to do so. This greatly impressed the Iranians because in Iran, as in most other Muslim countries, these are government decisions. So too are the appointments of the imams to lead the mosques.

Gaming Peace

After this second visit, I felt that the idea of building relationships and trust was all well and good; but I didn't think it could get us to where we needed to be as quickly as would be needed in light of the looming nuclear question. So, it caused me to wonder how one might short-circuit this process. A couple of years earlier, I had played a role in a war game at the National Defense University in Washington in which Iran was the assumed adversary; and I now began to explore what a "peace game" might look like.

After due deliberation, I came up with a concept one might call facilitated brainstorming (as contrasted with the kind of scenario-driven exercise one typically finds in most war games). The main idea was to bring together highly-capable individuals from both countries to meet for a week under the auspices of a world-class facilitator in order to discuss how the obstacles standing in the way of a cooperative relationship might be overcome. The participants would be religious leaders, academicians, and former government practitioners from a range of disciplines, who although no longer serving in their respective governments, were too respected to be ignored.

I then met with Roger Fisher, a former colleague from Harvard days, who co-authored the book *Getting to Yes* (in which he developed his now famous "win-win" negotiating strategy); and he agreed to serve as the facilitator. When I broached this idea with Javed Zarif, Iran's then Ambassador to the United Nations (and later its Foreign minister), he became quite enthused because he had read Fisher's book and, as a former college professor himself, was intellectually curious to see how Fisher's approach would work in practice.

In the course of our discussion, I told Zarif that I would prefer to conduct the Peace Game in Iran rather than in some neutral location, because it would provide greater incentive for the Americans to participate and, more importantly, would convey a note of humility that was all-too-absent from U.S. foreign policy at the time (by engaging in such an exercise on Iranian turf). This conversation took place just prior to a presidential election in which former President Rafsanjani was favored to win. Zarif said, "Well, if Rafsanjani wins, you can do it in Iran. With anybody else, it will probably have to take place in Europe."

When Ahmadinejad won, all bets were off. No one, including Ambassador Zarif, knew where they stood, so the Peace Game idea was tabled for the time being. Two years later, however, when President Ahmadinejad was in New York for the annual meeting of heads of state at the United Nations, I was able to present the idea to him; and he expressed his support for it. Despite his receptivity to the concept, though, I was unable to secure any traction within my own government, which was fixated on regime change as the only option worth considering. This should have come as no surprise, though, since the United States had not even bothered to respond to two earlier overtures from former President Mohammad Khatami to put everything on the table and begin a dialogue aimed at resolving all major differences.[50] The George W. Bush Administration wanted regime change, not dialogue. And that is exactly what it got, as Ahmadinejad and the hard-liners took over when Khatami and the reformists couldn't deliver.

In preparing for the possibility of a Peace Game, I crafted a paper on the potential benefits of an improved relationship between the United States and Iran. The number of issues in which we had overlapping interests was quite extensive and, among others, included stability in Iraq, Afghanistan, and Central Asia, defeating the Taliban, arresting the Afghan drug trade, developing increased policy options for bringing peace to the region, and exploring various economic opportunities.

But the above list will have to wait for a later time, after both countries have been able to overcome their deep-seated wounds from the past. In addition to those already mentioned, for Iran this also includes implicit U.S. support for Iraq's invasion of Iran in 1980 and the eight-year war that followed. Our more recent withdrawal from the multilateral nuclear agreement and simultaneous imposition of harsh economic sanctions only add to this list.

The Nuclear Question

In initiating our withdrawal from the nuclear agreement, it seems clear that no serious regard was paid by U.S. decision makers to the debilitating precedent that would be established by reneging on an international agreement for which the United States had been the leading proponent in the first instance and that was being scrupulously honored by all of the signatories. How could anyone ever trust the United States to keep its word in the future?

Nor was any serious consideration given to the significance of the *fatwas* (religious edicts) that had been issued by the country's current and previous Supreme Leaders—Ayatollah Khamenei and, before him, Ayatollah Khomeini—-against weapons of mass destruction (on the basis that such

---

[50] The first of these took place in 2002, following Iran's assistance in the diplomatic aftermath of our military victory over the Taliban government. Having every reason to expect a positive response, they were shocked to be included one week later in President Bush's "axis of evil" speech. The second approach took place a year later, following the fall of Baghdad to U.S. forces.

weapons are inherently un-Islamic because of their indiscriminate nature in killing innocent civilians).[51]

Buttressing this line of thinking is Iran's claim that it consciously chose not to respond in kind when attacked with chemical weapons by Iraq during the first five years of the Iran-Iraq War, attacks that resulted in an estimated 50,000 Iranian casualties. Also of note is a poll taken in 2008 of Iranian attitudes toward nuclear weapons, in which more than 70 percent of those polled expressed opposition to developing them, regardless of whether the respondents were conservatives, moderates, or reformists.

From a *realpolitik* standpoint, though, it is easy to see why Iran might want a nuclear weapons capability, if only to deter its neighbors, which already have them (Israel, Pakistan, India, Russia, and China). In view of the *fatwas*, however, and the fact that such edicts are taken seriously in a country where religion allegedly trumps all else (and constitutes the very glue that binds in a theocracy), it seems entirely plausible that Iran might want to be perceived as having a near-term capability to produce such weapons, if adequately provoked. However, if for any reason they should decide to develop them anyway, it would clearly be in America's best interest to reestablish communications with them sooner rather than later.

Lest one overreact in such a context, it is wise to take provocative gestures with a grain of salt, such as President Ahmadinejad's earlier, seemingly suicidal pronouncements relating to Israel's misdeeds and the imminence of the "end times." Iran is a highly advanced culture, with more philosophers per square hectare than can probably be found anywhere else on the planet. Such people do not value life lightly, and it seems highly likely that Ahmadinejad's pronouncements were intended solely to upstage the Gulf States rhetorically in opposing Israel.

How It All Began

My invitation to participate in the trip to Iran came through the Prayer Breakfast Fellowship and Doug Coe, who made the trip as well. Because

---

[51] Over a private lunch in his palace in Riyadh, I asked Prince Turki al-Faisal, former long-time head of Saudi Intelligence, about both *fatwas*. I told him we were keenly interested in seeing copies of each but had so far been unable to locate them. He assured me they both existed; but while he believed the sentiments behind Ayatollah Khomeini's edict to have been genuine, he thought those of his successor may be a bit disingenuous. Although I recognized it could be in the Prince's own best interest to question Iranian motives (because of the longstanding animosity between his country and Iran), he nevertheless appeared and sounded sincere.

there were ill feelings at the national level between Iran and the United States, normal diplomatic discourse was out of the question; and religion offered the only channel for meaningful engagement.

The groundwork for the trip had been laid by Marshall Breger, a Jewish professor at Catholic University's Law School, who had conducted a 20-day lecture tour in Iran the previous year. Upon his return, he briefed Cardinal McCarrick on his experience and noted, "If you want to talk with the Iranians, you have to enter through the portal of religion. If you start with a conversation about religious faith, you can talk about anything." This experience, in turn, led to the 2003 trip by our delegation.

Religious Diplomacy

Marshall's insight is important and should be taken into consideration in any future attempts at diplomacy. Iranians trust religion far more than they do politics. While there are hints of democracy in Iran, the trump card remains firmly in the hands of the unelected religious elite—yet another reason that interaction on a religious basis may hold the key to breaking future deadlocks.

To illustrate the above point, in 2004, Iran suffered a devastating earthquake; and the United States offered to send a delegation to help facilitate American recovery assistance. Iran, however, refused the offer. Senator Elizabeth Dole had been chosen to lead the delegation; and having previously served as head of the American Red Cross, seemed a logical choice. However, had the United States asked Cardinal McCarrick or some other prominent American religious leader to lead the "earthquake delegation," rather than a political figure, Iran in all likelihood would have welcomed the idea.

It was our delegation's experience that if one can begin serious discussions on important matters by building common ground around related religious values and goals (for example, by discussing how different belief systems might deal with the topic in question), it then becomes easy to segue to the more difficult specifics, whether they have to do with nuclear weapons, terrorism, or some other challenging topic. Politically speaking, they think Americans speak out of both sides of their mouths. One can only wonder why...

"Doug Johnston urged, and I agreed, that religious studies should be a major focus of education for American diplomats, and that our embassies should have people trained to reach out and engage with religious leaders across the globe."

Madeleine Albright
former U.S. Secretary of State

Chapter Thirteen

PAKISTAN

Once the pinnacle of learning excellence in the world, with curriculums that included medicine, mathematics, and astronomy, Islamic religious schools in Pakistan (at that time India) responded to the secular threat of British colonialism by retreating into limited, insular institutions focused on rote memorization of the Qur'an and the study of Islamic principles. Today's students emerging from a number of these institutions are not only indoctrinated in radical interpretations of Islam, but they are incapable of grappling with contemporary problems. This makes them highly vulnerable to recruitment by extremist organizations.

In January of 2003, I dropped by the Institute of Policy Studies (IPS) in Islamabad to visit with its Executive Director, Khalid Rahman, a friend with whom I had worked on an earlier project relating to development assistance in Afghanistan. The purpose of my visit was to brief Khalid on the state of play of our Center's project in Kashmir.

During the course of our visit, Khalid mentioned a major study his Institute had just completed on the madrasas (religious schools) in Pakistan. When he did so, I expressed keen interest because the madrasas were commonly thought to be central to the terrorism in South Asia, where students from poor families were schooled in the principles and techniques of violent religious extremism. Because of my obvious interest, Khalid asked me on my way out the door if our Center would like to partner with his Institute in reforming the madrasas. Sensing the strategic potential of this opportunity, I responded, "Would we? Absolutely, without question!" I later learned that, among other things, "partnering" meant I would have to provide all of the funding, so I spent the remainder of that year raising enough to get us started.

Shortly after making this commitment, I experienced a stroke of good fortune while attending a social gathering at the home of the Third Secretary of the Pakistan Embassy in Washington. I didn't know the host and to this day am unsure how I came to be invited. Anyway, while there, I ran into a young Pakistani-American couple, Azhar and Tazeen Hussain; and we immediately hit it off. Tazeen had recently given birth to twins and was actively seeking to reenter the job market. Because she had previously been involved in raising funds for an African-related non-profit, I invited her to join our Center to perform that same function on a half-time basis. She gladly accepted but lasted only a few months before she sensed that her kids were being adversely affected by her absence. Before she left, though, she mentioned that her husband, Azi, had expressed a keen interest in our Center's work.

At that time, Azi was working as a diversity trainer at the American Association for Retired Persons (AARP); but when we followed up over lunch to explore his possible involvement in our work, I immediately sensed that he would be a great fit for our yet-to-be launched madrasa project. So, over the next year and a half, I engaged him on a situational basis as we got it off the ground. When we needed him, he would either use his vacation time; or we would ask him to take leave without pay and reimburse him accordingly.

After securing the necessary resources to begin the project and making another trip to Islamabad to coordinate the final details with Khalid, the Institute for Policy Studies convened a two-week workshop on "Islam and Contemporary Thought" for madrasas leaders from each of the sects that sponsored these religious schools. Because of the sectarian strife that was all-too-common in Pakistan, getting these leaders to meet together was a huge challenge in and of itself. Fortunately, IPS had the credibility to convene such a gathering, stemming from its long-term involvement with the madrasas over the years and its more recent engagement in conducting the above-mentioned study.

Although IPS sponsored the workshop, we became responsible for most of its content, with Azi leading the way. Having spent his youth in Karachi and attended a madrasa himself, not only was he familiar with that milieu, but he had two other things going for him as well. I didn't know it at the time; but after seeing him in action, I quickly concluded he was one of the best trainers I had ever encountered (and I had seen my fair share during more than 40 years of public and private service). He was also one of the more likeable persons on the face of the planet, and this combination ultimately accounted for the lion's share of our success in working with the madrasas over the next eight years.

A Cautious Beginning

Because of the strained relationship between the United States and Islam more generally and the added animus stemming from America's then-recent invasion of Iraq, IPS introduced Azi to the workshop as a "friend from Karachi", without mentioning either ICRD or the United States. Even with that rather innocuous introduction, the workshop participants grilled Azi on exactly where in Karachi he was from and which madrasa he had attended. They also quizzed him on various passages from the Qur'an. Fortunately, he passed all of these tests with flying colors.

A number of the 29 workshop participants came with the intent of staying only a few days; but when Azi began talking about the inspiring scholarly contributions of the madrasas in Medieval times, they were hooked. Every one of them stayed the entire two weeks. Few of these leaders were aware that the madrasas had once been without peer as institutions of higher learning in the world and that it was only European exposure to them that had led to the establishment of today's university system in the West. Thus, it should come as no surprise that many of the traditions and mores of present-day academia trace their roots back to the madrasas— —such as the funding of chairs in various academic disciplines and the wearing of academic robes and mortar boards with tassels at graduation. Much like the madrasa leaders, though, few in the West are even remotely aware of this connection.

Azi further captured their attention by (1) noting that the oldest degree-awarding madrasa in the Muslim world (located in a mosque in Fez, Morocco) had been established by the daughter of a wealthy merchant, (2) explaining the central role played by the madrasas in facilitating the European Renaissance, and (3) pointing out how madrasas in as early as the ninth century had pioneered the concept of having students sit in small circles as they discussed academic subjects for extended periods of time (following which, they would be required to make presentations as "experts" on those same subjects the following day). After further noting that none of this in any way violated Islamic tradition, Azi emulated this practice each evening by dividing the participants into small groups to discuss what they had learned earlier in the day. Although a foreign concept to the madrasa leaders, they quickly adapted; and sectarian lines were cautiously broached as they began to recapture this lost heritage.

Why so much of this was new to the workshop participants was because of their more recent history in which the madrasas had undergone major change under the influence of British colonialism. Fearful of losing their Muslim identity when the British tried to secularize them, the madrasas purged themselves of all subjects deemed to be Western or secular in nature—to the point where the vast majority of these schools today confine their teaching to rote memorization of the Qur'an and the study of Islamic principles.

Thus, the aim of this workshop was to lay the groundwork for enhancing the madrasa curriculums by challenging the participants with new ideas and new pedagogical approaches in a comfortable, respectful and collaborative environment where free and open discussion could take place.

To build added camaraderie, Azi took the participants for a boat ride on a nearby lake, which turned out to be a first-time experience for most of them. The following describes that particular outing plus a typical workshop session and the hunger for more of the same that these activities created (as captured in an unpublished manuscript by Will Jenkins, a free-lance journalist and mutual friend of Azi's and mine).[52]

Boat ride

Azi rested one hand on the railing of the decrepit wooden pier, his eyes scanning the huddle of teachers.

"So, can everyone swim?"

Some smiled; others strained to maintain solemnity. Azi stepped into the first boat and helped several of the teachers join him. "All aboard now. We aren't leaving anyone behind."

The sun was warm and low in the sky as the boats motored out into the center of the lake. The breeze caught the teacher's flowing robes which struggled to billow freely.

In the neighboring boat, one of the IPS administrators continued to give Azi a wary stare. They had not approved of this little excursion; it might be deemed improper or disrespectful. And what if someone drowned? But Azi insisted that they needed to push the limits.

At a cue from Azi, the boats powered down and bobbed in the water in a loose circle.

"How are you doing?" Azi asked a senior cleric who hadn't spoken the whole trip.

"It is very good here." he replied. "We never do things like this in our schools."

"So, what do you guys do when you are in a good mood?"

---

[52] Manuscript excerpt reproduced with permission from Will Jenkins and Azhar Hussain. Copyright 2014 Will Jenkins and Azhar Hussain.

"I love to sing songs," said a young man in another boat. Heads turned in surprise to see it was a conservative Deobandi teacher speaking. Deobandis traditionally oppose music and art.

Azi smiled. "What songs do you like?"

The young man closed his eyes and in little more than a whisper began to sing a popular old folk song.

> *"Oh, my lover let's go,*
> *We can go across the moon together*
> *Because the moon is so beautiful now."*

Emboldened by this, others began to join him until everyone was singing—-young voices and old melted in haunting melody. They sang through a series of songs. They clapped and stamped during the rousing songs and held hands during prayerful ballads. The boats swayed with the energy of their singing. A few looked over the edge, fearful they might drown, but the singing pulled them back.

When the final chorus was finished, they all fell silent. The waves softly lapped against the sides of the boats. The sun touched the horizon.

"What do you think about when you sing?" Azi asked.

The young man who first sang gazed at the setting sun. "Sometimes there is a strong wish, a wish to escape all this…"

"Do you think that God will punish us for what we just did?" continued Azi.

"I don't know if God is going to punish us," said another teacher.

"I tend to feel the same way," replied Azi. "What harm has been done?"

Mandela

Azi motioned to a faded map on an easel as he began the morning session. Today we are going to talk about South Africa and a great African leader named Nelson Mandela. You may have heard of him."

"A few decades ago, he was a political activist who opposed the government of South Africa. At that time, South Africa was controlled by a small group of white people who oppressed the majority black population."

A few teachers nodded knowingly.

"Mandela was put into prison as a political prisoner. I'm sure you all know political prisoners here in Pakistan.

Now in African culture, just like Pakistani culture, if you are a grown man, only boys wear shorts. Men wear pants. But the prisoners all had to wear shorts.

I would like you to imagine there are lots of Africans there in prison, are they wearing shorts or pants?"

"Shorts." Responded the teachers.

"And who is wearing pants?"

"The white people. The guards."

"Good. I want you to picture the scene. Mandela was a prisoner. He would come to lunch, and pound the table, saying, 'I want to wear pants.'

The guards told him not to say that, but he did it again the next day. He was beaten. He was beaten for days and his prison mates started asking him why are you doing this? You'll be killed. His jaw was broken, he went to the hospital and came back. Do you think he stopped?"

"No!" the teachers shouted; feeling a connection with the underdog.

"That's right. He did the same thing every day." Azi told how Mandela finally found a pair of khaki pants in his cell with a note saying to be quiet. "The next day he came to lunch with the pants on his shoulder. He pounded the table and said he wanted everyone to have pants. He was beaten up; but after a while, everyone in the prison got pants.

Then Nelson Mandela went on to become President of South Africa." Azi passed around a photo of Mandela.

"Now you may be thinking that sounds pretty silly, right? All that just to get pants? Why not fight for his freedom? That was his real vision after all.

Mandela was in jail, but he proved that no matter where you are you can still do something about your vision. Now, why did he want pants for himself first? What would have happened if he'd asked for everyone first?"

"He would never have succeeded," offered a teacher. "It was too much."

"It would have caused more anger among the prisoners when they didn't get them." suggested another.

"Yes, Mandela showed that we need to have justice in our own lives first before we go out there to try to solve the problems of our country. So, let's think about Pakistan. How do your religious leaders motivate you?"

"They talk about how America is mistreating us. How our government is corrupt."

"We don't have money for food or books for our students. The government stole it all."

"What happens when we start to rationalize and blame the government or America for the state of Islam?" pressed Azi. "Mandela could have blamed the system, too, but even in the jail he realized his vision was for equality for everyone. He determined to win even small battles to achieve that ultimate goal. In Pakistan it seems everyone is waiting on someone else—America, the military, the government. But Mandela shows us there is always something we can do right now."

Azi asked the teachers to write down their own visions of what religious leaders could do now that would inspire the people and overcome injustice. That night, Azi read the teacher's visions for themselves, their students and their country. He began to cry at their honesty and hope.

"We have been teaching Islam all day for the last 10-20 years and missed the point that it is calling Muslims to live, work, and share life with others who are different from us." wrote one teacher. "We have been fighting to be left alone and live in isolation. No wonder people are so suspicious of madrasas because we are convinced that they are there to destroy our way of life."

"As leaders and teachers, we are so shocked to learn that our teaching methods can promote fear of losing our way of life and Islam," wrote another. "We keep thinking of these grand conspiracies about the others. What we need to do is build more confidence and trust in our students so they can trust the world they live in instead of rebelling against it. But we don't even know how to do that anymore."

One Down, One Thousand to Go

The next days blurred together. Azi would get up at 4:30 am for prayers and hurried discussions with the other facilitators. He worked to pace the exercises and lessons to draw out the teachers, encourage them to discover for themselves and not push too hard. Somehow it was working.

Despite the full schedule, he insisted that the whole group regather after evening prayers to debrief on the day's discussions and find points on which to take action. Then even if the program ended after only a few days, they would have something in writing to show for it.

Early on, the teachers were still very courteous to each other, partly because of the norms and partly because they just didn't know enough to be rude to each other yet.

No group activity lasted more than ten minutes because they weren't used to working in groups and would fall apart very quickly with normal group activities Azi had used with Western companies. They seemed to be enjoying the process. The goal was not only to build a community but also give the teachers knowledge and skills to be able to work together.

In addition to group exercises, the class explored the scientific and liberal arts disciplines, including religious tolerance and human rights.

One day, Azi saw a line of teachers waiting to use the telephone in the lobby.

"Azi, Azi," the man holding the receiver waved him over. "I have been telling my friend in Quetta about this program. He wants to meet you. Here, speak to him." The phone was thrust into Azi's surprised hands.

"You must promise to come to our madrasas," crackled the voice on the line. "Our students are very bright but they do not know this history you are teaching. Will you come?'

It turned out that every teacher in the line wanted to introduce Azi to friends around the country.

Thus, began a series of 10-day workshops for madrasa leaders from across Pakistan, workshops that focused on two principal goals: (1) expanding the madrasa curriculums to include the physical and social sciences (with a strong emphasis on human rights and religious tolerance), and (2) transforming the pedagogy to create enhanced critical thinking skills among the students. In these tradition-bound tribal cultures, there is little room for critical thinking, so this represented more of a leap for the students than just inspiring them to become more inclusive.[53] To illustrate its importance: whenever a local militant approached a madrasa student or a recent graduate and invited him to go fight Americans in Afghanistan or Hindus in Kashmir, that student had no ability to challenge or question the invitation. Almost without exception (or question), their response to such invitations was positive.

Reform Program Elements

The following are the key elements of the ICRD training program that we eventually developed for madrasa teachers:

- *Overcoming Barriers to Change*——It is critical to address the anxieties that many madrasa leaders feel with regard to change. In addition to fearing the possible secularization and Westernization of their curriculums, teachers who do not have the skills to teach subjects like math and science fear that they may become irrelevant and lose their jobs if these subjects are added to the curriculum. Some madrasa teachers also fear the prospect of failure if they try to implement new techniques or courses, worrying that they might lose face and come to be seen as incompetent by their students.

- *Honoring Islamic Achievements and Tradition*——The past accomplishments of Islam in selected areas of educational achievement and

---

[53] Closer to home in endorsing this same concept was a recent letter from Harvard University President Lawrence Bacow to the Harvard community in which he noted that "in order to differentiate signal from noise in a cacophonous world, a broad liberal arts education—and its emphasis on critical thinking and rational argument—has never been more important."

in promoting human rights and religious tolerance are emphasized and celebrated in order to inspire change.

- *Exploring Identity and Teaching Conflict Resolution Skills—* — Participants are encouraged to explore their own feelings in relation to perceived threats to their identity and how they respond to such threats. Workshop sessions also explore such concepts as the fundamentals of conflict, active listening, communication, mediation, and negotiation. These sessions help the participants develop conflict resolution skills which they can then apply in their own schools, communities, and society at large. Special workshops also focus on peace education and the Islamic basis for democracy.

- *Developing Awareness and Integration of Human Rights—* —Within the workshops, dialogue is initiated about the basis for promoting human rights in Islamic law and how human rights principles can be integrated into the madrasa curriculum and pedagogy. This approach promotes human rights not from a foreign point of view, but from a religious point of view consistent with the teachings of Islam.

- *Enhancing Teaching Methodology, Pedagogical Skills, and Foundational Knowledge—* —There is a strong focus on equipping the participants with enhanced pedagogical skills and educational knowledge. Efforts are made to help the participants determine how they can integrate concepts of tolerance, pluralism, identity, and human rights into their teaching methodology. Sessions address such topics as child psychology, ethics, responsibilities, interactive and student-centered learning, critical thinking and analytical abilities, and different styles of teaching and learning. These sessions are interactive in nature.

- *Integration and Experiential Exposure—* —In the final sessions, participants are encouraged to learn from one another and from non-traditional speakers with whom they would normally not interact (and who expose them to new ways of teaching and learning). These activities give the madrasa leaders the opportunity to put into practice new concepts they have learned in the training. Workshop sessions have included presentations by female Muslim scholars, and by leaders of other sects, religions, and nationalities.

During the first year of the project, the State Department learned of our effort and invited me to brief them on it. I agreed and explained our project to about 25 middle-level officials from various State Department offices, including the Agency for International Development (USAID). It was a receptive audience, and they urged me to apply for a grant from their Educational and Cultural Affairs Bureau, which had just issued a Request for Proposals (RFP), with which our Center's madrasa project would have made an ideal fit.

I was hesitant to do so, because our involvement in the project at that time was less than totally visible, and I was concerned that if of our Center's role became too public at this early stage, it might backfire and derail the project. By the same token, we desperately needed funding to continue the work; so, I decided to go ahead and apply. This was symptomatic of the fine line we have had to walk throughout our Center's history, maintaining a low-enough profile to do the work (without attracting too much opposition from vested interests that inevitably surround any conflict) versus maintaining a high-enough profile to attract the funding needed to make that work possible in the first place.

About three months later, I was called over to the office of a USAID luminary to meet with him and a senior official from State. They said, "This meeting never took place, because we aren't supposed to do this. But of the 50 proposals we received for the education project, yours is the most exciting and the one we would most like to fund. However, we need to discuss how we can overcome the political hurdles relating to Pakistani sensitivities that could stand in the way."

As luck would have it, our meeting was rendered moot later that same week by a pronouncement from President Mushareff effectively banning all foreigners from working with the country's madrasas. At that point, State lost all interest in our project. For understandable reasons, they didn't want to risk losing Pakistan as a partner in the Global War on Terrorism by supporting our work with the madrasas.

Playing Hardball

About a year and a half into the project— at about the same time I hired Azi on a full-time basis—I felt led to discontinue our partnership with IPS. Although we were raising all of the funding and had assumed all-but-total responsibility for the substance of the training, we were not receiving any credit for our efforts. We were essentially relegated to being silent partners, because of IPS's reluctance to make it widely known they were partnering with an American organization. Out of that same concern, they were only recruiting moderate madrasas to receive the training. Finally, IPS was institutionally associated with the Jamat Islamic sect, which had a very anti-Western agenda; and despite the inroads we were making with the madrasas, its anti-Western rhetoric remained as strident as ever.

After an amicable parting of the ways, we recruited two individuals as our new partners, one a Deobandi and the other Ahle Hadith (Wahhabi), the two hardest-line sects in the country. Each enjoyed considerable stature within his respective sect; and rather than being shy about working with Americans, saw it as advantageous to be doing so. They both felt that if they could showcase to their constituencies some good things Americans were doing, it might help stem some of the violence that was running rampant at the time.

It was not an easy game to play, and they periodically came under tremendous pressure to cease working with us. This was especially the case after U.S. bombing at one point destroyed a madrasa, which was thought to be harboring extremists. To address the resulting anger and anguish, I crafted a statement in which I made a strong case for why madrasas should be treated as sacred institutions, not subject to armed attack by anyone, nor misused by political forces to advance a violent agenda. Both partners prevailed on the local media to publish the statement widely, after which tempers subsided, and the partnership survived.

The above pressures were not the only kind with which our partners had to contend. We also leaned heavily on them to help us gain access to extremist madrasas in the more radical areas of the country. They did a stellar job in this regard, while often going in harm's way to make it happen.

Sometimes the threats became very personal in nature. For example, at one point, extremists kidnapped the son of our Ahle Hadith partner, Abdul Khamosh, and held him captive for a day before letting him go. The message to his father was loud and clear: stop working with ICRD, or there would be severe negative consequences to pay. In response to that threat, Khamosh sent his son, Ameer, to the United States; and we (ICRD) applied for political asylum on his behalf. After a number of months and a laborious legal process—including an entire afternoon in a Baltimore courtroom, persuading the judge of the seriousness of the request—Ameer gained asylum, graduated from college, became a citizen, and is now running a car dealership. Happily, with his departure from Pakistan, the extremists ceased making threats, and our partnership with his father continued until we completed our task. The friendship with both lasts to the present.

Out of the Closet

Despite Mushareff's earlier pronouncement forbidding foreign engagement with the madrasas, we continued doing what we had been doing, while keeping both governments (ours and theirs) at arm's length. After several years, though, because of the success we were having, we felt it inevitable that the Pakistan government would soon learn of our project and decided it would be safer if they heard about it from us, rather than someone else. So, Azi launched a charm offensive and succeeded in establishing a close relationship with the government's Secretary of Religious Affairs. The Secretary's boss was the Minister of Religious Affairs, who had a longstanding reputation as a religious hard-liner and someone who would probably not fully appreciate what we were doing. Hence, our focus on the Secretary.

Several months later, we invited the Secretary and the National Madrasa Oversight Board (ITMP) to visit the United States in order to provide them with a hands-on exposure to Islamic education in America. The Oversight Board, with whom Azi by then had established a close working relationship, consisted of the top religious leaders who oversaw the madrasas associated with their particular sects. (Because the madrasas are not government-funded, they are answerable only to these religious leaders.)

While in the United States, the delegates engaged in important discussions with a number of American educators, politicians, and religious leaders, who, in turn, benefited from an enhanced awareness of the complex realities of religious influence in Pakistan. At one point, I chaired a panel discussion on this aspect before a major gathering of policy-makers and pundits at CSIS, with the Pakistani delegates serving as the panelists. There were also helpful interactions with the Pakistani Embassy, other think tanks, university faculty, and selected officials in the Executive and Legislative branches of our government. By this time, the Mushareff restriction had died a slow death, and we were now out of the closet on all fronts.

In February of 2010, we hosted a second delegation of seven Pakistani madrasa and religious leaders for a three-week visit to the United States. This visit enabled these participants to (1) explore religious education in America, including best practices and how it is integrated with other subjects; (2) receive professional development training in teaching methodologies and conflict resolution skills; and (3) build relationships with American counterparts, while promoting greater intercultural understanding.

The delegation highlighted dialogue with Americans as one of the most powerful experiences of the program, as they became aware that Americans share many of their own concerns, that the values of the United States and Islam are not inherently opposed, and that it is possible to be both a devout Muslim and an active participant in American society. One participant stated,

> *"When I go back, I intend to tell the people of Pakistan that we should not look at US government policy only, but we should understand the mindset and the goodness of the American people as well...There should be much bigger exchanges like this beyond this small group."*

He subsequently founded a new school in his tribal area of Pakistan modeled after an American Islamic school he had visited during the program.

Because we pursued this madrasa enhancement project for eight years prior to turning it over to an indigenous NGO (for which we had established the legal framework some two years earlier), a thorough recitation of all that took place during that period would require several volumes to capture in its entirety. Instead, I will focus on a few anecdotal highlights and those measures we took on a systemic basis to make a lasting difference. The anecdotes also illustrate how faith-based diplomacy works at the local level and the significant impact it can have.

Anecdotal Change

In 2006, I took two ICRD board members, Harold "Rink" Jacobi and John Sandoz, with me to Pakistan to visit several madrasas that were clearly identified with terrorism. Rink is a sharp attorney from Boston (and my best friend) and John, also a friend, had been the Navy's first Commanding Officer of SEAL Team 4. Our Center had not previously been involved with any of these particular schools but was able to gain access based on the work we had been doing with other madrasas in the surrounding area. By way of background, there are five groups that sponsor these religious schools, of which the Deobandis and the Wahhabis, as previously mentioned, are the two hardest-line. In fact, the Deobandis, from which the Taliban emerged, are considerably more powerful and influential than all of the other four combined.

The first school we visited was a Deobandi madrasa outside of Karachi that housed some 7,000 students and was thought to provide most of the fighters for Chechnya and Kashmir. It was also known to have spawned the two most violent anti-Shiite terrorist groups in the country. Indeed, Azi had lost a cousin to an attack by one of these groups.

We walked into a sizeable room filled with madrasa leaders, administrators, faculty, and senior Islamic scholars. It was also full of rage, rage over U.S. foreign policy in general and, more specifically, over the conflict that was then underway in Lebanon between Israel and Hezbollah (with the United States credited for any perceived wrongs by Israel). I began by saying,

> *"We are not a government organization, nor have we ever received any funding from our government (which was true at that time). And while the United States may have made some mistakes of late, it's important for you to remember when they intervened on behalf of Muslims in Bosnia, Kosovo, Somalia, and Kuwait. Left*

unmentioned in most tellings of Somalia are the more than 100,000 Somali lives that were saved as a result of the humanitarian aspects of that intervention.

And while the United States may fairly be accused of operating with a double standard in the Middle East because of its strategic relationship with Israel, so too can Arab leaders be accused of doing the same as they complain mightily of Israeli mistreatment, and then turn a deaf ear to Palestinian pleas for humanitarian assistance. So everywhere you turn, there are double standards—driven by perceived national interest."

I was trying to get past the rage. And then I said,

"We are not here to talk about foreign policy, though. We are here to see if we can build meaningful relationships based on religious values that we share in common."

Then I quoted several passages from the Qur'an, which I had committed to memory, a consolidated paraphrase of which would go something like this:

"O mankind, God could have made you one had He willed, but He did not. Instead, He made you into separate nations and tribes that you may know one another, cooperate with one another, and compete with one another in good works."

I then said,

"I and my two colleagues are here to open the competition in good works. The three of us happen to be followers of Jesus, and we know you can't be a good Muslim unless you believe some pretty wonderful things about Jesus. So, let's ask ourselves, if He were here today standing in our midst, how would He want us to behave toward one another?"

By the time that discussion played out over the next hour, the rage had been converted to a spirit of acceptance bordering on fellowship. It was a remarkable transformation. Azi later told me that when I quoted the passages from the Qur'an, he heard an audible sigh of relief from the audience. That simple gesture of respect apparently dissipated much of the rage that had been present at the outset.

We then visited a madrasa near Lahore, which had been identified with the London bombers. Same scenario, same impact. Since then, the leader of that particular madrasa, who is a rather large, widely-revered and somewhat feared individual, has encountered Azi on several occasions. Each time, he has made specific reference to the question about Jesus, and said, "It caused me to ask myself on a daily basis, 'What would the Prophet have me do?'" And his madrasa, without the benefit of any of our training, has on its own convened seminars on peacemaking and conflict resolution. So, one never quite knows where the seeds one plants are going to bear fruit.

Following a similar presentation to an ICRD workshop that was taking place at the third madrasa, a madrasa teacher came up to me with his hand over his heart, a twinkle in his eyes and a smile on his face and said, "You have made me very happy. We thought all Americans hated us." I thought to myself, "Well, if one took the media as one's guide, one could easily come to that conclusion." I assured him that not all Americans felt that way.

After this third and final workshop, which, like the first, took place in Karachi, the three of us and Azi drove around town, at one point stopping to view the scenery at the city beach, which borders on the Arabian Sea. Because Karachi is a relatively violent city, with Taliban enclaves frequenting the suburbs, and because Americans were being taken hostage from time to time, we tried to keep a low profile as we ambled about. When we stopped at the beach, however, Rink and John jumped out of the car with their video cameras and started taking pictures of the beachgoers, while Azi and I sort of cringed in the back seat. To this day, I still haven't figured out what inspired them to act so impulsively. Bathing beauties dressed in *burkas* simply don't do it for me.

Bin Laden's Lair

Near the end of our trip, I was scheduled to make a presentation to about 300 madrasa leaders and Islamic scholars in Abbottabad, which is several hours north of Islamabad (and where Bin Laden was captured a few years later). It was not a particularly safe journey to make in light of the incidence of kidnappings that had been taking place throughout the country. So, at dinner the night before, Rink and John said they were exercising their authority as board members to forbid me from making the trip. I responded by saying, "Are you kidding me? Several hundred madrasa leaders will be attending this event (most of whom have never seen a Westerner). What am I going to say—-that I was too afraid to come? The two of you can stay, but I'm going." This sounds harsher than it actually was. The three of us are close friends and the dialogue was always cordial. Anyway, they backed off and decided to come as well.

The next afternoon when we arrived in Abbottabad and exited our SUV, bystanders began showering me with rose petals and put more than a dozen leis around my neck. I had no idea why, but it felt great to be treated like a rock star, however fleetingly. Once we were shuffled inside, the three of us sat on a stage with four other speakers, me at one end of the row and the two of them at the other. It was unbearably hot and humid, and I was scheduled to speak last, following the other four. The talking stretched on for about three sweltering hours before I was finally called on to speak.

Shortly after I began, several members of the audience started shouting and making threatening gestures in my direction. Meanwhile, John and Rink started looking for the nearest exit and discussing who would take the first bullet when they started shooting at me. At this point, our Wahhabi partner, Abdul Qadeer Khamosh, who was serving as the host of the event took the mike and out-shouted the protesters, until they eventually chose to leave. All of this took place in Urdu, so I didn't have a clue as to what was being said. All I recall was getting very calm and cool when it looked like things were starting to turn violent. That has always been my reaction in threatening circumstances. Not sure why, but it seems to serve me well in tight situations.

Another interesting moment from that event took place during the question and answer period when one of the madrasa leaders, referring to the passages I had cited from the Qur'an, asked if I could provide similar quotations from the Bible. This provided an opportunity to share Biblical verses relating to loving one's enemy and turning the other cheek. I told the audience that although these were tough verses to live out; it was what we aspired to do as Christians, much like their own aspirations as Muslims to form a community on earth that is pleasing to Allah.

Aside from the challenges in Abbottabad, we ended up having a rather close call on our return flight home. Apparently, the plane we took from London to Washington was targeted by a terrorist group that had just been apprehended for planning to blow it, along with nine other commercial carriers, out of the sky at roughly the same time. Clearly, the Lord had other plans.

Engaging the Government

Prior to leaving Pakistan, we called on Mohammedmian Soomro, Chairman of their Senate, to brief him on the project and seek his support for our efforts. During the course of our discussion, I mentioned that years earlier while teaching a Master's-level course at Harvard, some of the brightest students in my class were Pakistani foreign service officers. I told him that I was having difficulty reconciling that brilliance on the one hand with the abject poverty I witnessed while driving around Karachi on the other. It seemed incongruous in the extreme.

In response, the Chairman attributed the poverty to the heavy burden Pakistanis had borne in helping the United States free Afghanistan from the Soviets and now in opposing the extremists that were currently threatening their country. He said that Pakistan had paid a steep price on both counts in terms of lives and treasure and that his country needed another 200 million dollars from the United States to turn the corner and complete the task. (The real answer to my question as I later came to learn was that those on the top in Pakistan view life as a zero-sum game and are quite content to leave things as they are.)

As for ICRD's work with the madrasas, he applauded our efforts and recommended that we brief the Minister of Religious Affairs on the specifics of our project. Because, as previously mentioned, that particular minister had a reputation as a religious hard-liner, we chose not to do that.

A few months later, however, Azi and I met briefly with Soomro again, and he offered to help us secure additional support for our work by facilitating private meetings with the governors of Punjab, Baluchistan, and the Northwest Frontier Province. He also offered to accompany us on these trips. Soomro's reputation in the Senate coupled with his past service as Governor of Sind Province gave him tremendous credibility, so this was a highly meaningful gesture.

We also met with Rehman Malik, Minister of the Interior (under whose authority government oversight of the madrasas resided), followed by a longer meeting with the President of the country, Asaf Ali Zardari. The Minister was basically unsympathetic to the plight of the madrasas and felt they should be secularized and forced to become an integral part of civil society (the same approach that had failed miserably when attempted in the past).

The meeting with the President turned out to be far more personal in nature. About a year earlier, I had visited with him and his wife, Benazir Bhutto, over dinner in Washington. This was some months prior to Benazir's return to Pakistan to run for the Presidency in the 2008 elections. She had twice before served as Prime Minister, was highly popular, and as leader of the opposition Pakistan People's Party (PPP), seemed all-but-certain to be elected. Upon her return, though, she was assassinated following a political rally in Rawalpindi; and her husband subsequently rode his deceased wife's coattails to the Presidency.

After briefing President Zardari on our project and securing his moral support for the effort, I referred to our earlier dinner in Washington and told him how impressed I was to see how genuine Benazir's affection for him had been. (Prior to that dinner, I had been aware of his reputation as "Mr. Ten Percent," and of the fact that he had spent considerable time in prison on charges of extortion. I was also aware that theirs had been an arranged marriage, so I didn't know exactly what to expect).

He appeared touched by my comment and staring at the ceiling, while leaning back in his chair, said "Only she knows what I went through." I later learned from other sources that he had spent a total of eleven years in prison, and that she felt he had done it all for her. While in prison, he was offered the opportunity to go free if he would only agree to sign a document critical of the PPP (his wife's party). He refused to do so; and despite several attempts on his life during his incarceration, hung tough throughout.

Our 20-minute, late-night appointment turned into an hour and a half; and I suspect that if either of us won the other over, it was he who did the winning. In my eyes, he deserved far greater respect than his commonly-held reputation suggested. Bottom line: everyone deserves a deeper look.

Tribal Challenges

At one of the many other workshops that Azi conducted, a madrasa leader came up to him at the end and said, "There's a situation in my village that I feel a need to address." A young lady was apparently caught talking on her cell phone at two in the morning with a young man in another village, in whom she had an interest. The village elders felt this violated their code of honor, so she was to die, and the boy was to be severely punished.

The madrasa leader said, "These kinds of situations happen all the time, and I normally wouldn't get involved. But because of our workshop discussions on human rights, I feel compelled to go back and confront this on religious grounds." So, he did, but with a great deal of trepidation, since he was much younger than the elders. Nevertheless, he sat down with them, showed them there was nothing in the Qur'an that prohibited a woman from talking to a man; and by emphasizing passages that urge a peaceful resolution of differences, he was able to persuade them to forego the punishments. No one was hurt; and hopefully, that will serve as a future precedent in that village and perhaps others in the surrounding vicinity.

It is noteworthy that this was a situation where religion trumped tribalism in a context where even most Muslims can't tell where one ends and the other begins. And it's not always a given that religion will trump; because, as tribal members are quick to point out, their customs date back three thousand years; whereas Islam only goes back fourteen hundred. So, one still has to work at it.

On to Punjab

In another on-the-ground situation, we were conducting a workshop at a madrasa in Punjab that was known to be a major Al Qaeda feeder. Some 22 percent of its graduates went that route, but instead of deploying to fight Americans in Afghanistan, because of the geography, they went to Kashmir to become part of the militant movement there. Toward the end of the session, one of the madrasa leaders asked, "Is waging *jihad* in Kashmir sanctioned by Islam?" Azi said, "No it isn't, but I'm not a religious leader." So, he turned to Khamosh, our indigenous partner and a Wahhabi who enjoys at least honorary *mullah* status, who said, "No; *jihad* is only justified to defend the religion, never to acquire territory."

This led to an intense debate between the madrasa leaders, and they came to a consensus conclusion that the fighting in Kashmir was politically motivated, but not religiously sanctioned. After that, they began working to tone down the militancy of their graduates. On a later visit to Pakistan, I was surprised to learn that that this particular episode had been captured in a newspaper article in Balochistan, halfway across the country.

The Taliban

At another workshop and as briefly described in the first chapter, we were surprised to learn that one of the participants was a Taliban commander of some renown, who lamented the fact that neither he nor his colleagues knew what America wanted. This, in turn, led to an invitation for me to address this issue with their senior leadership, which I did two months later. Before going, I did my due diligence at State, Defense, and the Agency to ensure whatever I said was consistent with U.S. policy. After making these rounds, I concluded that the Taliban weren't the only ones who didn't know what America wanted.

I eventually had that meeting with some 57 Afghan Taliban commanders and several religious and tribal leaders at a private compound in the mountains of Pakistan. I started by telling them I was not there as a representative of the U.S. government, but rather as the head of a private center that practiced faith-based diplomacy. I said my goal was to determine if we could build on religious values that we shared in common to develop a confidence-building measure that could lead toward peace. I further said that for them to be able to participate in such an effort, they needed to understand the Western perspective on what was taking place. So, I told them what America wanted, which, simply put, was for the Taliban to lay down their arms, distance themselves from al Qaeda, and reconcile with the Karzai government.

Over the next couple of hours in which a great deal of venting took place, several key questions emerged, the first being, "What do the American people want?" At that, I breathed a sigh of relief because it meant they were still cutting us some slack, even though we had re-elected the same Administration that was the source of most of their problems. I told them that what Americans wanted was peace in the region, with democratically stable governments in Iraq and Afghanistan.

Then they wanted to know why we were attacking Islam. I assured them that we weren't, for the same reasons I cited during my earlier visit to the Deobandi madrasa. They then wanted to know why we were attacking Afghanistan, and I said,

> *"Well——to put it in terms that you hold dear: hospitality, loyalty, and revenge—-before we recognized certain members of al Qaeda as a threat, we welcomed them into our country and gave them hospitality. Then on 9-11 and without warning, they struck. We wanted revenge and asked the Taliban government to turn over al Qaeda's leadership, so we could bring them to justice. They refused, so we attacked.*
>
> *But we did so with a heavy heart, because most Americans have great admiration and respect for the Afghan people, stemming from our common struggle against the former Soviet Union.*
>
> *Furthermore, it's important for you to recognize that some of your own tribal leaders are now banding together against al Qaeda because they have violated your hospitality."*

At one point during the discussion, a young Taliban commander by the name of Abdul Hafeez stood up and told how he had always been opposed to the Taliban and al Qaeda until one day while out walking with his wife, they were stopped and searched by the U.S. military. Both of them were required to put their hands in the air as they were being frisked—all the while being subjected to a copious stream of profanity. Abdul said he was made to feel totally humiliated in front of his wife and at that point crossed over and joined the Taliban. At the time of our discussion, he was leading 350 Taliban fighters in Kunar, an Afghan province where the fighting was particularly intense.

After only a brief exposure to Abdul, I could immediately sense he was a born leader. He had a natural charisma, was fluent in four languages, and was addressed by his colleagues as "Engineer" —- a laudatory title, short for "one who gets the job done." Since meeting him, I have often wondered how many body bags have made their way back to the United States because the engineer has been "getting the job done." All because of a gratuitous insult in a culture where honor is everything (Addendum Q).

We later broke for prayer, and, with Abdul's help, came back in a smaller group to develop the confidence-building measure. During the earlier discussion, the participants had lamented the fact that of the billions of dollars flowing into Afghanistan, none of it had made its way to the village level. Almost all of it was being siphoned off either by the government or by the warlords. Thus, the confidence-building measure that emerged from the smaller group meeting called for establishing a secure zone in the western third of Nuristan, where things were relatively quiet, in order to facilitate private development assistance that would directly benefit the villages.

Nuristan is the Afghan province directly across the border from where we were holding our meeting (in the Malakand Agency of Pakistan), and Kunar is directly south of that. Although we were eventually able to facilitate additional U.S. development assistance in Nuristan, the confidence-building measure itself failed, because we were unable to gain sufficient traction with NATO to establish the secure zone.

During the course of this interaction, I came away with three distinct impressions. First, the Taliban leaders seemed to genuinely care about their people. Second, they nursed a visceral hatred for the warlords, who they felt frequently co-opted the U.S. military. Finally, they felt total disdain for Karzai, because of his failure to keep his promise to control the warlords.

The gentleman who owned the compound in which these meetings took place was Haji-Ayoub, rumored to have given sanctuary to Bin Laden in the immediate wake of 9-11. Haji had attended his first ICRD workshop with the expressed intent of killing Azi. However, when he didn't hear Azi promoting an American agenda and only heard him talking about how Muslims could become better Muslims, he changed his mind and soon became a champion of our work. That transformation eventually led to his willingness to host my meeting with the Taliban commanders, a gesture for which he subsequently paid a dear price. He made his living by renting construction equipment; and following my meeting, Al Qaeda confiscated his equipment. They also tortured two young men who had helped provide security for the event.

271

The Power of Culture

Several years later, when Haji traveled to Washington with a group of influential Deobandi and Wahhabi religious leaders to explore Islamic education in America, we ran into one another at the initial event. After rejoicing at seeing one another and exchanging the normal pleasantries, he invited me to come visit him again. I gladly accepted; but once he was out of earshot, I asked Azi how he could make such an offer after having paid such a huge price the last time I visited. Azi said, "I don't know; I'll ask him." After doing so, Azi said Haji's reply was, "I would rather die than not offer hospitality to someone I like and respect." A graphic illustration of what can be learned from other cultures, if we would open our hearts and minds to doing so.

The Ideas Behind the Guns

One final anecdote. In 2009, we were conducting a workshop for sixteen madrasas surrounding the Swat Valley, a resort area in the mountains of Pakistan which had recently been taken over by the Taliban. Near the end of the workshop, one of the participants stood up and said,

> *"I came here for one reason and one reason only, and that is to discredit everything you have to say. But after listening to what you have said, I now find myself filled with rage. Rage, because for 26 years I have been studying and teaching the Qur'an the way it was taught to me. But now, for the first time in my life, I feel I have sensed the soul of the Holy Qur'an and its peaceful intent. I now see that the right way to advance Islam is through peace, not conflict. I am going to change what I teach my students and tell them why."*

In addition to being a madrasa leader, he was also a commander in *Lashkar e Taiba*, the terrorist group that had earlier mounted a devastating attack against Mumbai, the largest city in India. Despite his status as a terrorist commander, it was nevertheless a brave statement to make in mixed company, when heads were rolling for considerably less.

A month later, we paid another visit; and this particular leader was doing exactly as he had promised. He also made that earlier statement about feeling enraged to a CNN crew that had come along to film our work. After that, he said, "Enough, enough" as he recognized he was skating on very thin ice.

This was only the latest of many examples of how courageous these folks are. Once you work your way past the veneer of rage and hostility and are able to engage them on the basis of religious principles, not only do they "get it", but many of them become champions of the new ideas, often at great personal risk to themselves. Once they believe in what you're saying, they go "all in."

In the U.S. contest with militant Islam, mention is often made of needing to "drain the swamp [of terrorism]." Bombs and bullets certainly have their place; but more often than not, they breed more terrorists as the cycle of revenge takes hold. And as the pool of future terrorists expands, so does the probability of evolving to a police state as one seeks greater security in an increasingly insecure world (a tendency that became all-too-apparent in the immediate wake of 9-11). However, as our work with the madrasas attests, if you truly want to drain the swamp, you need to win hearts and minds, which, in turn, becomes contagious.

Female Madrasas

Soon after we began conducting workshops for the boys' madrasas, we were asked by the female leaders of girls' madrasas to provide the same training for them. We were willing; but the male madrasa leaders were strongly opposed, so we backed off. After another three years (of pillow talk, I presume), the men asked us to conduct similar workshops for the women. This was important because women, particularly in the rural areas, are often stricter than the men in their adherence to Islamic precepts and, as in most cultures, enjoy a near-monopoly in shaping the formative years of their children (before they are old enough to enter a madrasa). Thus, they are a powerful grassroots influence in Pakistani society and must be engaged (in addition to the men), if religious tolerance and human rights are to take hold in that radicalized environment.

This commitment presented challenges we had never dreamed of, and we soon found ourselves jumping through some rather onerous hoops to teach the ladies without having direct contact with them. In one instance, this required speaking to them from outside a metal enclosure in which they were grouped—a hot (sometimes *very* hot) box, if you will. Such challenges aside, though, the women picked it up about twice as fast as the men in internalizing what we were teaching. Indeed, during the course of some of the workshops for females, we were also able to establish vocational training programs in their madrasas related to sewing.

Dancing with the FBI

Over the course of the madrasa project, we had two experiences with the FBI, one positive and the other less so. At one point in the early stages of the project, I thought it could be helpful for us to establish a formal partnership with the International Institute of Islamic Thought (IIIT), an NGO based in Herndon, Virginia, that focused on educational reform in the Muslim world. A Vice President of IIIT by the name of Jamal Barzinji had offered to be helpful in connecting us with Islamic scholars and potential funders for our madrasa effort, both of which would have been quite helpful at the time. However, in the wake of 9-11, IIIT had been accused of supporting terrorist activities. Even though nothing was ever found to substantiate such charges, IIIT was still under a cloud of suspicion at the time.

Because I had been involved with IIIT for quite some time on other fronts, I knew their officers well enough to be confident of their loyalty to the United States; and I was determined to cement the relationship. By the same token, I didn't want to do anything that might embarrass our Board or other supporters; so I met with the Assistant Director of the FBI for Counterterrorism, explained the situation, and asked his advice. He told me to give him three days to get back to me. On the third day, he called and said, "Full speed ahead, with your eyes open."

A few weeks later we consummated the partnership with IIIT in a formal signing ceremony; and although it didn't yield much in the way of support for the madrasa project, it did prove helpful in other areas. Payoff aside, I was grateful to the FBI for its responsiveness and willingness to provide the necessary top-cover for us to proceed ahead.

Our second experience with the Bureau took place the following year when two FBI agents visited our office. They said they had heard me speak at a conference on Capitol Hill, were aware of our Center's partnership with IIIT, and wanted to know if I would help introduce them to the American Muslim community. They were both former military, one a former Marine Recon veteran and the other from the Army's 2nd Ranger Battalion, so I felt an instant bond stemming from my own military service and told them I would be pleased to help.

Although their stated mission was to engage with the American Muslim community and they even offered to compensate us for our time in doing so (which we refused), I became convinced over time that their actual interests may have exceeded that. I based this on their intense interest in our Pakistan work and the kinds of questions they asked. They appeared particularly taken aback by my meeting with the Taliban commanders; and until

Azi showed them pictures of that encounter, they couldn't believe we had actually pulled it off.

At one point, Azi expressed a concern that our friends from the Bureau were attempting to influence his actions in Pakistan, suggesting to him in the process of doing so that they had us over a barrel because of the way we operated with our indigenous partners. These partners were instrumental in facilitating our workshops through their recruitment of the participants, securing of the facilities, and handling of the logistics. In exchange for their services, we compensated them monetarily.

Most of all, we needed their help in engaging the radical elements we were seeking to influence. Although neither of our two indigenous partners were on any of the U.S. government's terrorist watch lists, if they used any of the funding we provided to pay for their membership dues in some radical organization, then a case could be made that we were indirectly supporting terrorist activities. In short, the Bureau was starting to play hardball, and we were in a bit of a bind.

To address this problem, I scheduled an appointment with the Bureau's newly appointed Assistant Director for Counter-Terrorism (my earlier contact had since retired); and I asked Joe Reeder, an ICRD board member and lawyer who enjoys a "can do" reputation second- to-none in the ranks of Washington legal professionals, to accompany me. Because of the sensitivities involved, the meeting included several other Bureau officials in addition to the Assistant Director. I explained the situation to them in some detail and in the process persuaded them that (1) Azi would be in real danger if he were to do anything that raised even the slightest degree of suspicion, and (2) I was as patriotic as anybody in the room and that if we ever came across anything that I considered to be actionable intelligence, I would let them know right away. Meanwhile, they had to back off and leave us alone.

This approach carried the day, and the Bureau terminated their agents' involvement. Out of that experience, though, I developed a close relationship with the Bureau's Special Agent for the Washington Field Office (which for some unremembered reason was also responsible for Pakistan) and had the number of his private cell phone, which he assured me was never more than an arm's length away on a 24/7 basis. In short, a happy ending despite some tricky sledding along the way. Although that concluded our interaction with the Bureau, I ended up with enormous respect for its professionalism and its agility in responding to changing circumstances.

Systemic Initiatives

In 2008, I had the privilege of briefing James Glassman, then Undersecretary of State for Public Diplomacy and Public Affairs, on our madrasa reform project. The opportunity arose when a young lady by the name of Liora Danan, who was familiar with our Center's work, served as an intern in the Undersecretary's office and told Secretary Glassman about our efforts in Pakistan. The briefing went well, and he became an enthusiastic supporter (even later joining our Board after leaving government service). Shortly afterward and out-of-the-blue, we received a State Department grant for $150,000 to support our madrasas project, the first government support ever received for any of our work. A short while later, Secretary Glassman also briefed President George W. Bush on our Center's efforts in Pakistan.[54]

University Training

We used the State Department contribution to initiate a new program to provide university training for madrasa leaders and faculty. The first such effort took place at the University of Karachi in March of 2009, and included 29 sons or step-sons of the owners of the most influential madrasas in the surrounding area—in other words, the madrasa leaders of tomorrow. Preceding this initiative, Azi went over in advance and groomed the university faculty in what they should teach and how they should teach it.

An unspoken agenda in this effort was to break down the stereotypical disdain in which the madrasas are typically held by elite Pakistanis, including the universities. For their part, the madrasas generally felt isolated and looked-down upon by civil society, so this initiative involved a much greater challenge than the mere transfer of knowledge to madrasa teachers. When the 29 participants walked through the university gates and received valuable training devoid of arrogance or paternalism, the psychological feelings of acceptance were enormous.

Indicative of this transformation was the fact that every one of the participants invited his father or step-father to attend the graduation ceremony at the end of the six-week program. Further, 22 of the 29 participants applied to the university to undertake formal programs of study that would lead to teaching degrees. The success of that first university program led to similar

---

[54] A few years later, I attended a reception at the Pakistan Embassy at which Ambassador Husain Haqqani, who had become quite a champion of our madrasa project, told me he had briefed President Obama on the project earlier that day. He was quite enthused about it, and I happily shared his enthusiasm.

initiatives with a number of other universities and probably did more to bridge the madrasa community with the rest of civil society than anything that had ever been previously attempted.

The training itself focuses on equipping madrasa teachers with critical knowledge and skills in the following areas:

- Teacher Self-Awareness

- Learning and Development

- Critical and Higher-Order Thinking Skills

- Classroom Management

- Conflict, Conflict Resolution, and Peace

- Human Rights, Diversity, and Pluralism

Model Curriculum

Another systemic initiative consisted of developing a model curriculum for madrasa faculty that incorporated best-practices in Islamic education from throughout the Muslim world. To construct such a curriculum, we engaged noteworthy madrasa scholars in addition to other educational experts. And to buttress the best-practices aspect, Azi arranged for the National Madrasa Oversight Board (ITMP) to visit Turkey and Egypt in July of 2010, in order to see first-hand how these countries practiced Islamic education.

The Board itself went with a bit of an attitude— "What can these secularists teach us about religious education?" However, they returned with a much different view. They were humbled by the fact that not only were Turkish and Egyptian students every bit as able to handle religious questions as any Pakistani madrasa student, but they could handle questions in other academic disciplines as well, such as science, math and English, subjects that were clearly beyond the reach of the Pakistani students. They were most surprised by the importance these countries placed on teaching students about other religious faiths and other sects of Islam in an objective and tolerant manner. Indicative of their reactions were the following post-visit comments:

- "Seeing these religious school systems in other countries makes us realize how much hard work we have to do in our schools in Pakistan."

- "We should not let this learning opportunity pass without coming up with a workable plan of madrasa enhancement."

- "Keeping in view the current situation in our country, we should play our positive role to contain the environment of hate and hostility."

The Pakistani Minister of Education joined the trip as well, which added further gravitas to the effort.

New Standards

Upon their return, the ITMP levied a requirement that from that point onward, all future madrasa faculty would have to be certified through a university training program. Until then, there had been no standards. If one wanted to open a madrasa and had the funding, one could do so and teach without any qualifications whatsoever. Because of the ongoing deterioration of the public schools (in which many exist only on paper and a significant number of those that do exist pay teachers who don't show up for their classes), there has been an explosion in the number of madrasas—more than 20,000 at last count—that have sprung up to fill the vacuum.

The Elephant

The ITMP also agreed to register their madrasas with the government in exchange for funding to expand their curriculums by providing textbooks and teachers in the new disciplines. This agreement, like similar ones before it, ultimately came to naught because the government failed to provide the promised resources. This brings one to the elephant in the room that almost never gets discussed, the fact that those on the top of the social ladder in Pakistan are totally disinterested in empowering those at the bottom. In fact, they want to keep them there, which probably accounts for the country's incredibly low percentage of GDP devoted to education (one of the lowest in the world) and its exceedingly high illiteracy rates, especially among women in the rural areas. If they can read, they can vote; and that might upset the status quo.

This was especially driven home to me one evening when a high-level Pakistani friend invited seven of his well-heeled, philanthropic friends to dinner at his home in the hope of securing their financial support for our madrasa project. After a warm and friendly conversation around the table, I provided an in-depth description of what our Center was doing to improve the lives and performance of madrasa students. After doing so, my friend asked who at the table would be willing to hire a madrasa student that had successfully graduated from the new training. They were bankers and businessmen of various stripes, and not a single one of them raised his hand. They simply weren't interested in hiring anyone from the lower reaches of society.

I thanked everyone for their time, and after a round of cordial good-bys, left totally empty- handed.

In light of the above, one might reasonably ask why we were spending so much time and effort to improve the madrasas? The reason is that significant gains are possible, even without additional resources. In point of fact, changing attitudes is the key to all else. As confirmed by an independent, third-party evaluation of our training conducted in 2008, after experiencing an ICRD workshop, 98% of the participants felt the training had improved their understanding of how Islam can promote religious tolerance and 67% had incorporated these themes into their Friday sermons in the mosques—sermons that reach hundreds, if not thousands, of others in their communities.

Lest one underestimate the significance of these changes, the following statement of a madrasa oversight board member is representative of the prevailing attitude many of them had going into the workshops:

> *"We have the power to mobilize masses that can make our government shake in their boots, these people trust us and will follow what we tell them, not what the politicians want....you can tell that to [the] Americans."*

By penetrating the villages and taking advantage of the decentralized nature of Islam, which provides greater room for change in the madrasas than can be found in most religious institutions of other faith traditions (such as Catholic boarding schools), ICRD has had an immediate impact by enhancing religious education, mitigating the rhetoric of exclusion, and reducing the appeal of extremism and violence. In practical terms, this has equated to inspiring a number of madrasa leaders to become champions of peace, deterring madrasa students from becoming suicide bombers, and bridging the social gap between the madrasas and the rest of civil society.

Upon their return from a second trip to Turkey a few months later, the ITMP asked ICRD to train the "best of the best" of their madrasa teachers (from all sects) and to equip them to train others. This was given high priority, and it went well.

Promoting Peace

"Let us not seek to fix the blame for the past, let us accept our own responsibility for the future." —*John F. Kennedy*

Soon thereafter, Qari Muhammad Hanif Jilandhry, ITMP leader of the Deobandi madrasas, suggested that we develop a Peace Textbook based on Qur'anic principles for the use of all madrasa students, regardless of sect. I recall my later meeting with the appropriate State Department official in Islamabad to seek DOS funding to make it happen. I emphasized the critical opportunity this represented—a chance to put some of the toothpaste back in the tube—by creating an academic tool for promoting peace, in contrast to the extremist agenda we promoted in the madrasas during the 1980s (when we were growing holy warriors to evict the "godless" Soviets from Afghanistan).

At one point in that earlier process, the U.S. Agency for International Development awarded a $92,000 contract to the University of Nebraska to develop madrasa textbooks that would promote this extremist goal. Even in a math textbook – perhaps the most apolitical of all academic disciplines—one might find a question such as this: "If a Soviet soldier is standing on a hill 200 meters away and the bullet from your Kalashnikov travels 640 meters per second, how long will it take for your shot to hit him once you pull the trigger?" Eventually the Soviets left, then we left; and now the madrasas are doing what we trained them to do, only they've changed targets. Yet one more chapter in the book of unintended consequences!

The State Department ultimately provided the necessary funding for Azi to develop the peace textbook and also included sufficient funds to establish a Teacher Training Center in the headquarters madrasa of each of the five sects in order to institutionalize and sustain the madrasa reform process, including the teaching of the Peace Textbook.

To further reduce the call to violence and extremism in Pakistan and elsewhere, ICRD produced a video titled *Beyond the Brink: Countering Violent Extremism,* a 70-minute educational DVD created at the request of the State Department, which addresses the causes of violent extremism and how to counter them. The heart of this film is based on ICRD's work in Pakistan, with the remainder focused on the 1982 civil war in Lebanon and the challenges of gang violence in Los Angeles. It is a powerful film in which people who have lived through violent conflict recount the impact of that experience on their lives and how they came to renounce it and commit their future efforts to peacemaking.

The video leads off with the gang warfare piece (to avoid any specter of paternalism by showcasing the fact that America has its own problems in this area) and is designed to appeal to a wide range of audiences—targeting youth, teachers, parents, law enforcement officials, and foreign policy practitioners in various cultures and contexts. Perhaps most powerful is the section on

Lebanon because of the widespread denial which still exists in that country with respect to that conflict, some 40 years after its conclusion.

The Fourth Estate

Yet another systemic initiative took the form of a three-day workshop for religious journalists that we conducted in Bhurban, Pakistan in concert with Search for Common Ground, an NGO that works with local partners to transform conflict through collaborative problem solving. Conducted under the sponsorship of the United Nations, the workshop included representation from the country's leading religious journals, which reach an estimated half million subscribers across the country. Although there were a number of negative mindsets with which to deal, the workshop proved useful in promoting greater trust and less biased reporting. The journalists agreed not to publish incendiary material against other sects or schools of thought and each pledged to write at least one article promoting religious tolerance. Perhaps even more significant was the fact that Azi was able to inspire the Jamat-i-Islami journalists to begin adopting a positive vision for their party, as opposed to their normal negative, anti-Western agenda.

Course Changes

About this same time, two other developments took place that represented major changes in direction. For some unknown reason, the U.S. Embassy in Islamabad had cooled on our work with the madrasas and ceased to support it for an extended period of time. We never figured out why they took such a stance but supposed it to be either a concern relating to separation of church and state or, alternatively, that it was simply too hot for them to handle politically (if they openly acknowledged their support for an American NGO that was messing around with Pakistan's religious schools).

After five years of this stand-off treatment, a new Ambassador was appointed and things took a dramatic turn for the better. In fact, shortly thereafter, a contingent of State Department officials visited our Washington office and said they wanted to build their strategy around our work. They didn't say as much, but I assumed they had finally figured out that what we were doing in addressing the "ideas behind the guns" was every bit as strategic as anything else that might be taking place on or off the battlefield.

A short while later, I sat down with Azi and told him that from that point forward, I didn't want us to mention ICRD's name in Pakistan again. I felt we were becoming too well-known and too-targeted. I couldn't believe the timing; but less than a week later, a seven-page article appeared in the April 2011 issue of an on-line jihadist journal called *Nawa-e-Afghan (Voice of Afghan Jihad)*, specifically attacking our work. This journal, which reportedly goes out to selected terrorist cells in both Afghanistan and Pakistan, reflected a comprehensive understanding of all that we were attempting to do. In one particularly telling passage, they accused us of "promoting venomous concepts like civil society, human rights, women's rights, enlightenment, moderation, and freedom of expression"—all of which were deemed to be "caustic to Islamic family values."

This direct assault on our work inspired some of our indigenous supporters to flee the country and caused us to energize the dormant, previously mentioned indigenous NGO for which we had established the legal framework some two years earlier. Our original intent had been to take the new NGO operational at some appropriate time in the future and pass it the baton for the madrasa project, consistent with our ongoing commitment to always work ourselves out of a job (by creating capacity rather than dependency).

The journal article effectively forced our hand, and Azi left ICRD (as our Sr. Vice President for Operations) to take over as President of the new Pakistan-based Peace and Education Foundation (PEF). It was too dangerous in Pakistan, so he moved with his family to Dubai, where he could be close enough (by plane) to provide a sufficient on-scene presence to oversee the new NGO. The funding for the Peace Book and the Teacher Training Institutes provided sufficient capital for PEF to hit the ground running and to do so with considerably less risk because of the severed American umbilical.

Dining at the Marriott

This was the second time that extremist threats had slowed us down. The first occurred a few years earlier when I became aware that our every move with the madrasas was being closely tracked by the extremists. So close, in fact, that I began to give personal security a much higher priority than I had in the past. Consequently, on my next trip to Islamabad, I decided to stay in a hotel that enjoyed a reputation for tight security, of which there were only two: the Sabrina and the Marriott. The Marriott was the least expensive; but, even at that, the cost was pretty outrageous—-in excess of $300/night as I recall.

I chose the Marriott; and thanks to a referral from Ray Mahmood[55], an influential Pakistani-American friend, I was able to meet and have dinner with the hotel's owner, Sadruddin Hashwanni, shortly after my arrival. Of

---

[55] I had met Ray through the Prayer Breakfast network.

Iranian ancestry, Hashwanni was an incredibly hospitable gentleman, and we hit it off well.

As luck would have it, Hashwanni's generosity was put to a rather severe test two weeks later, when extremists attacked the Marriott with a truck bomb. Not only did it destroy most of the building, but a large number of the hotel employees were killed in the blast and ensuing fire. So much for enhanced security in Islamabad!

In the wake of that disaster, Hashwanni offered to educate the children of all employees who were either killed or severely wounded in the attack. Because another hotel that he owned in Lahore was similarly attacked a short while later, as was his home in Islamabad; he moved with his family to Dubai where they took up residence on the top floor of a rather majestic hotel. I later visited him there and was again impressed with his gracious hospitality. Although he applauded our work with the madrasas, I chose not to ask him for financial support. I felt the friendship was too special to burden it with anything that might be interpreted as self-serving.

One of the reasons for my trip (when I stayed at the Marriott) was to make another presentation in Abbottabad. However, just prior to my trip, we had a long-scheduled Board meeting at which the Board voted to prevent me from making that particular journey (much like Rink Jacobi and John Sandoz had sought to do on my earlier trip). Because this veto had the full weight of the Board behind it, I felt obligated to do as they said. So, when I got to Islamabad, I contacted Khamosh, who had arranged the event (just as he had the previous one) and begged off on making the trip, using ill health as a pretext. I was thus relegated to giving my presentation over the telephone via remote speakers. Later on, I learned that Khamosh had arranged for 127 former Pakistani Special Forces troops to protect me at the event. Had I known that beforehand, I would have made the trek in a heartbeat, Board or no Board.

Father of the Taliban

Years later, on a trip to visit Maulana Sami ul-Haq, widely known as "The Father of the Taliban" at his madrasa outside of Peshawar, I noticed a number of gentlemen walking around with machine guns. I didn't think anything of it, because it seemed a natural precaution in light of its dangerous location; but I later learned they were there solely to protect me. Yet another reminder of how serious-minded Pakistanis and Afghans are about hospitality.

During my visit with Sami ul-Haq, he gave me a personal tour of his madrasa, which was a large facility, that accommodated more than two thousand students. As with all madrasas I had visited in Pakistan, it had a room set aside for Islamic scholars to address practical questions that were channeled to them from madrasa faculty and others. They would attempt to answer them based on their interpretations of relevant Qur'anic scripture (or, on rare occasions, scripture from other religions).

In the course of showing me this room, Sami invited me to address the scholars. Though caught a bit off-guard, I congratulated them on their efforts to inform political decisions with their spiritual beliefs. I told them that in the West, we tended to treat the two separately and generally confined most of our spiritual thinking to a single day of the week. This, I said, was part of the reason why our Center was practicing Faith-based Diplomacy—to bridge religion and politics in support of peacemaking. We discussed this for a short while, and they clearly appreciated the role our Center was trying to play.

At one point during the tour, Sami mentioned that the day before, he had sent a letter to the Boko Haram terrorists in Nigeria, urging them to free the school girls they were still holding captive from their raid on the town of Chibok some two years earlier. In his capacity as the only extremist to have facilitated the takeover of an entire country (Afghanistan), his influence with other extremists was quite considerable. I don't know what, if any, response he received from Boko Haram, but his overture was almost certainly carefully considered.

At another point, he proudly showed me the preface he had written for the peace textbook mentioned earlier. As it turns out, his was one of five different prefaces. In a master stroke, Azi played to the fact that madrasas in different parts of the country pay homage to different religious leaders, so he had each of these leaders write his own preface for the book and then distributed them according to which leader had the most influence in any given geographical area. The book itself, which covers a wide range of topics, is both thoughtful and compelling. In fact, any country in the world would do well to have its own students exposed to such thinking, not to mention its political leaders. It is that good!

At the end of my visit, I thanked Sami for his generous hospitality, because it was clear he had rolled out the red carpet. I was later told by one of his assistants that it was highly unusual for him to go to such lengths because he was getting old and often had difficulty getting around. So much so, that even the U.S. Ambassador didn't command much of his attention whenever he or she paid a visit. Whatever infirmities Sami may have had, they didn't slow him down one bit during our tour.[56]

Although Sami and I clicked well on a personal level, I later concluded that the red-carpet treatment must have related to who it was that had arranged the visit. That someone was a retired Pakistani four-star Army General by the name of Ehsan Ul-Haq (no relation to Sami), who had last served as Chairman of Pakistan's Joint Chiefs of Staff Committee and, before that, as head of the ISI, Pakistan's somewhat notorious Inter-Services Intelligence Agency. To the extent the Pakistan military interacts with and attempts to control extremist elements, it is the ISI that carries this burden.

I had also met Ehsan through Ray Mahmood, and we had hit it off immediately. Not only did we know a lot of the same people because of our respective political/military backgrounds, but it turned out that both his father and grandfather had been religious leaders. Moreover, long before ICRD appeared on the scene, he had established a foundation of his own to provide university scholarships for deserving madrasa graduates. Later on, when it came time to establish the indigenous NGO, Ehsan agreed to serve as its Honorary Chairman.

Our relationship continues to this day. Whenever he comes to Washington, we have lunch and catch up on recent happenings around the world. On one occasion, I arranged for him to address a gathering of prominent U.S. national security practitioners over breakfast to exchange views on the latest developments in Pakistan.

By the same token, whenever our Center needed advice on how to handle a difficult extremist-related challenge in Pakistan, he provided it. Ehsan is an exceedingly impressive individual, and I've often said to anyone who would listen, Pakistan would flourish as never before if he were put in charge, even for a few months.

---

[56] While writing this section, I was saddened to learn that Sami had just been assassinated in Rawalpindi, the site of Benazir Bhutto's assassination several years earlier. Although, his killer or killers have yet to be identified, he had earlier predicted to Azi that he would be killed by the Taliban for supporting both the peace textbook and our later project to counter sectarian conflict. "I know them too well," he said. On a more encouraging note, when Azi attended his funeral, Sami's brother and son, who inherited his madrasa and associated political party, took Azi aside in the midst of the thousands in attendance and talked to him for a half hour, asking how he could help them convert the madrasa from an institution that was known for its radical roots to a center of great learning, much like Al Azhar University in Cairo (widely acknowledged to be the intellectual center of Sunni Islam). There could be no finer tribute to the influence of Azi's work over the previous 14 years than this inspiring request from Sami's son and sibling.

Before I leave the ISI as a topic of discussion, I should mention that the Center's first interaction with it took place during that visit to the Deobandi madrasa outside of Karachi with Rink and John. Two ISI agents had sat quietly in the back, monitoring all that was taking place. When the event concluded, Azi approached them and told them how pleased we were that they had attended. He then proceeded to show them the rest of our schedule for the coming week and invited them to attend anything and everything they desired. We never saw them again! Sometimes total transparency can be one of the more effective deterrents to unwanted intrusion.

A Meaningful Impact

After eight years of toiling in this vineyard, ICRD had engaged more than 2,700 madrasa leaders and faculty from about 1,600 madrasas in its workshops. And under PEF's auspices for the past six years, these numbers have now grown to almost three times as much. Because there are more than 20,000 madrasas in the country, our collective efforts have still only reached the tip of a very large iceberg. The national impact, however, has been considerably greater than these numbers would suggest.

In most cases, madrasa leaders are double-hatted as imams of their local mosques; and as their thinking becomes more enlightened, it feeds into their Friday sermons, which reach numerous others. In other words, our work has shown these leaders to be open to the kind of change that could ultimately enable them to become a national asset. Between the esteem they command as religious figures in their communities and the impact of their Friday sermons, their potential contribution to social stability is enormous.

Elements of Success

Key to ICRD's success with the madrasas (and in contrast to the failed attempts of others, including the Government of Pakistan) was a three-part strategy that informed our efforts throughout. First, we conducted the project in such a way that the madrasas leaders felt it was their reform effort and not something imposed from the outside. This was reflected in the degree to which they felt empowered to assume ownership of the change process, which they did in considerable measure throughout. Why such an approach was critical is because the madrasas are independently funded and fully capable of resisting any attempt at change that is not to their liking.

Based on typical media accounts, most Westerners and elite Pakistanis have negative views of the madrasas and look down on them as bastions of religious extremism. While the International Crisis Group estimated some time ago that only 15% of all madrasas have a *jihadist* agenda, it doesn't take many adherents to cause a lot of mischief. However, most of the remaining 85% are well-intended and employ reasonably capable teachers. Indicative of the latter is the following paragraph, which has served as the opening statement in our "Teacher Awareness" module for the workshops. It was crafted by a madrasa teacher:

> "I have come to a frightening conclusion that I am the decisive element in the classroom. My personal approach creates the climate. My daily mood makes the weather. As a teacher, I have a tremendous power to make a child's life miserable or joyous. I can be a tool of torture or an instrument of inspiration. I can humiliate or humor, hurt or heal. In all situations, it's my response that decides whether a crisis will be escalated or de-escalated and a child humanized or dehumanized."

I would have been hard-pressed to do half as well.

The second ingredient in our success involved inspiring them with their own heritage, not only of the schools themselves, but going back to the early days of their religion, when a number of the pioneering break-throughs in the arts and science, including religious tolerance, took place under Islam (at a time when Christianity was woefully intolerant). Whenever this is mentioned, the madrasas leaders tend to walk a bit taller and start thinking "maybe we can do better too."

The third element was the fact that we grounded all suggested change in Islamic principles, so the participants could feel they were becoming better Muslims in the process; and they were.

There was a fourth factor as well, but one I seldom mentioned. We operated from a posture of total humility driven by our awareness that the United States was complicit in planting the seeds of jihad in the madrasas in the first place (as mentioned earlier). On the few occasions that I did mention it, the madrasa leaders were taken aback by my candor and responded surprisingly well to it.

Inter and Intra-Religious Harmony

Finally, the keys to promoting tolerance in the madrasa environment and reducing religiously-motivated extremism more generally were our efforts to promote increased understanding and cooperation across the religious and sectarian divides. We did this through a three-track approach consisting of (1) a series of Muslim-Christian workshops to promote interfaith tolerance, (2) establishment of an Interfaith Leadership Network to advance protections for minority religions, and (3) development and implementation of a strategy to counter sectarian conflict.

In 2006, ICRD sponsored a series of interfaith workshops that brought together Pakistani Muslim and Christian religious leaders in order to develop personal relationships and to formulate and implement joint plans of action for countering religious extremism and discrimination. As a result of these workshops, the participants joined together in visiting mosques and churches to speak to one another's congregations about interfaith tolerance and cooperation. The Muslim leaders also engaged imams in the more radical areas of the country in promoting intra-faith harmony and reducing extremism. These relationships have continued, as has the associated outreach. Indicative of the psychological impact of these workshops is the following comment from one of the graduates:

> *"One thing was absolutely clear to me; we cannot be religious if we are burning with hatred. Those who are involved in bloodshed in the name of religion are only misusing it to serve their own agenda."*

As for the practical impact of this training, a few years after its conclusion, a young mentally-challenged Christian girl was accused of violating Pakistan's Blasphemy Law by allegedly burning some pages from the Qur'an. In response, ICRD was able to mobilize some of the workshop veterans, who traveled to the scene and met with local Christians and the mosque's officials. After determining what really happened, they elicited media statements from high-level Muslim religious figures, condemning the obvious attempt to victimize the girl. In addition, the local imam was taken into custody for fabricating the allegations. The incident itself was part of a larger scheme to use the Blasphemy Law to drive the Christians away and confiscate their property.

In Nepal in January of 2014, ICRD established a U.S.-Pakistan Interfaith Leadership Network (ILN) by bringing together conservative religious and interfaith leaders from Pakistan and from the United States to address the plight of religious minorities in their respective countries. The single theme that emerged repeatedly in their meetings was that any perceived mistreatment of religious minorities in one country directly influences radicalization in the other. Extremist groups in Pakistan cite perceived Western hatred of Islam to increase recruitment and justify preemptive violence. By the same token, violence against Christians in Pakistan fans the flames of negative opinion in the West toward Islam. Collectively, the ILN participants decided to collaborate in protecting their religious minorities. The first step in this new-found resolve involved the Pakistani wing of the ILN aiding in the establishment of the new Teacher Training Centers for training madrasa leaders and faculty in peace-building and religious tolerance.

The ILN also supported another ICRD- initiated project that was designed to promote peace within Islam itself by countering the longstanding sectarian conflict that has dominated most of Pakistan's history. In partnership with the PEF, the strategy for doing so included three elements: (1) development of a locally-informed, theologically-grounded counter- narrative to negate the messaging of sectarian divisiveness, (2) recruitment of Peace Advocates from each sect who, after undergoing extensive reconciliation training, take steps to live out the new narrative through community-based activities, and (3) establishment of multi-sect, Rapid Reaction Teams that deploy to troubled areas to defuse sectarian tensions before conflict erupts.

Foremost among the indicators of the effectiveness of this latter approach was the total absence of violence in 2018 during the holy Day of Ashura (the tenth day of the Islamic calendar, during which Shia adherents commemorate the death of Husain ibn Ali, grandson of the Prophet Muhammad (PBUH), who was killed in the Battle of Karbala in 680 AD). This religious observation customarily takes the form of processions of Shia adherents throughout the country.

In the past, these Ashura processions have often been targeted by Sunni terrorists, with major loss of life. However, owing to the collective efforts of the Peace Advocates, selected religious leaders, elected representatives, and state security officials, Ashura, in 2018 passed without incident in all of Pakistan's major cities.

As expressed by a madrasa teacher from one of the more violent sects following a PEF workshop:

> *"I had several stereotypical and biased images of people who belong to other sects, those who have studied in modern secular institutes, those who wear modern dress and those who have no beard. I used to think that these people are not to be talked with. Through this workshop I have discovered that the people who belong to other sects can also lead a moral life and they too had valuable knowledge which I badly lack. I have discovered humanity and great learning in my Shiite brothers. I have made a promise with myself that I would dedicate my whole life, my madaris and*

my every moment to spreading messages of peace, harmony and brotherhood. This workshop has been a turning point in my life."

Although ICRD secured the funding for this initiative from the State Department and exercised general oversight throughout, the credit for its impressive success rightfully belongs to Azi and his Peace and Education Foundation. In this initiative, as with all others before it, he demonstrated the same superb leadership qualities that caused me to nominate him twelve years earlier for the widely-coveted Peacemaker of the Year Award from the Tanenbaum Center for Inter-Religious Understanding in New York. He won the award hands down, with no close second. As well he should have, for to my way of thinking, he was a hero twice-over. Not only did he bear the burden of being an American, but he is Shia' as well. In the radical areas of Pakistan where we did most of our work, Americans are always at risk; but these are extremist Sunni areas where they do unmentionable things to Shiites. Fortunately, Azi is so amiable that by the time they figure out that he's Shia', they like him too much to want to do him harm. That is a horse we rode with some abandon throughout our involvement.

Why It Worked

Because of the length of our involvement in Pakistan and the multiple dimensions to our work there, it might be instructive to explore how past experience contributed to our success in that highly challenging environment. In short, why did we succeed where all others had failed?

First and foremost, when I asked Khalid Rahman why he had invited us to partner with his Institute in reforming the madrasas, he said it was because we had "religion" in our title and operated on a faith-based basis. Otherwise, the angst relating to the then-recent U.S. invasion of Iraq would have precluded any such arrangement.

The second most important factor was Azi's steadfast commitment to improving the lives of (and opportunities for) the children being served by the madrasas. He grew up in Pakistan, and with children of his own, has a real heart for kids. That coupled with his superb intellect, unrivaled training skills, and deep understanding of Islam collectively equated to an exceedingly capable change agent. In addition, his amicable personality and extraordinary "street smarts" in navigating an often-perilous landscape were also instrumental in getting us to where we are today. If Azi was the point of the spear, I was more akin to a carrier of that spear.

At the outset in 2003 (before I met Azi), when I was raising the initial funds and conducting the preliminary research, I recognized as a formidable asset the illustrious history of the madrasas during the Middle Ages, when they were the absolute peaks of learning excellence in the world at the time. With that as a touchstone, I felt we might be able to position ourselves as a vehicle for helping the madrasa leaders help themselves in recapturing the glories of their past.

During the succeeding eight years of our involvement prior to turning the project over to our indigenous counterpart, there were various points along the way in which past personal experience also became a helpful asset. For example, I found the dismissive attitude of Pakistani universities toward the madrasas to be as self-defeating as Harvard's was toward its NROTC program during the Vietnam War. It was this analogy that inspired me to channel our first increment of State Department funding into developing university training programs for madrasa leaders and faculty.

By the same token, I found my previous involvement with Cities in Schools helpful in understanding the needs of disadvantaged youth and how best to address them. From that same experience, I also drew on my exposure to the racially-charged sensitivities of the inner-city in navigating the similarly-demanding sensitivities of extremist madrasa environments. Finally, my past government service proved helpful in interacting with Pakistani government officials, once we came out of the closet and decided to share our work more openly.

Current and past connections also proved helpful. For example, it was through National Prayer Breakfast channels that I met both Ray and Shaista Mahmood. Ray later became Pakistan's Ambassador-at-Large in the United States, and Shaista became a member of ICRD's board. And for about five years, they graciously hosted our annual Faith-in-Action Award dinners at their majestic home on the Potomac. Even more importantly, Ray introduced me to General Ehsan Ul-Haq, whose invaluable insights helped us traverse any number of difficult obstacles in the radical reaches of Pakistan.

The fact that Ehsan was well-connected with a number of Washington decision-makers, not only gave us a lot to talk about, but it also inspired me to capitalize on past CSIS connections and Flag-rank friendships from Harvard days in arranging important meetings for us when he came to town.

Finally, my lengthy discussion with President Zardari, was arranged through the Prayer Breakfast network, as was the earlier dinner with him and his wife about eight months prior to her assassination. In short, there is seemingly no limit to which past involvements and experience have helped facilitate the Center's success.

Looking Ahead

In thinking about possible approaches for mitigating the never-ending angst between Sunnis and Shiites, one which leaps to mind is that suggested by the research of Ashutosh Varshney, a Political Science Professor at Brown University. In the wake of the Hindu massacre of some 2,000 Muslims in the western Indian state of Gujarat in 2002, he examined why other states with similar mixes of Hindus and Muslims were able to live together peacefully, without any recourse to violence. (The violence that took place in Gujarat was so brutal it is difficult to describe without feeling sick.)

Professor Varshney concluded that the overriding factor which enabled mixed populations to live peacefully was their joint participation in civic associations. In other words, the experience of Hindus and Muslims working together in pursuit of common goals has been a major contributor to communal peace. Perhaps a concerted effort to encourage Sunnis and Shiites to do the same, much like we have been doing with the Peace Advocates, could bear similar fruit.

Conclusion

The most dangerous places in the world today are those places where religious extremism and armed conflict come together. And it is in those places that ICRD has been operating since its inception, Pakistan being among them. As for Pakistan itself, it is crucial that the country not slide into the status of a failed state with nuclear weapons. There are any number of actions that will be essential to preventing this dire outcome, but it is clear that broad educational reform—particularly among the estimated 20,000 to 25,000 madrasas—is chief among them.

Madrasas, by and large, are supported by their local communities because they answer real human needs, providing education, food, and shelter to many children who would otherwise go without. They have a long and rich history, and they will not disappear anytime soon. The good news is that with internally motivated reforms of the sort we have been talking about, madrasas can play a powerful role in countering religious extremism. The hearts and minds of those who commit acts of terror in the name of Islam are best changed not by persuading them to become less pious Muslims, but by helping them to understand the peaceful intent of their own theology.

It is estimated that between two and three million children between the ages of 5 and 19 attend madrasas on a full-time basis and more than 20 million part-time. Since ICRD's initial workshop in 2004, more than 8500 madrasa teachers and administrators, religious leaders, and religious journalists have been collectively trained by ICRD and PEF. The number of students who, in turn, have been experiencing the effects of this training is difficult to estimate. Although it is no doubt an impressive total, the number of madrasas that have been engaged to date is probably no more than a fifth of those in existence. So, there is still much to be done.

While many in the West advocate the closing of these religious schools, our work has shown them to be open to the kind of change that could ultimately transform them into a national asset of major importance. ICRD's approach of helping the madrasas to help themselves has already displaced many of the extremist ideas that have previously led to violence. Ultimately, this initiative will help secure a better future for the children of Pakistan and, to the extent that it counters religious extremism, for our own children as well.

> *"I felt all the anger and rage I have carried for so many years about Americans washed away from my being...the ten days spent on learning and in reflections helped me put the pieces together to reach out in peace instead of constantly burning with anger."*

> —Madrasa Administrator

Chapter Fourteen

AFGHANISTAN

When the Taliban government of Afghanistan refused to turn over Osama Bin Laden to the United States for his suspected role in the terrorist attacks of 9-11, the US in concert with the British and the Afghan Northern Alliance overthrew that government. Bin Laden was found hiding in Pakistan ten years later and was killed, but ongoing Western efforts to build a stable nation in Afghanistan have proven elusive in light of the continuing resistance of the Taliban which, after 20 years of conflict, controls a significant fraction of the countryside outside of Kabul.

In July of 2007, 23 South Korean missionaries were taken hostage by the Taliban while traveling by private bus from Kabul to Kandahar. The next day, the Taliban demanded that all South Korean forces be withdrawn from Afghanistan within 24 hours and that the government of Afghanistan release all of its Taliban prisoners. Over the course of the next week, the Taliban demands shifted a bit; and they executed two male hostages when it became apparent their demands weren't going to be met.

The Challenge

On July 31ˢᵗ, I received a joint call from my friend Doug Coe (from the National Prayer Breakfast fellowship) and Lee Tae-Sik, Korean Ambassador to the United States,[57] asking if our Center could help secure the release of the hostages. I told them I'd see what we could do and then contacted Khalil Ahmed, a Deobandi leader from Baluchistan, who was serving as our indigenous partner in that region of Pakistan (not far from the Afghan province of

---

[57] I knew Lee personally because we both participated in a prayer breakfast for Ambassadors that met every Tuesday morning at the Cedars. Throughout the course of ICRD's engagement on this matter, my relationship with the Ambassador was a helpful asset.

Ghazni, where the hostages were being held). He, in turn, contacted a number of Afghan religious leaders who were then living in Pakistan.

The timing wasn't great because our request to Khalil came only six days following an unsuccessful attempt on his life by terrorists because of his involvement in our Center's work. Ordinarily when something of that nature occurs, the intended victim flees the country until the situation calms down and tempers subside. But in this case, Khalil's wife was on the verge of giving birth; and Khalil decided to hunker down in his madrasa. This is the state he was in when we called, and it is a tribute to his courage that he didn't hesitate in the slightest to help when asked.

The Approach

In a short while, Khalil was able to recruit 15 religious leaders, several of whom had once had some of the captors as their students. With them, Khalil formed a makeshift *jirga*, a decision-making body of respected elders, which made its way to Ghazni under the cover of darkness to establish contact with the captors. With open Qur'ans, they challenged the captors' actions on religious grounds, particularly in relation to the female hostages. One of their first questions was: "When are you going to let the women go?" Because all but five of the hostages were women, it was not an inconsequential question.

Over the next six days, the *jirga* engaged in a sustained dialogue with the captors, meeting with them at least once or twice a day and challenging them to provide Islamic justification for the kidnapping of innocent victims. In the course of their discussions, the Taliban representatives made it known that (1) no further harm would come to the hostages while this dialogue was taking place, (2) because an international extremist organization was involved at a higher level, they (the Taliban) didn't have the final say in the matter, and (3) because of a recent nearby bombing by Coalition forces, the hostages had been divided up and were being held in several different locations.

Although the *jirga* originally argued for the return of all hostages, once it became known that the hostages had split up, they took a step back and asked to have four or five of them released as a sign of "good intent." On August 8th, ICRD was informed by its team that several female hostages would be released as a "goodwill gesture." The *jirga* also encouraged the Taliban to meet with a delegation that had been sent from Korea some time earlier, but with whom contact had not yet been established. Following this, the *jirga* returned to their homes to recover from what had been an exhausting ordeal, made all the more difficult by the fact that most of them were sick from drinking the local water.

Throughout this process, the *jirga* never offered the Taliban any concessions. However, because the captors had complained on several occasions
that the Government of Afghanistan (GOA) was holding innocent women
captive simply because they were "guilty by association," through their marriage to Taliban fighters (who had either been captured or who were actively
being pursued), I recommended to the Korean Ambassador that the GOA be
pressured to accelerate its judicial process for these women, with a goal of
determining their guilt or innocence within a three week period and then setting free those who were found to be innocent (in short, a face-saving way
for everyone to win). When the Korean Ambassador met with the Afghan
Ambassador to the United States to suggest this approach, he received a favorable response. However, when he shared it with the U.S. Assistant Secretary
of State for that region, he did not. So, it didn't happen.

On August 10th, the Taliban negotiators met with the Korean delegation.
Because of inordinate time delays between actions that were taking place on
the ground and reports of those actions reaching ICRD (owing to the absence
of a secure communications capability between ICRD personnel), the Korean
delegates were unaware of the Taliban's previous commitment to the *jirga*.
Accordingly, they asked the captors to release those hostages who were ill.
Because only two were ill, only two were released (both of them women).

Round Two

"A winner never quits, and a quitter never wins." —Napoleon Hill

At the same time, we weighed in on several other fronts by sending Azi to
Kabul where he persuaded the GOA's Secretary of Hajj and Islamic Affairs
to form a team of religious leaders and local politicians to engage with the
captors. A team was formed, and it had one meeting, without apparent effect.

Azi also prevailed upon other Taliban leaders to intervene, including three
former Ministers of the Taliban government (when it was in power), who
asked not to be named but who retained considerable influence, were close
to the Taliban Council, and had a personal relationship with the Taliban negotiators. A new team was then formed to intervene, consisting of these three
gentlemen plus four members of the earlier *jirga*.

On August 13th, the two sick hostages were released; and on August 16th,
the newly fortified ICRD team reengaged with the captors. Because the South
Korean delegation was in active dialogue with the Taliban at the time, this
reengagement initially took place by telephone. Following a breakdown of

the talks with the Koreans on August 19th, our team met face-to-face with the captors and began its final push for a full release of the captives.

The Breakthrough

On August 26th, our team leader called to say there would be good news forthcoming within a few days. He indicated that the Taliban negotiators had agreed to release all of the hostages, with some minor demands for clean drinking water and for better teachers for their schools. Two days later the Taliban formally met with the Korean delegation and announced their agreement to release the remaining hostages.

Postmortem

"Trust everybody, but cut the cards." –Finley Peter Dunne (1867-1936)

With the actual return of the hostages, there was considerable speculation about whether or not the Korean government had paid a ransom to facilitate the process. It was later rumored that they had—to the tune of $40,000 for each hostage. However, one of the Taliban negotiators mentioned to our team leader that a sizable sum had been offered to free the hostages but that it had been turned down as a matter of religious principle. So there appears to have been competing views on the matter, at least among the captors. This same negotiator also said that had it not been for our religious intervention, they never would have let the hostages go until their full demands had been met. The full truth may never be known; however, the strategy of capitalizing on religious principles to trump other considerations does appear to have been helpful.

A sad P.S. to this particular episode took place when an attempt was made to honor Khalil during his next trip to the United States. The Korean Embassy in Washington was primed to roll out the red carpet for the central role he had played in securing the release of the hostages, as was our Center for that same reason. When he arrived at the airport, however, Customs Officials refused to let him in. Azi was at the airport to meet him; and when he called with the news, I was on my last day of vacation, playing golf at a course in Rhode Island with my son, Keith. As my cell phone rang with the news, I was about to hit a 7 iron and attempt to put my ball somewhere near the pin. It was a close contest, and I needed to make that shot. However, the bad news took its toll; and I didn't even hit the green (at least that's my excuse, and I'm sticking with it).

A few minutes later, I called the two FBI agents who had asked us to help them connect with the American Muslim community, and they immediately drove out to Dulles International Airport to break the log jam. However, they were unable to secure Khalil's release, and he was put in handcuffs and forced to go back. The only good news is that at a later meeting at the White House precipitated by this encounter, this practice was changed going forward. In future instances of this nature, any disagreement between Customs and other law enforcement organizations will be resolved at a higher level before forcing a visitor to return home.

This particular situation was apparently a case of mistaken identity; but adding insult to injury, not only had Khalil played an instrumental role in freeing the Korean hostages, but several years earlier, he had actively assisted U.S. military forces in Afghanistan as the Soviets were pulling out. He was a hero twice over, and this was his reward.

Charlie Wilson's War

During an interview that I had in January of 2008 with Willis Witter of the *Washington Times*, who was doing a story on our rescue mission, he made reference to "Charlie Wilson's War," a movie that had recently hit the theaters. It told the story of how Texas Congressman Charlie Wilson had all-but-single-handedly evicted the Soviet forces from Afghanistan through securing vital military assistance for the Afghan *mujahedeen*. He did so by influencing the budget of the House Foreign Operations Subcommittee (on which he sat) and by facilitating additional support from the governments of Saudi Arabia, Israel, Egypt, and Pakistan.[58]

Charlie was a graduate of the Naval Academy (Class of 1956) and at one point, Willis asked me what it felt like for one Academy grad to be picking up the pieces from another graduate's war. I said I supposed it might look like that, but as far as I was concerned, Charlie had done the heavy-lifting in getting the Soviets out. I further expressed my view that there would have been no Taliban takeover, if Congress had supported his proposed end-game

---

[58] At about the same time as my interview with Willis, I had lunch with Hank Crumpton, the former CIA Operations Officer who led the successful on-the-ground effort to topple the Taliban government following 9-11. Hank had just left government service to set up his own consulting practice, and we were meeting to exchange views on Afghanistan. Toward the end of our lunch, I brought up the subject of "Charlie Wilson's War" and mentioned the scene in the movie in which Gust Avrakotos, the rogue CIA Operative who had assisted Charlie in his efforts to evict the Soviets, was shown smashing the glass door of his boss's office in a fit of rage. Hank chuckled and said Gust had once worked for him and the way he was depicted in the movie was one hundred percent accurate. Gust was a wild man!

of helping the Afghans get back on their feet after the Soviets left. Power vacuums almost always create unintended consequences, and this was no exception.

Reconstruction

In the wake of our successful attempt to free the hostages, the Afghan Minister of Hajj and Islamic Affairs asked ICRD to lead an effort to bring Afghan political and religious leaders together to discuss how they could collaborate in supporting reconstruction throughout the country. The greatest challenge of this task would be securing the participation of the religious leaders, most of whom had a negative attitude toward their government. Moreover, they were the lifeblood of the Taliban, and the Taliban was actively sabotaging Western development assistance.

Our plan called for addressing this and a number of other challenges through a series of regional workshops, which, in turn, would culminate in a major International Islamic Summit on Peacemaking in Afghanistan. These workshops would not only bring together political and religious leaders from a specific region who normally had little, if any, contact with one another, but they would also seek to inspire and empower the religious leaders to play a more constructive role by engaging them in serious discussions designed to promote peace.

The first of these bridge-building workshops, which took place in Kabul on December 29-30, 2007, included major national religious leaders and federal government officials in addition to the regional representatives. In all, a total of 80 religious and political leaders participated. Because most of these religious leaders were, in fact, close to the Taliban, they were clearly uneasy about being there. However, their concerns soon abated as it became clear that a major purpose of the conference was to engage them in a meaningful way.

The workshop addressed three key questions: (1) What role should religious and local political leaders play in developing a peaceful society? (2) What role should the Government of Afghanistan play? and (3) What can participants do in an individual capacity to promote peace? Despite coming from diverse backgrounds and holding conflicting ideologies, the participants were able to work together in developing a common vision for the way ahead. Among the recommendations:

- Religious leaders need to play a larger and more structural role in working with the government to promote reconciliation and to develop action plans for addressing specific problems and conflicts in the country.

- More such workshops should be conducted to promote greater unity among the various parties, and to develop appropriate recommendations for the Government of Afghanistan and the international community.

- Ex-combatants should be re-integrated into society.

- The Constitution of Afghanistan should be upheld and form the basis for addressing the political, social, security, and judicial problems in the country.

Indicative of the conference's success was the uniform opinion of all involved that this was "exactly what Afghanistan needs."

Two additional workshops took place as well: the second in Jalalabad in February of 2008 and the third a month later in Herat, with each attracting more than a hundred participants and producing similarly encouraging results. At that point and despite the promising results, the well ran dry in terms of funding; and the project had to be discontinued.

Looking to the Future

"Men occasionally stumble over the truth, but most of them pick themselves up and hurry off as if nothing happened." — *Winston Churchill*

The key finding to come out of the above process, which U.S. and NATO policymakers would be well-advised to consider, is the overriding importance of the religious leaders. It was clear from the outset that most Afghan religious leaders felt isolated and ignored by the Afghan government, in contrast to life under the Taliban (when it was in charge) when they were consulted frequently.

If religious leaders feel respected and engaged, they will be far more inclined to cooperate with the government and support development assistance initiatives. Thus, the overriding need to acknowledge and respect the critical role that they play in their communities. Indeed, there was strong agreement in all three meetings that the role of the religious leaders will be pivotal to Afghanistan's future.

It will also be critical to recognize and accommodate the influence of tribal elders, who will be key to the country's social cohesion, and former combatants (*ex-mujahedeen*), including both those who fought in the Russian occupation as well as those involved in the more recent hostilities. Both groups will need to feel ownership in the political process, if it is to succeed in bringing peace.

A Washington-based group that helped negotiate the release of 21 Korean hostages last summer hopes to build on that experience by promoting reconciliation between Afghanistan's political and religious leaders....

The lessons learned from the whole episode, Mr. Johnston said, were "the wisdom of talking with one's enemies" and that "policies of isolation and demonization almost never bear the intended fruit."

Willis Witter
The Washington Times
January 9, 2008

Chapter Fifteen

THE UNITED STATES

At the outset of the new millennium, few would have predicted the dramatic change that lay ahead for the United States. In the blink of an eye, the sleeping giant was rudely awakened by planes crashing into the Trade Towers and the Pentagon. Any opportunity for further hibernation was foreclosed for the foreseeable future as the US and the West more generally faced a long-term struggle to defeat this latest manifestation of religious extremism.

Several years after 9-11, it occurred to me that the American Muslim Community (AMC), which numbers about four million members, could be one of our country's greatest strategic assets in its global contest with militant Islam, if we treated it right. However, not only was its potential not being recognized, but we were unwittingly alienating it over time through public displays of Islamophobia, onerous customs procedures, and various other discriminatory practices. So, in 2006, ICRD co-sponsored a conference with the Institute for Defense Analyses (IDA), the Pentagon's leading think tank, and with the International Institute of Islamic Thought (IIIT),[59] which brought 30 American Muslim leaders together with a like number of U.S. government officials to explore how they could begin working together for the common good.[60]

Developing an Asset

"Attitude is a little thing that makes a big difference." — Winston Churchill

---

[59] The fact that I knew the leaders of both organizations (Admiral Dennis Blair and Dr. Jamal Barzinji) made it an easy-sell. Not only did their participation enhance the credibility of the initiative, but they were both helpful in recruiting some of the participants.

[60] 4 One such official was Ambassador-at-Large Hank Crumpton, who was then serving as the State Department's Coordinator for Counterterrorism.

We looked first at what could be done to address legitimate American Muslim grievances. Following that, we sought to determine how our government could capitalize on the extensive paths of influence the AMC enjoys with Muslim communities overseas, many of them in areas of strategic consequence to the United States. We also explored what could be done to provide U.S. policymakers and diplomats with a deeper understanding of the Muslim perspective in order to minimize future missteps in foreign policy and public diplomacy. During the Cold War, we used to "red team" important national security initiatives by mentally putting on a Soviet hat and figuring out how they were likely to respond to whatever we were thinking of doing. We have not been so enlightened in dealing with religious extremism.

Finally, we examined how the AMC could play a leadership role in the further intellectual and spiritual development of Islam.[61] When I explored this idea with high-level Muslims overseas, I found them surprisingly receptive. In fact, I was told there exists within certain Muslim circles an undercurrent of thinking that the future "Sun of Islam" will rise in the West. Perhaps this is because the AMC enjoys greater freedom of thought than most other Muslim communities around the world and because it bridges the gap between modernity and the contemporary practice of Islam on a daily basis (unlike the majority of Muslims elsewhere).

All things considered, the conference went well and represented a good first step in moving things in a better direction. Immediately following the conference, the conference findings became the subject of a televised panel discussion in which I participated that was broadcast over *Al-Aribya* to 33 million Arabs in the Middle East and Persian Gulf region. Among other benefits, the broadcast provided an excellent opportunity to share with a significant Muslim audience how well Muslims are generally treated in America (significantly better than most Arabs have been led to believe).

A year later, we reconvened the same participants to follow-up on the recommendations of the first conference and to explore a number of important new ideas. Out of these efforts, American Muslims formed an advisory body called American Muslims for Constructive Engagement (AMCE), which

---

[61] A ready-made vehicle for doing so already exists in the form of a concept known as *ijtihad,* or independent reasoning, which once played a significant role in the intellectual history of Islam. As explained earlier, this concept provides a degree of latitude in adjusting how one's religious dictates inform one's daily existence in response to major changes in the external environment. Although *ijtihad* was widely practiced when Islam was in full flower, it later fell into disuse as Islam felt it was no longer needed. There are any number of Muslims who think it should be resurrected to help meet the challenges of today's fast-changing world.

has been taking steps to provide the U.S. government with Muslim-related insights on a range of foreign policy issues. They also produced a directory of Islamic experts on various topics for the use of U.S. government officials and the media whenever they need a Muslim viewpoint or additional information on any particular situation. For the government's part, the doors at the Departments of State, Defense, Justice, and Homeland Security opened wider to the inputs of their Muslim citizens; so the progress, while slow, has been both meaningful and helpful.

Policy Forums

To jump-start the process of informing U.S. foreign policy and public diplomacy with a Muslim perspective, ICRD and the newly-formed AMCE jointly sponsored a series of monthly Policy Forums on Capitol Hill for key Congressional and Executive Branch staff, and leading representatives of the American Muslim Community. The purpose was to discuss relevant and timely issues under consideration by the government that could affect U.S. relations with Muslims either at home or overseas. These focused, off-the-record, non-attribution discussions were roll-up-the-sleeves sessions over a working lunch in which a Legislative or Executive Branch official would begin the dialogue by sharing problems or questions that he or she was wrestling with that pertained to the topic under discussion. This would then be followed by a lengthy exchange between those in attendance, which always included outside experts as well as other government officials having a stake in that particular issue.

Illustrative of the kinds of exchanges that took place during these discussions was a question that emerged from a session on Libya, which took place during the peak of the popular uprising in that country (and the NATO action reinforcing it) against Colonel Qadhafi. One of the participants, who worked for a humanitarian NGO, mentioned that his organization had received considerable donor funding earmarked for Libya but that it was facing major difficulties in distributing it. He voiced a need for greater clarity from the Treasury Department and, more specifically, the Office of Foreign Assets Control (OFAC) on what material support could legally be provided to Libya in light of the existing uncertainties. He also expressed a desire to share with U.S. Intelligence officials important insights gleaned from their on-the-ground involvement there. The forum gave him the opportunity to connect with the appropriate government points of contact for addressing both of these needs.

These forums, which lasted for two and a half years, were well-received; and, with no known exceptions, those who participated (between 25 to 30 in any given session) left feeling enriched and better informed than when they arrived. Not only did policymakers benefit from the collective wisdom of those in attendance, but the larger goal of imparting a more nuanced understanding of Islam to U.S. policymakers was clearly advanced, as was that of building more effective bridges between the government and the American Muslim Community.

Countering Islamophobia

"A great many people think they are thinking when they are merely rearranging their prejudices." —William James (1842-1910)

In October of 2015, the year following the establishment of the International Leadership Network (ILN) in Nepal, both the American and Pakistani wings of the Network participated in a major two-day conference on "Countering Islamophobia" held at Temple University in Philadelphia. Sponsored by ICRD in partnership with Peace Catalyst International and the Dialogue Institute at Temple University, the conference addressed all aspects of the problem, ranging from attacks against Muslims in the West on the one hand to the role played by American social conservatives in fanning the flames of intolerance on the other. A common symptom of Islamophobia is the failure to distinguish between American Muslims and Islamic extremists overseas.

Aside from its unfair implications for law-abiding Muslim citizens, Islamophobia is a self-defeating proposition for other reasons as well. To the extent American Muslims are perceived to be marginalized or otherwise discriminated against, that perception plays directly into the hands of the extremists and enhances their ability to attract additional recruits. And, as mentioned earlier, it also exacerbates the mistreatment of Christians and other minority faiths in Muslim-majority countries. Finally, Islamophobia risks alienating the American Muslim community, which is arguably our first line of defense against Muslim extremism. As of 2007, for example, American Muslims had alerted U.S. security officials to an estimated 40 percent of all terrorist plots against the United States since 9-11.

Evangelical pastors from across the country were the target audience for the conference and its subsequent outreach. The purpose was to explore with them the ways in which Islamophobia manifests itself and the role they could play in arresting its spread and impact. The conference findings, which dealt with everything from sleeper cells to religious liberty, were subsequently captured in a special edition of the Dialogue Institute's periodic journal. Later, and perhaps more importantly in light of our target audience, the proceedings and findings were also captured by Fuller Theological Seminary, the leading evangelical Christian seminary in the United States, as the sole focus of the Fall 2016 issue of its own journal (titled, "Evangelicals and Islamophobia: Critical Voices and Constructive Proposals").

The Japanese internment camps of World War II provide a stark reminder of how fear often drives us in directions we later come to regret. If we are not careful, current attitudes in some circles toward American Muslims could drive us in that same direction.

"The more you sweat in peace, the less you bleed in war."

—Asian Proverb

Chapter Sixteen

SAUDI ARABIA

At the heart of the Islamic world and steward of its holiest sites, Saudi Arabia has a unique and powerful influence on the Muslim faith and, in turn, global stability. One of the five pillars of Islam requires that all Muslims undertake a sacred pilgrimage to Mecca and Medina at least once during their lifetimes, if they have the means to do so. Moreover, an enormous pool of foreigners migrates to Saudi Arabia for employment. Collectively, these two influxes expose a disproportionate number of the world's Muslims to the more extreme interpretation of their faith found in the Wahhabi doctrine that has prevailed in the Kingdom since its birth in 1932 (and which has unwittingly inspired the activities of terrorist groups like Al Qaeda and ISIS).

Background

Following the attacks of 9-11 (in which 15 of the 19 hijackers were Saudi nationals), the Kingdom faced strong external pressure to curb its spread of Wahhabism, the earliest, most Puritanical form of Islam, which had transitioned over time from its original apolitical stance to a more militant interpretation, calling for jihad against those having dissimilar beliefs. One of the more prominent vehicles for spreading this latter interpretation has been the Kingdom's public-school textbooks, which have been used or misused in various parts of the world to inspire the activities of extremist groups like ISIS and al-Qaeda. In an attempt to address this aspect of the problem, the US Department of State (DOS) engaged ICRD in 2011 to assess the discriminatory content in these textbooks and to evaluate its global impact.

Approach

The immediate catalyst for the study was a visit to the Kingdom in 2011 by the U.S. Special Envoy for Anti-Semitism. While there, she had complained to

Saudi officials about the pejorative references to Jews in their public- school textbooks. The officials denied their existence; and in effect, said, "Show me." Hence, the study's purpose was to do just that and to hit the Saudis over the head with the truth of our findings.

However, as we began our task, we soon discovered that the Saudis already had a reform effort of their own underway; and while its progress was glacial at best, it was nevertheless a credible effort. Accordingly, instead of approaching our task by "cursing the darkness," as had typically been done in earlier think tank studies, we opted to "celebrate the light" by giving the Saudis full credit for any reforms they had already implemented, including those associated with their deradicalization program, while being unsparing in our detail of what yet remained to be done. This approach was designed to keep things moving in a positive direction through quiet diplomacy, rather than attempting to force further change through additional criticism.

As we began to understand the full scope and sincerity of the Kingdom's reform efforts, we prevailed on State to keep our study's findings out of the public eye, lest Western critics use offensive passages that yet remained to increase the volume of their criticisms and risk provoking a defensive back-lash from Saudi hard-liners, who might then nip all further progress in the bud.

Findings

ICRD's review of the texts, which encompassed a total of 99 books (primarily from courses on religious studies, history, the social sciences and language arts) was the most comprehensive that had been conducted to date and provided an analysis of (1) textbook changes that had taken place over the previous decade, (2) remaining areas of bias and intolerance that still existed, especially at the high school level, and (3) how the Wahhabist content of these textbooks compared to Quranic admonitions on the same topics (unfavorably, in almost every instance) and to the provisions of the Cairo Declaration on Human Rights to which the Kingdom was a signatory (again almost uniformly unfavorable).

In short, we were holding them to their own standards, not those of the West. The study provided a comprehensive baseline for future analysis and offered helpful recommendations for immediate improvement. However, it also concluded that the impact of the texts was rather minimal when compared to the influence of teachers and the training they receive.

Implementation

In 2013, the DOS extended ICRD's funding for another two years to help implement some of the study's recommendations. Toward this end, I traveled to Riyadh in 2014 with Abubaker Ahmed, our part-time Vice President for Preventive Engagement, to discuss in greater depth the findings of our study with a contingent of Saudi education experts. Although Azi Hussain had originally directed the study, it would have been difficult for Sunni educators to accept a critique of their education system from a Shia'h scholar. By the same token, it would also have been difficult for them to listen to it from a Western Christian. So, I took Abubaker, who not only had impeccable credentials as a Sunni scholar and government practitioner, but also had a keen sensing of what the Saudis would need to hear, based on his long involvement in promoting educational reform in the Muslim world.

Although Abubaker had not been involved in conducting the study itself, I briefed him on its essentials; and we gave a tag-team presentation to the Saudis in which I set the stage strategically by providing an unvarnished overview of the misgivings harbored by Washington policymakers toward the Kingdom because of the offensive nature of its textbooks. Following that, Abubaker briefed them on our study's findings. It was a successful encounter, and we concluded our briefing by proposing that a follow-up meeting take place in the United States between Saudi and American educators to engage in a general discussion of educational reform strategies.

With the backing of the Saudi Minister of Education and the personal approval of the King, the proposed meeting took place at Georgetown University in November of the following year. In organizing the meeting, I thought it important that both sides come to the table as equals to discuss a problem they shared in common, that being the problem of bias and intolerance in national education systems. Although the Saudis' problems are far more onerous than our own, we have more than enough shortcomings to justify our own presence at the table. In short, it was important to facilitate an atmosphere of shared problem-solving, while avoiding any specter of paternalism.

To provide a substantive framework for the discussion, I shared the results of a study our Center had conducted prior to the meeting, which examined how a dozen other countries had dealt with similar problems. The meeting, which included officials from the Saudi Ministry of Education and from the U.S. Departments of State and Education (in addition to selected scholars and other practitioners) also addressed a number of key principles for advancing educational reform in both the Muslim world and the West.

After an extensive discussion of various aspects of one another's educational systems, the head of the Saudi delegation gave a detailed presentation on his country's recently announced National Strategy for Educational Reform, a strategy that had been announced a year after ICRD's study had made its way to the Kingdom through diplomatic channels. This new strategy, which was being funded at a level of $22 billion over a four-year period, focused on additional textbook revisions, teacher training, new curriculum standards, and the development of 21st century skills, including those relating to cross-cultural communications. The ultimate goal was to create "global citizens" who, in addition to being professionally competent, would be instilled with values that promote religious and sectarian tolerance, human rights, and critical thinking. The meeting concluded with both delegations agreeing on the range of topics to be researched prior to a second meeting in the Kingdom six months later.

At the second meeting, which took place in Riyadh the following May, the above-mentioned topics were discussed; and recommendations were developed for the consideration of both governments. In August of that same year, I was able to present the recommendations for the Saudi government to their Minister of Education, when he visited our Center's Washington office to chair a roundtable discussion on educational reform in the Kingdom.

Summary

Over the course of the first five years in which we were involved with Saudi policymakers and educators, we:

- Conducted the most in-depth study to date of Saudi public-school textbooks and established a comprehensive baseline for measuring further progress.

- Developed near and long-term recommendations for improvement of the Saudi educational system.

- Informed the implementation of the Kingdom's new National Strategy for Educational Reform by exposing Saudi educators to (1) the pros and cons of related aspects of the U.S. educational system, e.g. the teaching of critical thinking skills and the challenges of moving toward a more decentralized system, and (2) how the dozen other countries mentioned above had handled problems of bias and intolerance in their national educational systems.

- Established important personal relationships with high-ranking officials in the Saudi Ministry of Education and other important organizations like the government-owned Tatweer Company for Education Services, that was leading the development and implementation of the Kingdom's educational reforms, and the King Abdulaziz Center for National Dialogue, which was building bridges with previously excluded segments of Saudi society.

- Facilitated the official retrieval of unrevised Saudi textbooks from around the world.[62]

While it is impossible to determine the degree to which our study influenced the development of the Saudi's new strategy, it seems likely that prospective change was less a product of Western criticism than it was a result of perceived national self-interest. The goal is to give Saudi youth the ability to compete effectively in the globalized marketplace (as a more appealing option than running off to join ISIS).

Shortly before our contract extension was due to conclude, I received a call from a friend, who in his capacity as a Washington attorney, was responsible for managing part of the Saudi lobbying portfolio. He had been aware of (and keenly impressed by) our madrasa project in Pakistan and knew that we were now involved in facilitating Saudi educational reform. He asked how things were going with the Saudis, and I gave him a quick summary of all that we had done. He asked if I could put it in writing so he could use it to help forestall new legislation pending in the Congress that would enable victims of 9-11 to sue the Saudi government for their losses. I did so, and upon reading my summary, he called again and expressed great enthusiasm both for our approach and for the results we were achieving. I cautioned him not to get too excited, because our contract with State would be ending in another two weeks. He asked about the possibility of securing funds from the Kingdom to continue our efforts, to which I replied, "Absolutely not. We would lose all credibility if we were perceived to be in the pockets of the Saudis."

---

[62] In the November exchange between U.S. and Saudi educators at Georgetown University, the Saudi official in charge of implementing their reforms expressed doubt that the Kingdom's public-school textbooks were being used in other parts of the world, because there was a law specifically forbidding their use beyond the Kingdom's borders. I told him they were, in fact, being used outside the Kingdom and apprised him of our study of the global impact they were having. I then passed him a copy. He later responded by sending a directive to all Saudi embassies around the world, urging their Cultural Affairs Officers to retrieve any older textbooks that might be in use within their respective geographic areas and to replace them with the latest revised editions.

We left it at that until he called back a week later to say that the Saudi Foreign Minister, with whom he enjoyed a close relationship, had called the U.S. Assistant Secretary of State for Near East Affairs (NEA) and asked her to please continue funding ICRD's project, because the Kingdom was finding it extremely helpful. NEA agreed and eventually provided funding for a second reexamination of some of the high school textbooks and for an in-depth assessment of the religious and social influence of Saudi educational materials in several counties of significant concern: Spain, Kenya, Indonesia, and Ethiopia.

At the same time that we were re-examining the high school texts, they were undergoing further revision by the Ministry of Education. Rather than risk having our own efforts rendered moot by their changes, I suggested to my Saudi counterpart that we feed him our findings on an incremental, real-time basis every other month, in order to give him the benefit of an ongoing Western interpretation of what was wrong. He secured the approval of his Minister as did I from NEA, and we proceeded as suggested. Not only did this working partnership yield the hoped-for changes, but it was indicative of the kind of trust that can develop over time through respectful engagement. It may take a while, but it works.

Congressional Hearings

"In my many years, I have come to a conclusion that one useless man is a shame, two is a law firm, and three or more is a Congress." –John Adams

In July of 2017, I was invited to testify on "Saudi Arabia's Troubling Educational Curriculum" before the House Foreign Affairs Subcommittee on Terrorism, Nonproliferation, and Trade. Each of the three other witnesses had a long-standing reputation for being a tough critic of the Saudi educational system, so I felt the most important contribution I could make would be to provide a semblance of balance to the deliberations by noting the progress that was being made toward improving the textbooks and highlighting the challenges yet to be addressed, without appearing to be an apologist for the Saudis.

During the course of the hearings, I suggested that as long as the U.S. government was willing to sell $150 billion worth of military equipment to the Kingdom, it was doubtful they would take Western criticism of their textbooks as seriously as they should. Instead, to inspire a more helpful engagement, I suggested an alternative approach called "organic suasion,"[63] which

---

[63] The term itself is explained more fully in *Religion, Terror and Error.*

our Center had developed in working with next-generation leaders in Kashmir and with madrasa leaders in Pakistan, an approach based on respectful engagement that promotes reform from within. I then explained how we were using that approach in Saudi Arabia.

Toward the end of the hearings, the Chairman of the Subcommittee asked what grade each witness would give the Saudis on their reform efforts to date. The other three gave them a resounding "F," while I chose to give them a "D."[64] Despite the "D," I received an email the following day from Dr. Mohammed Al-Zaghibi, the official in charge of the Kingdom's educational reform process who had watched the hearings from Riyadh, thanking me for my balanced presentation. Similar comments were also forthcoming from the State Department and from the Subcommittee itself, so our Center gained a bit of added credibility that would serve us well later.

Teacher Training

Textbooks are one thing; teacher training quite another, and far more important than the textbooks. After sharing this thought with then Minister of Education, Dr. Ahmed Al-Aessa, and suggesting that ICRD could provide such training based on Islamic principles, he agreed that a training program could be useful and suggested "Globalization" as an overarching theme. Happily, that theme was not only consistent with the Kingdom's desire to equip its youth to compete effectively in the globalized marketplace, but it would require training in many of the same disciplines that we needed in order to purge the Saudi educational system of its inflammatory content–such as tolerance, human rights, religious literacy, pluralism, critical thinking, and cross-cultural communications.

With this fortuitous opening to train Saudi teachers in all the right disciplines, we approached the Counter Terrorism Bureau (CT) at the State Department for an initial tranche of funding to support such an effort. They were supportive; and a short while later, an opportunity arose to apply for the additional funding that would be required from the Department's Bureau of Democracy, Human Rights, and Labor (DRL). To secure the latter, DRL required official certification from the Saudi Ministry of Education, indicating the Kingdom's willingness to cooperate with us in developing, testing, and

---

[64] In a presentation to State Department staff some months later on our progress with the textbooks, one staffer commented, "In the Congressional hearings, you only gave the Saudis a "D" on their progress," to which I replied, "That answer was politically driven." She then asked what the real grade should be?" I said, "C minus," which provoked a bit of laughter around the table.

implementing the teacher training initiative. After a great deal of to-and-froing between ICRD, DRL, and the Ministry, we were positioned to receive a Letter of Cooperation from Tatweer Educational Services that would satisfy DRL's need.

At that point, however, the planets fell out of alignment when Saudi officials murdered Jamal Khashoggi, a widely-respected Saudi journalist and contributing columnist to the *Washington Post,* who had been highly critical of the Crown Prince and his approach to change. Because of heightened anxiety in the Kingdom in the wake of this scandal, the Minister of Education imposed an additional condition on the Letter of Cooperation, requiring that we also secure the approval of the Ministry of Foreign Affairs (MOFA).

A short while later, both the Minister of Education and the Minister of Foreign Affairs were replaced by officials having closer ties to the Crown Prince. Over the eight years of our involvement with the Saudis, we had established significant credibility with both of these gentlemen, so their loss was keenly felt. In effect, the planets were not only misaligned; they were scattered all over the landscape.

Pulling Out the Stops

"Let us never negotiate out of fear but let us never fear to negotiate."
—*John F. Kennedy*

Meanwhile, despite pulling every string we possibly could to obtain the MOFA's approval, it was nowhere in sight. In a last-ditch attempt to secure the DRL funding, which was scheduled to disappear if we didn't have the needed certification by February 1st, I and several colleagues traveled to the Kingdom at the end of January to make that happen. Our alleged agenda for the trip was to brief the Education Ministry on the results of our latest examination of their 11th and 12th grade public school textbooks, but the real task in our minds was to bring home the needed approval for the teacher training. This was no small undertaking in light of the fact that the added requirement for MOFA approval, had effectively elevated the status of the Letter of Cooperation to the equivalent of an official Memorandum of Understanding (MOU), which we later learned requires at least several months to approve.

Through the back-channel maneuvering of friends in the Ministry, we were able to secure an appointment with the newly appointed Minister of Education on January 31st, our last day in the Kingdom (and the final day for meeting DRL's requirement). He had a reputation for boldness, in addition to being very bright, so we were hoping to have him sign an MOU without any requirement for further approval. At the last minute, though, I changed our MOU to a Letter of Endorsement for the Minister's approval, hoping that by doing so, we would eliminate any possible need for additional signatures.

While sitting in the waiting room prior to seeing the Minister, the CEO of Tatweer cautioned me against raising the subject of the training project with the Minister. I told him that ship had already sailed, and it was now or never. So, at the outset of the meeting, I mentioned to the Minister our need for the Ministry's approval of a teacher training project that we had developed with his predecessor. He responded by saying that his staff would have to study our proposal and get back to us. We then discussed the political state of play between our two countries, after which I briefed him on our textbook findings. Then I returned to the need for his approval of the letter we had crafted (which effectively called for everything an MOU would require, only under a different label).

I apologized for violating all bounds of protocol by returning to the original topic and telling him that Allah, in his infinite wisdom, was not allowing sufficient time for additional staff processing of our teacher training project. Instead, we would need his approval that very day, or we would lose the needed funding for the initiative. I further told him, that He (Allah) had awakened me at 2:30 AM that very morning to list ten compelling reasons why he (the Minister) should sign the letter. I then asked him if I could share those reasons. He said, "Of course;" and I offered the following (in no particular order other than that in which I happened to think of them):

- ICRD's services would be cost-free, since the U.S. Department of State would pay for the training.

- Advance approval of the proposed curriculum by the MOE would be required before the training could take place.

- All suggested changes would be grounded in Islamic values.

- Such an initiative would have significant PR value in Washington in the midst of the ongoing criticism of the Kingdom relating to its textbooks and other matters.

- It would provide an opportunity to address points of continuing confusion in the textbooks.

- ICRD had recruited a highly capable team of American Muslim scholars to develop and teach the curriculum.

- ICRD's President and Project Director would provide close oversight of the project throughout.

- ICRD enjoys a stellar reputation in Washington policy circles. Here I mentioned that two days following our return to the United States, the Center for Strategic and International Studies (CSIS) would be sponsoring a major event to celebrate the 25th anniversary of the publication of *Religion, the Missing Dimension of Statecraft*, the book that had launched ICRD. And the day after that, I would be speaking to several hundred foreign officials and others on religion and diplomacy at the National Prayer Breakfast. (During the course of this discussion, I showed the Minister a copy of the book, which he graciously accepted as a gift).

- ICRD is experienced and can be trusted.

- Everything to be taught would be totally supportive of the Crown Prince's 2030 Vision and its call for the Kingdom's youth to become "global citizens."

In response to the above, the Minister said he would read the letter, make any edits he felt were necessary, sign it, and have it hand-delivered to us that same afternoon prior to flying home. Then he did exactly that. And so it was, that faith-based diplomacy once again proved its worth in paving the way for helpful change (Addendum R).

A Sobering Challenge

With a perfect storm descending on Saudi Arabia in the form of low oil prices, two costly wars in Yemen and Syria, and a demographic tidal wave (youth bulge), the Kingdom finds itself at a crossroads. Fundamental to its future success will be effective implementation of the 2030 Vision and an education system to support it that provides the necessary professional and cross-cultural skills to succeed in an increasingly integrated and competitive world.

"If we are to reach real peace in the world, we shall have to begin with the children."

—Mahatma Gandhi

National Library of Bosnia and
Herzegovina during the shelling by the
Serbs (public domain)

David Steele, head of
the CSIS training team
that became trapped
in Sarajevo during the
bombardment

After the shelling (public domain)

Olga Botcharova,
Russian member
of the team

After reconstruction (public domain)

Evening presentation by Hassan al-Turabi (center) at ICRD meeting of religious leaders in Khartoum. Respondents include myself; Enock Tombe, General Secretary of the Sudan Council of Churches (far right); and Mumir Shafiq, a Jordanian journalist. Dr. Abubaker Ahmed, ICRD's Vice President for Preventive Engagement, is at far left.

At the Pyramids of Bajrawia (north of Khartoum) with Enock Tombe from the Council of Churches, and Ahmed Abdul Rahman, head of the International Peoples' Friendship Council, whose organizations co-sponsored the meeting of religious leaders with ICRD. Thought by many to predate the pyramids of Egypt, we journeyed to Bajrawia following the meeting, to celebrate its success in addressing the religious issues underlying Sudan's long-running civil war.

The incomparable Al Tayib Zein Al-Abdin, first Executive Director of the Sudan Inter-Religious Council.

Sudan Inter-Religious Council Chairman Abdallah Ahmed Abdallah welcoming Catholic Archbishop Zubair Waco to the initial meeting of the Council.

Imam Feisal Rauf, a fellow member of the U.S. delegation to Iran in 2003, founded and chairs the Cordoba Initiative, an international organization that works to reconcile conflicts between Muslims and the West. Although he was the subject of undeserved notoriety in 2013 as prospective imam of the "Ground Zero mosque," he received ICRD's annual Faith-in-Action Award the following year.

. With Rabbi Jack Bemporad outside of Persepolis, capitol of the Persian Empire when it was at its peak. Also a member of our delegation, Jack was later instrumental in reconciling longstanding tensions between Israel and the Vatican, stemming from the Vatican's perceived complicity in Hitler's mistreatment of the Jews. Jack was also a recipient of ICRD's Faith-in-Action Award.

Meeting at the Cedars of Iranian delegation with selected leaders of the American Muslim community

Discussing important similarities and differences between their respective religious communities over lunch

Madrasa students in Pakistan
memorizing the Holy Qur'an

ICRD Senior Vice President for
Operations Azhar Hussain ("Azi") and
me connecting with madrasa students

Girls in rural Pakistan meeting
on a voluntary basis in their own
"madrasa" (without a teacher) to
study and dream together of one
day becoming doctors, teachers,
or engineers. One young lady
with whom Azi spoke, rose each
morning at 4:30 am to complete her
daily chores so she could attend.

Kids, the same the world over

Addressing a madrasa workshop with
board members John Sandoz and Rink
Jacobi sitting to my left. To my right,
Khalil Ahmed, our Pakistani partner from
Baluchistan, who later played an instrumental role in our rescue of the Korean
missionaries from the Taliban in 2007.

Abdul Qadeer Khamosh, ICRD's other indigenous partner in Pakistan, addresses our
training team in Lahore, with Azi joining
in. Khamosh played a key role in arranging
a number of our initiatives in the more radical areas of the country, including my
meeting with Taliban commanders and tribal
leaders in 2006.

Azi and Khamosh with the religion journalists

Azi teaching a workshop for the ladies.

With Khamosh and Haji Ayoub (who hosted my meeting with the Taliban at his compound in the mountains)

Strategizing with "the Engineer"

General Ehsan ul-Haq, former Chairman of Pakistan's Joint Chiefs of Staff and former Director General of the ISI, describing the latest security-related developments in Pakistan at ICRD's annual dinner in 2010 (Marsha Vander Mey photographer)

321

First meeting of the U.S.-Pakistan Interfaith Leadership Network (ILN) at Kathmandu, Nepal in January, 2014

Muslim and Christian delegates of the ILN explaining the nuances of their respective prayer rituals to one another.

ICRD Executive Vice President James Patton with two other U.S. delegates to the Nepal meeting of the ILN: on the left, Dr. Muhammad Shafiq, Executive Director of the Center for Interfaith Studies and Dialogue at Nazareth College, and on the right, Imam Mohamed Magid, Chairman of the International Interfaith Peace Corps (and another ICRD Faith-In-Action Award winner)

Co-sponsors of the ILN-inspired Conference on Islamophobia at Temple University. On the left, Rick Love, President of Peace Catalyst International; on the right, Howard Cohen, Board Member of the Dialogue Institute at Temple (and a long-time friend from Cost of Living Council days).

Chapter Seventeen

EXTENDING THE REACH

Alexander, Caesar, Charlemagne, and I myself founded great empires: but upon what did the creations of our genius depend? Upon force. Jesus alone founded His empire upon love, and to this day millions would die for him.
Napoleon Bonaparte

Because of the global acclaim that accompanied the publication of *Religion, the Missing Dimension of Statecraft*, I began receiving numerous invitations for speaking engagements and media interviews. Most of them were in the United States, but a significant number were overseas as well (a combined total of 152 between the two in the five years prior to establishing ICRD). The same also held true with respect to our Center's work once ICRD was established.

One of the earliest of the overseas engagements took place in London at the invitation of MRA. Two of the book's chapters featured MRA's work in promoting reconciliation on a large-scale, personal level between the French and the Germans following World War II and in facilitating a peaceful transition from the colonial, white-minority government of Rhodesia to the majority-ruled government of Zimbabwe. In the course of its reconciliation efforts with the French and the Germans, Konrad Adenauer and Robert Schuman met for the first time and eventually gave birth to Jean Monet's European Coal and Steel Community Plan (which later morphed into the European Community and, ultimately, into today's European Union).

Although MRA makes no claim to having had any involvement in Monet's Plan, it was clear from our research that the Plan could never have taken hold had it not been for the reconciliation achieved across industry groups and labor unions from both countries at Caux. In Rhodesia, but for MRA's intervention, the transition from a colonial to a popular government would most certainly have turned violent.

Religion at Oxford

To increase public awareness of these past involvements, MRA invited me to spend a week in London, where I was to speak about the book to a number of live audiences in addition to various media outlets, including the BBC (both television and radio) and the London *Financial Times*. Among the live audiences, two stood out in particular. The first was a presentation to a room-full of Oxford Dons at All Souls College. Although I expected it to be a tough audience when it came to discussing religion, it proved quite the opposite, as any number of them stood up during the discussion period to comment on their own personal and highly positive experiences relating to past religious involvements in their lives.

During this presentation, I sat next to Sir Christopher Zeeman, Principal of Hertford College at Oxford and a renown mathematics professor who had been knighted by the Queen in 1991 for his pioneering applications of catastrophe theory[65] to the biological, behavioral, and physical sciences. He would do this by gaining sufficient mastery of a selected field, like biology, become conversant in it, and then subject it to the rigors of catastrophe theory (since renamed singularity theory). This, in turn, would lead to significant breakthroughs in that field through new, pathbreaking insights that emerged from his work.

We had a great conversation over lunch during which I asked if he had ever applied his theory to the field of psychology and, more specifically, to the challenges of manic depression. He said that he had and would be happy to show me the results of his research in his office following the lunch. I shared with him that a close acquaintance suffered from that condition, and I was interested in learning as much as I could about it.

After lunch, we proceeded to his office, and he passed me a copy of his assessment of that particular condition. Perhaps the greatest insight I gleaned from his study and our exchange was that the transition between the manic and depression phases is abrupt (like a bistable function in electronics) and not the gradual sine wave that I had assumed. I also marveled at how capable

---

[65] Catastrophe theory is closely related to chaos theory, but while the latter concerns itself with the sensitivity of systems to changes in their initial conditions, catastrophe theory focuses on the different ways a system will respond to changes at a later point. A straightforward example of an application of catastrophe theory would be a study of the change in shape of an arched bridge as the load on it is gradually increased. A metaphorical and widely-cited example of chaos theory, on the other hand, would be the impact of the proverbial butterfly flapping its wings in Moscow and the wind currents it creates eventually resulting in a thunderstorm in Santa Fe.

some manic-depressives are when in their manic phase, as contrasted with their occasional inability to do even the simplest things when depressed. Once I became more familiar with this affliction, I came to realize how so many of the great artists in different fields have suffered from its grasp, ranging from Hemingway to Beethoven to Van Gogh (and numerous others in between). When in their manic phase, we mere mortals can't touch them. That greatness, however, often comes at a sometimes-terrible price.

As it turned out, the good professor and I shared another interest in common, albeit on a totally different front. We were both huge fans of William Tyndale, the Catholic priest who brought holy scripture within the grasp of the common man by translating the Bible into English from the original Greek of the New Testament and the original Hebrew of the Old Testament. Because this disrupted the *status quo,* he was branded a heretic by the church and burned at the stake in 1536. His dying words were "Lord, open the King of England's eyes." A prophetic utterance as it turned out, because the following year King Henry VIII licensed a new Bible that contained all of Tyndale's translation. Even more far-reaching was the fact that when the King James Version of the Bible was produced 75 years later, 90% of it was pure Tyndale.[66]

Several months before my visit, Professor Zeeman had given an address titled "On the Life and Work of William Tyndale" in which he highlighted the priest's masterful touch in creating phrases that have become the "very tapestry of our everyday language" such as:

> *"Wherever two or three are gathered in my name…,"*
> *"The spirit is willing, but the flesh is weak."*
> *"Am I my brother's keeper?"*
> *"Let not your hearts be troubled"*

and numerous others. In some respects, Sir Christopher, who passed away in 2016, did for science what Father William did for religion, with both making invaluable and lasting contributions in their respective fields.

That same surprising influence of religion at Oxford emerged again when I later addressed a foreign policy audience at Chatham House (less commonly called the Royal Institute of International Affairs), a public policy institute in London that is somewhat similar to CSIS in terms of its impact and outreach.

---

[66] The fact that Tyndale authored so much of the King James Version is a singular tribute to the accuracy of his translation, which survived all-but-totally intact the collective scrutiny of a substantial number of the best biblical scholars and translators of the time, who had been recruited by the King to come up with an official translation. All the more remarkable is the fact that Tyndale was self-taught in both Greek and Hebrew.

At the outset of the event, the Director of Chatham House, who was chairing the event, made the following comment, "*A number of you here must be wondering why I am chairing this session, since I so seldom do. What none of you know—and certainly Doug doesn't know—is that in an earlier incarnation, I was once a religious broadcaster on the East Coast of the United States.*"

And so it went, with all sorts of past religious involvements working their way out of the closet. Even more gratifying was a strong endorsement of our work five years later in the House of Lords by Sir George Carey, then Archbishop of Canterbury. Richard Chartres, the Bishop of London, paid similar tribute in a number of his speaking engagements as well. More importantly, they found our work helpful in inspiring initiatives of their own:

> "In the United States, the American expert Douglas Johnston, has undertaken ground-breaking work on religions and diplomacy. His efforts are now being carried forward in a number of initiatives blending theory and practice. Closer to home, in the City of London we watch with admiration the project to build a Centre for Reconciliation and Peace from the rubble to which St. Ethelburga's Church was reduced by a terrorist bomb."

The Archbishop of Canterbury
House of Lords, *Hansard,*
October, 1999

It was clear from these and other reactions that the book had indeed struck a responsive chord around the globe—and in some of the most unpredictable settings. Through such engagements, the book reached a great many people, a number of whom said it had affected their lives in meaningful ways, often inspiring them in new directions. And, in the interest of full disclosure, it had a significant effect on my own life as well.

In the Wee Hours

In the final chapter of the book, for example, I described a decision taken by Joseph Lagu, leader of the rebel forces in the south of Sudan during its first civil war (following the country's transition to independence in 1956), to free 29 northern Sudanese who had just survived a plane crash in rebel territory. The government forces had recently burned down a church in which rebels and their families had been praying, so the urge for revenge was little short of overwhelming.

In reaching his decision, Lagu asked himself, "What would Jesus have me do?" After wresting with that question for the better part of a restless night, and recalling the advice that a chaplain had once given him as a young man ("If I ever have a thought in the cool hours of the morning, I should act on it and not dilute it by consulting others. God was talking to me, not them."), he decided to let them go. He did so in the hope that they would become ambassadors for peace; and that is exactly what happened. As news of his humanitarian gesture spread, it made it more difficult for the government to continue the fighting. Ever since Joseph shared his thinking with me, I too have been acting on that chaplain's advice, thus far to good effect.

Baptism in the Galilee

Another of the numerous overseas speaking engagements involved a trip to Israel, which led to yet another of life's periodic epiphanies. After making a presentation to a group of scholars at the Tantur Ecumenical Institute just outside of Bethlehem, I joined Scott Appleby, a highly accomplished scholar from Notre Dame, and an Israeli friend of his for a tour of the Galilee in the friend's automobile. Along the way, we visited the Golan Heights where I was able to see up-close how strategic they really are to Israel's security. Another reality that sank in during our brief journey was just how compressed the geography is in that part of the world. Nothing in Israel is very far from something else.

Back to our tour. After standing on the Mount of the Beatitudes and internalizing its spiritual significance, we visited the synagogue in Capernaum where Jesus preached a number of his sermons. Unfortunately, we arrived five minutes too late, and it was locked tight as a drum. Not to be deterred, I suggested that we attack from the sea. After driving to a spot about a half mile away where we could access the water, Scott and I dove in and swam to the water's edge of the synagogue only to find that entrance locked tight as well. So, we retraced our steps, with Scott opting to walk back along the shore while I swam. In the late afternoon, the Sea of Galilee often gets a bit rough; and as I slowly made my way through the choppy waters, I experienced my next epiphany, driven by the realization that I was swimming where He once had walked. On this particular occasion, there was a physical as well as an emotional dimension to that sense of closeness.

Closer to Home

Perhaps the most significant of my U.S. engagements, which led to numerous others, was an hour-long interview on National Public Radio in January of 2007. Some years earlier, I had been invited by Krista Tippett, hostess of "On Faith," a widely-acclaimed public radio program, to be inter-viewed on her show about the book and its impact. I agreed; and the interview went well, until we discovered when it was over that because of a technical glitch, it had not been recorded. As we amicably parted ways, Krista said she would be coming after me to try again in the not-too-distant future.

Another five years or so went by before I received another invitation from Krista, this time to speak about Iraq, following the release of the Iraq Study Group's final report, which came out in in December of 2006. Although I didn't know much about Iraq beyond what I read in the daily news, I readily agreed and dreamed up some new approaches to that situation, which had not yet been tried but which I thought could conceivably do some good. Iraq aside, when I sat down for the interview, Krista said, "On second thought, why don't we just talk about your Center's work?" I said, "Great," and we had at it (Addendum S).

Because the interview was totally off-the-top, it probably flowed better than it would have had I prepared for it. In any event, the public response was over-the-top. Not only did the broadcast result in numerous invitations for other speaking engagements, but the feedback that NPR received inspired them to re-broadcast the exact same interview one year later (which gave rise to yet another wave of invitations).

Fast-forward another seven years, and I have remarried. My wife, Dareen, is reading about the work of ICRD, which had captured her interest. As she was doing so one evening, I passed her a copy of the transcript of Krista's inter-view, thinking she might find it of interest. As she began reading it, though, she recognized that she had heard it before—some years earlier, while listening to my interview over her car radio. She heard it, that is, until I started talking about helping Muslims to become better Muslims, at which point she turned it off. The lingering impact of 9-11 had taken a toll on the attitude of many Americans toward Muslims, and she was no exception. However, by the time she read what I gave her, her view of Muslims had significantly improved. So, we had a good laugh; and that was that until we ran into Krista Tippett a few years later, when she was speaking at a synagogue in downtown Washington. After the event, I introduced the two of them and told Krista about Dareen's reaction to our earlier interview. At that point, Dareen said, "Yeah. I turned him off. Now I turn him on." Yet one more catalyst for uproarious laughter.

Subsequent to our interview, Krista changed the name of her show from "On Faith" to "On Being" in order to include those who had no faith as well as those who did. In 2014, she received the National Humanities Medal from President Barak Obama and to this day continues to inspire countless listeners with her thoughtful commentary on deeper issues that matter.

The Magic of Chautauqua

One of the more interesting speaking engagements resulting from the NPR interview took place at Lake Chautauqua in Western New York. Prior to the invitation, I had not heard of this 145-year-old gathering, which brings people together from near and far throughout the summer for a full-immersion experience in lectures, music, theatrical performances, and recreational pursuits. The range of topics they addressed was truly amazing, as were the quality and interests of those who attended.

As a speaker, it was humbling to know I was speaking from the same platform that once accommodated the likes of Ulysses S. Grant, Susan B. Anthony, Booker T. Washington, Theodore Roosevelt, and Amelia Earhart. Indeed, it could conceivably give one an inflated sense of self-importance, if one were to forget that, at least in my instance, it was the subject matter and not the speaker that inspired the turnout. As I experienced at Oxford, most people have a natural hunger to discuss the role religion has played or is playing in their lives or to learn how it is being used in helpful ways to address pressing problems or inspire better behavior.[67]

Land of Lincoln

Yet another NPR-inspired engagement, took place in 2009 at Knox College in Galesburg, Illinois. What made it particularly meaningful was the context. It was during the bicentennial celebration of Abraham Lincoln's birth, and the college encompassed the only preserved site of the historic debates that had taken place in 1858 between Lincoln and Stephen Douglas. Lincoln, Republican candidate for the Senate from Illinois, was running against the Democratic incumbent, Senator Douglas. The principal topic of all seven of their debates was the future of slavery in the United States, particularly with respect to its expansion into new territories. Although Lincoln lost that election, his exposure in these debates proved instrumental in his later election to the Presidency.

Shortly before my visit to Knox I learned that I was tangentially related to Abraham Lincoln's step-mother, who, when she married his father, brought with her a sizeable personal library which, among other volumes, included the complete works of William Shakespeare. She and Abraham grew quite

---

[67] This was also the case when I spoke one evening at Saint Anselm College in Manchester, New Hampshire only five hours after Mitt Romney had spoken from the same rostrum while running for President. The auditorium was large and completely full, and it wasn't because anyone knew who I was. It was because they knew what I would be talking about.

close; and with her strong and loving encouragement, he spent countless hours immersed in the classics. Lincoln was later quoted as saying, "All that I am and all that I hope to become, I owe to Sarah Bush Johnston."

Providing further confirmation of the close relationship between Lincoln and his step-mother (and perhaps conveying a kinder-than-normal portrait of his wife) is the below letter from Mary Todd Lincoln in December of 1867, which accompanied some gifts she was sending to Sarah (as captured in a 1952 book by Charles Coleman titled, *Sarah Bush Lincoln: The Mother Who Survived Him*).

> *My dear Madam:*
>
> *In memory of the dearly beloved one, who always remembered you with so much affection, will you not do me the favor of accepting these few trifles? God has been very merciful to you, in prolonging your life and I trust your health has also been preserved—- In my great agony of mind I cannot trust myself to write about, what so entirely fills my thoughts, my darling husband; knowing how well you loved him also, is a greatful [sic] satisfaction to me. Believe me, dear Madam, if I can ever be of any service to you, in any respect, I am entirely at your service... I will be pleased to learn whether this package was received by you. Perhaps you know that our youngest boy is named for your husband, Thomas Lincoln, this child, the idol of his father—I am blessed in both my sons, they are very good and noble. The oldest is growing very much like his own dear father, I am a deeply afflicted woman, and hope you will pray for me.*
>
> *I am; my dear Madam, affectionately yours,*
>
> > *Mary Lincoln*

Although Mary and Sarah never met, the above testifies to the affection Lincoln held for his step-mother. As Thomas Malone put it in an article in *American Legion Magazine in February of 1939,* "Abraham Lincoln was step-mothered to greatness."

After he won the Presidential election, Lincoln reportedly rode his horse a hundred miles out of the way to say goodbye to her. I don't know if they ever saw one another again after that, but it was clear that she had a significant impact on his life. I haven't seen any reference to it, but I strongly suspect that his wholistic approach to problem-solving was heavily influenced by his deep-seated familiarity with Shakespeare.

When I sat in the chair Lincoln used during the Galesburg debate, I sensed a surreal connectedness to him. Later, when it was announced that a play centered around the Lincoln-Douglas debates would soon be coming to Washington, I immediately purchased an advance ticket. Shortly before the performance, however, I contracted a case of walking pneumonia while on a trip to Norfolk, Virginia, to speak at the Joint Forces Staff College. When I returned, it was time for the play; and although I felt miserable beyond words, there was no way I was going to miss it. So, I went and was glad I did. It was one of the best stage performances I think I've ever seen.

The actor who played Stephen Douglas was forceful and highly articulate as he made his strong and seemingly persuasive arguments that decisions relating to slavery should be left to the individual states. Then a tall, gangly Lincoln would amble out, respond to his arguments with a combination of folk-like humor and iron-clad logic and effectively cut him off at the knees. The play itself was drawn from the actual debates, so it had an authentic ring to it.

Lincoln once expressed an early desire to "leave the world a little better for my having lived in it." A tall order, even for a tall country lawyer, but one he clearly achieved as he became a role model for the ages.

Pure Mountaintop

An invitation to speak in Salt Lake City to the annual gathering of the North American Interfaith Association (NIA) also left a lasting impression. The point of contact for this event was a Utah State Government official by the name of Brian Farr, who was also affiliated with the NIA. As we spoke over the phone prior to the event, Brian suggested that I come out a day early, so I could hear the Mormon Tabernacle Choir at a Sunday church service. He also mentioned in passing that after the choir finishes the televised portion of its performance, they often sing a couple of additional numbers, at which point I said, "If that's the case, I have a request to make." He asked what it was, and I immediately said, *"The Battle Hymn of the Republic."* He chuckled and allowed as how that was their most-requested number. Nevertheless, he was a close friend of the President of the Choir and said he would see what he could do.

Several weeks later, I found myself listening to that choir sing that hymn and concluding when it was over that there was no way the South could have ever won the war, not with *The Battle Hymn* inspiring the North. It was beyond mountain top; it was transcendent.

About a year later, through unrelated channels, I became a Senior Fellow at the Wheatley Institution at Brigham Young University (BYU) in Provo, Utah. There, over a four-year period, I would spend a week or two each year giving presentations, teaching classes, and organizing major conferences, all having to do with faith-based diplomacy (Addendum T).

Aside from appreciating the intense interest that BYU students had in the subject matter, I particularly enjoyed the opportunity to understand Mormonism in greater depth and to observe close-hand the priority they give to living out exemplary family values in the home. I was also tremendously impressed with the depth of their commitment to (and impressive capability for) providing emergency assistance to others around the world of any and all religious persuasions whenever natural disasters occur.

At one point, while having lunch with eight BYU professors, I asked each of them to tell me how many children they had. As they responded, it turned out that the lowest number anyone had was five, and only one of them had that few. All the rest had more, some quite a few more. However, the one with five was rapidly catching up, as two of his kids had already given birth to twins. I laughed and told them I now understood why Mormonism was the fastest growing religion in America.

Another observation I took away from my BYU experience emanated from several one-on-one lunches with BYU students. I was amazed to see the degree to which those who had already performed their two years of missionary work were wise beyond their years. I could only conclude that the combination of working in a foreign culture and having to contend with any number of unfriendly responses to well-intended knocks on people's doors must be an incredibly maturing experience.

Some of the nicest people I have known are Mormons; and one day while thinking about the role Joseph Smith had played in starting their religion, I thought to myself, "That's quite a tale." Then I paused and thought, "I have quite a tale of my own." I then thought about how the religious traditions that most people practice are largely a function of their birth. If you are born into it, chances are you will stay with it. This, in turn, brought to mind a book titled *A Wideness in God's Mercy,* authored by Clark Pinnock, an inclusive-minded Lutheran pastor. In this book, he shows through citing both New Testament and Old Testament scripture how God has blessed all people. As the Quakers say, there's a spark of God in everyone. Our job is to find it and show it the respect it deserves. In many cases, that is far easier said than done.

Dancing in the Square

A later overseas engagement that was yet another cultural eye-opener for me took place at a NATO conference in El Escorial, Spain, about an hour outside of Madrid. As I was going to bed the night before my presentation, I began hearing music from afar. Although it was past midnight, I let my curiosity get the better of me, donned my clothes, and followed my ears.

I soon came to what had to be the village square, fully illuminated and with the entire village dancing about. From the youngest child to the oldest adult, everyone was mixing it up and having a wonderful time. As the laughter and fun penetrated the surrounding darkness, I marveled at their sense of well-being and found myself more than a little envious of their community spirit.

Apparently, this was a normal occurrence that typically took place from midnight to about 3:00 am, aided and abetted by their mid-day siestas. Just as we could learn a lot from Afghan culture about hospitality, so too could we learn from the Spanish about enjoying life.

Providing Hope

Following a speaking engagement in Dallas on New Year's Day in 2007[68], I was surrounded by a number of attendees who had loved ones in the military, fighting in Iraq or Afghanistan, and who were hungry for anything that might offer some hope. The concept of using commonly-shared religious values to bridge differences between adversaries and the examples I was able to cite of its successful application in some of the world's tougher neighborhoods seemingly filled this need, and a large number of them not only bought copies of our books, but they volunteered to assist in the Center's work in any way they could. This was not an uncommon response.

Casting a Broader Net

As our book and the Center's work became increasingly known, we were invited to play a leadership role in broader gatherings as well. The first of these took place during the second year of our existence at the first World Peace Summit of International Religious and Spiritual Leaders held at the United Nations in the year 2000. Not only was this the first acknowledgement by the U.N. of the important role that religious leaders can play in peacemaking, but the event itself was staged so that its deliberations would inform the Millennial Heads-of-State Summit a week later. As a designated

---

[68] The occasion for speaking on New Year's Day was precipitated by an invitation from ICRD board member Steven Thompson for me to address his 300+ network marketers at their company's annual meeting in Dallas. During his introduction, he presented me with a check for $25,000 (made out to ICRD) in order to demonstrate to his sales force the importance of "giving back."

"strategic partner" for this later summit, we organized and moderated a panel on the religious aspects of the conflict in the Sudan.

Also tied to this later summit was a State of the World Forum chaired by Mikhail Gorbachev, for which our Center organized and orchestrated a half-day module entitled "Peacemaking and Reconciliation: The Religious Challenge". This effort involved a number of prominent speakers and, like the Sudan panel the week before, was well received.

The World Peace Summit that originally kicked it all off a couple of weeks earlier was heavily subsidized by Ted Turner as part of his billion-dollar philanthropic contribution to the UN. At one point, he spoke to the audience of 2,000 and elicited an unforgettable response. He mentioned that in his youth he had attended seminary for a year but dropped out after they suggested that only Christians would be going to heaven. Moreover, only his particular brand of Christianity would be welcome there. With tongue-in-cheek, he concluded that heaven was likely to be a very lonely place; and he wanted no part of it. At that, the Hindus and the Buddhists in the audience broke out in wild cheers and thunderous applause.

The Clinton Initiative

Another of these broader audiences took place in 2005, when I was invited to attend the first meeting of the Clinton Global Initiative (CGI), which took place in New York City. The purpose of this event was to bring worthy charitable causes together with potential private funders. Even though it cost each of the latter $15,000 to attend, they were present in significant numbers.

I was there to advance our Center's work in reforming the madrasas of Pakistan. Because Tony Blair, then Prime Minister of the United Kingdom, devoted most of his plenary speech to the urgent need to address the terrorizing influence of these schools, I felt confident that our Center's work would greatly benefit from my later address in which I explained all that ICRD was doing to counter that influence. As it turned out, we never received one penny of support for our efforts, not from that inaugural gathering nor from any of those that followed in later years. I came to suspect there was probably a degree of political favoritism at play in funding the philanthropic interests of major Clinton supporters, but never knew for certain.

During the course of the first day's activities of that initial gathering, we broke into small working groups of ten to a table. Among those at my table were the Rev. Jesse Jackson and Rev. Ian Paisley, the Protestant religious leader from Northern Ireland. Seated right next to me was Barbara Streisand, although it took me a short while to recognize her, since she was in casual attire and not made up in any sense of the word.

Even more memorable was my second encounter with Hillary Clinton. She joined the event during the afternoon to take part in a panel discussion and then stayed for the duration. As everyone gathered for dinner that evening, I saw her from a distance, surrounded by a sizable crowd. For no compelling reason, I decided to elbow my way through to say hello. Once there, I introduced myself and reminded her of our earlier conversation in the Congress about Iran. Then I told her that I was the bearer of personal greetings from a mutual friend by the name of Carl Oglesby (with whom she had become friends in the 1960's, when she was a flower child and he was head of the SDS). I said he wanted her to know that he would be delighted to come to Washington to help her run for President. This was long before she had declared her candidacy, and she acted suitably flattered by the suggestion.

Then she took me by the elbow, looked me straight in the eyes and said, "Ever since we spoke on Capitol Hill, I have been carrying your card in my pocket; hoping to find a way to help your organization." Then she said, "I'll find a way" and turned to mingle with the crowd. Although I didn't believe for a second that she had my card in her pocket or that she would find a way to help ICRD, I was mightily impressed with her artful ability to connect and concluded Bill wasn't the only politically-gifted one in the family.

Years later while I was in Pakistan advancing our continuing work with the madrasas, Hillary happened to be there at the same time. At the time, she was Secretary of State and was being interviewed on local television by a panel of Pakistani foreign policy experts. Relations between our two countries were severely strained at the time because of a recent incident in which a CIA operative had been found guilty of killing a couple of Pakistani citizens. Despite the strain, she took everything the panel threw at her and knocked it out of the park. Through her thoughtful responses, she single-handedly laid the groundwork for a restored relationship; and once again, this conservative-leaning observer left more than a little impressed.

Teaching Old Dogs New Tricks

"You can't tell the depth of a well by the length of the handle on the pump."
–Louis Prima (1910-1978)

In 2006, I was invited by the State Department to travel to Rome to spend a week with the Vatican Foreign Service. I gladly accepted but was initially puzzled as to what I could possibly have to offer that would be of help to the foreign policy arm of the Holy See. After all, they had been practicing religious diplomacy far longer than I. After my first couple of days on the scene, though, it became clear that my principal task was to inspire them to expand their horizons. The most recent success they could point to was their resolution of a potential conflict between Chile and Argentina in the 1970s over their mutual claims to the Beagle Islands.

The need for peacemaking in the world is little short of overwhelming, yet these foreign policy practitioners of the cloth were largely unengaged. Much of my time was thus spent in private meetings and making presentations to larger audiences on the range of our Center's involvements around the world, with an eye toward inspiring them to enhance the breadth of their own efforts.

Among my many appointments that week was one with Cardinal William Levada, whose predecessor, Cardinal Ratzinger, had just been elevated to Pope (as Benedict XVI). While waiting to see him, I scanned his biography and noticed he had been born in Long Beach, California. When we met, I said, "Before we get down to business, I would bet the farm that you and I were born in the same hospital." And that indeed proved to be the case, because the name of the hospital was St. Mary's. The Catholic connection was obvious, and I suppose my own birth there (three years after his) was simply because my folks, who were both Protestant, must have lived somewhere close-by at the time. Anyway, we both enjoyed a good laugh and a pleasant meeting.

Increasing Global Awareness

By the time I stepped down from leading ICRD some 23 years after the book's publication, I had literally made hundreds of presentations around the world to various civilian and military audiences on the need for (and demonstrated effectiveness of) faith-based diplomacy. In the year leading up to and encompassing 9-11, for example, I had some 33 speaking engagements and media interviews and authored six pieces on related topics for the *U.S. Foreign Service Journal,* the *Princeton Journal of Foreign Affairs,* the *Northwestern Journal of International Affairs,* the *U.S. Naval Institute Proceedings,* an edited volume on religion and peacemaking put out by the University of Victoria, and an edited volume on globalization by the National Defense University. This was typical and indicative of the hunger that existed for finding new solutions to age-old problems (Addendum U).

After 9-11, the pace picked up even more, especially overseas, addressing such groups as the NATO Defense College in Rome; the annual meeting of International Military Chaplains in Talinn, Estonia; a European Interparliamentary Conference on "Human Rights and Religious Freedom" in Brussels; and the keynote address to a UN conference in Baku, Azerbaijan on "Strengthening Cooperation in Preventing Terrorism."

A number of presentations I made in the United States relating to ICRD were to church audiences of one denomination or another. In this context, I would often begin by observing that if they took their cues from the media, they would more likely than not conclude that Islam was their enemy. I would then ask if this was so, what did Jesus say about how we are supposed to treat our enemies and what might that look like? Then I would proceed to tell them about our Center's work.

Beyond the speaking engagements, media interviews, and written articles about our Center's work, we began holding an annual dinner in the fifth year of our existence at which we presented a worthy recipient with the Center's newly conceived Faith-in-Action Award. For a number of the dinners, we also included a keynote speaker. The purpose of these dinners was threefold: to honor someone who deserved it, to raise much-needed funds, and to create a "buzz" within Washington circles about our work. The venue was always special, extending from the Evermay Estate in Georgetown to the palatial residence on the Potomac of the Ambassador-at-Large for Pakistan.

The awardees are typically prominent individuals, who have lived their faith in making important contributions to a better world. Representative of those who have been so honored is former Secretary of State Madeleine Albright, who authored *The Mighty and the Almighty* and has become a forceful champion of including religion as an important factor in the formulation of U.S. foreign policy. Because of her continuing influence in this regard, it seems doubtful that the "real" in realpolitik will ever again ignore the religious impulse. To quote from her presentation:

> *"Religion matters in foreign policy for the simple reason that what people believe about God and God's will is a major influence in how they act towards one another, how they conceive of their responsibilities, and where they draw the line between right and wrong…."*

Fundraising: It Takes a Village

For the first seven years of the Center's existence, our principal sources of revenue were private foundations and individuals. The former category almost always requires informed research, a thoughtful strategy, a compelling proposal, and a great deal of luck. The Ford foundation, for example, typically funds only about five percent of the proposals that they receive. Of course, one's "luck" can be considerably enhanced if one has a personal relationship with a member of the Foundation's board or senior staff.

The first foundation from which we sought support was the Hewlett Foundation based in Menlo Park, California. At the time, it was providing start-up money for new non-profits having conflict resolution as their principal focus. It took more than a year for us to win an award, primarily because of the adjustment in thinking required for donors to recognize religion's potential in the peacemaking arena. In seeking the grant, I prepared a business plan that described the geopolitical context as it then existed, in which religion was central to much of the strife that was taking place. I then made the case for establishing an organization that could "inspire religious activity in more positive and helpful directions," citing the case studies of *Religion, The Missing Dimension of Statecraft* as a basis for how this might be done.

I next discussed the approach such an organization could take in defusing tense situations and how it could go about doing so. Then I tried something I had not seen done before. I attempted to show what sort of difference such a center could make by taking a hypothetical, retrospective look back at the kinds of accomplishments one might expect to see at the end of the first, third, and fifth years of operations.

After much effort, we received a grant in the amount of $100,000 a year for three years. Ironically, we failed to achieve any of the accomplishments cited as possibilities in our retrospective look-backs. However, what we were able to achieve was of even greater importance; which just goes to show, one never knows which of the seeds one sows will land on fertile soil and of those that do, which will ultimately bear the intended fruit.

Another source of foundation funding that became a valuable lifeline of support over the Center's history came from the Stewardship Foundation in Tacoma, Washington. After supporting my efforts to disseminate the findings of *Religion, the Missing Dimension of Statecraft* as widely as possible, Stewardship began providing general operating support for our new center at varying levels of funding, peaking at $65,000 a year for an extended period of time. Bill Weyerhaeuser, who chairs Stewardship, is also President of the Sequoia Foundation, which in addition to providing support at that same level, also provided funding on a situational basis to support extraordinary opportunities that came along to move important mountains that needed moving in such places as Kashmir, Iran, and Syria.

None of the above was taken for granted, since every year's funding increment required a sound and all-encompassing proposal to justify the support.

The situational infusions, which also required compelling proposals, were always preceded by lengthy conversations over the phone with Bill, who never failed to ask penetrating and insightful questions about the request. I never ceased to marvel at how well-informed he was about whatever need we were hoping to meet, no matter where in the world that need happened to exist.

Another source of institutional support had its genesis in an invitation I received from a good friend from the Prayer Breakfast fellowship by the name of Doug Crane, who asked me to speak about our Center's work to 75 of his friends and acquaintances at a reception that he would host at the Portland Golf Club in Portland, Oregon. Present among those in attendance was one of three board members of the Murdock Charitable Trust, headquartered directly across the Columbia River in Vancouver, Washington.

Although the Trust generally confined its giving to the Pacific Northwest, their board was sufficiently impressed with our work that they invited us to submit a proposal, which they subsequently funded. As I write this a decade later, we are now completing our third cycle of three-year grants from Murdock, the first two for $75,000 a year for the three years, and the third for $100,000 a year for the same period. These were project-specific grants, each of which required a detailed and convincing rationale and all of which enabled us to work in some very challenging areas overseas. One year we struck out with them, so it was never something we could take for granted. In western parlance, one always needed to earn one's spurs.

In contrast to foundation funding, individual giving is inherently more opportunistic in nature and often involves taking advantage of unexpected openings as they arise. One such opening took place when John Kiser showed up in my office one day in the company of a mutual friend by the name of Yehezkel Landau, who had dropped by to pay a visit. John and I immediately hit it off and over time formed a close friendship. At ICRD's fifth anniversary dinner, I purposely sat him next to Azi in the hope that he might become interested in our madrasa work. The upshot of that evening was a trip to Pakistan in which John spent a full week visiting various madrasas to better understand their role and their needs. As a result, his family foundation, which he chairs, contributed more than a million dollars over the course of the next seven years in support of our efforts to enhance the curriculums and pedagogy of these religious schools.

On a more deliberate note, I lobbied for a year and a half to make a presentation to "The Gathering," an annual meeting of those individuals across the country who give at least $100,000 a year to support charitable Christian causes (now up to $200,000).[69] When I finally broke through and was accepted as a speaker for their next conference, which was taking place in Washington DC, my prospective presentation was given a great deal of advance publicity. However, the timing was awful and occurred before most of the participants arrived. So, instead of the 150 or so attendees that I was expecting, a total of six individuals showed up. One of the six, however, was Jack Willome, who that year happened to be chairing the event.

Despite the disappointing turnout, I gave it my best; and when it was over, Jack invited me to breakfast the following morning. Over breakfast, he told me he was very impressed with our Center's work (which at that time was heavily focused on Sudan and just getting underway in Kashmir) and said that he now knew why he had made the trip (from his home in Texas). He contributed $15,000 toward our work in Sudan and has continued as a supporter ever since.

Jack is a retired businessman from San Antonio, and on the next two occasions that I happened to be passing through town, he had me speak to different audiences that he thought might be interested in what I had to say. The third time, he invited 50 of his friends to lunch at his country club and told them to bring their checkbooks. After lunch, Jack introduced me; and I gave an impassioned pitch about our work and the need for funds to support it. Then I turned to former National Security Advisor Bud McFarlane, who spent the last ten minutes endorsing its importance. Bud, who was on our board and a son of the great State of Texas, had generously flown down from Washington to do this. The combination apparently worked, as those in attendance collectively pledged to provide $50,000 a year for three years and then proceeded to deliver as promised.

Although I think our presentation was pretty convincing, I strongly suspect that most gave out of their affection for Jack and the fact that he had supported their causes in the past. Whatever the reason, it was difficult to ignore Jack's pitch at the end:

> *"As a donor, I believe that our investments in the ICRD have been among our highest leverage opportunities. For every dollar that I give to the Center, I believe that thousands of lives are impacted in Sudan, Kashmir and other areas where the Center is active. I encourage you to become an investor in this ministry yourself."*

I too came to feel that same affection for Jack, and consider it an extraordinary privilege to count him as a spiritual brother.

---

[69] Strictly speaking, ICRD is not a religious organization but rather an organization that deals with religion. However, the fact that it was led by a Christian motivated by the peacemaking mandate of Matthew 5:9 was apparently close enough to qualify.

Speaking of spiritual brothers, when I was living in Wellesley while working at Harvard, I used to meet every Friday morning with a small group of men for a fellowship breakfast at a nearby Marriott in Newton. It was there that I met David Vander Mey and Harold Jacobi in 1980, both of whom became life-long friends. As mentioned earlier, Dave contributed the first $10,000 that enabled us to get the Center started and has continued to contribute as a longstanding member of its board. Harold (or "Rink" as he is better known), who was with me in Pakistan when we visited the terrorism-linked madrasas, has now been serving as board chairman for the better part of a decade. Beyond the fact that we became best friends (even though he dropped most of the passes I threw him while cavorting on a beach on Cape Cod),[70] he has been exceedingly generous in his moral and financial support for ICRD.

The Center is indebted as well to numerous other supporters who have also caught the vision. As I once had occasion to say to the board, "The work isn't about any one of us; it's about all of us being able to look our Maker in the eye when that day comes and saying, "We ran the race; we did our best."

Inroads in Academe

Beyond the inclusion of our three books on the reading lists for various graduate and undergraduate courses in a range of colleges, universities, and seminaries, we had an even greater indirect impact on academia in 2004, when I received a phone call from the Henry Luce Foundation in New York (named after the gentleman who started *Time Magazine*). They made reference to my first book and said they were considering the possibility of funding programs in religion and foreign policy and asked if they could meet with me to discuss the matter. I readily agreed and gave the meeting serious consideration. I also sent notes to the few young men and women who had worked for ICRD either as a research assistant or in an intern capacity, asking them what kinds of programs in this arena they would ideally like to see included in college curriculums.

A month or so later, I was visited by Luce's Board Chairman, its President, a Vice President, and a staff member, and we discussed a list of eleven recommendations that I presented to them. Of the eleven, they ultimately implemented ten. Of course, the one they didn't implement was that of funding project work like that which ICRD was doing.

Foremost among those they did implement was the establishment of academic programs on Religion and International Affairs in selected universities

---

[70] *Rink would undoubtedly quarrel with this characterization, but he will have to write his own book to refute it.

across the country. And I was very impressed with how strategic they were in their selections. For example, the grants, which typically ranged from $350,000-$400,000, went to schools like Harvard to influence future policymakers, to Syracuse University to influence future journalists, and to the University of Southern California, which has the largest international relations student body in the country. I believe Luce planted a total of eight or so programs; but whatever the number, the investments have had a lasting impact.

Government Recognition

Over this same period, the State Department evolved from a posture of tepid acknowledgement of ICRD's existence to one of outright enthusiasm for its work; and the Center's budget, which for the first seven years had no government support whatsoever, increased significantly once that ceased to be true. Capitalizing on the transcendent aspects of religious faith in overcoming the secular obstacles to peace has become a Center trademark, and the efficacy of this approach has become widely recognized by the foreign policy establishment, as it increasingly calls upon ICRD to achieve the impossible in highly-charged environments like Pakistan and Yemen.

As has been clear from the outset, though, there will always be some Center initiatives in which the political sensitivities will preclude the possibility of U.S. government support. Every government has its own political agenda, which may or may not coincide with the substantive thrust of any particular project. As mentioned before, balanced neutrality is a prerequisite in this business, and the nuances are legion. Hence, the ever-present need for a light touch, a thick skin, and endless patience. Finally, what women seem to know from birth and men occasionally figure out, all things are relational, particularly when it comes to establishing the kind of trust required to reconcile differences between people and nation-states.

> *"Your work gives us hope that not only are there people on all sides of these conflicts who are willing to work together for peace, but also that religion can be part of the solution."*

John V. Hanford
U.S. Ambassador-at-Large for
International Religious Freedom (2002-2009)

PART V
The Final Prize

Chapter Eighteen

LOOKING BACK

To each there comes in their lifetime a special moment when they are figuratively tapped on the shoulder and offered the chance to do a very special thing. What a tragedy if that moment finds them unprepared or unqualified for that which could have been their finest hour.

–Winston Churchill

About 15 years ago, I was getting dressed after a physical workout at the University Club in Washington when I struck up a conversation with a doctor who was dressing at the locker next to mine. He mentioned that it was his birthday, and he needed to dress quickly to get to his "surprise" party on time. I told him that for years I had always wondered why there was so much hoopla over birthdays. After all, all it takes to qualify is a little fog on the mirror. I then said, "but now I'm at an age where I've changed my tune and consider every birthday a miracle." He said, "You bet your sweet ass it is. Where else do you find 32 million parts moving in perfect harmony with one another?"

Speaking of such celebrations, I am reminded of the one that took place when I hit the big 5-0. Of the innumerable condolence cards that I received, the one from Lance took the prize. On the outside was a stern and rather authoritarian figure pointing at the reader and saying, "It's your birthday, so try to act your age!" On the inside, "Lie underground and remain very still."

Life is a Miracle

Several years later, my sister was visiting from Chicago and mentioned that she had been wanting to visit an exhibit on "Bodies" that had been making the rounds across the country and which just then happened to be in Washington where I was living at the time. So off we went, and it proved a memorable experience.

In this exhibit, the intricacies of the human body are on full display through the use of skeletons in various states of posed animation to which the body's muscles are physically attached. Internal organs are also positioned as in real life, much like one would expect to see through multiple overlays in an anatomy textbook, only far more graphic. In short, the inner workings and hidden mechanisms of the human body are brought to life in a poignant and unforgettable manner. As one exits the exhibit, there is a sign at the end which, as I recall, says something to the following effect:

> *In today's fast-paced world, any time for serious reflection is all-but-totally squeezed out of one's daily existence. However, it is our hope that having seen what a marvelous creation your body is, you will be inspired to honor it even more through proper diet and exercise.*

As we concluded our visit, I left with two distinct impressions: first, that the human body is indeed a marvelous creation; and second, it is a miracle that we ever feel good in light of the need for all "32 million parts" to be functioning well and working as one to achieve that happy state. The "32 million" is undoubtedly an exaggeration, but considering the fact that the human body has more than 600 different muscles and innumerable other support systems, that number may not be as outlandish as it sounds.

Out of all this, I concluded that life itself is a miracle and should be treated as such. While this could be interpreted as a statement against abortion and/or war, it could also be interpreted as a plea for practicing the Golden Rule, treating others as we would want to be treated ourselves. Related to this scriptural admonition, is the Second Law of the Prophets, which is "to love your neighbor as yourself." But how does that work if you don't love yourself (as our increasing national suicide rate would seem to suggest for any number of us)? Instead of using one's self as the standard, perhaps it is more useful to apply a different measure, one in which we attempt to understand why others view problems the way they do and use that as our benchmark. This is the standard to which ICRD has aspired since its inception.

ICRD Revisited

"Ultimately, leadership is about creating new realities." –Peter Senge

From the outset, the Center's principal strategic goal was to facilitate the incorporation of religious considerations into the practice of U.S.

foreign policy. Everything else we did flowed from that, including our stated objectives of:

- Serving as a bridge between politics and religion in support of peacemaking.

- Deploying multi-skilled, inter-religious action teams to trouble spots where conflict threatens or has already broken out.

- Training religious clergy and laity in the tasks of peacemaking, and

- Providing feedback to theologians and clergy on interpretations of their teachings that might be contributing to strife and misunderstanding and suggesting where some rethinking may be in order.

Superimposed on top of this were the criteria we used to determine where we would intervene, which included those situations (1) where we could do the most good for the most people, (2) that were of strategic consequence to the United States, (3) where we had access to established relationships of trust that could be brought to bear in addressing the problem, and (4) where neither our government nor other NGOs had already established a significant presence, either because of political constraints or limited accessibility. This latter criterion was driven by the fact that ICRD has always been a small organization, and we wanted to ensure that our efforts would have a value-added impact.

One of the above objectives that deserves special mention is the deployment of inter-religious action teams. Here, in addition to having the necessary secular skills to address the problems at hand, it is important to include on the team religious representation that mirrors that of the local population with which the team will be working. The locals need to feel reassured that someone on the team is mindful of their religious sensitivities. This goal was driven by common sense, as was most everything else that we did.

I recall with a chuckle sketching out our proposed methodology for tackling new situations on the back of an envelope, while riding the metro home one evening after work. It must have taken all of 40 minutes to create; but despite the abbreviated and informal nature of its creation, the resulting template served us well over a challenging span of involvements in any number of hot-spots around the world.

Perhaps the most critical element of the template was a requirement that wherever we choose to intervene, we partner with an indigenous organization that already commands a high level of trust with the local population. That way, we are always able to hit the ground running, without having to slow down to establish our own credibility from scratch. In constructing the template, the fact that I was unschooled in the nuances of the different religious traditions proved not to be an obstacle. What was essential, though, was a visceral understanding of how faith drives action.

Changing Course

"Good ideas are not adopted automatically. They must be driven into practice with courageous impatience." —Hyman Rickover

To achieve our strategic goal of informing U.S. foreign policy with religious considerations, we confined our involvements to foreign policy challenges that were of critical importance. I felt this would be the most effective way to sensitize policymakers and practitioners to the importance of religion in foreign affairs (by seeing our impact as we addressed the religious dimensions of those challenges). Thus, our involvement over time in such places as Kashmir, Pakistan, Iran, Afghanistan, Syria, Saudi Arabia, and Yemen.

The above approach finally bore fruit in February of 2015, when the State Department established a new Office of Religion and Global Affairs. Although our strategy took nearly 16 years to have a discernable impact, changing course on the Ship of State has never been an easy proposition. Beyond overcoming some rather deep-seated assumptions, there are also the harsh, generic realities of change with which one must inevitably contend, as were so ably captured five centuries ago by Nicollo Machiavelli in his classic work, *The* Prince:

> *It ought to be remembered that there is nothing more difficult to take in hand, more perilous to conduct, or more uncertain in its success, than to take the lead in the introduction of a new order of things. Because the innovator has for enemies all those who have done well under the old conditions, and lukewarm defenders in those who may do well under the new. This coolness arises partly from fear of the opponents, who have the laws on their side, and partly from the incredulity of men, who do not readily believe in new things until they have had a long experience of them.*

The charter of the new office called for it to facilitate active cooperation between the Department and religious leaders and institutions around the world in promoting mutually beneficial interests. As conveyed in a third-party posting on the *Huffington Post* blog site in reference to the new office:

> *"The office in some respects will be following in the footprints of a small, non-government organization—The International Center for Religion and Diplomacy (ICRD) – which for the past 14 years has been using religious values to bridge differences between adversaries and to counter religious extremism in conflict-prone regions of the world."*

A similar piece in the *Washington Post* also cited our Center's role "on the front lines of religious engagement." Although major bureaucratic surgery will be required before religious imperatives receive their just due in the daily course of doing business at the State Department, the establishment of the new office was clearly a step in the right direction.

Some of the Center's objectives and criteria changed following the establishment of the new office, but the basic mission of bridging religious considerations with the practice of international politics in support of peacemaking remained the same.

In Retrospect

"Never doubt that a small group of thoughtful, committed citizens can change the world; indeed, it is the only thing that ever has."
—Margaret Mead (1901-1978)

The most dangerous situation that we tackled while I was in the saddle, was our work with the madrasas in Pakistan. Over our eight-year involvement there, we spent most of our time in the more radical areas of the country, penetrating any number of extremist strongholds to conduct our workshops. The most dramatic involvement, on the other hand, was when we intervened with the Taliban in Afghanistan to secure the release of the Korean missionaries they were holding hostage.

Finally, our most strategic engagement has been the work we have been doing to reform the educational system of Saudi Arabia. As custodian of the two holiest sites in Islam, the Kingdom's influence in the Muslim world is unrivaled. Although it will take some time for our efforts there to make a noticeable difference, once they do, the impact is likely to be far-reaching.

Education has been the focus of our efforts in Pakistan and Saudi Arabia, but that has not been the case elsewhere. Every situation is unique and requires a tailored approach that both accommodates the on-scene personalities and circumstances and pursues whatever strategy is thought to offer the greatest potential for achieving the desired result. It also has to be recognized that most situations will require lengthy involvements to make a lasting difference. In Sudan, it was five years, Kashmir six, Pakistan eight, and in Saudi Arabia, ten and counting.

Although every engagement requires its own approach, the overarching challenge, particularly for these longer-term involvements, has been that of acquiring the necessary resources to do the job. Fortunately, although we started on a shoestring, within the first nine months we were able to raise a total of $600,000, which put us on a much stronger footing.

At least part of that initial fundraising success was attributable to the pioneering nature of our work. For example, when we applied to a widely-respected, security-related foundation for a grant of $217,000 to support our madrasa work in Pakistan, the foundation's board sensed its strategic importance and awarded us $347,000. The fact that their board included both a former National Security Advisor and a former Army Chief of Staff with whom I had previously worked undoubtedly helped as well; but whatever the reason, it was the only time in that foundation's history that they ever awarded more than had been originally requested.

For the first year and on at least two other occasions along the way, I went without pay for extended periods of time in order to make ends meet; but that was never done with any sense of personal sacrifice. When doing something out of a sense of calling, you do whatever it takes to keep things moving.

A Touch of the Divine

People have the "candle of the Lord" by which to see and act
—John Locke (1632-1704)

In the final analysis, the genesis of ICRD was my decade-plus involvement with the National Prayer Breakfast fellowship and the model it provides in building bridges of understanding across religious and political divides. To that, I have sought to add a professional dimension by systematically applying the resulting relationships of trust to solving practical problems, like making peace and advancing social change.

On a Personal Note

The Lord doesn't call the equipped; He equips the called. —anonymous

It may also be instructive to contemplate how my disparate job experiences might have also contributed to the Center's success. For example, with regard to our Saudi project, I can see how the perseverance I internalized at the Naval Academy served me well in coping with the eternal timetable required to accomplish anything of consequence in the Kingdom. Dealing with the multiple sensitivities inherent in this project also drew deeply from my experience with the racially-charged environment of Cities in Schools. Finally, whatever subtleties of diplomacy I picked up at CSIS undoubtedly played a role as well.

These same ingredients (and others) not only played a role in other ICRD projects, but in transitioning from one job opportunity to the next as well. A good example here would be when I moved from Cities in Schools (CIS) to the Center for Strategic and International Studies (CSIS). Because of the skills acquired in handling highly difficult personnel situations at CIS, I was able to resolve rather quickly several problems that had plagued CSIS in this same area for many months. In one instance, it involved letting a program director go who didn't want to go and who had the full backing of the Israeli Cabinet to stay. And it was done amicably. Next to CIS, CSIS was a walk in the park.

In reviewing the specific projects in the earlier chapters of this book, I was surprised at how often my connection to the Prayer Breakfast fellowship had actually played a role either in a project's conception or in its implementation. When asked by anyone familiar with the National Prayer Breakfast what ICRD is about, I usually describe it as a loosely-affiliated operating arm of the Fellowship. And even though I felt that was a bit of an exaggeration (since there has never been any sort of formal ties between our two organizations), I was surprised to learn in looking back how accurate that characterization has proven to be.

In three instances, the Fellowship was responsible for the genesis of a particular project, those being the initial invitations to visit Sudan and Iran and the later call-to-arms to rescue the Korean missionaries. In most cases, however, the connection played out in some other form. Thus, I feel tremendously indebted to the Fellowship and all that it stands for, not only for inspiring me to capture in book form some of the magic for which it has been responsible, but also for supporting my later efforts to walk-the-talk through my work with ICRD.

I have spent the last several decades of my life attempting to live out the principles that inspire the Prayer Breakfast. However, I should note in the interest of full disclosure that the Fellowship itself has periodically come under heavy criticism. Because the norm for its activities is to keep many of them in confidence so that those involved will feel free to express their private thoughts and feelings, the Fellowship is often accused of having a secret agenda. Once tarred with that particular brush, if it's "secret," then it must *ipso facto* be negative. And since their network includes so many world leaders, it falls victim to various conspiracy theories relating to a negative global agenda.

Finally, just as Jesus met with and talked to all "the wrong people," inspiring them to rise above themselves (the harlots, the tax collectors, and the like); so has the Fellowship engaged any number of disreputable leaders in that same spirit. Some of these have been in areas of the world, which for one reason or another, have been beyond the reach of the State Department (thus giving rise to even further suspicion). Although such engagements have often led to improved behavior on the part of these leaders, mere involvement with them has also been the subject of some criticism.

Beyond the above kinds of suspicions raised in the secular press, the inclusive nature of the Breakfast has also inspired adverse reactions, albeit from a different direction. For example, at the 47th National Prayer Breakfast in 1999, the presence of PLO leader Yasser Arafat as an invited guest created quite a stir among conservative Christians, causing some of them to boycott the event. Negative reactions from this same quarter were even greater at an earlier Breakfast when then Saudi Ambassador to the United States, Prince Bandar bin Sultan, was invited to read about Jesus from the Qur'an to the audience of 4,000 mostly card-carrying Christians.

Last year, the 2020 National Prayer Breakfast gave birth to yet another form of criticism. For the first time in its 68-year history, it was criticized because of the President's remarks. The keynote speaker who preceded him was Harvard professor Arthur Brooks, who spoke about the "crisis of contempt" in America and the need to "Love Your Enemies." He gave an inspiring message; but when President Donald Trump (who just the day before had avoided impeachment) spoke, he openly disagreed with the concept and complained bitterly about the "dishonest and corrupt" detractors who had put him, his family, and the country through a "terrible ordeal." In short, he directly refuted the heart of Christ's mandate.

In the criticism that followed in the wake of this event, one columnist began his piece by saying, "At the 68th, and perhaps last, National Prayer Breakfast...." He then went on to build a seemingly persuasive case for why the Breakfast had "ceased to be useful." Although this reporter is one of my favorite commentators on religious matters and far more thoughtful than most, I totally disagreed with his conclusions about the Breakfast.

While the Fellowship selects the keynote speaker, who always does a wonderful job of conveying insights consistent with the teachings of Jesus, it has no influence over what the President of the United States is going to say. Nor do most critics have any idea of how extensive the influence of the Prayer Breakfast is through the example it sets in inspiring similar breakfasts in numerous states, cities, and towns; and, most particularly, in other countries (more than a hundred at last count). It also inspires weekly breakfasts of small fellowship groups around the world, each formed around the spirit of Jesus and led not by religious figures, but by inspired lay persons who want to better serve their local communities or the institutions of which they are a part. The collective efforts of these groups constitute an incalculable force for good across the globe and should be encouraged wherever possible.

Illustrative of the good that can result from such gatherings is the following case in point: when South Africa was escaping the bonds of apartheid, there was a moment in time when it looked like a full-scale war might break out between members of the African National Congress Party (ANC) under Nelson Mandela and the Inkatha Freedom Party (IFP) under Mangosuthu Buthelezi. Followers of both leaders were already killing one another.

In an attempt to avoid greater bloodshed, a team of international negotiators under the leadership of U.S. Secretary of State Henry Kissinger and British Foreign Secretary Lord Peter Carrington attempted to defuse the situation. Despite their best efforts, they were unable to persuade Buthelezi, who wanted an independent Zulu nation, to participate in the country's first democratic elections, scheduled to take place a few weeks later. Washington Okumu, the Kenyan diplomat with the "invisible means of support" mentioned earlier, accompanied the team as a Special Advisor.

Following the failed mediation attempt, Okumu, who had become friends with Buthelezi when both of them attended a National Prayer Breakfast in Washington some twenty years earlier, wasn't prepared to give up. So, he arranged to meet privately with Buthelezi at the airport in Johannesburg. When he arrived at the airport, though, Buthelezi's plane had already taken off; and Okumu thought he had missed his chance. However, a short way out, the plane's compass began to act erratically. Standing regulations required that any aircraft with a malfunctioning compass must return to home base, if it takes place less than ten miles away. So, it did; and the two gentlemen were able to meet.

During the meeting, Okumu was able to persuade Buthelezi to reconsider his earlier decision. Shortly thereafter, the two of them and Mandela spent five days in intense negotiations at a secret location in Johannesburg. Buthelezi finally came around; and after the elections (in which he participated), was appointed Minister of Home Affairs in Mandela's new government of national unity. Moreover, in an added gesture of reconciliation, Mandela appointed

Buthelezi as Acting President of South Africa on 22 separate occasions, when both he and his deputy, Thambo Mbeki, were out of the country.

The fact that South Africa was able to rid itself of apartheid without undergoing a revolution of any sort is little short of a miracle and is due, at least in part, to the kind of lasting friendships that are developed at the National Prayer Breakfast. Until he passed away in 2013, Mandela always paid tribute to Okumu whenever they were together, acknowledging him as the principal architect of the deal that saved South Africa.

Amazingly, the technicians never found anything wrong with the compass.

Crossing the Divides

The Breakfast has had its lighter moments as well. One year the principal speaker was the Irish singer and rock band leader Paul Davis Hewson, better known by his stage name, Bono. At the time, he was leading a major initiative to relieve Third World debt by persuading Western countries to support the idea. So, showcasing his work on behalf of the poor to the Prayer Breakfast audience was a natural fit. As he led into his remarks, wearing his trademark black jacket and sunglasses, he said, "I'm sure all of you are wondering why I'm up here speaking to you today. Certainly, I'm not a man of the cloth—unless your cloth happens to be leather." He went on to give a wonderful talk that undoubtedly attracted significant additional support for his cause.

Because of my own involvement with the Prayer Breakfast, I have at times been approached for comments by some of the would-be critics. In every instance, I have attempted to set the record straight on the Fellowship's impact by citing (1) the integrity of its mission in promoting peace and serving the poor by changing hearts and minds at the top, (2) the purpose of the Breakfast itself, which is for attendees to set aside their differences and come together in the spirit of Jesus to develop personal friendships, and (3) the inspiring aspects of its work, which collectively attempt to emulate the teachings of Jesus in quiet ways that attract people of all religious persuasions. Nowhere was the latter more driven home to me than when I met with six Japanese businessmen in a restaurant atop the ANA Hotel in Tokyo to discuss their interest in translating *Religion, the Missing Dimension of Statecraft* into Japanese.

Although they were all exceedingly busy in their respective professions, each of them had volunteered to translate a portion of the book out of their commitment to honoring the spirit of Jesus. Each of them was personally involved with the Fellowship, but I was nevertheless amazed to see how intensely they felt about Jesus. All of them were Shinto, yet none of them felt any need to change his religion.

Whether one believes Jesus was the son of God, one of many Gods, or merely a great prophet, there is universal respect for His teachings that transcends all religious divides. And if properly harnessed, there is a unique ability to leverage that respect in achieving laudable goals that would ordinarily defy accomplishment by other means.

Respectful Engagement

Another important contributor to the Center's success (as mentioned earlier) was the fact that we had "religion" in our title. I had been advised at the outset and periodically reminded along the way by various friends and acquaintances that we could improve ICRD's lot financially if we were to remove that word from our title. They felt, and I agreed, that its presence could be a deterrent to securing government or corporate support for our work; because at that stage, and as mentioned earlier, whenever either of these entities heard that word, they typically backed away for fear of appearing to favor one faith tradition over another. However, I felt that the helpful aspects of including the word when working with Muslims and others who integrate their religion and politics probably outweighed any downside on the fund-raising front. And our experience bore this out. The madrasa project, for example, would not have come to pass without "religion" in our title.

In important ways, the challenge for ICRD was far more spiritual than it was political. The mandate was disarmingly simple: to capitalize on the good that religion can do by bridging religion and politics in support of peace-making. If one were to encapsulate what this equates to in simpler terms, it would be "respectful engagement." And key to pursuing that successfully is the ability to empathize.

The Power of Empathy

When I first started out at ICRD, I used to argue that what was needed to bridge differences between people was not an attitude of tolerance toward others but respect for their values. Tolerance, which essentially means "I recognize you are different, and I'm willing to put up with you," is all too often little more than a thin veneer of accommodation to paper over that which divides.

A good example of respect in action, though, occurred during that visit I made with ICRD board members Rink Jacobi and John Sandoz to the Deobandi madrasa outside of Karachi (as described in Chapter 13); where we encountered considerable rage because of the conflict then taking place between Israel and Hezbollah in Lebanon. As later attested to by Azi, when I quoted several Qur'anic passages during my remarks, there was an audible sigh from the audience as the rage dissipated because of the respect being shown for values they held dear.

After several more years, though, I came to think that showing respect is also inadequate. Instead, I concluded what is really needed is a finely-honed sense of empathy in which one does the hard work of determining why others see problems the way they do. Sometimes it may be a function of cultural imperatives or religious beliefs. In other instances, it may have to do with some unresolved wound of history. Whatever is driving their perspective and attitudes, though, one should do whatever it takes to understand at a deeper level what that is and to adjust one's own approach accordingly, as one seeks a "win-win" outcome.

To do the above most effectively, one should operate on the premise that everyone on any given side in a conflict isn't bad. And even those who are bad, aren't bad all the time. Thus, one should always, as a matter of course, play to the angels of their higher nature.

The Basics

"If we could read the secret history of our enemies, we should find in each person's life sorrow and suffering enough to disarm all hostility."
—*Henry Wadsworth Longfellow (1807-1882)*

Empathy, at its most basic level is the act of identifying with someone else, of seeking to understand their point of view and looking at the problem at hand through their side of the prism. Although empathy is normally viewed through a personal lens and can be a critically important element in peace-making, it has implications for national security as well. And there, I'm afraid, we as a nation aren't doing very well either. By failing to take into account the reasons behind our adversary's actions, we fall victim far too often to the law of unintended consequences. The revered Chinese military strategist Sun Tzu advised that we should "know our enemy" – an unachievable ideal without the practice of empathy. Indeed, it is as critical to engaging an enemy effectively as it is to avoiding conflict in the first place.

Adversaries in today's conflicts typically leave empathy out of their calculations, as each side tends to dehumanize the other in pursuing its own political ends. Although a natural response, dehumanizing effectively condemns both parties to unending conflict until one side or the other capitulates. In other words, if one wants to resolve a dispute with minimal loss, it is essential to empathize.

Part of the reason that most foreign policy and national security practitioners overlook the importance of empathy is because they associate the concept with weakness. It lacks the perceived weight or gravitas of other terms like "power" or "justice". In some circumstances, empathy becomes close to unthinkable. Speaking in relation to the events of 9/11, analyst Gaetano Llardi with the Security Intelligence Group observed, *"To demonstrate any degree of empathy, regardless of how slight, implied conceding some validity to the act... to empathize was to sympathize. To sympathize was unimaginable, unforgiveable."* This is a stigma that needs to be broken. Empathy is not weakness; empathy is critical to informed and effective decision-making.

To illustrate the problem, one has only to think about the passengers who overwhelmed the hijackers on the plane that crashed in Pennsylvania. As expressed by Islamic theologian Farid Esack:

> *"...The sure prospect of their own deaths didn't keep them [the passengers] from doing what they had to do to prevent greater harm, essentially to save a larger part of humankind.*
>
> *Difficult as this may be for us to understand, in the twisted minds of these suicide bombers, they too saw themselves as giving their lives so that a larger part of humanity may live. For them, the United States is the enemy, Satan incarnate, who is causing chaos and destruction around the world."*

Is one weaker for having figured this out? I think not. Does it mean that one has to roll over for the suicide bombers in order to address their grievances? Most probably not. Does it mean one's future choices will be better informed? Most assuredly yes.

When former Secretary of Defense Robert McNamara was asked the most important lesson he learned from the Vietnam War, he said, "the need to empathize with the enemy." And as he further lamented in his book, *In Retrospect: The Tragedy and Lessons of Vietnam* published in 1995, "Our misjudgment of friend and foe alike reflected our profound ignorance of the history, culture, and politics of the people in the area..." Although he was later vilified by the public for confessing his misgivings about a conflict he had overseen in which numerous families had lost a loved one, he expressed those same sentiments to me over dinner about two years before he crossed over in 2009.

Commenting on American management of the war in Iraq, Harvard professor Larry Diamond concluded that the United States hurt both its own interests and Iraq's recovery through a lack of empathy by American officials. This became particularly apparent when the Coalition Authority's plan for implementing the peace following our invasion was rendered dead on arrival because it lacked any input from Ayatollah Sistani, the country's leading religious figure.

General David Petraeus, whose strategy later turned the corner in Iraq, suggested yet another role for empathy in his *Counterinsurgency Field Manual:* "…leaders {should} feel the pulse of the populous, understand their motivations, and care about what they want and need. Genuine compassion and empathy for the populous provide an effective weapon against insurgents". The General understood that empathy strengthens both military and peacebuilding capacities alike in zones of conflict, because it helps win the support of local populations.

Some critics suggest that empathetic leaders may have greater difficulty in making tough decisions than those who are not. This, they say, would be even more likely if they were unpopular decisions. While there may be some truth to this, one way to minimize the possibility is by delegating the function itself to leaders below you (if there are any) after thoroughly briefing them on your expectations (a recent Gallup study showed that the greatest influence on employees' happiness and productivity is the degree of support they receive from their direct supervisor). Then you can decide important matters in the manner that suits you and the organization best. Otherwise, although showing empathy may slow your decision process for the reasons cited; in more cases than not, its application should lead to wiser outcomes.

Yet another important dimension of empathy that former Secretary of State George Schultz highlighted on the occasion of his 100th birthday is the basis it can provide for building trust. As captured in an article he crafted for the December 13, 2020 edition of the *Washington Post* on "The 10 most important things I've learned about trust in my 100 years," he said the following:

> "Often in my career, I saw that genuine empathy is essential in establishing solid, trusting relationships. In 1973, when I was treasury secretary, I attended a wreath-laying ceremony at a World War II memorial in Leningrad with the Soviet foreign trade minister, Nikolai Patolichev. As we walked, Patolichev, a tough old guy, described the staggering death toll in the Battle of Leningrad. Tears streamed down his face, and his interpreter was sobbing. When we were about to leave, I said to Patolichev, 'I, too,

fought in World War II and had friends killed beside me.' Looking out over the cemetery, I added, 'After all, these were the soldiers who defeated Hitler.' Facing the cemetery, I raised my best Marine salute, and Patolichev thanked me for the show of respect. Later on, to my surprise, I found that I had earned the trust of Soviet leaders as a result of this visit."

Do Unto Others

Beyond our national failings to empathize, we also fall victim to hypocrisy when we fail to recognize that we as a country would not stand for a minute to be treated by some other country the way that we so cavalierly treat others. A recent case in point is the hue and cry across the county over Russian interference in our 2016 elections. If we were being honest, we would have to admit that they beat us at our own game, particularly in view of the numerous attempts we have made to influence the elections of other countries, up to and including deposing popularly-elected leaders.

One of the many cases in point was the previously mentioned effort in 1953 to overthrow Muhammad Mosaddeq, Iran's Prime Minister, who we and the British feared was about to draw closer to the Soviet Union. His removal, as described earlier, unwittingly paved the way for the ultimate take-over by Ayatollah Khomeini and the seizure of our embassy personnel. When one puts on the hats of both parties, it becomes easier to understand why relations have remained strained ever since.

Assistant Professor of Political Science Lindsey O'Rourke at Boston College has calculated that the United States attempted to change the governments of other countries a total of 72 times between 1947 and 1989 (66 of which were done covertly). While this might appear to be an understandable byproduct of containing the Soviet Union during the Cold War, in some respects, one could consider the recent Russian meddling in our own elections as more of the same, only in reverse (as post-Cold War payback).

Certainly, we should do everything we can to avoid future interference in our elections; but we should do so with a keener appreciation for how hypocritical we must look if we ourselves meddle elsewhere. Moreover, we even do it to ourselves. Skewing the thinking of our own electorate on important issues is essentially what the "dirty tricks" departments of most presidential campaigns are all about, but to that we turn a blind eye. If it can be proven that a candidate has resorted to deceitful practices to mislead the public, as was done, for example, by the Nixon campaign in sabotaging the election of Edmund Muskie (by forging his name to a document in order to create a false impression), why shouldn't that also be considered off-limits with punitive consequences?

Yet another aspect of empathy that is less apparent is that of perspective. Perhaps a good illustration of this can be found in St. Augustine's classic, *City of God,* in which he cites a reply given to Alexander the Great by a pirate who had just been captured. When Alexander asked the man what he meant by "keeping hostile possession of the sea," he answered, "What thou meanest by seizing the whole earth; but because I do it with a petty ship, I am called a robber, whilst thou who dost it with a great fleet art styled emperor."

Another, more recent but equally poignant, illustration of this aspect took place when I was on vacation some years ago. While riding in the back seat of a taxi in Mexico City, the driver pointed to a building that had housed the Spanish Inquisition until its demise in 1820. I expressed great surprise that the Inquisition had lasted that long, and I will never forget his response, "Yeah, they came in and tore down all our idols to replace them with their own."

Although nation-states in today's conflicts tend to under-appreciate the power of empathy, ICRD actively brings it to bear in its project work as a matter of routine. One project that illustrated the worth of empathy particularly well was our initiative to reform the madrasas in Pakistan. We did so by empowering the madrasa leaders to feel it was their reform effort, inspiring them with their own heritage, and grounding all suggested change in Islamic principles.

A more recent example has been our project work in Saudi Arabia where we have been working with the government to help reform their educational system. Throughout, we have been sensitive to the constraints under which the Saudi government is forced to operate. First and foremost, under the agreement between the House of Saud and Muhammad ibn Abdal-Wahhab that established the Kingdom in 1932, education was to be strictly under the purview of the religious establishment. Thus, the government has had to proceed carefully as it seeks to assert its own influence in this area. Further, in his role as Custodian of the two holiest sites in Islam, the King has to be careful about the example he sets for the whole of the religion, taking care to avoid any perception that the Kingdom is being unduly influenced by the West.

Summing Up

"Steady drops hollow the stone." — *Italian proverb*

Several years ago, I attended a day-long conference at the State Department sponsored by its Office of Religion and Global Affairs. As I looked around the packed auditorium, it occurred to me that ten years earlier it would have been difficult to attract even a handful of people to such a gathering. Indeed, since the publication of *Religion, the Missing Dimension of Statecraft* first made the case in 1994, it had taken no fewer than 20 years for the foreign policy establishment to recognize and attempt to accommodate the positive role that religion can play in international affairs.

In the meanwhile and as detailed in earlier chapters, ICRD by incorporating religious considerations into conflict resolution strategies: (1) helped end the 21-year civil war in Sudan, (2) eased tensions between the Muslim, Hindu, and Buddhist regions of Kashmir, (3) opened back-channel communications to promote improved relations with Iran, (4) secured the release of 21 Korean missionaries held hostage by the Afghan Taliban in 2007, (5) worked with madrasa leaders and faculty in Pakistan to enhance their curriculums and transform their pedagogy, (6) advanced educational reform in Saudi Arabia to improve the treatment of religious minorities, and (7) informed U.S. foreign policy and public diplomacy with a more nuanced understanding of Islam.

Left unmentioned in the above is (1) a social contract which ICRD facilitated between the Kurds and Syriac Christians in the Al Hasakah region of Syria, that would enable them to live in peace once the conflict subsides—only to have it later rendered moot when ISIS overran the area, (2) a network of indigenous conflict resolution experts that ICRD has been training in Yemen to help resolve inter-tribal disputes, thereby serving as a buffer against the further intrusion of Al-Qaeda and its affiliates (which had been providing these same services because of the government's inability to do so), (3) the extensive effort ICRD has had underway in Colombia for a number of years working with religious leaders and women's networks to facilitate the effective reintegration of former combatants into civil society, and (4) the exploratory work the Center has been doing in Morocco, Tunisia, Yemen and Pakistan to enhance the role of conservative Muslims in countering the forces of extremism.

> *Once Assad falls, will you come to Syria to stand with us in rebuilding our nation? You have brought the very message that is needed to galvanize the people of Syria. You have spoken not just to our minds but to our hearts…*

> *As a Bedouin tribal leader, I have had a bitter relationship with one of the Kurdish leaders from Hasakah at this conference. We had not spoken in decades. After the lecture on forgiveness, we reconciled with each other.*

The U.S. government's pursuit of justice and retribution following the attacks of 9-11 was understandable and entirely warranted, but it did little to win the hearts and minds of those who had already demonstrated a willingness to die in order to make a statement against the United States and its policies. What is needed instead (or in addition to) is an effective strategy of respectful engagement in which one makes a concerted effort to understand and respond as feasible to the cultural imperatives that are driving the extremists to see the world as they do.

As the late Samuel Huntington rightly pointed out in his *Clash of Civilizations,* religion is the defining element of culture. And that is where ICRD comes in with its inter-religious action teams, addressing cause rather than symptoms, giving priority to preventing conflict over dealing with its consequences after the fact, and using faith-based diplomacy coupled with organic suasion to even the asymmetric playing field—-all the while broadening religious understanding, tempering the rhetoric of exclusion, and reducing the call to extremism and violence. Said differently and a bit more poetically is this poignant summary by my successor in his address at our annual Faith-in-Action Dinner in 2017, as he was taking over as President:

> *ICRD is a small operation in a magnificent and complex world. But I contend that it is a special place. It is a place where integrity and risk come together in the low places to advance the most difficult faith—faith in one another.*

On a concluding note and repeating an earlier admonition, the stigma of weakness associated with empathy should be discarded and replaced with a keen appreciation for its unrivaled potential in understanding others and identifying the most promising avenues for bridging existing differences. It is also abundantly clear that in the absence of an empathetic understanding of other world views, the United States will face major difficulties in advancing its interests in an emerging multi-polar world.

Chapter Nineteen

PERSONAL REFLECTIONS

Lord, teach us to number our days that we may gain a heart of wisdom.
Psalm 90

As I think back on life from the twilight zone, I find myself filled with gratitude and humility. It has been a full life—to the point where the varied nature of my life's experiences makes it seem as though I have lived at least five different lifetimes—in the military, in government service, at Harvard, at CSIS, and at ICRD, with various other experiences sprinkled in, from empowering inner-city youth to complete their schooling, to developing a course for MBA students at a Business College, to crafting a course for Prospective Commanding Officers at the Naval War College (plus any number of other disparate consulting tasks). I suspect that the distinctive chapters in my personal life also contributed to this feeling of different lifetimes.

I have often joked to others that deep down I'm pretty shallow, but it has only been half-jokingly. Because I have held so many different jobs, often proceeding from one to the next—sometimes, from one career field to the next—without feeling in total command of the one I was leaving, I did feel a bit shallow at times.

Nevertheless, I always felt that wherever I worked, there was an important mountain to be moved; and although I might not possess the optimal credentials for any given assignment, I always thought it was possible to make a helpful difference, if one had the desire to do so, a modicum of common sense, and wasn't afraid of failure. Perhaps the most glaring examples of this that leap to mind are (1) when I was appointed Deputy Administrator of the Office of Wage Stabilization (effectively number two in charge of wage controls) during the final phase of the Economic Controls Program, with only a year of experience and no relevant educational credentials to speak of, and (2) when I became Executive Vice President and Chief Operating Officer of Cities in Schools and suddenly found myself fully immersed in the problems of the inner city and the innumerable racial sensitivities that went with it, without any prior exposure whatsoever to the social services milieu.

Blazing New Trails

"Everyone is ignorant, only in different subjects." –Will Rogers (1879-1935)

I have felt unusually blessed by the fact that every job I ever held had an exciting dimension to it. None of them were what I would call maintenance functions. All-too-often, folks are appointed to important positions in government where they perform whatever tasks might be required, enjoy the perks that come with the office, and move on to whatever comes next without leaving any sort of legacy accomplishment behind. When offered such opportunities, it is important to take sufficient time to get one's bearings, reflect on the possibilities for positive change, and identify the two or three major accomplishments you want to achieve before you leave. Happily, I was able to do this on at least several occasions because of the extensive opportunities that came along to plow new ground in a number of first-ever situations.

In more than half of the jobs I ever held, I was either the first person to hold the position or, alternatively, the job had been specifically created for me.[71] That was more luck of the draw than anything else; but regardless of how it happened, there is an inherent excitement to blazing new trails and it's a fun way to live one's life.

As I write this, I am reminded of Sir Christopher Zeeman from my brief time at Oxford, who would familiarize himself with a new discipline to the point where his command of that discipline was sufficient to achieve new insights through subjecting it to his catastrophe theory, after which he would move on to a new field. Although I doubt that anyone ever accused him of being shallow in anything he ever attempted, my own path was much less deliberate. In fact, one might say it was totally opportunistic, taking advantage of whatever new challenges came along.

---

[71] Coming out of Annapolis, I was fortunate to be a part of that first, small group of direct inputs to the nuclear submarine program and later had first choice of which nuclear sub I would serve on when I graduated from Submarine School (which almost certainly saved me from going down on the *Thresher*). As a civilian, every position I held in the Economic Controls Program was a first, because none of them had previously existed. At the Pentagon, I was the first Director of Policy Planning and Management in the Office of the Secretary of Defense and later the first Deputy Assistant Secretary of the Navy for Manpower. At Harvard, I was the Founding Director of the Kennedy School's first Executive Program. Finally, I ended up pioneering the inclusion of religious considerations in US foreign policy.

I have always felt that the best way to advance in life is simply by doing the best you can in whatever job you have and letting the future take care of itself. Prior to founding the International Center for Religion & Diplomacy, I had held a total of 14 positions in several different career fields. In only three of those positions, though, did I ever actively look for another job: first, when leaving the Navy; second, when leaving the economic controls program; and third, when leaving Harvard to return to Washington. Otherwise, the job opportunities came of their own accord.

The Best-laid Plans

"Never make predictions, especially about the future."
—*Samuel Goldwyn (1879-1974)*

When I left the Navy, I thought what I would most like to do was hold a high-level position at the State Department where I could advance our country's interests in a more significant way. By the same token, I was far enough along in my naval career when I left the service that I was unwilling to start all over again by taking the entry-level Foreign Service Exam. Instead, I decided I would climb the ladder elsewhere and make a lateral transfer to State once I was closer to the top. And, it almost worked.

After my first year of running ICRD, I received a call from Andrew Natsios, who had just been appointed by the George W. Bush Administration to be Administrator of the U.S. Agency for International Development (USAID), a State Department-related agency that oversees our foreign assistance to other countries. He invited me to become his Deputy; and, knowing I had just started my center within the previous year, said, "Before you say no, please think about it over the weekend."

I did think about his offer and found it appealing for several reasons. First, although Andrew had just come from overseeing "The Big Dig" for the Massachusetts Turnpike Authority (which involved tearing up much of downtown Boston to reroute the central artery through the heart of the city), I knew him from before that when he served in a senior-level position at World Vision, a global Christian humanitarian organization; and I liked him a lot. Beyond that, he was exceptionably able, had a great sense of history and, in all likelihood, would want to make a little history himself. Second, he said he wanted me to represent AID at future Inter-agency meetings, which include the deputies of the major national and international security-related departments of government, and are where the rubber meets the road in hammering out the details of public policy. Finally, I was in a position where I only needed one additional year of government service to qualify for a Civil Service retirement.

While it was a tempting offer, I concluded it probably wouldn't work for two compelling reasons: (1) I was very reluctant to leave an enterprise I had just started, and (2) I strongly suspected in any event that I wouldn't be able to pass the White House political screen (and told Andrew as much at the outset). In any new Administration, political appointments are typically awarded to those loyalists who played an instrumental role in getting the President elected. In my own case, I hadn't even voted for him, because I was in Sudan on the date of the election and hadn't made any arrangement to vote in an absentee capacity. That is exactly how it played out, and I was greatly relieved when the door finally closed.

Although Andrew had a superb reputation and it would have been a great experience working in the upper echelons of government, my heart was with ICRD; and I really didn't want to risk leaving it in a lurch. Throughout its history, the Center has typically been hanging by its fingernails financially; and at no time was that more the case than during this early period.

With the USAID position off the table, the last two civilian positions I held were exceptions to the "deep down pretty shallow" rule, my 12 years at CSIS followed by the 18 at ICRD. CSIS played to my abiding interest and training in national security and foreign policy, and I felt totally at home dealing with the nuances of those disciplines. And while I can never pretend to know as much as I should about the different faith traditions, I did feel comfortable dealing with the intersection of religion and politics.

Ironically, my political-military background was precisely what was needed to get ICRD off the ground and onto a solid footing, largely because of the corresponding need to convince foreign policy practitioners of religion's importance. Moreover, because the Political/Military arena is where most life and death decisions are made; if you can traverse that minefield, you can make just about anything work. When I finally stepped down from ICRD with that phase well-behind us, my successor was fully ready to take the helm, with a very different and more appropriate set of credentials to do so.

Passing the Baton

"Success without a successor is failure." —*Mack McCarter*

Five years earlier, I had been visited by a young man by the name of James Patton. We were meeting because his father, Jim, was aware that we shared a great deal in common. His dad was a classmate of mine from the Academy with whom I had roomed when we were going through Advanced Nuclear Power School following graduation. About 50 years later, Jim had somehow learned what I was up to and knowing that his youngest son had some of those same interests, encouraged the two of us to connect. When we finally did after more than a year of "Dad's prompting", the half-hour courtesy call turned into a two-and-a-half-hour discussion.

ICRD didn't have any job openings and James wasn't looking for one, since he was doing quite well at the State Department. So, that aspect wasn't even on the table during our discussions. However, I woke up the following morning fully convinced he was the right one to take charge when I stepped down. Over the next few months of a rather active courtship, I succeeded in luring him to become our Executive Vice President; and he served in that capacity for five years before taking over in May of 2017.

Although my credentials were well-suited to the Center's needs during those initial years, once the organization was solidly established, it needed an entirely different skill set. In contrast to my own dearth of credentials in religion, conflict resolution, and diplomacy, James was a graduate of the Harvard Divinity School and sported a Master's Degree in Conflict Resolution from the Fletcher School of Law and Diplomacy at Tufts University. Further, not only was he well-versed in State Department protocols, but he also had extensive field experience stemming from various overseas assignments in government and with several NGOs for which he had worked. More importantly, he had the streets smarts to go with it.

When I was advancing James's candidacy with ICRD's board, I told them that the principal finding from my review of the literature on succession was that the majority of those candidates who relieve a founder don't last a year in the job. This is exactly what had happened at CSIS after I left and what was then happening at the Heritage Foundation, the most prominent conservative think tank in town. I reassured the board this was not going to happen with James. He was the right person to take the Center to the next level, and I would do everything I could to help facilitate that.

The Vision Thing

"What you leave behind is not what is engraved in stone, but what is woven into the lives of others." —Pericles

A number of post-Cold War commentators criticized then-President George H.W. Bush for lacking what he himself once rather disparagingly referred to as "the vision thing." As confirmed by a diary entry at the end of his first year, "I'm not seen as a visionary, but I hope I'm seen as steady, prudent and able." One can quarrel as to whether or not that was an accurate self-portrait (especially since history is already characterizing his shaping of the post-Cold War world as nothing less than brilliant), but the subject itself deserves a closer look.

It has been said that two percent of the people make things happen, 18% watch them happen, and 80% say, "What happened?" While there may be a grain of truth to this, I suspect that at the end of the day, most of us would like to be able to answer (at least for ourselves) the overarching question of "Why did I exist?" Implicit in this question is a search for significance.

We want to make a difference; we want to leave a legacy. For many who might think along these lines, their responses may relate to what they have been able to do for their children, who, after all become living legacies of those who have gone before. However, the other normal trappings of suc-cess—rank, status, or wealth—can grow hollow, if we are unable to satisfy this deeper longing for meaning. This hollowness, in turn, can lead to living what Henry David Thoreau, referred to as *"lives of quiet desperation."*

As my good friend Os Guinness pointed out twenty years ago in his book, *The Call,* there are at least two factors fueling an unprecedented search for sig-nificance in our time. First is the seemingly unlimited opportunity for choice and change we have in all that we do, which has greatly contributed to an expectation that we can, in fact, live purposeful lives. And second is the fact that the fulfillment of this search for purpose has largely been thwarted by one stunning fact: "Out of more than a score of civilizations in human history, modern Western civilization is the very first to have no agreed-upon answer to the question of the purpose of life." Thus, there is more ignorance, confusion, and longing surrounding this topic than at almost any other time in history.

With the absence of purpose in our lives, we tend to slip into cycles of confusion and uncertainty, which, in turn, lead to a life of wandering—a life without focus. The mere fact that you may have overcome any number of obstacles to get to where you are today suggests a tenacity and drive that will serve you well in the future; but to what end? As Ralph Waldo Emerson once said, *"Hitch your wagon to a star"*. That star, to my way of thinking, is vision; so let's take a look at what that word really means.

Vision is that compelling noble idea, which, if courageously and effec-tively pursued, will provide you with the answer to how you can leave this world better off than you found it. Mahatma Gandhi once said, *"Be the change you want to see in the world."* This short yet powerful statement challenges us to consider our unique calling in life. If we honestly allow ourselves to address this challenge, vision will soon follow.

Because we all have different gifts, different understandings, and different outlooks, vision is highly personal. Your vision doesn't have to appeal to everyone, rather, it needs to respond to the deep longing for meaning within your own heart—indeed, within your very soul. Perhaps, it would be useful to examine some of its other characteristics.

First of all, why is it important? On a cosmic level, we are reminded in Proverbs 29:18 "Where there is no vision, the people perish." A bit closer to home it's important because so many Americans and others around the world spend most of their lives as "trappers of dollars", earning and accumulating as much money as they can, and then leaving an inheritance when they die. Sounds pretty empty, doesn't it? Indeed, when you stop to think about it, there is almost nothing you can buy for yourself that will feed your soul—except perhaps a new *Ferrari*. More seriously, the leading candidate for feeding the soul is the extent to which one reaches beyond one's self to enrich the lives of others, including as Jesus encouraged, "the least of these."

Vision can manifest itself on any number of levels. Perhaps it is best captured on a personal level in a book titled, *How Will You Measure Your Life?* by the late Harvard Business School Professor Clayton Christensen:

> *"While many of us might default to measuring our lives by summary statistics, such as number of people presided over, number of awards, or dollars accumulated in a bank, and so on, the only metrics that will truly matter to my life are the individuals whom I have been able to help, one by one, to become better people."*

Implicit in his statement is a desire to never be the reason that others think less of themselves.

As for the timing of when you acquire your vision, that is totally unpredictable and not something you can necessarily plan. In my own case, to the extent I can be accused of having a vision, it was acquired circuitously and largely by default. One might conclude that change was in my blood, probably as a result of growing up in a military family where we were constantly on the move. With that constant movement, though, came a sense of versatility and perhaps a subliminal self-confidence that one could handle just about anything that came along. Internalizing this mindset is probably one of the better deterrents to living a staid existence in which one becomes intimidated, if not fearful, of venturing beyond the comfort zone of one's training and expectations. As my own journey attests, though, and if you are open to it, opportunity and new directions will have a way of finding you, particularly if you are doing well in meeting whatever challenge you happen to be addressing at the time.

My own sense of vision came rather late in life. When I set out to produce *Religion, The Missing Dimension of Statecraft,* I intended the book to be an end in itself. Because of the favorable global response it received, though, I became inspired to walk the talk and founded ICRD at the age of 60. If I had set out with that as a goal earlier in my career, I would have undoubtedly focused my studies on religion and conflict resolution. Had I done so, though, it is doubtful my vision would have ever acquired sufficient traction to succeed. As luck would have it, the new ground that needed to be plowed leaned heavily on my political-military credentials.

When we launched the Center, policymakers still generally believed that religion was irrational and therefore unworthy of their attention; and conflict resolution, as previously mentioned, was thought to equate to pacifism. Turning that mindset around would *ipso facto* require someone with proven credentials in their own field to make the case. In short, one would have had to have "earned the right to be heard." This is why my resume' always included the fact that I had once been the youngest officer in the Navy to qualify for command of a nuclear submarine. It was not a big deal, but it sounded like it was and was almost always mentioned by others when introducing me before any speech I was about to give. Because of that, the various audiences paid greater attention than they might have otherwise, as I described faith-based diplomacy and ICRD's track record in practicing it.

By the second decade of the Center's existence, the concept of bridging the religious and the political in support of peacemaking had developed to the point where someone with proven leadership qualities from the peace community or the conflict resolution field could readily step in to lead the effort, as James is doing today. And he is doing it because the work is exciting, and it feeds the soul.

But what about the possibility of failure? Author and motivational speaker, Liz Murray, while reflecting on her unprecedented rise from homelessness to graduation from Harvard, said it was the *"what-if"* questions in her mind that ultimately inspired her to apply to one of the most reputable universities in the world. On the face of it, a seemingly illogical and impossible goal. It was the fact that she dreamed big and allowed herself to focus on the potential, the opportunity, the *"what-if I did get accepted"* that drove her to take a risk and shoot for the moon. Vision accompanied by a *"what-if"* attitude unlocks the impossible. We will never realize our full potential if we don't dare to think big and act accordingly.

Finally, vision carries with it yet another unpredictable dimension. Who would have guessed that the inspiration to write a book in the 1980s would lead to the rescue of 21 Korean missionaries in 2007? While the book's hopeful impact on the vocational pursuits of college students might have been predicted (Addendum V), little else that followed could have been.

Thankfully, it is not required that we know in advance where our vision may take us. It is only necessary that we be open to having one in the first instance; that we feel it is right for us (based on our capabilities and interests), and that we commit ourselves fully to its implementation, wherever that may lead. As Albert Einstein once said, *"A ship is always safe at the shore—but that is NOT what it is built for."* So, as one dreams big, it becomes necessary to accept the fact that there will be risks ahead and times when things will go off course. When they do, it helps to have those "invisible means of support" on which to lean. It also helps to appreciate that adversity can strengthen resolve if you let it do so, by using that experience to become better rather than bitter.

This may be a good point to digress a bit. There is adversity and there is adversity of a seemingly overwhelming nature, when something truly drastic has taken place. Spiritually speaking, if one assumes there is a God and that God is omnipotent, it has always been difficult to understand why bad things happen to good people. To be sure, there is more than a little mystery to much of life, but at least some of it in relation to this particular imponderable may again have to do with perspective.

In an exchange that took place in August of 2019 between CNN's Anderson Cooper and late-night host and comedian Stephen Colbert, Cooper asked Colbert how he had dealt with the loss of his father and two brothers when they were killed in a plane crash in 1974 (when Colbert was ten years old). More specifically, Cooper asked him to elaborate on how he had come to "love the thing which he most wished had not happened." Colbert replied, that his mother's faith had been instrumental in helping him deal with it. Although he didn't want the tragedy to have happened (in fact, would have given anything not to have had it happen), through her, he concluded that life is a gift, with suffering an inescapable part of it. Ergo, "if you are grateful for your life, you have to be grateful for all of it. You can't pick and choose what you're grateful for." He went on to explain that a sense of loss can at times actually become a gift, to the extent it enables you to connect more compassionately with others who have experienced similar loss (much like Jim Whittaker concluded when hospitalized with two broken legs in chapter seven).

When you live a meaningful life and have a vision that carries you beyond yourself, you will be surprised at the impact you can have on those around you and even on others in distant parts of the globe. This aspect was elevated to an even higher, perhaps ethereal plain by the late Rabbi Abraham Joshua Hescel, former Professor of Ethics and Mysticism at the Jewish Theological Seminary of America, when commenting in the 1960s on the nature and role of humankind:

> *The greatest sin of man is to forget that he is a prince—that he has royal power. All worlds are in need of exaltation, and everyone is charged to lift what is low, to unite what lies apart, to advance what is left behind. It is as if all worlds…are full of expectancy, of sacred goals to be reached, so that consummation can come to pass. And man is called upon to bring about the climax slowly but decisively.*

In other words, life is a miracle and should be treated as such. And as the good Rabbi implies, treating life like a miracle should find us spending a sizable fraction of our time marching to the beat of a higher drummer, as we climb our way toward a higher calling.

EPILOGUE

There is no cure for birth and death save to enjoy the interval."
George Santayana (1863-1952)

To end on a lighter note and saving the best for last, allow me to share a bit about the tallest peak and my source of greatest joy.

There we were, a thousand feet above Waikiki and Diamond Head, parasailing side by side while honeymooning in Hawaii, when Dareen pointed to what looked like the entrance to a cave beneath the surface of the water. At first glance, it looked rather foreboding. Then I broke into laughter when I noticed it was moving at the same rate that we were. It was the shadow from our parachute, and we both laughed uproariously the whole time we were up there. The Mai Tais came later as we celebrated one of those personal mountaintops that adds a bit of zing to life.

How it All Began

"By all means marry. If you get a good wife, you'll become happy. If you get a bad one, you'll become a philosopher." –Socrates

On Labor Day in 2014, I arrived late to a picnic at the Cedars, the home of the National Prayer Breakfast fellowship. It was raining at the time, and the picnic was just starting to break up. As was always the case whenever I was in a bachelor mode, I was keenly aware of my surroundings; and my internal radar started flashing "full alert" when it homed in on Dareen.

We connected and after a whirlwind courtship tempered by our mutual determination to take things "low and slow," we were married a month later by a Justice of the Peace whose office was across the street from the Arlington Court House (where we had just obtained our marriage license). The Justice himself was a pleasant fellow with an abiding interest in early American history, as clearly reflected in his office furnishings.

Although there is no requirement that a witness be present for weddings in the state of Virginia, we had one anyway. Joining us in our wedding picture was a young Tom Jefferson, looking keenly interested, while watching from close behind. To top it all off, there was still time on the meter when we returned to the car (which must have caused every one of my Scot ancestors to swell with pride).[72] Happily, after a fun-filled seven years, the magic on this tallest of mountaintops has only increased with the passage of time.

The Valleys

My personal story, as stated at the outset, has focused on the good times and the more humorous moments in life, of which there were many. Left largely unaddressed are the valleys and inevitable reverses that occurred along the way. Although that was purposeful and will remain the case, it is the setbacks that build one's character. And there is probably no one whose life's experience illustrates this more than that of Abraham Lincoln (this book's favorite role model).

As is widely known but seldom talked about, Lincoln's life was replete with personal failure and tragedy. At the age of nine, his mother died; and although a loving step-mother soon stepped in to fill the void, it was nevertheless a major loss and significant readjustment for young Abe. At 22, he lost his job as a store clerk and the following year incurred significant debt to become a partner in another store. When his business partner died three years later, the even larger debt he was left with took him years to repay.

He later ran for Congress and after two defeats, was finally elected at the age of 37. On the personal front and prior to his first run for Congress, he experienced prolonged heartache over the death of a young lady by the name of Ann Rutledge, with whom he had apparently shared a quite-serious romance. It is believed that he never completely got over the loss. Two years later and after a hesitant courtship, he married Mary Todd; and they started a family. When Lincoln was 41, his second son died from Typhoid Fever at the age of three.

Although Lincoln served in the Illinois legislature for four terms, his future runs for national office were less successful. At the age of 41, his first campaign for the U.S. Senate ended in defeat, as did his nomination for Vice President two years later. In 1858, he ran again for the Senate and lost to Stephen Douglas.

---

[72] This approach was not without precedent. A classmate and good friend by the name of Dick Pariseau blazed this same, highly-efficient matrimonial trail a few years earlier.

Despite his discouraging track record at the Federal level, Lincoln was elected to the Presidency in 1860 at the age of 51. That was almost immediately followed, though, by the prolonged anguish of the Civil War and the devastating loss of yet another son, Willie, who was eleven at the time and who shared an exceptionally close bond with his father. Finally, at the pinnacle of success, with the war having been won just five days earlier, his life was cut short at the age of 55 by an assassin's bullet. As he lay dying in a rooming house across the street from Ford's Theater, Edwin Stanton, his Secretary of War and a former detractor of Lincoln's said, "There lies the most perfect ruler of men the world has ever seen...[and] now he belongs to the ages."

In addition to Lincoln's extraordinary leadership in preserving the Union, he was second to no one in his ability to inspire others through the spoken and written word. It is difficult to imagine any other self-educated person having a comparable ability to scratch on the back of an envelope something as profound as the Gettysburg Address, shortly before giving it publicly. The depth of feeling and sense of national purpose captured in that brief but eloquent statement could only have come from someone who was exceedingly well-read and who had experienced at a deeper level the pain of personal tragedy and the disappointment of repeated failure. As Lincoln once said:

> *"I have been driven many times to my knees by the overwhelming conviction that I had nowhere else to go. My own wisdom, and that of all about me, seemed insufficient for that day."*

In important respects, the Address was also a poignant reminder that heading the list of those who most deserve to lead are those who have paid their dues. Two other examples who leap to mind are Theodore Roosevelt and his cousin, Franklin. Prior to his Presidency, Theodore had to overcome the double blow of losing his wife and his mother, the two women he loved most in this world, when they died unexpectedly on the same day (Valentine's Day in 1884). And Franklin Roosevelt had to overcome the constant pain of polio both before and throughout his three terms as President. All three of these individuals made lasting marks on history and left legacies that endure to the present. So, please don't be misled by this book's failure to give equal time to the valleys nor underestimate their importance in advancing toward a more perfect world.

A Departing Challenge

In the first chapter, I expressed the hope that this book might inspire readers to reach beyond their comfort zones in seeking a higher purpose to which they can devote themselves and in which they can find added meaning for their lives. In the final chapter, I spoke a great deal about vision; and although vision and purpose came together for me, they don't necessarily coincide for everyone. To illustrate the difference between the two, I hearken back to my swim in the Galilee in the mid-1990s.

As described in the Book of Matthew, the disciples of Jesus were crossing that sea when a storm arose. As they strained against their oars, Jesus appeared, walking toward them on top of the water. He extended a hand and an invitation for Peter to join him. Peter did and was doing well, until he stopped to think about how impossible it was.

Whereas the sense of purpose that might come out of such a situation could be a determination to build better boats that are more capable of weathering such storms; the vision might equate to Peter's willingness to step out of the boat in order to prove a new concept for traversing deep bodies of water.

In my own case, I sort of stumbled into my vision and eventual purpose. Professionally, I became mindful of that missing dimension in statecraft; and I was able to lean on my spiritual convictions to inspire me to do something about it. In other words, the counterproductive neglect of religious considerations in the practice of U.S. foreign policy coupled with the encouragement of Matthew 5:9 to become a peacemaker collectively made it an easy call (Addendum W).

To give an idea of just how challenging it can be to initiate a purposeful journey, I recall reading a book while on Polaris patrol titled *Civilization in the West*, which included a couple of paragraphs describing Max Weber's interpretation of the Protestant Ethic. I was a lieutenant in the Navy at the time and in my mid-20s. Weber, a deceased German sociologist, philosopher, and political economist is widely regarded as one of the world's foremost authorities on the development of modern Western society. As I read those paragraphs, I found myself mortified by how accurately they seemed to describe me. Not just their general thrust, but their every word—hard work for the sake of working hard, sacrificing the present on the altar of the future, frugality, self-discipline, and the list went on. I felt like an unthinking automaton, totally captive to these broader social currents. Ever since, I have sought to become my own person.

Adding to the challenge of living a purposeful life is an observation by French statesman Alexis de Tocqueville, who in his classic tome *Democracy in America* said, "I think in no country in the civilized world is less attention paid to philosophy than in the United States." Now philosophy can mean many things; among them, the system of values by which one lives, the investigation of causes and laws underlying reality, and inquiry into the nature of things based on logical reasoning. In essence, it equates to a search for deeper meaning, which in today's fast-paced world is probably considerably more challenging than it has been in the past.

German philosopher Friedrich Nietzsche captured well the liberating nature of this search: "He who has a why to live can bear almost any how." Moreover, such a search is also good for your health. A recent survey by researchers at Washington University in St. Louis, Missouri, concluded that having a higher purpose promotes greater well-being (happiness, and lower stress), even in the midst of a COVID-19 pandemic. Other surveys show the same to hold true for organizations as well. Employees who work for a company that has a written statement of purpose which keys to the betterment of society (rather than merely to shareholders), are generally happier than those who do not. When working for such an organization, employees not only tend to trust their leaders to make socially-responsible decisions, but better business decisions as well.

Victor Strecher, a professor at the University of Michigan School of Public Health and pioneer in the field of behavioral science, has also examined how purposeful living affects quality of life and longevity in a book titled *Life on Purpose: How Living for What Matters Most Changes Everything*. For example, his research shows that those who do not "repurpose their lives" at retirement, are 2.4 times more likely to suffer from Alzheimer's disease seven years later than those who adopt an "authentic higher purpose."

Once you determine your purpose, it enables you to transcend the noise in your life and focus on what matters most. If life is a boat, it becomes your rudder. Regardless of whatever purpose you settle on, it is important to remember that life is fundamentally about relationships; and while the ultimate goal is to leave the world better than you found it, it is to do so while loving well and ending well.

The Goal

"An aim in life is the only fortune worth finding."
–Robert Louis Stevenson (1850-1894)

And what might that better world look like? Here, I am reminded of a joke I once heard that defined heaven on earth as a place where the police are British, the chefs are Italian, the mechanics are German, the lovers are French, and it's organized by the Swiss. Conversely, hell is where the police are German, the chefs are British, the mechanics are French, the lovers are Swiss, and it's organized by the Italians.

More seriously and on a less spiritual note, the farewell message in my Naval Academy yearbook provides a worthy challenge:

8 June, 1960

Message to the American People...

To the concept that through world-wide cooperation, man may eventually find the means to everlasting peace: that hates may wither, that prejudices may die, that wars be forgotten, that only amity and good-will prevail—-To the concept that by this cooperation we will improve our standards of living, eliminate the wastes of conflict and needless argument, and elevate the world-wide society to its highest level—-To the concept that this cooperation will bring to our earth the peace of mind and tranquility man has so long striven for; that it will bring to him the light to see perfect harmony—-To these ideals, this book is dedicated.

...The Class of Nineteen-Sixty

I don't know which classmate crafted this message of 60 years ago, but whoever it was captured in succinct and compelling fashion the standard to which we should all aspire. Although we have thus far fallen woefully short of that mark, we must never give up pursuing it. And while we're at it, having a bit of fun along the way.

James with prison inmates in Colombia discussing the challenges facing former combatants as they reenter civil society.

ICRD Senior Program Manager Rebecca Cataldi conducting a conflict resolution training workshop in Yemen.

Signing a formal partnership agreement with Ken Starr, then Dean of the Pepperdine University Law School, to formalize the training of graduate students in faith-based diplomacy under the tutelage of ICRD Senior Vice President Brian Cox (left rear). In overseeing that program, Brian has drawn on insights from his earlier experiences in this arena coupled with those he acquired while directing ICRD's projects in Kashmir and Syria.

Conversing with Ed Meese and Azi at the National Press Club

My first mountaintop in Utah

Kicking off the book event for *Religion, Terror, and Error,* with Undersecretary of State Jim Glassman preparing to speak

An ICRD Faith-in-Action Award Dinner gathering at the Mahmood's residence on the Potomac River in Mt. Vernon, Virginia. (Marsha Vander Mey photographer)

ICRD board member David Vander Mey spreading good will at the gathering. David put up the initial seed funding that enabled ICRD to begin its work. (Marsha Vander Mey photographer)

Part of ICRD's agenda in working with BYU's Wheatley Institution was to establish and lead a biennial International Affairs Conference on Religion and Diplomacy for college students from across the country. Pictured above is BYU's winter facility in Sundance, Utah at which we and 80 students gathered for three days in 2016 to wrestle with the challenges of how the two disciplines can work together to defuse conflict and promote reconciliation.

Former ICRD Board Chairman Jim Wootton and his wife Ellen enjoying the reception before dinner, along with Board Vice Chairman Jim Stanley in the background. (Marsha Vander Mey photographer)

ICRD Board Chairman Harold "Rink"
Jacobi presenting Ray and Shaista
Mahmood with a token of ICRD's
appreciation for their generous hospitality
(Marsha Vander Mey photographer)

General Anthony Zinni, former
Commander in Chief of the U.S.
Central Command and former U.S.
Special Envoy to the Middle East,
addressing ICRD's dinner audience in
2009 on the importance of religious
factors in global stability.
(Marsha Vander Mey photographer)

Brian Cox bringing a dinner audience
up to date on our work in Syria
(Marsha Vander Mey photographer)

Azi doing the same for Pakistan
(Marsha Vander Mey photographer)

Andrew Natsios, former Administrator
of the U.S. Agency for International
Development, giving the keynote
address at our 2011 dinner.
(Marsha Vander Mey photographer)

Thanking former National Security Advisor
Bud McFarlane for his keynote address in
2014. (Marsha Vander Mey photographer)

End of dinner celebration by ICRD
junior staff and interns in 2016.
(Marsha Vander Mey photographer)

Former Secretary of State Madeleine
Albright paying tribute to ICRD upon her
acceptance of the Center's 2017 Faith in
Action Award. (Ben Barber photographer)

Sharing a laugh before dinner with
Jim Patton (rt.), fellow submariner,
USNA classmate, and father of James.
(Marsha Vander Mey photographer)

James taking it to the next level
(Marsha Vander Mey photographer)

The end of my rainbow at a rainy-day picnic

(Photo by Warren Kahle)

After honeymooning in Hawaii, we transitioned from Mai Tais
back to mountaintops in the Canadian Rockies.

GLOSSARY

AMC	American Muslim Community
BYU	Brigham Young University
Canoe U	U.S. Naval Academy
CGI	Clinton Global Initiative
CIS	Cities in Schools
CNO	Chief of Naval Operations
CO	Commanding Officer
COLC	Cost of Living Council
COMSUBLANT	Commander, Submarine Force Atlantic
CSIS	Center for Strategic and International Studies
DASN	Deputy Assistant Secretary of the Navy
Deobandi	Hardline Pakistani religious sect that gave birth to the Taliban
DEPSECDEF	Deputy Secretary of Defense
DRC	Dutch Reformed Church
FBD	Faith-Based Diplomacy
First Classman	A senior at the Naval Academy
Flag-rank	Admiral or General officer military rank
HMS	Her Majesty's Ship
ICRD	International Center for Religion & Diplomacy
IDA	Institute for Defense Analyses
IPFC	International People's Friendship Council (Sudan)
IIIT	International Institute for Islamic Thought
ITMP	National Madrasa Oversight Board (in Urdu)
JCS	Joint Chiefs of Staff

Jirga	A decision-making body of respected elders
Knesset	Israeli Parliament
LOC	Line of Control (Kashmir)
M&RA	Manpower and Reserve Affairs
Madrasa	Religious school
Midshipman	Lowest officer rank in the Navy
MOE	Minister of Education
MOFA	Minister of Foreign Affairs
MRA	Moral Rearmament
NGO	Non-governmental organization
NIA	North American Interfaith Association
NIU	National Intelligence University
NPB	National Prayer Breakfast
NPEB	Nuclear Power Examining Board
NROTC	Naval Reserve Officers' Training Corps
O-5	Navy Commander (equivalent to Lieutenant Colonel in the Marine Corps, Army and Air Force)
OEP	President's Office of Emergency Preparedness
OOD	Officer of the Deck
ORE	Operational Readiness Exercise
OSD	Office of the Secretary of Defense
PEF	Peace and Education Foundation (Pakistan)
Plebe	Freshman at the Naval Academy
Polliwog	Anyone who has not crossed the equator in a ship
ROTC	Reserve Officers' Training Corps
SCC	Sudan Council of Churches
SDS	Students for a Democratic Society
SECDEF	Secretary of Defense
Second Classman	A junior at the Naval Academy
SERE	Survival, Evasion, Resistance, and Escape
Shellback	One who has crossed the equator in a naval vessel and undergone appropriate initiation

SIRC	Sudan Inter-Religious Council
Skipper	Commanding Officer (CO)
Sonar	Sound Navigation and Ranging
SSBN	Nuclear-powered ballistic missile submarine
SSN	Fast attack nuclear submarine
Steamer	A naval person with an unconstrained ability to have a good time when ashore on liberty
Task Group	A group of maritime military assets assigned to work together for a specific purpose
The Hill	U.S. Congress
Track Two	Unofficial diplomacy
U boat	German submarine
USAID	U.S. Agency for International Development
USS	United States Ship
Wolf Pack	A group of German submarines
Youngster	A sophomore at the Naval Academy

ADDENDA

A. Local news

B. Note from the President

C. Vintage Wine

D. Harvard bound (2)

E. Executive Program (8)

F. Teaching stint

G. Letter from Herman Wouk

H. Departing academe

I. War College engagement (2)

J. Siege option (2)

K. Pacific Forum merger (2)

L. Monument to greatness

M. CSIS farewell (5)

N. Letter to Mike (3)

O. Getting our feet wet (2)

P. Kashmir Agreement (2)

Q. Cultural initiative

R. MOE Letter of Endorsement

S. Krista's Journal (2)

T. BYU engagement

U. NDU invitation

V. The next generation

W. Personal encouragement

Local News

Bullis Natators Submerged by Mercersburg

The Bullis Swimming Team, shepherded by Bob Hayes, made a dreary trek to Pennsylvania one Saturday morning last month and suffered defeat in every event at the hands of the more thoroughly trained tankmen from Mercersburg Academy. The Little Admiral swimmers realize that they must take a back seat to the more highly touted football, baseball, and basketbal teams, however, and their spirits are just as high as if they had won every event of the meet.

Nevertheless, Bullis men placed in many of the races:

Doug Johnston
    3rd; 2000 yard free-style
Lloyd Burkley
    3rd; 50 yard free-style
Gerry Montague
    3rd; 100 yard backstroke
Tommy Kurtz
    3rd; 150 yard medley
Ross Bremer
    2nd; 100 yard breast stroke

(Ever swimming)

DOUGLAS M. JOHNSTON, JR. ENTERS NAVAL ACADEMY

On 25 June 1956, Douglas M. Johnston, Jr., enrolled at Annapolis, after placing seventh in the nation-wide presidential examinations for academy entrance.

Doug received his secondary education at schools in Astoria, Oregon; Long Beach, California; and Charleston, South Carolina. He graduated second in his class from Bullis School in Silver Springs, Maryland, in May of this year. During this four year period, he earned letters in several sports, including swimming and football. He also received an excellence in mathematics award in his senior year.

Doug has been very active in scouting. He earned his God and Country Award, and became an Eagle Scout at 13. He went on to earn a Silver Award, the highest award in scouting.

Doug is the son of LCDR and Mrs. D. M. Johnston, who reside at 524 Caffee Road.

Middies Represent NA In Swim Meet

In the recent Pensacola Swimming and Diving Championships held at Bayview Park, the Annapolis Midshipmen fielded a couple of teams in the open division and did themselves proud.

The Middies entered two teams in the 200 meter freestyle event and placed second and third in that event. The team that finished second was comprised of Tom Marit, who also finished third in the free style event, Jim Lippolo, Mario Zambre, and Al Miller. The team that finished third was made up of Bob Ianucci, Bill Lee, Doug Johnston (who also finished second in the butterfly and backstroke events), and Carl Ingerbretesen.

(Never winning)

1. Excerpt from Spring 1956 edition of *The Bulldog*, school newspaper of The Bullis School, Silver Spring, Maryland.

2. Excerpt from July 1956 edition of *The Prover*, U.S. Naval Proving Ground, Dahlgren, Virginia.

3. Excerpt from a July 1958 edition (specific date unknown) of the *Pensacola Journal*, Pensacola, Florida.

THE WHITE HOUSE

WASHINGTON

May 25, 1990

Dear Mr. Johnston:

My belated thanks for your good letter about
my opinion of broccoli. Your story gave me
a chuckle. My comments were an expression
of my personal taste, even though I recognize
many Americans enjoy this vegetable.

I appreciate your lighthearted comments and
hope that all is well with you.

Best wishes.

Sincerely,

[signature]

Mr. Douglas M. Johnston
Executive Vice President
Center for Strategic and
    International Studies
Suite 400
1800 K Street, N.W.
Washington, D.C. 20006

Page 2 THE DAILY ASTORIAN, Astoria, Oregon, Tuesday, December 30, 1975

Addendum C

Former Astorian named to high Pentagon post

A former Astoria High School student who went on to graduate from the U.S. Naval Academy and earn a master degree at Harvard University has been named deputy assistant secretary of the Navy for manpower.

Douglas M. Johnston Jr., whose parents, Mr. and Mrs. Douglas Johnston Sr., live near Port Orchard, Wash., was sworn into the high-ranking post Nov. 14.

At the same time Johnston received the Secretary of Defense Civilian Meritorious Award for his previous assignment as director of policy planning and management for manpower and reserve affairs.

A Navy press release said, "Under Johnston's direction, great progress was made for the first time in establishing programs for the joint training of U.S. and NATO forces."

Johnston celebrated his 37th birthday two days after he was sworn in.

The Johnston family moved to Astoria in the 1950s. The elder Johnston was a career Navy man, retiring in 1958 while his son was attending the Naval Academy. Douglas Johnston attended grades eight and nine here.

While here, Johnston joined a Scout Troop headed by Bob Lovell and earned Eagle Scout standing and the Order of the Silver Arrow.

Johnston finished his schooling in Long Beach, Calif., Charleston, S.C. and Silver Springs, Md. before entering the Naval Academy and graduating with honors in 1960.

At 27 years old, Johnston became the youngest man ever to qualify for command for a nuclear submarine. He was one of the first 25 Navy officers selected for nuclear submarine training by Adm. Hyman J. Rickover.

Among the positions he has held since his Navy service are planning officer with the President's Office of Emergency Preparedness, special assistant to the director of the Cost of Living Council, deputy administrator of the Office of Wage Stabilization and staff assistant to the secretary of defense.

Johnston has received the Navy Achievement Medal for Leadership, Freedom Foundation awards in 1967 and 1970, outstanding performance awards from the Cost of Living Council and Office of Emergency Preparedness and two letters of commendation from the president.

His parents, sister Kathleen and brother Mike from Los Angeles attended his swearing in ceremony in Washington, D.C.

DOUGLAS M. JOHNSTON

OFFICE OF THE ASSISTANT SECRETARY OF DEFENSE

WASHINGTON, D. C. 20301

August 16, 1977

MANPOWER,
RESERVE AFFAIRS
AND LOGISTICS

Mr. Peter Zimmerman
Assistant Dean of the Kennedy
  School
Harvard University
Cambridge, Massachusetts 02138

Dear Mr. Zimmerman:

This is followup to our conversation of June 30 concerning Douglas Johnston.

As I said on the phone, I've known Doug quite well since 1974, and have been impressed greatly with his abilities. I also made the point that I think I understand the nature of the program with which he'll be associated since I have been involved in similar enterprises and in the selection process related to them.

Doug is a brilliant fellow who doesn't try to carry his brightness on his sleeve. He listens to others, learns from them, and frequently reshapes and improves their ideas. He is terrifically well organized -- always seems to have a goal and a logical plan to reach it.

I would call Doug an analyst if the word had fewer pejorative connotations. By whatever name, he has a remarkable ability to sift through the elements of a problem and examine the alternatives to its solution.

One is tempted to say he is more concerned with substance than with form -- but that may give the impression that he lacks social graces. Nothing could be further from the truth. He is an interesting, affable person -- fun to be with. He has a fine sense of humor and the ability to laugh at himself.

What I mean about substance and form is that in establishing an educational program, for example, Doug would get more joy from analyzing the course content than he would from designing the public announcements; be more interested in critiquing research papers than in arranging a graduation ceremony; and so on. That's not to say that he wouldn't do a good job on the logistical side (he would); only that his interests would probably be in other directions.

Doug seems an ideal choice for an educational program concerned with leadership, for he is an outstanding leader himself. His Navy exploits are legend; and he enhanced his reputation during the time he served as a civilian in the Pentagon.

Finally, I guess I should mention that Doug is an excellent writer and speaker. He presents solid ideas with a flair, and he reacts spontaneously and well to his audience.

Would I hire Doug for the sort of thing you discussed with me? You bet I would -- and feel lucky to get him!

Please call if I can be helpful.

Sincerely,

/s/

Thomas W. Carr
Director
Defense Education

bc: Mr. Douglas M. Johnston

Addendum E

NATIONAL AND INTERNATIONAL SECURITY

An Executive Program of the
John F. Kennedy School of Government

Harvard University
August 22 – September 3, 1982

E - 2

"Without reservation,
the finest short
program I have ever
attended. It was
tremendously
effective, stimulating,
and masterfully
conducted."

Air Force Reserve
Major General, 1981

"It furnished a
quantum jump in
my substantive
knowledge of major
issues and of the
policy formulation
process."

CIA Official, 1979

"I was quite
impressed. It [the
final exercise] was
very realistic and the
responses were very
good, indeed."

Secretary of Defense,
1981

E - 3

"It would be virtually
impossible to achieve
the higher level of
expertise I have
reached here in any
other way."

Army Brigadier General,
1981

"It's rather like being
lifted to the rim of a
funnel and observing
the view for miles
around."

OMB Branch Chief, 1980

"I have already
applied skills and
insights gained from
Fisher and Raiffa in
dealing with a major
internal conflict."

Department Manager,
Battelle Labs, 1981

E - 4

MAY THIS BRIDGE
BUILT IN MEMORY OF
A SCHOLAR AND SOLDIER
CONNECTING THE COLLEGE YARD
AND PLAYING FIELDS OF HARVARD
BE AN EVER PRESENT REMINDER
TO STUDENTS PASSING OVER IT
OF LOYALTY TO COUNTRY
AND ALMA MATER
AND A LASTING SUGGESTION
THAT THEY SHOULD DEVOTE
THEIR MANHOOD DEVELOPED
BY STUDY AND PLAY
ON THE BANKS OF THIS RIVER
TO THE NATION AND ITS NEEDS

Photography: Lew Hepburn, Sandra Johnson, Michael Nagy, Terrence White

Harvard University
Gazette

September 4, 1981

Visit by Weinberger Brings Note of Reality to Security Managers Program

In a seminar room at the Kennedy School last Friday, a group of 78 admirals, generals, defense and intelligence analysts, Congressional staff members, other civilian government officials, and selected participants from the private sector were preparing for an important meeting with the National Security Council and the President of the United States.

A crisis had arisen in the night; terrorists had blown up key installations in major Saudi Arabian oil fields, general strikes in the oil fields had widened, and it appeared from intelligence reports that a full-scale revolution was underway. The lives of American workers were threatened, and members of the Saudi royal family were incommunicado.

The group met to consider possible American action. What were the options? Should troops be deployed? Should the President go on television? What would happen to international oil and stock markets? Should we just sit tight and wait for more information on the nature of the event? Were the rebels friendly or hostile? Was this action secretly supported by the Soviet Union?

The group worked out their alternatives, sometimes in disagreement. The players were real, but it was all an exercise, part of a role-playing game in a unique pro-gram at the School of Government for national and international security managers.

Reality

But then, the exercise took on a touch of reality. Secretary of Defense Caspar Weinberger walked into the room. He sat watching the presentations and deliberations and, afterwards, spoke to the group. "I was quite impressed," Weinberger said. "It was very realistic, and the responses were very good, indeed." He then spent 45 minutes taking questions from the group on various aspects of defense policy. The presence of the Secretary of Defense is only one example of the respect with which the program is viewed in the government. Now in its fourth year of summer sessions, the program seeks to provide special tools to people who are in (or moving into) posts "where their personal decisions or recommendations can affect the critical political economic or military interests of the United States," as the program description states.

Douglas M. Johnston, Jr., Executive Director of the program, who also teaches International Affairs and Security at the Kennedy School, says, "We are trying to improve the national security process by bringing together people who, to some extent, work in isolation from one another.

Harvard Gazette, September 4, 1981

E - 6

Defense Secretary Weinberger handling questions at Kennedy School. (Photo: T. White)

Weinberger Talks at Security Conference

(Continued from page 1)

We attempt to help them understand the larger perspective, from the point of view of other players in the process."

Johnston says the program also provides viewpoints for participants from a wide range of concerns so that they "draw some conclusions on how to relate to Congress, the media, other agencies, the private sector, and even other countries."

The program is an intensive, two-week series of seminars, lectures, exercises, and discussions built around the case-study method. Says Johnston, "Nothing is as good as hearing a participant's own thoughts and perspectives." He underlines his point by revealing that the class has a combined cumulative experience of more than 2,000 years of service.

Fifteen faculty members bring an equally high range of experience and expertise to the sessions. Johnston has served as Deputy Assistant Secretary of the Navy, Director of Policy Planning and Management in the Office of the Secretary of Defense, and Planning Officer with the President's Office of Emergency Preparedness. Faculty Chairman of the Program is Professor **Ernest R. May** (History), who has served as a consultant to the Joint Chiefs of Staff, the Office of the Secretary of Defense, and the National Security Council.

Other faculty members include: Professor **Joseph S. Nye, Jr.** (Government), who recently served as Deputy to the Undersecretary of State for Security Assistance where he was instrumental in framing U.S. policy on nuclear nonproliferation; Professor **Arthur R. Miller** (Law); **Howard Raiffa**, Frank Plumpton Ramsey Professor of Managerial Economics at the Business School, and a pioneering researcher in the uses of formal analysis in decision-making; **Hugo E. R. Uyterhoeven**, Timken Professor of Business Administration and Senior Associate Dean for External Relations at the Business School, who is a specialist in the interaction between business, government and the international economy; Professor **Albert Carnesale**, (Public Policy), a member of the Kennedy School's Center for Science and International Affairs, who was a participant in the Strategic Arms Limitation Talks; and

Director of the Institute of Politics **Jonathan Moore**.

Johnston says, "The faculty performance this year was nothing short of dazzling. They've been refining and learning from this process for four years now." But he stresses the fact that faculty are in a learning experience themselves. "Nothing can beat the real experiences of these people in the real world," he says.

He continues, "What you see over the two weeks is the merger of the worlds of the practitioner with that of the theorist. While the practitioner needs to be able to put the daily crises into a broader perspective and think above the level of his or her 'inbox,' so must the academic temper theory with the real world constraints of the art of the possible."

This year's program featured, along with Friday's final exercise, two sessions on "Dealing with Conflict," with Professor **Roger Fisher** (Law); and several classes on aspects of security in various world regions led by Associate Professor **Michael Nacht** (Public Policy), who is Associate Director of the Center for Science and International Affairs. A session on "Grain Policy" was conducted by **Roger B. Porter**, currently on leave from the Kennedy School to serve as Special Assistant to the President for Policy Development. "Congress and Parliament" was discussed by Professor **Don K. Price** (Public Management, *Emeritus*) former Dean of the Kennedy School, and food policy discussed by Professor **James E. Austin**, (Business Administration), Senior Lecturer on Nutrition Policy at the School of Public Health.

E - 7

Johnston points out that a byproduct of the program is a set of continuing relations, both between the School and program graduates, and among the participants themselves. In January, the first Alumni Day was held at Dumbarton Oaks in Washington, D.C. Close to 100 of the 150 graduates from across the country gathered to discuss Presidential transition.

Johnston says that the experience of having graduates of past programs meet was very successful, and plans are being made for future alumni weekends to be held. "The idea is to have some contact among the different year groups in the program. While it undoubtedly helps future recruiting, I think it clearly benefits the country as well."

E - 8

CHAIRMAN OF THE JOINT CHIEFS OF STAFF
WASHINGTON

15 September 1983

Mr. Douglas M. Johnston, Jr.
Executive Director
Executive Program, National
   and International Security
John F. Kennedy School of Government
Harvard University
Cambridge, Massachusetts 02138

Dear Doug,

    Just a short note to let you know how much I
enjoyed particpating in your final exercise. I
was glad I could get away from Washington, even for
a short time, to be with you at Harvard.

    Please pass along my special thanks to Larry
Murphy and the Harvard police for their fine support.

    I wish you continued success with the program
and look forward to seeing you again in Washington.

                        Sincerely,

                        JOHN W. VESSEY, JR.
                        Chairman
                        Joint Chiefs of Staff

P.S. The events of the afternoon — and
next few days in Washington brought
out all the lessons of the seminar!

HARVARD UNIVERSITY

JOHN F. KENNEDY SCHOOL OF GOVERNMENT
CAMBRIDGE, MASSACHUSETTS 02138

Addendum F

OFFICE OF THE DEAN

79 JOHN F. KENNEDY STREET

Memorandum for the Files   DATE: February 16, 1983

FROM: Graham T. Allison

RE: Teaching Status of
        Douglas M. Johnston

Doug was hired in September 1977 to become the Executive Director of
a new Kennedy School executive program in national and international
security and to assume part-time teaching responsibilities in the area
of international affairs. Since he subsequently decided to pursue a
doctorate in Political Science, he was precluded by University rules
from acquiring official faculty status. Despite the lack of formal
status, however, he did, in fact, carry out the intended teaching responsibilities, taking the lead in setting up and co-teaching a new core
course in International Affairs and Security. Although the grades he
assigned legally required the endorsement of a colleague having faculty status, he performed all the functions expected of any Harvard professor. Indeed, he received unusually high evaluations from his students, averaging 4.63 out of a possible 5.0. At the same time, he established an extremely successful executive program and satisfactorily
completed his Ph.D.

In summary, I would highly recommend Doug for a teaching position at any
institution of higher learning.

GTA
cc: Douglas M. Johnston

HERMAN WOUK   Addendum G

3255 N St NW

DC 20004   9 Nov 80

Dear Mr. Johnston,

Very few of the many letters I've received
about my War Novels have given me
as much satisfaction as your kind
note. Your background, + the work
you're doing now, makes your
commendation especially gratifying
+ valuable.

The Executive Seminar sounds fascinating,
+ if I were not immersed in a new
novel I'd apply to join one. Your Ben
Hauan told me how much he enjoyed
your course. He found it decidedly
illuminating; + he's another "old pro"
like yourself.

My warm thanks for your generous comment —

Sincerely

Herman Wouk

HARVARD UNIVERSITY

JOHN F. KENNEDY SCHOOL OF GOVERNMENT

CAMBRIDGE, MASSACHUSETTS 02138

Addendum H

OFFICE OF THE DEAN

79 BOYLSTON STREET

March 8, 1983

Dr. Douglas Johnston
25 Cypress Road
Wellesley Hills, MA   02181

Dear Doug:

Just a note to reiterate what I've said to you many times:
yours is among the most outstanding performances during my term
as Dean of the JFK School. I can think of no higher accolade in
a job than the enhancement of the value and status of the position
during one's watch. By this test, and by the fierce competition
among such extraordinary talents to be your successor, you have
succeeded beyond all expectations.

Your steady, sound, sensible, thoughtful, even-handed, fair-
minded, and unstinting commitment to this enterprise has been an
inspiration to us all.

You've acquired a real equity position here. I trust that you
will consider yourself a member of the School's extended family and
a very active participant in our National Security Management Programs
over the years ahead.

Personally, I value our professional relationship, and our
friendship.

On behalf of the School, and me personally, thank you.

Yours sincerely,

Graham Allison

DEPARTMENT OF THE NAVY
NAVAL WAR COLLEGE
NEWPORT, RHODE ISLAND 02841-5010

Addendum I

26 May 1986

Dear Doug,

You asked me sometime ago to keep you posted on the long-term impact of your earlier redesign of the Post Command Course. Since your recommended changes were implemented in 1984, we have held 7 sessions to rave reviews ever since. This contrasts sharply with the dissatisfaction associated with the earlier design which suffered from excessive breadth, a disjointed flow and an overly passive pedagogical approach. The key to this success was clearly your decision to focus the course around integrated warfare, at the Battle Group (and higher) level within the Navy, on joint operations with the Army and Air Force, and on combined operations with our allies. We are, for perhaps the first time, treating the threat on a holistic basis, with due consideration for the total spectrum of capabilities afforded by the U. S. arsenal. As you rightfully pointed out at the time, our recent attempts at joint operations have typically left a great deal to be desired, so the change has been long overdue. All of this, of course, dovetailed nicely at the time with the CNO's and SECNAV's emphasis on "warfighting."

Aside from the substantive changes in curriculum design and flow, your recommendations in other areas proved every bit as critical in effecting the change. Your thorough grasp of the politics of change, both internal and external to the college, enabled us to (1) implement your proposed management configuration (Al Bernstein and Tim Somes proved to be a dynamite combination), (2) take advantage of the ongoing presence of senior foreign naval officers, and (3) tie the course into other related programs of the college, i.e., the Center for Advanced Research and the Operations and Strategy Departments. It has simply provided a long overdue coherence and synergism to what we are doing around here, not to mention the long-term benefits to the senior officers who attend. We also use it as a training course for military faculty as they arrive--there is no faster way to bring them up to speed.

I have often thought of how Admiral Service's attendance at your Executive Program at Harvard led to your involvement here and to what has become one of our finest courses of instruction. Without that twist of fate, we would probably still be plodding along on the same old heading.

Beyond the impact of what you did with the Integrated Warfare course, I might also add that your earlier assessment of the then newly established Center for Naval Warfare Analysis (including the Strategic Studies Group) proved instrumental in integrating the center's activities into the rest of our program, greatly increasing the effectiveness of both the center and the college in the process.

I am afraid this letter has turned out considerably longer than I intended, but I do think we owe you a debt of gratitude for what you did and I wanted to let you know that your assistance was of a very profound and enduring nature. The college, the Navy, and the country are certainly better off as a result. Your breadth of perspective and objectivity were essential and perfectly suited to our former set of problems. Knowing of your continuing strong interest in your Naval Reserve affiliation and duty, I assume you won't object to my sending a copy of this letter to the Bureau.

Thanks again for the help and please drop by to see us when you can. I should be here until August of 1987 when my 30 years' service will regrettably come to an end. As always, the spring weather in Newport is, though late, magnificent.

With best personal regards,

ROBERT B. WATTS
Captain, U. S. Navy
Deputy to the President

Mr. Douglas M. Johnston, Jr.
Cities in Schools
1110 Vermont Ave, N.W.
Suite 1120
Washington, DC 20005

𝕿𝖍𝖊 𝕾𝖆𝖓 𝕯𝖎𝖊𝖌𝖔 𝖀𝖓𝖎𝖔𝖓
SAN DIEGO, CALIF.
D. 268,450
CA-590

JAN 14 1991
BURRELLE'S

Exploring the siege option –

8020

By Douglas M. Johnston

The President does have an alternative to attack — but it isn't peace either: a siege. Such an approach would combine limited military action with a more effective exploitation of the U.N. sanctions.

Certainly President Bush has done all that he can to persuade Saddam Hussein of the seriousness of U.S. intent, a strategy that may yet bear fruit. If it does not, however, the siege option may provide a way out of the Hobson's choice between attack, with its potentially severe human and economic consequences, and maintaining the status quo, with its loss of credibility.

Although the effectiveness of the U.N. sanctions is being questioned on the basis that Saddam Hussein can impose upon his people whatever hardships he wants in order to stay the course — much as he did in the war with Iran — there are important and telling differences between the economic support Iraq received during its earlier confrontation and that which it is now receiving.

As pointed out by a number of the nation's most capable strategists during recent congressional hearings, there is very good reason to believe that sanctions can, in fact, do the job over time. The factors that make this true, relating to the serious vulnerability of Iraq, are the same factors that warrant consideration of siege warfare.

The following actions should be considered:

▣ On Jan. 15, sever diplomatic relations and declare war against Iraq — but one to be waged by siege.

▣ U.S. and allied naval and air forces should confiscate or destroy (after first removing the crews, if possible) all Iraqi ships and aircraft found to be carrying contraband goods. The U.N. provisions relating to medical supplies and "humanitarian" foodstuffs would continue to be honored.

Janusz Kapusta/United Feature Syndicate

▣ Encourage Turkey to take strong measures to eradicate the minor smuggling across its border with Iraq.

▣ Hold U.S. air forces in place for immediate retaliation against any Iraqi incursion into Saudi Arabia or Turkey or against any acts of Iraqi-sponsored terrorism.

▣ Gradually adjust U.S. ground forces to accommo-

— an alternative to attack

date the siege strategy, substituting Arab forces wherever feasible (in recognition of the ultimate need for an Arab solution), but retaining the capability for rapid reinforcement to launch offensive operations on short notice. To facilitate meeting this latter requirement and to move toward greater Arabization of the conflict, selected U.S. equipment could be left in place for use by the "U.N. contingent."

To keep the other side guessing, the toughened sanctions should be given an unspecified period of time in which to work. The administration's actual timetable would be made known only to top congressional and allied leaders. A posture of ongoing troop rotation should be adopted and every effort made to maintain the international coalition. If it begins to break down, however, the United States should be prepared to continue implementation of the U.N. resolution on a unilateral basis.

It is axiomatic that, in a democracy, war should be the instrument of last resort and, once contemplated, should have strong popular backing. This approach, in effect, would trade administration restraint for congressional support and help depersonalize the confrontation; it would be the nation taking a stand, not George Bush. At the same time, the prospect of avoiding all-out war coupled with continuing oil price stability should have sufficient appeal to our allies to elicit continuing (and possibly even greater) commitments over the longer term.

A siege strategy includes the capacity to launch a later attack, but at a time when Iraq's military capabilities have been seriously weakened through shortages of critical spare parts and other war-time essentials. If effective, it would also avoid the tragic loss that could befall numerous American (and other) families in order

to do little more than move from one condition of instability in the Middle East to the next.

Some may feel that such an approach would be perceived as backpedaling or that it represents too small a departure from the current strategy and is the same kind of incrementalism that plagued us in Vietnam.

The cardinal lesson of Vietnam was that one should employ whatever force is required to do the job. In this case, the added noose-tightening, coupled with the clear endorsement that the nation stands with the President, dramatically alters the situation and, over time, has a good chance of working, with minimum loss of life.

The declaration-and-siege approach may also be criticized on the basis that televised pictures of starving Iraqi children will be no more acceptable to world opinion than would a frontal assault involving significant casualties. But by continuing to permit the humanitarian aid authorized under the U.N. resolution, it will be clear to all that Saddam can end the suffering by vacating Kuwait.

In many respects, the United States has seldom been in such a strong position. The trillions of dollars we invested in winning the Cold War have finally paid off — we no longer have to worry much about the Soviets. And but for the reserves, our forces would have to be somewhere anyway. Why not in Saudi Arabia making an immediate and valuable contribution? We clearly have the upper hand. If Saddam Hussein doesn't budge by tomorrow, let's hold onto it a while longer.

Johnston is the executive vice president of the Center for Strategic & International Studies in Washington, D.C., and former deputy assistant secretary of the Navy.

Pacific Forum, CSIS

Pauahi Tower, 1001 Bishop Street, Suite 1150, Honolulu, Hawaii 96813
(808) 521-6745 Telex: 634474 FORUM Facsimile: (808) 599-8690
Ref. no.: 01CRA04003

PRESIDENT
Lloyd R. Vasey

DIRECTOR
Thomas H. Miller

April 27, 1990

The Honorable Anne Armstrong
Chairman, Board of Trustees, CSIS
Center for Strategic &
   International Studies
1800 K St., N.W.
Washington, D.C. 20036

Dear Anne:

On the eve of my relinquishment of command here to Joe Jordan, I do so with some sadness of course, but with tremendous pride in our accomplishments through the years, consummating in our joining with CSIS. The merger was a master stroke which puts Pacific Forum, CSIS, in the forefront of the emerging policy debate as the Asia Pacific region undergoes fundamental transformation in the period ahead. No other institution is positioned to equal our strength and credibility in helping to define changing American national interests and policies in the increasingly competitive economic environment of this region.

My original goal in establishing a private international network for cooperative policy assessments around the Pacific rim has served well and I foresee a larger mission ahead in being a highly respected forum where governments can participate informally and out of the limelight in debating the issues and options. In a region of great diversity of faiths, interests and politics, and with unforeseen political and strategic changes on the horizon, this role can be of particular value in bringing into focus the impact of Western policies toward the socialist countries as the latter transform their societies, hopefully to the Western mode.

I have had the privilege of working with two exceptional persons, Dave Abshire and Doug Johnston. Dave seized the vision that together we could enjoy a scope of work in Asia Pacific that will surpass all our competition. He provided the course and steady hand at the tiller. Working with Doug in the day-to-day, management of issues and details, some thorny and sensitive, made everything seem easy. Doug is one of the finest operational executives and leaders I have known in my half century of public service, and he is a gentleman whose word you can trust. Thanks to him the Forum's relationship with CSIS staff is superb, as the Chinese say, "as compatible as the lips and teeth".

-2-

Thank you for your support and confidence, and for sharing the vision that we are building a fine structure that is worth the labor. God bless you and your leadership, and I hope you will call on this old sailor if he can ever be of service. As you may know, I will have an office in residence here and will be doing what I can to help promote the continued success of Pacific Forum, CSIS.

Sincerely,

L. R. Vasey

bcc: Dr. David Abshire
Dr. Douglas Johnston

Addendum L

MAR 3 1 1989

MAR 3 0 1989

M E M O R A N D U M

TO: Doug Johnston

FROM: Sam Armstrong
         Jim Barkley
         Mike Mazarr
         Bill Stokes

DATE: 30 March 1989

SUBJ: Immense gratitude

In order to express our enormous gratitude for your great generosity, we have voted unanimously in favor of the following action. On the evening of April 20, 1989, before our first softball game (against the White House, no less) we will officially dedicate the Douglas M. Johnston Memorial Beer Cooler.

We would, of course, be honored if you were able to attend what we are certain will be a solemn and moving ceremony. If, however, you are unable to be there, we promise not to let your "meal" go to waste.

Thank you once again for making possible another spectacular summer of fun in the sun and employee bonding.

Addendum M

Remarks of Stan Burnett, former CSIS Director of Studies
At Doug Johnston's farewell ceremony (July 26, 1999)

When thinking about life with Doug, I naturally recall best the laughs and good times. But we all know from hard experience that these are very personal moments that just don't tell well on occasions such as today's. So, Doug, each of us will cherish those moments without being capable of sharing them very effectively.

Therefore, I hope you'll forgive me if I'm a bit more serious. Of the many chapters one could write in the volume of *Life with Doug,* two stand out, one well known to all in the room, one perhaps not known at all.

Well known is Doug's fundamental warmth and human kindness. I picture Doug as unable to steer his submarine on a true course because he would have tried to avoid bumping into any innocent fish. Doug helped so many people, with personal concern and real action, action that cost him, that in the days when he was the chief executive officer of the Center, half the people in any assembly like this would have had their lives touched by Doug Johnston—from a young man whom Doug bootstrapped into a good job at the International Club, to program directors whose budget had sprung a leak, to colleagues afflicted by the most dire twists of fate.

He showed solidarity with people, not when it was easy, but when the going was difficult.

I think, however, that most of you know this about Doug Johnston. Let me turn to what a few of you know, a characteristic of which I happen to have close personal knowledge.

You have to start by understanding the joy of being Director of Studies. It's the job that, if you have a mind to play it this way, is the very ideal of licentious irresponsibility. While others worry about donors and cash flow, about sensitive senators and unpleasant undersecretaries, the Director of Studies can speak for methodological propriety, intellectual rigor, academic respectability, and God help us, good writing style. He can allow himself to be a force for missed deadlines, cost overruns, and irritated clients.

Now Erik entered on the scene already knowing the players. I didn't, and so I started with a series of lunches and meetings with the scholars and analysists who were my special concern. For all their diversity, I found that most of them agreed on two things. One of them, that they didn't want a Director of Studies, we'll ignore. The other was more interesting.

Over and over, I was told that CSIS was divided into two cultures. These were not exactly C.P. Snow's two cultures, but they were related. On one side were those from an academic and scholarly background. On the other side was, in effect, the military-industrial-governmental complex. And these folks who were initiating me were certain that they knew how the battle lines were drawn.

Doug Johnston, as the chief executive officer, was the crucial figure in the daily life of these people. Ignoring some parts of Doug's biography, they were certain that they had him pegged, and it was on the other side of the line.

What some of you don't perhaps realize, even if you were at the Center through all this period, was how absolutely wrong these analyses were. Not that we lacked for battle lines; when I once spoke of the task of synergizing the Center as being like trying to herd kittens, everybody knew what I meant.

But <u>without fail</u>, in every struggle to insist on sound methodology, intellectual rigor, and, yes, good style, Doug came down on the side of maintaining high standards. Since these debates were mostly in closed rooms, few people realized how much the <u>quality of the Center's work</u> had its greatest hero, and the Director of Studies his greatest ally, in Doug Johnston.

And some of these issues were truly poignant and difficult. For example, I was charged with examining the publications and academic background of people whom the Center was considering taking on. Many of them were figures of real stature in Washington. Whatever the recommendation, a purely scholarly recommendation, abstracted from the surrounding politics of the case, Doug <u>always</u> supported it, even in the face of the most intense pressure to compromise.

This quality was seen most dramatically in the project that was closest to Doug's heart, the one that produced the book on religion in diplomacy and was a step on the path to Doug's great new adventure.

Doug knew where his passions lay in this, yet he loaded the working group with gadflies and trouble-makers. Half the meetings seemed, to most of us, to be disastrous. Someone would bring in a spurious construct of social scientific whimsy and we'd all shoot it down mercilessly. While the char force was cleaning the blood off the floor, I'd try to get back to my office without running into Doug, who, I was sure, must have been crushed; we had taken three steps backward from ever producing anything. Instead, he'd be all smiles and say "<u>That</u> was a great meeting!" He genuinely loved the challenge. He was determined to speak with honesty in this area, even if it meant giving up some of the scientific trappings that would have made some people more comfortable with it. He considered the worst of the snipers to be allies who were simply keeping the findings true to the evidence.

So this was Doug Johnston as I knew him—sort of out of step with his surroundings.

—In a community of scholars who expected something different from him, he was the staunchest ally of high standards.

—In a city of front-runners and fair-weather friends, Doug was there to support people at the bad times, at the moments of greatest difficulty.

—In a city of compromise and corner-cutting, Doug <u>always</u> voted for rigor.

CSIS has an unequalled record of turning research and analysis into important political action. We always <u>think</u> we're on the side of the angels when we do this work, but since our work lives in the context of the normal ambiguity of politics, you never really know.

But Doug's new adventure, on which we all wish him well, is probably the only case where we can say with certainty that, to the extent that he succeeds, the world will be a better place.

Happy landings, Admiral.

M-4

SAM NUNN
191 PEACHTREE STREET
ATLANTA, GEORGIA 30303-1763
404/572-4600

4/5/99

Dear Doug,

You have made a wonderful contribution to our Nation and the world through your leadership at CSIS and your personal example of commitment and integrity.

I am excited about your plans for the Center on Religion and Diplomacy with its great potential for promoting understanding and

M - 5

peace among various religious and ethnic groups.

On behalf of all of the CSIS family — we thank you Doug for your outstanding leadership and wish you every success in your important new work.

Sincerely,

Sam

Addendum N

Christmas, 2009

Dear Mike,

I decided some months ago to devote most of this Christmas day to writing my long-overdue response to your letter of several years ago in which you articulated the reasoning behind your doubts relating to Christianity and the role that Jesus plays in that narrative. I am mindful that your letter was precipitated by my own suggestion that we exchange views on the matter, and that I have until now seemingly reneged on my part of the bargain. Frankly speaking, the reason for my delayed response is that I have not felt capable of doing justice to the deeper dimensions of your doubt or of capturing the depth of my own feelings on the subject. I still don't feel entirely capable of carrying the freight on this, but you have waited long enough.

Unfortunately, I don't have your letter in front of me; but as I recall, it was highly thoughtful and played to understandable themes relating to Christian hypocrisy and any number of other predictable failings of so-called "believers." The case I will make in response is two parts intellectual and one part emotional.

Going back to first principles, it is probably more rational to believe that the creation had a creator, rather than chalking it up to particles, chance, and the impersonal laws of physics. I think I may have mentioned some time ago that a good friend of mine by the name of Dean Overman authored a book entitled *A Case Against Accident and Self-Organization*. In this book and as the title suggests, he proves mathematically that the world as we know it could not have been created by chance. As I recall, (which at this advanced age may be off more than a little), the mathematical definition of impossible is something like one chance in 10^{50}. The power of 10 in Dean's calculations totally dwarfs that at 10^{300}. To put that number in context, there are only 10^{80} atoms in the entire universe. Moreover, his conclusions have withstood the scrutiny of the toughest scientific critics. That aside, though, I know from what you have told me in the past that you consider nature itself to be a form of divine revelation. I suspect that anyone who has witnessed nature up close and personal and spent any time at all reflecting on the incredible interdependence and complexity of it all would probably come to that same conclusion.

On a related note, I have long been of the opinion that science doesn't really have much to say about origins. Isaac Newton observes an apple falling from a tree and comes up with a formula for predicting the rate of speed at which future apples will fall. All of a sudden, we "own" the phenomenon of apples (and by extrapolation, all objects) falling, when in actuality all we did is describe what we saw. I find the observation below by Robert Jastrow, a self-proclaimed agnostic astronomer to be quite telling in this regard:

> Now we see how the astronomical evidence leads to a biblical view of the origin of the world. All the details differ, but the essential element in the astronomical and biblical accounts of Genesis is the same; the chain of events leading to man commenced suddenly and sharply, at a definite moment in time, in

a flash of light and energy. . . . The scientist's pursuit of the past ends in the moment of creation. This is an exceedingly strange development, unexpected by all but the theologians. They have always accepted the word of the Bible: *In the beginning God created heaven and earth*. . . . For the scientist who has lived by faith in the power of reason, the story ends like a bad dream. He has scaled the mountains of ignorance; he is about to conquer the highest peak; as he pulls himself over the final rock, he is greeted by a band of theologians who have been sitting there for centuries.

So, starting with the premise that there is a God, what does that have to do with Jesus? Well, for starters, it alerts one to the fact that with every passing year, there is added archeological confirmation of what the Bible has to say. This includes the Messianic background presented in the Dead Sea Scrolls. And here, as one ponders the figure of Jesus and the fact that the life he lived and the role he played fulfilled more than 30 Old Testament prophesies from earlier centuries, one is transported far beyond the outer bounds of coincidence.

A very telling point for me in the New Testament narrative is the fact that following the crucifixion, all of Jesus' disciples were totally disillusioned and in a state of deep despair. What is it then that could have turned them around to the point of risking everything they had to preach the "Good News" (with all but one, suffering a martyr's death for their efforts)? The only explanation that I find at all plausible was their absolute conviction that Jesus had returned from the dead.

When Nero was going to crucify Peter and offered to let him go if he would renounce Jesus, Peter not only refused, but declared that he wasn't worthy to die in the same manner as Jesus and asked to be crucified upside down instead (which he was). When Paul was similarly offered the chance to live by renouncing Jesus, he too turned it down, indicating that he had not been living a fable; it was the real deal (my words, not his). Incidents like this coupled with the eyewitness testimony of the many others who saw Jesus following his death more than meet the standard proofs for historical accuracy. I say this based on well-argued explanations offered by professional historians.

Beyond the foregoing intellectual arguments, I have also been influenced by a personal experience that I may have shared with you during our sailing trip off the coast of Maine. I am referring to the time I was struck by a car while crossing a street in London (it was night and he didn't have his headlights on). After I picked myself up off the pavement, I experienced a strange and overwhelming sense of peace that defies description. Beyond the fact that it triggered an immediate reordering of priorities on my part (which lasted all of two weeks), it also sensitized me to the fact that there were others who had experienced something similar. Although I had never heard of such a phenomenon prior to my mishap, it was the subject of later research by a Swiss psychiatrist who interviewed numerous people who had returned to life after being pronounced "clinically dead." According to her, they had experienced this same sense of peace, had seen a blinding white light, and had in some cases met Jesus and/or relatives who had gone before. After my own experience, I could readily understand why many of those interviewed said they were no longer afraid to die. In fact, in a number of cases, they expressed resentment at having to "come back."

So these are some of my reasons for believing that Jesus was a transcendent figure who paved the way for us to reconcile our sinful natures with God. As for the disquieting but accurate observations that you made about Christians falling short of the teachings to which they supposedly subscribe, I suggest that you read the enclosed book. Although it's a novel, it incorporates a heavy autobiographical dimension, addresses the issues you've raised, and is the only thing I have ever read that integrates the here and now with the hereafter in an understandable and seemingly plausible manner. It is also the only book I have ever read that left me with a tear in my eye as I finished.

Again, I apologize for taking so long; but you're a great brother (in fact, the greatest I've ever had) so I wanted to do justice to the argument and, even more importantly, to you.

December 26, 2000

Mr. Doug Johnston
President
International Center for
  Religion and Diplomacy
1156 15ᵗʰ Street, N.W., Ste. 910
Washington, DC   20005

Dear Doug:

I cannot tell you how impressed I was at what you were able to accomplish at the reconciliation conference with political and religious leaders in Sudan last month.

Frankly, my expectations were not all that high given the hostilities in the region, particularly since the outbreak of civil war 16 years ago. However, your efforts to establish common ground through an intentional process involving leaders from both Christian and Muslim communities succeeded in a manner that was, in my opinion, nothing short of a miracle. While you deserve much of the credit, God's hand was clearly in this.

I was amazed as I heard Christians from the south venting their feelings over the pain and suffering experienced there at the hands of a Muslim dominated government. I was even more amazed by the conciliatory tone of the Muslim response to the extent that they admitted that the "application" of their beliefs (Sharia) was "possibly in error." Further, that you were able to achieve resolution on the 14 points of agreement — embodying expansion of human rights and religious freedom — was, again, nothing short of a miracle.

Doug, I truly admire your efforts and congratulate you on making such an auspicious beginning. While I know that much rough road lies ahead, you have made an excellent start.

May God bless you in your future undertakings.

Sincerely,

Albert D. Ernest, Jr.
ADE/kac

1560 Lancaster Terrace, Suite 1402, Jacksonville, Florida 32204 Telephone (904) 355-1930

431

The Right Reverend Frank S. Cerveny
Sixth Bishop of Florida (retired)

November 28, 2000

Dear Doug,

What an extraordinary accomplishment you achieved in the Sudan. Yours was a masterful performance of moving conference leaders from talking at each other to reaching compromise and agreement on very difficult issues.

As I listened attentively for four days, I was particularly impressed by the way you directed the conference without having to take center stage. Months of planning went into the agenda yet you remained open to modification with your colleagues. Your addresses were <u>good</u>, <u>brief</u>, and to the point and your comments on the dynamics of each session were gentle yet firm. As the conference ended, Muslim and Christian leaders genuinely <u>owned your</u> agenda and you could feel a growing spirit of cooperation and collegiality - Remarkable!

It was a brilliant beginning, Doug, but as we all know, the <u>real</u> test lies ahead. Religious leaders, <u>particularly</u> those in ecumenical gatherings, will rarely move from dialogue to action without an <u>outside mover</u>! Collective memory fades, so time is critical for the implementation of peace resolutions as well as the Center's credibility as a peacemaker.

The reason why I am drawn to the Center is that I am a visionary. It is one of my spiritual gifts – and I like your vision! I believe if you can dream <u>and</u> the spirit is in it – <u>it can be done</u>!

Thank you for your vision. The dream is very much alive. I hope you will not spread yourself over other global areas until conflict resolution follows dialogue in Sudan – and Muslims/Christians can finally live in peaceful coexistence.

Blessed are the peacemakers,

Frank

3711 Ortega Boulevard • Jacksonville, Florida 32210
Telephone: 904 384-1611 • Fax: 904 384-8902 • Email: BishopFSC@aol.com

Addendum P

Joint Statement

We the members of civil society of the state of Jammu and Kashmir gathered in Kathmandu, Nepal on November 11-14th, 2005, under the auspices of the International Center for Religion and Diplomacy based in Washington D.C. We come from both sides of the Line of Control and from regions of Azad Kashmir, Kashmir Valley, Jammu & Laddakh. We are people of faith. We are Muslims, Hindus and Buddhists who believe that faith-based reconciliation is a key to the peace process and to the future prosperity of the Kashmir region.

We are committed to a pluralistic vision of the community and the restoration of human values. As such, we believe that the return of Kashmiri Pandits and all displaced persons to their homeland is central to the peace and normalcy. Therefore, we urge both the governments and civil society to facilitate this process as a matter of great priority.

We are committed to an inclusive community and to demolish the walls of hostility that exist among the various identity-based groups. As such we express appreciation to the governments of Pakistan and India for creating the opening in the Line of Control. However, we encourage any means possible to allow the free flow of the Kashmiris so that there might be healing and restoration among us. We also deplore violence in any form from any side.

We are committed to the peace process between India and Pakistan, especially as it relates to Kashmir. As such, we see the need for a unified Kashmiri voice to emerge so that the legitimate aspirations of the people of the State of Jammu & Kashmir might be heard, understood, and be given proper respect by India and Pakistan. We also urge the members of civil society to take an active role in the peace process.

We are committed to social justice as a key foundation of Kashmir society. We are committed to sharing power and privilege among different identity based groups. As such we urge the governments to setup the mechanisms to facilitate the economic restitution and restoration of land and businesses to Kashmir Pandits and all other displaced persons.

We propose that the principles of Human Rights and the essential moral and ethical values of religions be made a standard part of all school curriculums and that security forces be trained in respectful treatment of citizens.

We are committed to a process of forgiveness among Kashmiri people as essential to creating a better future together. We are committed to healing the wounds of our history. Collectively we grieve the sale of Kashmir by the British in 1846 and ask them to apologize. We call for the establishment of a "Kashmir Truth & Reconciliation Commission" as a means of exposing human rights violations and other wrongdoings with an eye towards justice and healing rather than revenge.

We urge the international community to support the ongoing peace process between India and Pakistan. We urge the governments of India and Pakistan to involve all identity-based groups and regions in the dialogue and negotiations leading to the resolution of the Kashmir Conflict. We urge all Kashmiris regardless of their religious traditions to pray for peace and reconciliation in our land.

We depart from Kathmandu with a sense hope and joy at having been together from across the Line of Control and different regions of the State of Jammu & Kashmir. We believe that faith-based reconciliation in Jammu & Kashmir is an idea whose time has come.

Shah Ghulam Qadir
Dr. K.L.Chowdhary
Sardar Amjad Yousaf
A.R.Hanjura advocate
Sardar Usman Ali Khan
Dr. Dauood Iqbal Baba
Sardar Azhar Nazar
Rakesh Kar
Chaudhary Ilyas Advocate
Hamid Nasim Rafiabadi
Sardar Tahir Aziz
Muhammad Ramzan Khan
Iftikhar Ahmed Bazmi
Uzera Shah
Tsering Tsomo
Maria Iqbal Tarana
Vir Ji Saraf

Brian Cox ICRD (Witness)

Addendum Q

DEPARTMENT OF THE ARMY
DEFENSE LANGUAGE INSTITUTE FOREIGN LANGUAGE CENTER
PRESIDIO OF MONTEREY
MONTEREY, CALIFORNIA 93944-5000

February 27, 2012

REPLY TO
ATTENTION OF

Office of the Commandant

Professor Douglas Johnston, PhD
Georgetown University
Berkley Center for Religion, Peace & World Affairs
3307 M Street, Suite 200
Washington, DC 20007

Dear Professor Johnston:

As the Commandant of the Defense Language Institute Foreign Language Center (DLIFLC), I would like to extend my sincere gratitude for your contribution to our cultural training product, "The Force of Faith." This DVD series is the collaborative result of both the US military and professional contributions from experts such as yourself.

The Force of Faith instructional film series is intended to train and educate service members and all Department of Defense personnel to become more culturally competent in terms of understanding global beliefs, text, narratives and symbols from various faith communities. Although this series was under development for the past few years before its recent approval through the US Army Training and Doctrine Command, the now completed product has had an immediate and long-term impact on the cultural and religious training of our Soldiers worldwide.

Once again, on behalf of the Soldiers, Marines, Sailors, Airmen, faculty and staff here at the Defense Language Institute Foreign Language Center, I thank you. We have included a copy of the DVD series as a symbol of our appreciation for your participation in the creation of this exceptional product and for your continued service, support and dedication to our nation.

Sincerely,

Danial D. Pick
Colonel, US Army
Commandant

Addendum R

المملكة العربية السعودية

وزارة التعليم

(٢٨٠)

مكتب الوزير

Letter of Endorsement

The purpose of this letter is to endorse the International Center for Religious & Diplomacy (ICRD) development of a teacher training module on Globalization for the Ministry of Education (MOE). This training will be designed to help Saudi students to become "global citizens" (as called for in the 2030 vision) by increasing understanding of and commitment to tolerance, inclusiveness, critical thinking, and cross-cultural communications.

Once the content of the globalization module is developed and the MOE has approved it, ICRD will pilot-test it with two separate groups of Saudi teachers, who will be chosen based on selection criteria established with the MOE.

Once the module has proven its worth to the MOE, ICRD will work with the MOE to strategically determine the most effective approach for embedding the training contents within existing suitable activities. We mutually agree that the goal of this pilot training will be to refine the Globalization module and expand its reach through successive iterations to a wider audience of teachers within the MOE.

The Ministry looks forward to working with ICRD on this important initiative.

Minister of Education

Dr. Hamad Al AlSheikh,

Addendum S

The piece below was crafted by Krista Tippett in conjunction with a January 2007 NPR interview with Dr. Douglas Johnston.

Krista's Journal
(www.speakingoffaith.org)
January 25, 2007

TRANSITIONING FROM COLD WAR POLITICS TO "FAITH-BASED DIPLOMACY"
I've been following Doug Johnston's work for a decade, ever since I read his 1994 book, *Religion, the Missing Dimension of Statecraft*. Remember, this was well before 9/11 thrust religion to the fore of international relations at the highest level.

In the mid-1990s I attended a regional Council on Foreign Relations meeting at which Johnston spoke about his findings. Many of the attendees, raised in a Cold War world dominated by secular power politics between nation-states, were openly scornful of the idea that religion should have any place at all in a legitimate foreign policy discussion.

But Johnston was COO and executive vice president at the Center for Strategic and International Studies (CSIS), one of the top foreign policy think tanks in Washington, D.C. And he presciently saw that as the Cold War division of the world unraveled, potential conflicts would again be ethnically and regionally driven, with religious dynamics front and center. He also saw that understanding and working with religious people and passions could be key to what he calls "preventive diplomacy." His book documented case studies around the world where religion helped mediate and end conflicts that traditional diplomacy could not.

In 1999, he left CSIS to create and run the International Center for Religion and Diplomacy. History has borne out Johnston's sense of religion's centrality in the foreign affairs of the future in ways he would never have wished for. Johnston is taken seriously in corridors of power by way of classic military and strategic credentials — a graduate of Annapolis, he was the youngest person ever qualified to command a nuclear submarine. He's worked in the office of the Secretary of Defense and the President's Office for Emergency Preparedness. His case studies have been used in the instruction of new American military and diplomatic leaders.

Douglas Johnston's primary and most active contribution to world affairs in recent years has come through the work he describes in this program — initiatives of Track-II, or unofficial diplomacy, which are deeply consonant with the urgent recommendations of the December report of the Iraq Study Group. He has helped foster religious openings with deep humanitarian and political implications between the governing Islamic regime of Sudan and its Christian south. This is an aspect of the complex and tortured recent past and present of Sudan that simply does not make the news.

Johnston has also orchestrated some of the highest level contacts that have taken place between religious and political leaders in Iran and the United States in recent years, in an era of hostile impasse in the official diplomatic relationship between the two countries. I decided that it was finally time to interview him when I read a thought-provoking and helpful memo he crafted last year titled, "What Iranians Want Americans to Know About Iran."

438

Douglas Johnston is not easy to classify in the handy categories of America's culture wars. He is not a liberal, nor is he a hawk. He is an evangelical Protestant who has created a center with a multi-religious staff; personally he's most involved these days in crises with an Islamic interface. He is quick to note that his kind of faith-based, preventive diplomacy cannot negate the fact that sometimes "brutality must be met by brutality." He is a staunch advocate of the U.S. tradition of separation of church and state, and yet he says that we have used it as a crutch not to do our homework on the different role religion has in cultures with which we must learn, as a matter of self-interest, to relate respectfully.

Among the most hopeful images Douglas Johnston leaves me with, perhaps, are his stories of the unprecedented work he and his center are doing in Pakistan to help reform and modernize *madrassas* — religious schools which U.S. officials have cited as frequent breeding grounds for terrorism. His pictures from that project, posted on our Web site, are astonishing in themselves. Pakistani religious and educational leaders — including "hard-line" Wahhabi and Deobandi sects — have taken him as a trusted partner because of his expertise and his respectful, faith-based approach to cultural engagement and diplomacy. At the very least, he says, this is a worthwhile investment in the children of Pakistan.

And this effort at the source of current global violence, Johnston argues, is as pragmatic a use of resources as the money we're spending upping security at airports to catch the symptoms of full-blown militancy. In that sense Doug Johnston's work is an investment in the future of all of our children, one I'll keep following.

Douglas Johnston

From: David Kirkham [kirkhamd@lawgate.byu.edu]
Sent: Monday, May 02, 2011 6:50 PM
To: dmj@icrd.org
Subject: RE: Confirmation: Class visit "Ethics and International Affairs" 16 Feb 2011 - Walzer Readings

Dear Doug,

I just received your very timely and appropriate note on what should be our reaction in the wake of the death of Osama bin Laden. Thank you for being the man you are, taking these kinds of initiatives, and encouraging us to perhaps restrain a little of the football victory rally exhibitions which tend to be part of who we are.

I wanted to tell you two things as follow up to your last two stays at BYU.

1) My wife read, studied even, the booklets you obtained for her the night of the Islam and the West conference keynote. She was very impressed and, honestly, though she read a great deal and a great deal of variety, I was a bit surprised to see how much time and attention she gave to your work.

2) I gave my students from the "Ethics and International Affairs" course a final exam essay question on countering ideological extremism. Almost everyone cited your work and usually you by name as a positive example of the kinds of things that need to be done and as a real concrete example of how the theory can be translated to the good work of individuals.

Again, it was a pleasure having you with us. I hope we will see you again and thank you very much for the post-Bin Laden message.

With warmest regards,

David

David M. Kirkham, J.D., Ph.D.
Senior Fellow for Comparative Law and International Policy
International Center for Law and Religion Studies
J. Reuben Clark Law School

Brigham Young University
452 JRCB
Provo, UT 84602

Tel. (801) 422-9236
Fax (801) 422-0399

5/3/2011

Addendum U

Dr Douglas Johnston, President,
International Center for Religion and Diplomacy
1156 Fifteenth St., NW, Suite 910 Washington DC 20005

7 March 2008

Dear Doug,

Please consider presenting ICRD and the work that you do to all of our students and faculty at
National Defense University on one of the last two Wednesdays in April, and again with the new
class next fall.

I am still stunned after hearing you speak at the International Institute for Islamic Thought in
Herndon this week. I told the deans at the University that it was the most profound and
strategically relevant presentation that I've heard in the past four years in Washington.

The innovative type of religious diplomacy that ICRD advances is a topic that all of our students
and faculty should know about to expand their thinking about cross-cultural diplomacy and
conflict resolution. Unfortunately, with so many topics competing for our time, we don't
adequately explore this kind of "moral imagination" in our year-long curricula, so your
presentation would give our students the exposure to this critical subject matter and a model for
how to employ it.

Doug, I'm still in a state of shock over how you and your elite and small team at ICRD brought
about such major reconciliations in the Sudan, in Kashmir, among the Taliban, in freeing the
Korean hostages, and even in reforming Pakistan's madrassas. It simply doesn't sound believable
until one actually hears you describe it. For that reason, I firmly believe that you need to lead our
leaders through this faith-based diplomacy concept so they can go out and help multiply ICRD's
kind of thinking around the world.

Especially in this age of religious revivalism in all major faiths, and the age of seemingly
intractable faith-based conflicts that we're now in, your presentation to us would be a great
capstone for our Master's degree in strategy and global leadership.

Sincerely,

David Belt
Captain, US Navy and Assistant Professor, National Security Studies
National Defense University (ICAF), Washington DC 20319-5066
beltd2@ndu.edu, 202-685-4498 (Office), 703-965-5918 (Mobile)

Gmail

Douglas Johnston <dmj@icrd.org>

Leaving ICRD
1 message

Nick Acosta <nick@icrd.org>   Fri, Apr 9, 2021 at 2:24 PM
To: Douglas Johnston <dmj@icrd.org>

Dear Doug,

I wanted to write you and let you know that I will be leaving ICRD on April 20. I've been offered a digital communications position with the Alliance for Middle East Peace, where I will be overseeing all of their social media, website, email marketing, and strategic communications.

Reflecting on my four years with the Center, it has been an honor to work alongside you and to carry on your vision for ICRD. Your pioneering work has been a formative inspiration and a driving force behind my career, ever since I first read *Religion: The Missing Dimension of Statecraft* as a college student. You laid the groundwork for international relations professionals like me - who recognize that the transformative power of God's love in the world can transcend borders, heal divisions, and move mountains.

I never imagined that we would one day be coworkers, colleagues, and friends. Thank you for your guidance and mentorship. I am blessed to have been a part of something so special.

Forever grateful,

--

Nick Acosta (He/Him)
Director of Communications and Development

International Center for Religion & Diplomacy
www.icrd.org
(202) 331 - 9404

Dear Doug,

Thanks very much for your note and kind invitation to the Center's annual meeting and ICRD's Changing of the Guard. I would surely love to be there Doug, to join with others in honoring you; the visionary founder and source of inspiration throughout ICRD's history.

Doug, I only hope that you – and just as important because of your own humility – someone else will write your biography. You've surely earned a very praising treatment of your life Doug. Your founding vision was accompanied by a sense of realism toward the daunting dimension of the challenges ahead when dealing in crisis areas. Yet, you took it on; and with such dogged determination and joyful abandon – and truly phenomenal results. You knew always that the Lord had your back and would lift you up and get you through times when despair was the most logical sensation and any basis for hope was tenuous.

Congratulations Doug. You ought to be terribly proud. Now go take your pack off and pay attention to that wife of yours. You two heroes deserve a break.

Warm regards,

Bud

P.S. Unfortunately my 92 year-old sister Mary, is coming up from our home-town in Texas on Friday for the christening of her 11th great grandson (and our great nephew). He is the son of a Marine Major whom I've mentored for years here in town in the president's helicopter squadron. I'm so sorry Doug. I'd much rather be at your annual gathering to help in honoring you.

Robert C. McFarlane
Co-Founder
U.S. Energy Security Council
2700 Virginia Ave. NW (Suite 901)
Washington, DC 20037

ACKNOWLEDGEMENTS

Outside of a dog, a book is man's best friend. Inside of a dog, it's too dark to read.

Groucho Marx

First and foremost, I must pay homage to my incredibly supportive wife, Dareen. In addition to serving as a valuable sounding board for many of my ideas, she patiently typed multiple drafts of multiple chapters until I got them right. Why that is so worthy of tribute is because I know I will one day be listed in the Guinness Book of World Records as the only person on the face of the planet who actually types at a negative rate of speed. In the seventh grade, I had to make a choice between typing class and going out for football. At the time, I thought I could always hire a secretary. That turned out to be the first of many strategic blunders along life's way.

Second in the order of merit is my brother, Mike, to whom I turned not once, but twice at different stages in the manuscript to provide a sanity check on such questions as: Is it interesting? Does the notion of blending a light-hearted half with a more serious half work for the reader? To the extent the answers to these questions and selected others is yes, much of the credit for that goes to him for his invaluable suggestions.

And to my sister, Kate, heartfelt thanks for her herculean efforts in pre-paring the images that grace the book from stem to stern. Her reputation as a magician with Photoshop is more than well-deserved and remains intact. The same holds true for Marsha Vander Mey and her gifted ability with a camera to capture for posterity the highlights of important events. Others who weighed in with helpful suggestions relating to the manuscript were my good friends Will Jenkins and Ben Barber and my gifted nephew, Mark Ulett (Kate's oldest).

Professionally, I am particularly grateful to the staff and interns of ICRD, who over the 18 years of my tenure, took a chance on serving a mission, which although exciting in nature, was largely untested and occasionally required going in harm's way. I am particularly grateful in this regard to James Patton,

Steve Hayes, Rod MacAlister, Bob Bovey, and Miles Kimber for having served for varying terms as the Center's Executive Vice President, and in James's case, as my successor-in-residence.

Special thanks are also more than due to those who served at various times as (1) Chairman of the Center's Board, including Harold Jacobi, Jim Wootton, and Bill Flynn and (2) as Chairman of the Executive Committee (of the Board), John Kiser and John Sandoz. I can only hope that whatever return these folks feel they may have reaped from their major investments of time, energy, friendship, and financial support at least begets a smile. God knows, every one of them has been a blessing to me, as have all other current and past members of the Board, the Advisory Council, the staff, our interns, and the multitudinous donors who have helped keep the ship afloat through often stormy seas.

A special note about staff and interns. Indicative of the superb quality of both have been the contributions of Senior Program Manager Rebecca Cataldi, who has now been at ICRD longer than anyone else. She joined the Center in 2006 after graduating *summa cum-laude* from Georgetown University's School of Foreign Service. She then went on to earn a Master's Degree in Conflict Analysis and Resolution from George Mason University in her spare time, while carrying a full workload supporting our Center's work in Pakistan. Again, on her own time (and at her own expense), she made her way to Yemen where she worked for a short while on a volunteer basis, training local religious leaders and NGO personnel in conflict resolution techniques. Her efforts there laid the foundation for several major ICRD projects in that war-torn country which are already proving to be of strategic consequence. All because Rebecca had a vision.

A note of thanks as well to Henry "Duke" Burbridge for his many years of selfless toil in the ICRD vineyard, first as a volunteer, later as a key member of our staff, and finally as a contractor. Never before have I met anyone so devoid of academic credentials on the one hand and so naturally gifted as a strategic thinker and doer on the other.

Finally, I am indebted beyond words to my immediate and extended family and to the many wonderful colleagues and friends along life's way—some mentioned in the book and others not (no slight intended)—who have made it all both meaningful and fun. They have clearly been a large part of the miracle of this pilgrim's life.

ABOUT THE AUTHOR

D ouglas M. Johnston is President Emeritus and founder of the International Center for Religion & Diplomacy (ICRD). A distinguished graduate of the U.S. Naval Academy, he holds a Master's Degree in Public Administration and Ph.D. in Political Science from Harvard University and has served in senior positions in both the public and private sectors. Among Dr. Johnston's government assignments, he was Deputy Assistant Secretary of the Navy; Director of Policy Planning and Management in the Office of the Secretary of Defense; and planning officer with the President's Office of Emergency Preparedness. He has taught courses in international affairs at Harvard and was the founding director of the University's Executive Program in National and International Security.

Immediately prior to ICRD, Dr. Johnston was Executive Vice President and Chief Operating Officer of the Washington-based Center for Strategic and International Studies (CSIS). In addition to his managerial duties, he chaired the Center's Preventive Diplomacy Program and its Maritime Studies Program. His publications include *Religion, the Missing Dimension of Statecraft* (1994); *Foreign Policy into the 21ˢᵗ Century: the US. Leadership Challenge* (1996); *Faith-based Diplomacy: Trumping Realpolitik* (2003); *Religion, Terror and Error: U.S. Foreign Policy and the Challenge of Spiritual Engagement* (2011); and *Religion and Foreign Affairs: Essential Readings* (2012).

In 2011, *Religion, Terror and Error* won the "Book of the Year Award" from Foreword Reviews, the rating agency for universities and independent publishers. In October 2014, Dr. Johnston was honored by Georgetown University on the 20th Anniversary of the publication of his earlier work *Religion, the Missing Dimension of Statecraft*. Five years later, CSIS sponsored a similar celebration on the book's 25th anniversary. In February 2015, the International Studies Association presented Dr. Johnston with its inaugural Distinguished Scholar Award for Religion and International Affairs.

Dr. Johnston's hands-on experience in the political/military arena coupled with his work in preventive diplomacy, guided ICRD's early efforts to bridge religion and politics in support of peacemaking in Sudan, Kashmir, Pakistan,

Afghanistan, Iran, Syria, Yemen, Colombia and Saudi Arabia. He is a retired Captain in the U.S. Naval Reserve and a Grand Commander in the Knights Templar Order of Merit. He holds an Honorary Doctorate in Humane Letters and in 2008 was identified in *Christianity Today* (a leading Christian journal) as "The Father of Faith-based Diplomacy."

ICRD ENDORSEMENTS

"Congratulations to ICRD for the terrific work you are doing to promote respect across religious barriers in the Middle East, South Asia, and elsewhere…If we don't make religion a basis for reconciliation, it may well be an ongoing source of conflict in the future as it has been in the past."

The Honorable Madeleine Albright
former U.S. Secretary of State
(Acceptance remarks upon receiving ICRD's
Faith-In-Action Award, May, 2017)

"Let me begin by thanking Doug and his colleagues for the unbelievable work that you do. You are truly doing God's work here on earth…So, on behalf of the President and on behalf of the American people, I thank you for that work."

Dennis McDonough
White House Chief of Staff
(Keynote Speaker, May 2016
ICRD Faith-In-Action Award Dinner)

"You are giving voice to the voiceless…...Words can't explain our gratitude."

Southern Yemini activist
July 2016

"Johnston's groundbreaking academic work as well as his on-the-ground success have made room for other organizations to work in faith-based diplomacy, including my own. Doug is John the Baptist out there in the wilderness, saying, 'wake up' to international relations people."

The Honorable Robert Seiple
first Ambassador-at-Large for
International Religious Freedom,1999-2001
(from "The Father of Faith-Based Diplomacy" by
Rob Moll in *Christianity Today*, September 2008)

INDEX